DEFIANCE AND DEFERENCE IN MEXICO'S COLONIAL NORTH

DEFIANCE AND DEFERENCE
IN MEXICO'S COLONIAL NORTH

Indians under Spanish Rule in Nueva Vizcaya

SUSAN M. DEEDS

UNIVERSITY OF TEXAS PRESS
Austin

First edition, 2003

Requests for permission to reproduce material from this work should be sent to Permissions, University of Texas Press, Box 7819, Austin, TX 78713-7819.

♾ The paper used in this book meets the minimum requirements of ANSI/NISO Z39.48-1992 (R1997) (Permanence of Paper).

LIBRARY OF CONGRESS CATALOGING-IN-PUBLICATION DATA

Deeds, Susan M.
Defiance and deference in Mexico's colonial north : Indians under Spanish rule in Nueva Vizcaya / Susan M. Deeds.
         p.   cm.
Includes bibliographical references and index.
ISBN 978-0-292-70551-7

1. Indians of Mexico—Mexico—Chihuahua (State)—History.   2. Indians of Mexico—Mexico—Durango (State)—History.   3. Indians of Mexico—Cultural assimilation—Mexico—Chihuahua (State)   4. Indians of Mexico—Cultural assimilation—Mexico—Durango (State)   5. Jesuits—Missions—Mexico.   I. Title.
F1219.1.C46   D44   2003
972'.150049745—dc21   2002153961

For Ellen, Gabriela, and Colin

CONTENTS

MAPS

FIGURES

TABLES

ACKNOWLEDGMENTS

Even if you're on the right track, you'll get run over if you just sit there.

WILL ROGERS

I have managed to avoid being run over by moving on many tracks. Over the years that I have worked on this book, I have joked with many of my colleagues about the likelihood of its completion. Perhaps the lowest blow came from a former fellow graduate student who quipped, "Gee, Susan, I never thought you would become a grandmother before finishing your book!" In a more serious vein, however, such pointed reminders have stimulated many memories of all the people who have helped me along a journey that has been equally intellectual and affective. Although I could find roots going even further back (and risk incurring even more taunts about how long it has taken me to finish this project), the genesis of this book can most truly be traced to 1963, when I arrived in Mexico City for my junior year abroad, courtesy of a scholarship from the U.S. State Department arranged by Stanley Ross and Roberto Esquenazi-Mayo, at the University of Nebraska, Lincoln. For a Nebraska girl from a sparsely populated agricultural heartland, the experience was startling, humbling, and stunning. From my *madre mexicana*, an indigenous woman from Guerrero, Ofelia Ramos de Lezama, I learned extraordinary things about the beauty of Mexican peoples and their cultures. At El Colegio de México, I underwent the terrors of becoming suitably prepared for classes in Latin American history with a formidable María del Carmen Velázquez and equally demanding Carlos Bosch García, as well as no less talented fellow students such as Alejandra Moreno Toscano, Enrique Florescano, and Clara Lida. In that particular year of the topsy-turvy 1960s, I experienced epistemological and cosmological shifts that insinuated Mexico into the core of my being and largely determined the paths that my life would take. This land of striking cultural contrasts kindled my desire for social justice, my need for intellectual challenge, and my curiosity about the persistence of cultures and peoples.

Back at the University of Nebraska, this passion for Mexico was further stimulated by Michael C. Meyer and David Warren, and even a detour with the Peace Corps to Brazil from 1968 to 1973 did not shake my resolve to continue to explore Mexican history and culture. First drawn to the regional intricacies and personalities of the Mexican Revolution, I changed gears in the doctoral program at the University of Arizona in the late 1970s, taking advantage of an opportunity to study colonial history with Ursula Lamb. In a rare experience, this remarkable female pioneer in Latin American history pushed me to blur the lines and stretch the confines of my thinking. All in all, I am grateful to my mentors at the University of Arizona. With George Brubaker, I studied Andean and cultural history. Charles W. Polzer, S.J., introduced me to my thesis topic and hired me as a translator and documentary editor at the Documentary Relations of the Southwest project of the Arizona State Museum. Donna J. Guy made me realize the importance of economic history, and her early attention to gender was especially influential; her encouragement has never wavered. Michael Meyer renewed his role as mentor and *patrón,* promoting my scholarly efforts and employing me as the editorial assistant on the *Hispanic American Historical Review,* where I had the opportunity to see the strengths and weaknesses of the academic enterprise. Subsequently, he hired me as the Assistant Director of the Latin American Area Center. At Arizona, my scholarly endeavors were also enriched by my interaction with fellow students, including Tom Barnes, Lupe Castillo, Roger Davis, Tim Finan, Dianne Kercheval, Al López, Vesta Manning, Tom Naylor, and Barbara Silvers. Dana Deeds shared my love for Latin America and encouraged me for many years.

The year 1981 marked the completion of my Ph.D. dissertation, "Rendering unto Caesar: The Secularization of Jesuit Missions in Mid-Eighteenth Century Durango," the nucleus of the larger project represented by this book. The research in Mexico was funded by a Fulbright Dissertation Fellowship in 1976 and 1977. I benefited from considerable assistance in Mexico City from directors and archivists at the Archivo General de la Nación. Both there and at the Biblioteca Nacional, Roberto Beristaín provided invaluable help, and he has continued to do so until today. Dr. Manuel Ignacio Pérez Alonso, archivist of Jesuits' Mexican

Province, gave me access to its collection of original documents. In Durango, Licenciado José Ignacio Gallegos C. afforded me the opportunity to investigate relevant civil documents. Some of the great treasures for this study came from the Cathedral Archive of Durango, where Padre Antonio Díaz most kindly allowed me to work long before parts of the archive were microfilmed.

From the dissertation research, I had managed to paint a picture of a part of the Jesuit mission enterprise, one in which Acaxees, Xiximes, Tepehuanes, Tarahumaras, and Conchos all still seemed to be "peoples without history." Encouraged, perhaps naively, by theoretical trends of the 1980s that I could overcome this deficiency, I broadened the scope of the study and continued to carry out research, first in Spain with a Tinker Foundation Field Research Grant (1984), and then in Mexican archives with the assistance of summer grants from Northern Arizona University's Organized Research Program (1987–1992). Support followed in 1993 and 1994 from the National Endowment for the Humanities, the American Philosophical Society, and a Fulbright Senior Scholar Award. This research, as well as summer support for research from Northern Arizona University in the late 1990s, enabled me to complete a number of articles that focused on resistance, rebellion, and cultural change among the five Indian groups. In 1999 I worked in the Vatican Film Library at Saint Louis University with the assistance of an Andrew W. Mellon Travel Grant.

During my sabbatical in Mexico in 2001, I completed this study. I am grateful to many colleagues in Mexico who have helped me over the years, especially to Elsa Malvido, who extended to me the hospitality of her home, reviewed my presentations, and arranged for me to be a visiting researcher at the Dirección de Estudios Históricos of the Instituto Nacional de Antropología e Historia in 2001. There I also received support from the director, Salvador Rueda, and his assistant, Guillermo Turner. At the Universidad Nacional Autónoma de México, I have benefited from the counsel of Clara Bargellini and Marie-Areti Hers in the Instituto de Investigaciones Estéticas; Ignacio del Río, Sergio Ortega, and José Luis Mirafuentes in the Instituto de Investigaciones Históricas; and Luis González Rodríguez and Carlo Bonfiglioli in the Instituto de Investigaciones Antropológicas. I owe special thanks to Cecilia Sheridan Prieto (Centro de Investigaciones y Estudios Superiores en Antropología Social), to Chantal Cramaussel and Salvador Alvarez (Colegio de Michoacán), to Carmen Castañeda (Colegio de Jalisco), and to Agueda Jiménez Pelayo (University of Guadalajara).

Over the years, so many colleagues in Latin American history have provided feedback and encouragement that I will surely leave someone out of this list, but let me thank Dauril Alden, Linda Arnold, William Beezley, Richard Boyer, Amy Bushnell, John Chance, Edith Couturier, José Cuello, Frank de la Teja, Susan Deans-Smith, Ross Frank, Kevin Gosner, Richard Greenleaf, Ramón Gutiérrez, Linda Hall, John Hart, Rebecca Horn, Evelyn Hu-Dehart, Robert Jackson, Lyman Johnson, Jane Landers, Erick Langer, Asunción Lavrin, Sonya Lipsett, Colin MacLachlan, Cheryl Martin, Elinor Melville, Leslie Offutt, Ray Sadler, Linda and Richard Salvucci, Susan Schroeder, Fritz Schwaller, Stuart Schwartz, Thomas Sheridan, William Sherman, Susan Socolow, Daniela Spenser, Barbara Tenenbaum, John TePaske, Ann Twinam, Eric Van Young, Mary Kay Vaughan, and Mark Wasserman. Several other colleagues have provided valuable detailed critiques of my work over the years: Linda Curcio-Nagy, Susan Kellogg, Murdo MacLeod, James Saeger, Patricia Seed, and David Weber.

I will never be able to adequately thank Cynthia Radding and William Merrill for their painstaking criticisms of this manuscript, and for the ways in which their scholarly work and commitment to indigenous peoples have inspired me. I am likewise especially indebted to Karen Vieira Powers, my fellow ethnohistorian and constant friend at Northern Arizona University, for many fruitful exchanges about how we approach our work. From Jennifer Nez Denetdale, I learned how much I did not know and could never know about indigenous peoples. Interchanges across theoretical and disciplinary lines with other colleagues at NAU have also been invigorating, thanks to Sanjam Ahluwalia, Judy Giesberg, Sanjay Joshi, John Leung, George Lubick, Sheryl Lutjens, Irene Matthews, Eric Schenk, Julie Schimmel, Mary Ann Steger, and Cynthia Talbot. Many of my graduate students have pushed me to be current and creative, among them Lance Blyth, Jim Callard, Laura Camp, Tracy Goode, Ray Gonzales, Lomayumtewa Ishii, Kristin Mann, Gretchen Merten, Gabriel Rhoades, Victoria Apodaca Spencer, and Scott Wolf.

I would also like to thank my editors at the University of Texas Press, Letitia Blalock, Theresa May, Leslie Tingle, and Carolyn Cates Wylie, whose professionalism and skills have made the process of bringing this book to fruition a happy one. Thanks are also due to Ron Redsteer and Cynthia Kosso for assistance with the maps.

When a project takes so long for one to complete, it is inevitable that many of its inspirers will not survive its completion. I regret that I cannot share this book with the ten people mentioned in these pages who have died. My parents also would have been pleased to see this return on their many investments in me. I am thankful, however, to be able to celebrate the book with my extraordinarily gifted and giving children: Ellen, Ana Gabriela, and Colin (whose gestation exactly coincided with the production of my dissertation and whose adulthood corresponds with the publication of this book). They are the true survivors of this project, and they are the ones who made me keep its importance in perspective. From my sister Beth I received unconditional acceptance and support throughout periods of discovery and struggle.

In the final analysis, though, I could not have written *Defiance and Deference* except on the bodies, acts, and legacies of the Xiximes, Acaxees, Tepehuanes, Tarahumaras, and Conchos who crossed paths with their would-be colonizers in the seventeenth and eighteenth centuries. My efforts to record parts of their lives are wanting in many ways, but I hope I have done them no injustices.

DEFIANCE AND DEFERENCE IN
MEXICO'S COLONIAL NORTH

INTRODUCTION

"Three hundred Tarahumara, Pima, Guarijío and Tepehuan governors came to the appointed meeting. One more time they listed their needs: the 70,000 Indians of the Sierra Tarahumara lack job opportunities; the ejidal sawmills barely operate, not only because of the scarcity of credit, but also the high cost of technical assistance in forestry; and in addition to chronic malnutrition there is hunger in the sierra because the harvests were affected by frost and hail."[1] This contemporary newspaper report continues to enumerate problems: land conflicts; lack of adequate medical care, education, and potable water; the struggle for indigenous autonomy in the face of growing brokerage from outside the community; and finally drug trafficking. The gathering of Indian leaders in Creel, Chihuahua, was suffused with a high level of frustration over perpetually ineffectual dealings with municipal, state, and national government institutions. One of the *ejidatarias*/communal property holders in attendance, Doña Teresa, challenged officials. "I almost didn't come here. I am really angry. To whom can I address my complaint? I've already gone through all the proper channels. Now I am tempted to go to Chiapas to ask for help." Echoing the concerns of indigenous peoples throughout Mexico, these northern groups continue to seek self-government in the areas of the Sierra Madre Occidental where they live.[2]

Four hundred years after Europeans invaded this region, the contemporary scene bears a striking resemblance to the seventeenth and eighteenth centuries. As Spaniards imposed a structure of colonial rule in the northern Mexican province of Nueva Vizcaya, indigenous concerns also centered on the struggle to preserve cultural autonomy, the need to obtain sustenance from the land and other natural resources of the rugged and unpredictable sierra environment, and recurrent battles with disease and malnutrition. The strategies for survival were multiple and included rebellion. That colonial problems persist today in neocolonial guise comes as no surprise to the student of Mexican history. The story is an old one, you say; why read yet another story of colonial oppression?

Domination and repression, of course, figure in the story to be retold here, but they are only some of the threads of the history of the native peoples of Nueva Vizcaya. Undoubtedly they must be invoked, among the other strands, to explain the historical disappearance of many Indians of eastern Sinaloa, Durango, and Chihuahua in the Sierra Madre Occidental and the central plateau stretching between the cities of Durango and Chihuahua. What of those people who don't appear in the newspaper article: several hundred thousand individuals who once inhabited the territories of the Xiximes, Acaxees, and Conchos, as well as sizable parts of protohistoric Tepehuan and Tarahumara areas? How are we to explain the persistence of ethnic identity in some cases and not in others under conditions of conquest? This is the central question of *Defiance and Deference,* one which I intend to probe by using a comparative and chronological approach to the study of these five semisedentary and nonsedentary groups. Although excellent ethnographic studies of Tarahumaras and Tepehuanes exist for the national period,[3] we have no comprehensive history of any of the five groups for the colonial era. This book provides a multifaceted analysis of their past from the time the Spaniards first attempted to settle them in missions, at the end of the sixteenth century, to the middle of the eighteenth century, when secular pressures had wrought momentous changes. Its examination of ethnic persistence among less hierarchical and stratified peoples offers clues for our understanding of the paradox of ethnic identity in a postmodern world.

As we know from the escalating array of monographs on indigenous responses to colonialism that has been produced in the past few decades, outcomes varied widely across the Americas.[4] The need to redefine and understand the Columbian quincentenary in an academic environment beset by postmodern and postcolonial concerns served as a powerful stimulus for this research. The bulk of this literature focuses on sedentary peoples with more complex polities and lineages who have persisted as ethnic groups until today[5] and, in the case of Mesoamericans, has been enhanced by the mining of native language sources.[6] Nonsedentary and semisedentary peoples, often on the margins of the Spanish empire, have received less scrutiny both because the relative paucity of sources hampers complex analysis and because most of these groups disappeared as distinct indigenous entities.[7]

In order to make sense of the remarkable diversity of human beings who inhabited the Americas when Europeans arrived, social scientists and historians have proposed models that distinguish between indigenous peoples on the basis of modes of production and organization. One of the main focuses of such models has been the degree of Indian sedentism. The models have also been used to correlate indigenous forms of organization with their responses to colonial conquest. Edward Spicer, for example, classified Indians of northwestern New Spain in four different types of economy: *ranchería*,[8] village, band, and nonagricultural band. In his schema, ranchería peoples were the most accepting of Spanish forms of religious and social life, while the villagers were more tenacious in preserving customs, through mostly passive means. Band peoples aggressively resisted but also experienced the greatest alteration in their way of life. Spicer did describe a range across the north, and he effectively dispelled the myth that northern Indians were all *chichimecas* or ahistorical nomadic hunter-gatherers who had little significance in the enormous landscape.[9] In a different blueprint designed to sort out all of Latin America, James Lockhart and Stuart Schwartz employ the categories sedentary imperial, sedentary nonimperial, semisedentary, and nonsedentary to describe different forms of social and economic organization, prevailing technologies, and adaptations to certain environments, as well as to predict their responses to European intrusion on a continuum emphasizing the potential for accommodation and resistance.[10]

Although both models are useful for explaining diversity in very general terms, these schemas cannot capture the enormous complexity that existed (as all of their authors recognize). Looking closely at specific ethnic groups, we find wide variation within each of these categories which are themselves quite porous. This book will address this conundrum for groups that apparently fall outside the category of sedentary but experienced heterogeneous outcomes between and among themselves in terms of the persistence of ethnic identity. What accounts for these differences? As I collected archival data for this study over many years, a bewildering number of variables presented themselves. Among them were demographic patterns; ecology; geography; autochthonous sociopolitical organization, subsistence patterns, religion, aggressivity, and mobility; availability and accessibility of labor and natural resources valuable to Spaniards; the institutions of colonial control; and the intensity of extractive pressures.

In my effort to make sense of the impact of such a multiplicity of heterogeneous factors, I discovered that some emerged as the most palpably pivotal for this northern region. These fall into two broad clusters. One is the interplay of preconquest social structures and cultures with disease and Spanish labor demands. Within this set are (a) the *precontact* degree of sedentism and population concentration, relations with other indigenous groups, and use of the environment, and (b) the *Spanish intro-duction* of disease and unremitting demand for labor in a mining economy. The second general set of factors, inextricably related to the first, encom-passes the role of missions on frontiers in structuring and mediating the relations between Indians and outsiders, as well as between Indians and their belief systems and ritual practices. How these elements interacted in combinations of disintegrative and integrative ways provides the key to understanding diverse outcomes in terms of subsistence and resistance strategies and of the persistence of ethnic identities among these semi- to nonsedentary groups.

This explanatory framework begs several questions, perhaps the most obvious of which is whether missions were different from other reduction strategies. In the Spanish system, *misiones* were distinguished from *doc-trinas,* or Indian parishes of central and southern Mexico, even though neither was a *parroquia,* that is, a fully developed Christian parish. The difference is based on the extent of (1) sedentism of particular indige-nous groups, (2) isolation from Spanish settlements, and (3) subsidization provided by the state and political control by missionaries. Missions had the more formidable task of imposing entirely alien forms of organization in sparsely populated areas. As Cynthia Radding has observed, "Among the seminomadic peoples of northern New Spain, the missions were to achieve religious evangelization and a new political order, goals which re-quired an agrarian economic base and often the physical relocation of the Indians."[11] Even though sedentary peoples were often recongregated in other regions of Spanish America, they did not face such foreign modes of production. Furthermore, as outposts in frontier areas, missions required financial support from the crown.

Another question concerns how the analytical blueprint I have con-structed corresponds with general theoretical approaches to issues of colo-nialism, cross-cultural contact, and ethnic or cultural identity. My own peregrinations in writing this book over a twenty-year period are confir-mation of the maxim that what we say as historians is determined and shaped by our historical and ideological circumstances.[12] From my earlier work on labor, land, and demography centered in the "new social history" of the 1960s, I turned to culture, resistance, and gender. Generationally, I fall within a group of Latin American historians first influenced by neo-

Marxism and Gramscian perspectives on hegemony, but later moved to engage in postcolonial critiques and cultural studies. The tensions generated by this mingling have been described by Florencia Mallon as "fertile" and necessitating that we become stunt riders who hang on to or negotiate between different theoretical horses.[13] One of the problems in using theory to approach colonial situations from a comparative perspective is the great variation across time and space. Spanish colonialism of the sixteenth century was very different from British colonialism in the nineteenth, due largely to the distinct roles of religion, variant types of capitalism, and demographic dissimilarities.

Nonetheless, much of the fruitful debate over the tensions between a Gramscian project that aims to uncover the agency of oppressed peoples and the postmodern/postcolonial positing of pervasive power structures that limit agency has taken place within the rubric of subaltern studies, the movement begun by South Asian historians to revise theories of nationalism and postcolonial social formations.[14] In a parallel vein, political scientist James C. Scott tackled issues of peasant responses to domination and Gramscian forms of hegemony, in effect elevating forms of everyday resistance over outright rebellion through his formulations of "weapons of the weak" and "hidden transcripts" that located agency in less militant actions such as foot-dragging, flight, pilfering, sabotage, gossip, and slander.[15]

Still another concurrent track that includes Michel Foucault and Edward Said emphasizes language or discursive practices in the dissemination of power and the constructedness of identity.[16] The "linguistic turn" has most prominently insinuated itself in the historical discipline as the "new cultural history" explicated by Lynn Hunt and others, a move away from the social to the cultural as influenced heavily first by Foucault and Clifford Geertz and then by Hayden White.[17] Latin American historians debated its meaning and influence in an issue of the *Hispanic American Historical Review* devoted entirely to this subject in 1999. For me the not so new cultural history is simply the latest approach to reconciling materialist and culturalist explanations of history.[18] As a fad that acts as a provocateur to keep historians thinking outside the box, it is useful but not a panacea for unraveling complex relationships in the past. Just as helpful have been the many ethnohistorical approaches to emerge in the past decade. Although Eric Van Young has suggested that ethnohistorians of Mexico have not been very successful in reconciling the social scientific and hermeneutic approaches within our already cross-disciplinary perspectives,[19] I see a good deal of sophisticated work that takes a critical and self-reflexive stance toward sources on indigenous peoples and cultures/mentalities/symbolic systems and focuses on the social construction of ethnicity.[20] Nor do I agree with Thomas Abercrombie's critique: "No matter what inroads the various postmodernisms have made into the profession, the discipline of history remains that of objectivism, and the historian's work is judged by the adequacy of his or her writing as a representation of 'what actually happened,' or at least 'what was actually written.'" For Abercrombie ethnohistory "has simply served as a label for the ghetto into which we place the pasts of peoples without writing."[21]

Conversely, I see Abercrombie's masterful study of the K'ulta peoples of Bolivia as a remarkable synthesis of the approaches that can be taken or invented within the porous boundaries of ethnohistory. I have found ethnohistory to be the borderland most conducive to exploring my chief preoccupations: (1) to recover the forms and configurations of ethnic persistence (or to understand the lack thereof), despite the problems of recovering nonliterate indigenous voices,[22] and (2) to overcome the overwhelming emphasis of postcolonial theories on representation, ideology, and power that has overshadowed the material or everyday conditions of people's lives and distorted notions of agency.[23] The result is a theoretical eclecticism that develops the history of Acaxees, Xiximes, Tepehuanes, Tarahumaras, and Conchos in missions through a conceptual construct that I will call mediated opportunism. If ethnogenesis is the larger process through which ethnic cultures re-create themselves over time, mediated opportunism provides a framework tailored to understanding how material and mental barriers limit the capacity for change in these particular groups. Local hybridities could be very ethnocentric, just as local transformations could ultimately produce stagnation and strangulation. Based upon the interaction of the variables I have outlined above, mediated opportunism is the crossroads between cultural and environmental opportunism on the one hand and moral boundaries and biological barriers on the other.[24] It is the sequenced process in which cultural ferment splashes against behavioral and physiological walls. The extent to which indigenous peoples could formulate mixed strategies and exercise choices in adapting to changing cultural and ecological circumstances was tempered by many factors, perhaps the most important of which were the mortality produced by diseases, the endemic warfare that characterized precontact history, and the incapacity to accept changes that violated the most basic principles for assuring life's balance. Mediated opportunism took unique forms across and within the groups studied here.

My idea of a mediated opportunism bears comparison with the concept of social ecology formulated by Cynthia Radding in *Wandering Peoples*, a highly influential work on the responses of Sonoran indigenous groups to colonialism. Drawing on ecological history and ethnogenesis, she defines social ecology as "a living and changing complex of relations that developed historically among diverse human populations and with the land they occupied. It refers both to the social structures through which different ethnic communities re-created their cultures and to the political implications of resource allocation in the region."[25] She goes on to develop the idea of a colonial pact in which both subsistence practices and reciprocal obligations shaped ethnic divisions and social stratification. My study examines some of Radding's concerns, especially those involving subsistence and ethnicity, but while she is more focused on later social stratification, I am more intent on explaining how early colonial structures affected ethnic persistence among semisedentary and nonsedentary peoples. These different purposes are largely linked to the variance in our time frames: my study begins and ends a hundred years earlier. This allows me to look more closely at certain variables, especially demographic and labor pressures, from the beginning of effective contact, but inhibits my ability to comprehensively trace social stratification through ethnic, class, and gender intersections, because the data for the period before the second half of the eighteenth century are fewer and inadequate to such a task. Nor does my study place the same emphasis on the evolution of the *común*/community or on a colonial pact between monarch and frontier Indians in the same way that Radding's does, primarily because I think these are later colonial developments.[26]

Within somewhat different theoretical formulations, both Radding and I have responded to the call of a still powerfully present figure in the ethnohistory of northwest Mexico, Edward Spicer, to focus critically on the reasons for the survival of ethnic enclaves or "enduring peoples."[27] This work is also situated within an evolving "new mission history."[28] Recent studies have explored the ties between missions (Jesuit and Franciscan) and surrounding Spanish settlements, especially in terms of the relationships between ethnicity, demography, and subsistence patterns. Some very early studies had pointed the way; for example, Robert West's 1949 study of silver mining in Parral alluded to labor and commercial relationships with mission Indians. But long after that, now outdated portraits of missions portrayed them as bounded, disciplined communities, forged out of conditions of savagery by heroic, occasionally martyred, and highly paternalistic religious fathers.[29] A quite different panorama emphasizes not only the material ways they were linked to the outside world but also their persistent cultural and ethnic interchanges, explaining why they were inherently unstable. Scholars have revealed demographic patterns and other previously unexplored facets of mission history, highlighting, in particular, their porous boundaries and the ways in which they were "contested ground."[30] Robert Jackson's demographic studies have advanced our understanding of the relationships between congregation, disease, gender, and ethnic survival. And we now have nuanced explanations of the complex economic motives and activities of the Amazonian Moxos of northern Bolivia and the Guaycuruans of the Gran Chaco in relationship to Jesuit missions. James Saeger's study critically questions the notion that nonsedentary people could not function in missions or participate in complex economies; it is also especially useful for explaining the missions' impact on gender relations and economic roles. Cecilia Sheridan has given us the most comprehensive study to date of the "cultures of the desert" in Mexico's northeast, exploring the complex inter-relationship of hundreds of nomadic groups, Franciscan missions, and the Spaniards' effort to dominate this space. She documents, with remarkable clarity, the use of force that resulted in the overwhelming of indigenous groups who were highly resistant to the destructuring of their way of life throughout a long, contentious process.

Defiance and Deference connects missions and indigenous peoples to the regional economy of Nueva Vizcaya, contributing to the small but growing body of literature on the socioeconomic evolution of the area. Until recently, regional studies of Nueva Vizcaya focused primarily on administrative institutions, both civil and ecclesiastic.[31] Cheryl Martin's analysis of the social dimensions of governance in eighteenth-century urban Chihuahua is a welcome antidote to the administrative genre. Economic history has been part of the promising evolving work of Chantal Cramaussel and Salvador Alvarez on land, labor, agricultural and mining production, and ecology. They have made explicit connections between the military and missionary conquests of the region, an evolving labor pool, and the formation of mining and hacienda elites.[32] They are primarily responsible for obtaining and analyzing the data that provide a larger context through which we can see missions and presidios as organic parts of a whole.[33]

This book approaches regional history from the focal point of missions. Nueva Vizcayan missions were never closed communities. They were transactional and transitional crossroads where ethnic identities, subsistence patterns, cultural beliefs, and gender relations were forged and changed over time in a frontier only slowly conquered by non-Indians.

The delays and intermittent character of this conquest were dictated by unfavorable geography and ecology, logistical problems of distance and supply, and the hostility of indigenous groups unused to incorporation in a state (albeit a weak one in this frontier situation). Over time the balance shifted to facilitate incorporation of mission pueblos into the Spanish orbit. Of course, not all indigenous peoples acquiesced to pueblo life; that is the story of those Tarahumaras and Tepehuanes who fled west to establish rancherías in the rugged and inhospitable canyons of the Sierra Madre. Yet not even those survivors rejected all outside influences, as their subsistence came to depend heavily upon animals introduced by Europeans. At least in the colonial period, the indigenous population clusters, whether rancherías or pueblos, were permeable either culturally or ethnically. The interethnic connections that characterized these areas are difficult to identify and document, since the main source of documentation for missions is the body of reports by the missionaries who would not serve their own interests by demonstrating the absence of boundaries and control.

This last point raises the question of sources for this study. There are virtually no native language sources for these groups, except for a very occasional document produced in Nahuatl. Indigenous representations and petitions in Spanish are also few and far between. The principal sources for what purports to be an indigenous voice are judicial records, generated by Indians whose testimony was given — quite infrequently before the eighteenth century — either in civil or criminal cases.[34] Records of military and other courts convened to deal with rebellions also contain Indian testimonies.[35] These declarations were recorded in Spanish after being filtered through a translator and a scribe. This small body of indigenous testimony is dwarfed by the much larger corpus of Jesuit and other ecclesiastical reports and correspondence, as well a substantial number of administrative and military reports.[36] Records of commercial and land transactions provide some traces of indigenous lives, as do parish registers which, mostly incompletely, record their births, marriages, and deaths.[37] The latter, along with criminal and Inquisition cases, are the most likely to reveal information about ethnic interactions and evolving multiethnic folk practices. Yet in its totality the documentation on indigenous peoples in Nueva Vizcaya from 1600 to 1750 is limited in comparison to the records generated in the late eighteenth century.

Nonetheless, from this dispersed, fragmentary record a surprisingly multidimensional history of missions emerges. This account encompasses the daily economic labors and transactions that went on with or without missionary supervision, as well as the tantalizing glimpses of beliefs and attitudes, reported sexual liaisons, and shared local knowledge of cures and remedies. It recounts the movements, not only of the nominal residents as they went to and from their fields and pastures or those of Spanish landowners, but also of assorted travelers who tarried at mission crossroads. The fluid, porous boundaries of Nueva Vizcayan missions accommodated multiple types of transactions, licit and illicit, that produced varying patterns of material, cultural, and ethnic change.

Within the new mission history, much has been said about the need to present the past from an indigenous perspective or at least to focus more centrally on the indigenous experience.[38] Although I have tried to suffuse this book with the experiences of the Acaxees, Xiximes, Tepehuanes, Tarahumaras, and Conchos who lived in missions, this is not the story they would tell. Clifford Geertz has described the conundrum for anthropologists and historians of "getting an imaginative entry into (and admittance of) an alien turn of mind" as a "question of writing out other peoples' consciousness for them, scripting their souls."[39] Such an endeavor cannot replicate; it can only (mis)construe or mirror imperfectly. For as much as I have tried to deduce and intuit what these northern peoples thought or felt, this is a history filtered through the many others they came into contact with. The first European invaders certainly did not understand their systems of government, subsistence, kinship, and relationships with other indigenous groups. The book begins with the Spanish accounts, brash and uninformed as they were, of the early *entradas*/expeditions and indigenous responses (Chapter 1). The discussion of geography, environment, and precontact cultural characteristics (Chapter 2) seeks to shade in the gaps left by the incomplete and biased Spanish accounts and to probe more deeply into differing initial responses. The book then reverts to the colonial context, which is developed in the next six chapters in chronological fashion. The fractious and contemptuous "peace" that followed the rebellions of the early seventeenth century (Chapter 3) flew violently apart in the 1690s, under the scourge of new exploitations, epidemic disease, and subsistence crisis (Chapter 4).

The 1690s ended in a new demographic low for indigenous peoples in Nueva Vizcaya and marked the end of direct insurrection, as many Tarahumaras—the most recent rebels—deliberately chose to migrate west to rugged and inhospitable canyons in the Sierra Madre Occidental, away from the silver and ranching economy of the central plateaus of Durango and Chihuahua. Those Indians who remained in missions experimented with other options to avoid the most onerous aspects of their colonial status, but even their slight demographic recovery was thwarted in the late 1730s by a brutal epidemic of *matlazahuatl*, at the same time that they were being demographically swamped by a growing non-Indian population (Chapter 5). Before long, the missionaries, whose influence was being undermined by royal (Bourbon) and local initiatives, as well as by raids mounted by Apaches and even mission Indians, were forced to take stock of the deterioration of their enterprise (Chapters 6 and 7). *Mestizaje*/racial mixing and the influx of outsiders into the missions accompanied the integration of these villages into the regional mining and agricultural economy, and in some of them it was difficult to distinguish between Indians and non-Indians (mestizos, mulattoes, and poor Spaniards) as they sought to augment subsistence farming by seeking work in silver mines and on agricultural estates, or by engaging in petty commerce. In the 1740s, the Jesuits acknowledged the political and economic transformations by turning the majority of their Nueva Vizcayan missions over to the secular clergy (Chapter 8). In the former mission communities, the processes of mediated opportunism had engendered changing intersections of ethnicity and identity. The mix of new faces and alliances that characterized the missions in 1750 was far removed from the polar distinctions that marked the entradas of Europeans into these indigenous territories two centuries earlier.

ONE

SPANISH ENTRADAS AND INDIGENOUS RESPONSES IN TOPIA AND TEPEHUANA, 1560–1620

The initial impact of Spanish invasion in Nueva Vizcaya was cataclysmic for indigenous peoples. Within a half century of sustained contact with Europeans, the native population was reduced by more than half.[1] Despite this dilution in numbers, the agents of invasion—miners, grain producers, merchants, soldiers, and missionaries—met with determined opposition as they attempted to impose their visions of "civilization" on groups whose organization was antithetical. Although this resistance was at first piecemeal and halting, within a generation every contacted group was engaged in a concerted attempt to turn its world right side up. First-generation millenarian rebellions were directed by precontact war leaders and shamans, reacting to their own loss of status and prestige as well as to generalized distress resulting from the dislocations imposed by massive deaths and Spanish enterprise.[2]

By the time Francisco de Ibarra reconnoitered the region in the 1560s, Indians had already felt the Spanish presence in the form of slaving expeditions from Sinaloa and probably epidemic disease.[3] Ibarra's explorations in the newly created province of Nueva Vizcaya (1563) resulted in the founding of a number of settlements, including the villa of Durango in 1563 and *reales de minas*/mining towns at Indé in 1563 and Santa Bárbara in 1567.[4] Outnumbered by Tepehuanes and Conchos who inhabited these areas and could not at first be compelled without force to work in the silver mines, Spanish settlers were forced to seek mining and agricultural laborers outside the region. In addition to importing black slaves, Indians, mestizos, and mulattoes from areas to the south, they conducted slaving expeditions into Sonora and New Mexico and resettled these Indians in camps near their enterprises.[5]

Before the end of the century, however, *encomiendas* or grants of local

Indians were being made in the Santa Bárbara–San Bartolomé region and in the sierras, where new silver strikes spurred the founding of Spanish settlements at Guanaceví, Topia, San Andrés, and San Hipólito. Encomiendas in northern Mexico allowed a Spanish settler (by virtue of his role as conqueror) the use of a specified group of Indians for labor only. In the absence of sizable surpluses and because of the hostile conditions of the frontier, by 1582 the crown determined not to exact commodity tribute in Nueva Vizcaya (although it was assessed on the Sinaloan coast).[6] Even though some of the Indians actively resisted, a combination of Indian population reduction, concomitant disaggregation, and increased Spanish presence now made local procurement of labor more feasible. The first recorded epidemic in the Nueva Vizcayan heartland was the 1577 *peste*,[7] which has been variously identified as a combination of typhus, typhoid, and dysentery, as well as bubonic plague.[8]

The first encomiendas of Conchos, Tepehuanes, and some Tarahumaras, dating from the 1570s, operated under conditions that were little different from slavery in spite of the restrictions imposed by the crown.[9] The distances between Spanish settlements and locations of encomienda grants ranged from a few miles to several hundred. In particular, Conchos were brought from as far north as the Río Grande (Río Bravo). Prospective *encomenderos*/recipients of encomiendas took the initiative of sending Indian scouts to search for isolated population clusters (rancherías) and deliver their residents. Grants of encomienda were issued by Nueva Vizcayan governors to legitimize a fait accompli once the Indians had been relocated.[10] Because many Indians were moved considerable distances from their homes, resettlement near Spanish enterprises amounted to a permanent change. The length of their labor service invariably exceeded that allowed by law (three weeks per year), and some of them became permanent residents of haciendas. These *naboríos*, along with counterparts who had been procured from slaving expeditions conducted even farther away, endured a condition of servitude that, if not technically slavery, effectively bound them and their few children (their reproductive rates were extremely low) to their masters.[11]

A large portion of early encomienda labor was dedicated to the livestock ranches and grain farms established in the Valle de San Bartolomé (today Valle de Allende in southeastern Chihuahua). This area was the main breadbasket for the region, as Bishop Alonso de la Mota y Escobar noted in his late-sixteenth-century inspection. Wheat, maize, vegetables, and fruits were cultivated along the affluents of the Río Florido.[12] Land grants were issued in areas north of Durango by Governor Ibarra as early

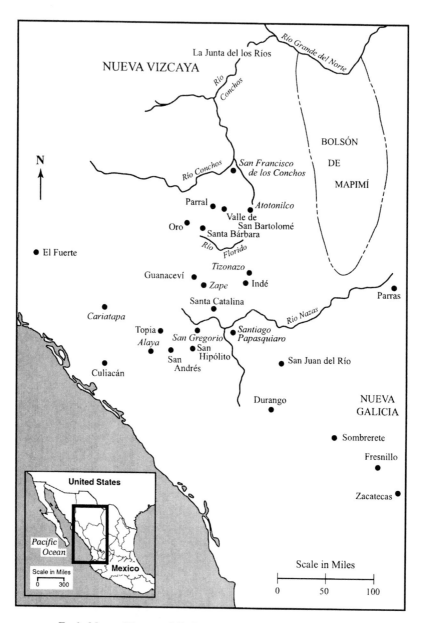

MAP I. *Early Nueva Vizcaya. Mission names in italic type; towns and presidios in roman type.*

as the 1560s, and the early miners continued to receive land near silver deposits and in the Valle de San Bartolomé. Those who were able to establish continuous access to water and labor came to constitute a landed oligarchy that persisted throughout the colonial period through its connections with the intermittently developing mining economy.[13] Franciscan friars helped encomenderos meet their obligations to convert the Indians by establishing doctrinas in the Valle de San Bartolomé. By the beginning of the seventeenth century, their missions at Atotonilco and San Francisco de los Conchos attempted to congregate Toboso and Concho Indians.[14] Since most agricultural labor was seasonal, encomienda Indians who worked on haciendas commonly fled during slack periods and had to be rounded up periodically by Indian captains or intermediaries who cooperated with the Spaniards.[15] Encomiendas also furnished a significant component of mining labor in the western sierras. In the 1580s and 1590s, Acaxees and Xiximes were pressed into encomiendas to work at the mines and ranches of Topia and San Andrés. Not surprisingly, they were also the discoverers of many new veins of ore.[16]

On the heels of the increased labor coercion, smallpox and measles spread through the area in the 1590s and the first decade of the seventeenth century. Typhus, smallpox, and measles struck again in the second decade. After the first (virgin-soil) epidemic of smallpox in any given location (which could take 40 percent of its inhabitants), the disease probably became endemic, often recurring every generation.[17] We have more information on the effects of these epidemics because, probably not coincidentally, this is the period when Jesuits began to establish themselves in what came to be the Tepehuana/Tarahumara Baja and Topia mission provinces. Relative latecomers to colonial Mexico in 1572, the order found a niche in educating criollos at the many *colegios*/secondary schools they established throughout New Spain. Not to be denied opportunities for evangelization and martyrdom, they sought mission fields in northwest Mexico.[18] Franciscans had already established missions in the north central corridor from Zacatecas to New Mexico. The fortunes of the Franciscan establishments tended to parallel those of the adjacent mining *reales* and Spanish settlements, on which they depended heavily for fees for sacraments and charity to support their missions. Their ability to attract and retain Tepehuanes, Conchos, and Tobosos, however, was inhibited by fierce competition from encomenderos in the mining reales and agricultural enterprises around the Valle de San Bartolomé.

Jesuits were more successful at building an infrastructure that provided a cushion in bad times. Their colegios in central and southern Mexico

TABLE I.   CHRONOLOGY OF EPIDEMIC DISEASES RECORDED
FOR MISSION AREAS

Years	Diseases	Years	Diseases
1576–1577	Peste	1647	Peste
1590	Smallpox	1650–1652	Peste
1596–1597	Smallpox, measles	1662–1663	Peste
1601–1602	Measles, smallpox, typhus(?)	1666–1667	Peste
		1692–1693	Smallpox, measles
1606–1607	Measles, smallpox	1696–1697	Smallpox
1610	Smallpox	1718	Smallpox
1616–1617	Smallpox, measles	1728–1729	Measles
1623–1625	Smallpox	1738–1739	Peste
1636	Smallpox, *tabardillo* (typhus?)	1748	Measles

Sources: Reff, *Disease, Depopulation, and Culture Change;* Jesuit annual letters: 1596, 1597, 1598, 1607, 1608, 1610, 1612, 1613, 1638, 1646, 1651, 1662, 1663, 1668, 1719–1720; report of P. Diego de Alejos, Teguciapa, May 18, 1617, AGN, Archivo Provisional, Misiones, caja 2; parish records from Santiago Papasquiaro, Santa Catalina, Parral, Valle de Allende, Huejotitlán, San Pablo; AGI, Audiencia de Guadalajara, legs. 104, 105, 110, 151, and Patronato, leg. 236; ACD, Varios 1749.

Note: The epidemics entered the north from areas to the south.

came to control efficiently administered agricultural enterprises. Profits from these and bequests from colonial elites contributed to the order's financial success.[19] By the early 1590s, the Jesuits had founded colegios in Sinaloa and Durango, providing a base from which conversion efforts could be carried out. The missionary enterprise also received support from the crown, which provided an initial endowment for constructing the physical plant and furnishing livestock, plus between 300 and 350 pesos annually as a stipend for each mission that it authorized. Although Spanish and other European "Black Robes" made up more than half of the early Jesuit missionaries in Nueva Vizcaya, by the 1630s Mexican-born Jesuits were more numerous, constituting about 60 percent.[20]

From Durango in 1596, Padre Gerónimo Ramírez moved beyond the Franciscan missions among Tepehuanes to the north. At first he was escorted by Spanish soldiers, but he came to see them as too severe in their treatment of Indians and made a number of forays accompanied only by lay brother Juan de la Carrera. Some of these Tepehuanes already had been exposed to Franciscans preaching in Nahuatl and Spanish, as well as to Spanish settlers and their central Mexican Indian and mestizo workers and black slaves. Ramírez began to make converts among the Tepehuanes, swayed in part by his knowledge of their language. He, in turn, was impressed by the fact that some of them had already been taught parts of the catechism by neophyte Tepehuanes and by central Mexican Indians, like the Tarascan who had married a Tepehuana from the Río Papasquiaro area. Some of these Tepehuanes were working in Spanish mines and on livestock ranches, perhaps attracted by Spanish goods and horses, as well as the fiestas and processions of Holy Week.[21]

Most, however, had opposed the Spanish presence, periodically attacking their settlements.[22] Now Ramírez found many Tepehuanes dying of *cocolitzli*/epidemics in their rancherías. In 1596 and 1597, both smallpox and measles reportedly killed thousands of Indians.[23] Initially, the devastation of disease provided fertile ground for conversion, and Jesuits actively sought out the infirm.[24] Physically weakened and psychologically more receptive to outsiders who offered comfort, materially and spiritually, Indians often allowed padres to come in and baptize them. Jesuits viewed epidemics as God's will, and rather than dwelling on the number of deaths, took comfort in the number of souls they could save.[25] Choosing sites along the rivers in the Santiago Papasquiaro and Santa Catalina valleys, Ramírez and other Jesuits, with assistance from paid laborers (often Tlaxcalans brought from central Mexico to establish agricultural colonies that would serve as models for nonsedentary peoples), constructed makeshift churches and encouraged Tepehuanes to move into the villages where they were assigned plots for building houses and planting (*milpas*). At least in the beginning, Jesuits noted that Indians from specific rancherías resided in separate *parcialidades* and *barrios* in the mission pueblos, suggesting the continuance of precontact patterns of sociopolitical organization likely based in kin networks. The existence of two governors, one each for the settlements on both sides of the river in the early days of mission Santa Catalina, provides additional evidence for this view. The fact that the term "parcialidad" disappears from the documentation very quickly seems to indicate that the missionaries were successful in eroding distinctions between these earlier kin-based associations.[26] Material inducements which included cloth, tools—especially axes—seeds, and cattle did attract many Tepehuanes, although some refused to enter the churches because people had been buried there. They carefully explained that according to their beliefs it was important to avoid the "souls" of the dead who would try to draw them into their world. Such reasoned arguments also countered other Jesuit teachings. One Tepehuan, when told that his sins would be washed away by baptism, responded that he was careful to bathe frequently in the river.[27]

Civilized life (*vida política y cristiana*) in the view of Spaniards meant living in towns with a prescribed form of government. The Jesuits organized their missions in a structured fashion. All of the missions were under the control of the *padre provincial* of the entire Jesuit province of New Spain, and they were visited periodically by a Jesuit inspector from Mexico City. Seven large administrative divisions came to comprise their total mission fields in northern Mexico. The Nueva Vizcayan districts of Topia and Tepehuana included several subdivisions called *rectorados;* each rectorado had several *partidos,* further subdivided into *cabeceras*/head missions and *visitas*/satellite stations. The head missions brought together many separate ranchería clusters, and smaller visita pueblos not uncommonly had as their nuclei groups of Indians who had been part of an encomienda.[28] A single missionary resided in the cabecera and ministered to the visitas (often a considerable distance away). As enumerated by one padre, this single individual played multiple roles, including curate, sexton, notary, preacher, confessor, doctor, property manager, and innkeeper.

In accordance with rules of hierarchy, Jesuits named Indian officials for each pueblo. At a minimum these included a *gobernador* and a *capitán*, as well as *alcaldes, fiscales,* and *alguaciles* or *topiles.* In the beginning, the most prestigious position, that of governor, was accorded by Jesuits to the representatives of the rancherías with whom they had negotiated and regarded as *caciques.* Captains who were responsible for protecting the mission from outsiders and mobilizing troops to serve the Spaniards were former war leaders. Alcaldes, along with the governor, oversaw the daily affairs of the mission, particularly the economic aspects. Fiscales and alguaciles were expected to enforce the Jesuits' rules. Only the governor received the *bastón* or staff of office symbolizing authority.[29] Through former leaders or persons who commanded authority, the missionaries hoped to exercise their authority. It is probable that, failing to understand the lack of formal hierarchies in most of these societies, the Spaniards also picked war leaders for the post of governor because they were traditionally the individuals chosen to negotiate with outsiders. As the Jesuits became more familiar with local practices, they identified shamans or inspirational practitioners who tried to undermine them. But they also recognized other principal elders whose counsel was valued. Employing persuasion and gifts, they tried to pull the latter into the Spanish sphere, where they bestowed varying measures of authority and the title "Don." Titles and privileges were conferred by Spaniards, whenever possible, in feasts staged to impress the *naturales*/natives.[30]

The contingent nature of indigenous leadership in these situations has been characterized in many ways, ranging from positive to negative outcomes for the Indian officials' communities, but in any case it was precarious. How could these intermediaries satisfy both constituencies? The Spaniards expected them to enforce a new order and provide laborers. Their people expected them to mitigate abuses and to uphold practices that were thought to ensure their spiritual and material well-being. The degree to which these officials retained moral authority in the colonial order varied a great deal. In the beginning, they often tilted toward the indigenous world, a factor that prompted the missionaries to cultivate other sources of leadership, more amenable to doing their bidding. Old or new, such leaders were compromised by the special privileges accorded to them by the missionaries or fees for supplying laborers. When the padres allowed them to participate in the allocation of community resources, they may have been able to maintain bonds of reciprocity. As time went on, however, their conferred status tended to erode the consensus-building nature of indigenous leadership.[31]

Jesuits also concentrated their energies on establishing monogamous unions, and they moved quickly to establish seminaries where the brightest young boys in catechism classes were groomed to take over the offices related to religious conversion.[32] Until that could be accomplished, Jesuits often used Christianized Indians or other outsiders as catechists/*temastianes*, and they tried to establish religious routines that emphasized repetition and memorization. On Sundays and religious feast days, the Tepehuanes were expected to attend mass and hear the sermon. Saturdays were for praying the rosary and singing hymns of praise/*alabados*. Children were expected to recite the catechism/*doctrina* on weekday mornings and afternoons. Adults and children were always segregated by gender. The patron saint's day, Holy Week, Corpus Christi, and the Virgin Mary commanded special celebrations.[33]

Jesuits pressed the Tepehuanes to plant fields near the missions. In the earliest years of the Santiago Papasquiaro mission, hired workers (Indians from central Mexico and mestizos) began to lay out fields and to build irrigation ditches/*acequias*. Expenses, which included wages for laborers, oxen, plows, and a variety of tools, were paid from royal treasury funds in Durango by order of the viceroy.[34] At least in the early years of the Jesuit mission enterprise, the crown commonly provided substantial initial assistance in establishing missions. Gifts of cattle to stock mission ranches were particularly useful, because providing meat at religious fiestas proved a strong incentive in attracting Indians. "When the Society [of Jesus] begins to evangelize, it has to go with the gospel in one hand, and meat and corn in the other."[35] Sheep were also valued by the natives, who substituted wool for cotton or *pita*/agave fiber in making more durable and tightly woven cloth. The viceroy donated 2,000 sheep to the first Tepehuan missions.[36] Formal land titles were not issued, although the land allotment/*fundo legal* of a mission came to be recognized as a square league at least by the eighteenth century.[37]

The Jesuits designated certain lands to be used for the maintenance of the church and supplying the needs of the mission as a whole. Wheat was being cultivated and sold by 1604. In general, the irrigation canals and ditches were constructed to water the wheat fields, while corn was raised in nonirrigated fields. Indians were expected to divide their labor between mission lands and their own plots; theoretically they were to spend three days in each, but this was not always the practice. The common lands were used to produce grain both for mission consumption and for sale, although the priests were enjoined not to make more profit than necessary for supporting the mission itself. Indians were also expected to provide labor for constructing and caring for churches, herding livestock, and maintaining a packtrain. The division of labor in missions was to a certain extent gendered, with women occupied in the preparation and storing of foods, in weaving cloth, and in cleaning the churches. Although the men were primarily responsible for agricultural tasks, women also aided in these at times, and they, along with their children, became responsible for herding sheep and goats. Both men and women engaged in gathering activities.

Jesuits compensated Indian labor in the missions through commodity gift giving, primarily of clothing and cloth, but also of tools, tobacco, and other sundries. These articles were supplied to a mission from Mexico City after their cost was deducted from the mission's annual stipend. The most cooperative Indians, especially the appointed officials, received preference in the distribution of gifts. The value of the goods ranged from 300 to 350 pesos per year, depending upon the accessibility of mission sites. The extra 50 pesos was comparable to a modern-day hardship allowance for diplomatic posts.[38] The Jesuit order got these funds from the royal treasury in the viceregal capital, but the missionaries actually received the emolument, given in the form of alms (and actually called *limosna*), as goods.[39] Although some Tepehuanes did begin to cultivate corn, beans, and squash on mission lands, few took up residence in the pueblos. They were discouraged, not only by their own shamans who promoted the idea that the Jesuits brought sickness, but also by the awareness that congregation made them an easier target for Spanish labor needs.[40] Nonetheless, as their raiding activities became more circumscribed, the prospect of alternative food sources was alluring.

A similar process was taking place to the west, where the Jesuit Hernando de Santarén, coming from Culiacán in Sinaloa, entered the sierra of Topia in 1598. Spaniards, black slaves, and paid Indian (predominantly Tarascan), mestizo, and mulatto laborers from the south had been working silver mines in this area for more than a decade, having founded settlements at Topia, San Andrés, San Hipólito and Las Once Mil Vírgenes de Cosalá.[41] Franciscans accompanied them but had made few inroads in converting Indians outside the towns.[42] Several hundred Spaniards immigrated from Chiametla (Sinaloa) after mines there played out in the 1580s (and after they decimated their Indian slave labor pool).[43] From the reales de minas, Spanish encomenderos mustered enough force to compel Acaxee rancherías to work in the new mines. Acaxee resistance to the new colonists may have been diverted or diluted by the depredations of Tepehuan raids from the east and Xixime threats from the south.

Santarén was welcomed by the encomenderos, who recognized that the Jesuits could help consolidate dispersed rancherías ravaged by the recent epidemics of smallpox and measles and resettle the survivors near the mines. In addition to providing mining labor, Indians could also produce grain to supply the mines. In this alliance with the Jesuits, the encomenderos were able to fulfill their obligation to provide religious instruction to the Indians at the crown's expense. The Jesuits were apparently willing to cooperate if the labor and commodity exchanges took place under their supervision. They were able to stipulate that a fine would be imposed on any Spaniards who entered the missions without permission. Padre Santarén accompanied Captain Diego de Avila and other encomenderos, supported by Indian allies from the south and the Sinaloan coast, on a tour of the sierra in 1600. In what they called a pacification campaign, Spaniards presided over ceremonial formalities intended to awe the Indians with the power of the Spanish king. Spanish soldiers paraded on horseback in front of assemblages of Indians and then fired salvos to the Spanish king. Captain Avila explained the proper forms of deference to the king's representatives and taught the Acaxees to kiss the padre's hand. Threatening to return in greater force to enslave Indians who did not comply, the encomenderos ordered them to build houses and plant milpas on lands granted to them in the name of the king. These sites were intended to merge Acaxees from several rancherías into larger, more compact villages. The Indians were also ordered to build a *casa de comunidad*/community house, to wear clothing, and to cut their very long hair. Following the stick with a carrot, the Spaniards furnished cloth, seeds, tools (knives and axes were especially popular), and livestock to each pueblo. Individuals identified as caciques were named to offices and admonished to see that all these instructions were carried out. A school was established to train Indian boys to serve the church. An added incentive from the Spaniards was their promise to protect the Acaxees from frequent Xixime incursions. One of the main goals was to get the Indians to turn over images and bones (stored away from settlements in caves) that served as war trophies and fetishes. When they did comply, the Spaniards burned these items in huge bonfires. Exemplary beatings were administered to some Indians who demonstrated their insubordination publicly. This act of "taking possession" was carried out over several months; the case of the Acaxees is the only one for which we have detailed documentation, but the procedure must have been similar in subsequent "conquests." Since the Spaniards had only one permanent military garrison or presidio, enforcement of their orders had to be carried out largely by encomenderos and Indian allies who brandished arms but also made effective use of performance and ceremony.[44]

Efforts to convert the Xiximes to the south proceeded slowly. Shamans were particularly active in trying to discredit the Jesuits, linking them to plagues of sickness and hunger. They were able to convince most Xiximes that building churches would only invite more suffering. Nonetheless, the Jesuits continued to preach and baptize in makeshift ramadas/open-sided shelters. With Spanish soldiers from the presidio of San Hipólito, they concentrated on persuading the Xiximes to stop attacking the Acaxees. The Xiximes were particularly recalcitrant about giving up their customs and showed no fear in boldly taunting their adversaries. Playing a game of words, they exploited Spanish concerns about their apparent ritual cannibalism, no doubt taking some delight in embellishing their culinary preferences. As they explained to the padres, Indian flesh was ordinary, similar to beef. Blacks tasted more like salt pork, but Spaniards, savoring of lamb, were the most delicious of all. To what extent did the Jesuits take these revelations seriously? Much has been made recently of the colonial discourse on cannibalism and how the practice was exaggerated or contrived to magnify the savagery of the colonized. Scholars have also considered the degree to which indigenous peoples feigned cannibalism to terrify

Europeans or exaggerated the practice where it existed for ritual purposes. As Gananath Obeyesekere has observed, this was a perhaps more potent weapon than their real weapons in comparison to European guns. Certainly the Xiximes tried to use it as a threat, provoking unease if not the exodus of the padres.[45]

The Jesuits were more encouraged by their progress with the Acaxees, who not only provided labor for the mines and planted corn but also learned the catechism and continued to turn over their stone icons to the padres. The priests performed thousands of baptisms and continued their efforts to enforce monogamous unions.[46] Gift giving and protection from their former enemies seemed to mask the intrusions. Acaxees quickly caught on to the custom of allowing mine laborers a *pepena*/small portion of silver ore, but it is not clear whether unskilled workers shared this benefit.[47] Other Acaxees bartered their corn to petty traders, who took advantage of them and sometimes their women.[48]

Grievances were mostly aired away from the villages. Vigilance did not extend to woods and caves, where native rituals continued to be nurtured by shamans. There Acaxees still venerated former icons representing gods of war and fertility. Through dances and offerings of food and drink, Acaxees attempted to appease the old gods as well as a more recent addition to the pantheon: the icon symbolizing bloody stools. Elders warned that turning over more idols would bring starvation and death; it was imperative that the Indians make haste in restoring the relations of reciprocity that assured their survival by paying homage to their own gods.[49] Forced resettlement was expedited by the arrival of more Jesuits and soldiers in 1601, and prospects of taking refuge away from Spanish intruders were narrowing.

A Sobaibo Acaxee from the area of Alaya, a significant source of mining labor for Las Once Mil Vírgenes de Cosalá to the south and San Andrés to the west, listened to these shamans' predictions and imbued them with some meanings that were not completely autochthonous. After several months of communicating with other Acaxee headmen through messengers, Perico inspired a rebellion in late 1601.[50] He called himself God, Holy Spirit, and Bishop. It is probably no coincidence that the bishop of Guadalajara, Alonso de la Mota y Escobar, was at the time undertaking a pastoral visitation in Sinaloa. Claiming to have come from heaven to save the Indians from the false doctrine of the Jesuits, Perico performed the sacraments of baptism and matrimony. He also dissolved marriages that had been performed by the priests. He said mass, taught the Indians new prayers, and named disciples, including Santiago and San

Pedro, to carry news of the revolt to other pueblos and rancherías. The object was to exterminate all Spaniards, and Perico even claimed that he could change Spaniards into livestock to make them easier to kill. Within the next few weeks, Spaniards and other non-Indians were attacked in the mining camps and on the roads of the sierra, resulting in as many as fifty deaths. Churches and other buildings were destroyed. Acaxees who refused to join the rebellion were also targets.

Initial attempts by Governor Rodrigo de Vivero to negotiate with the rebels and then inflict decisive defeats failed, as Acaxees took up well-protected positions in rocky outcroppings where they had stored substantial provisions. The insurrection was only suppressed in 1603 by the incoming governor, Francisco de Urdiñola, who led an encomendero militia to the rugged summits of the sierra. Capitalizing on former intergroup hostilities, Spaniards had recruited troops from the Tepehuanes and Conchos; there were even some Acaxee allies. Mining activities had come to a virtual standstill during the two years of the insurrection. The campaign was particularly brutal, marked by summary trials and executions of hundreds of captured rebels. Forty-eight of the rebel leaders were executed by hanging and their heads displayed on pikes along the roads. Other rebels were sold into slavery. Most official accounts emphasized the role of *hechiceros* or shamans, considered agents of the devil by the Spaniards, in provoking the rebellion.[51] Not only for the religious, but also for lay Spaniards steeped in medieval Christianity, the devil was a force to be reckoned with, just as real as agents provocateurs of modern insurrections. They did not doubt that the devil could change humans into animals or make his idols weep. It had to have been the devil who caused the revolt.

Some Jesuits also blamed it on the exploitation of Indian labor by greedy Spaniards. Bishop Mota y Escobar went even further, using the pulpit to castigate encomenderos for their abusive behavior and informing the viceroy that these Spaniards could turn sheep into lions.[52] Nonetheless, the tendency of the invaders was to minimize dissension within their own ranks. So it was that Jesuit superiors could argue that lay Spaniards wished the Indians no ill, that they had committed no offense by entering their land and opening the mines that the Indians did not have the good sense to exploit. The benefits of salvation and material accumulation clearly outweighed the aggravations.[53]

The Acaxee revolt initiated a series of "first-generation" rebellions which affected the Nueva Vizcayan heartland in the seventeenth century. Many of its features reappeared in subsequent uprisings.[54] In its aftermath, Spaniards renewed efforts to impose their minimum requirements for "civilized" living and to create conditions for the resumption of mining. Twenty-five thousand pesos had already been spent in suppressing the revolt. Some seventy rancherías, diminished in size from casualties and starvation, were congregated into twenty-four villages by eight Jesuits.[55] Because many of the rebel leaders had been converts occupying positions of leadership, the fathers exercised more control in appointing Indian governors and officials whose loyalty was assured, in part through gifts and privileges. Some of these officials accompanied Jesuits on visits to Sinaloa, where they were supposed to observe in the more settled missions the benefits of compliance.[56] To overcome conditions of scarcity after the revolt, the new mission sites were located near rivers on lands that could be cleared and planted.

Conversion efforts met with mixed results. Receptivity was greatest among children and youth, who were boarded in the new villages and taught the doctrina in their own language in hastily constructed churches. Adults were not neglected, since the Jesuits recognized the powerful influence of former leaders and elders in the recent rebellion. Nonetheless, long conversations with elders yielded far fewer rewards than the molding of youthful minds. Jesuits took great pride in telling stories such as that of the thirteen-year-old girl who on her deathbed disavowed her natural parents and celebrated her imminent reunion with her "true" father in heaven.[57] These deliberate attempts to drive a wedge between parents and children rankled, inciting new attempts by shamans and elders to discount Christian teachings.[58]

Their credibility was enhanced by the appearance of Halley's comet, that ancestral omen of pending disaster, in 1607. Shamans predicted great mortality from disease and continued to emphasize the association between Christian baptism and death, encouraging people to flee the missions. When smallpox struck the next month, thousands succumbed, especially the young and the very old—as one Jesuit noted, all those who had escaped it the last time.[59] Vindication of the prophecy did little to promote active resistance, however, as the survivors of the epidemic struggled to avoid starvation.

Xiximes also felt the effects of the epidemic. Because of their long-standing enmity with the Acaxees and because they still held the upper hand in power relations with the Spaniards, they had not joined the revolt. After it was suppressed, Spaniards turned their attention to bringing the more immovable and bellicose Xiximes under control.[60] In particular, they wanted to stop Xixime incursions into areas of the Sierra de San Andrés where Acaxees had just been resettled. Spanish soldiers from

San Hipólito occasionally captured marauding Xiximes, chained them, and forced them to work in the mines. It is probably no coincidence that it was in 1607, as the smallpox epidemic penetrated the area, that some Xiximes sought assistance in the mining camps. The Jesuits began to congregate them at the mission of San Gregorio, attempting to lure others with lavish religious celebrations; these fiestas were also venues for impressing upon the Indians a hierarchy of command. Converted Acaxees were also settled nearby to serve as examples. At least one Jesuit argued that these efforts had some positive results among Xixime women, noting that the religiosity and virtue of these women were powerful enough to deter Spanish soldiers from molesting them.[61] This is a telling reference to what must have been a common problem for native women, but one rarely mentioned explicitly since it merited no sanctions.

The epidemic of 1607, coming after a severe drought, exacted a heavy toll among Xiximes, both children and adults. Shamans blamed the padres and convinced many Xiximes to stay away from their churches, but the disruptions and distress caused by smallpox and probably measles postponed a conflagration. Inevitably it came when Xiximes renewed their attacks on Acaxee settlements in 1610, after the latter refused to join them in the fight against the Spaniards. Acaxees appealed for aid to Governor Urdiñola, who first tried to negotiate with the Xiximes. The emissaries were rejected with a jibe about savory Spanish flesh. When several Spaniards were killed in the San Andrés area, the governor decided to make a decisive strike. He assembled a force of 200 armed Spaniards and more than 1,000 Indian allies to engage approximately 1,000 rebels. After pursuing the Xiximes through rugged terrain (often on foot) to two large armed camps, the Spaniards and their allies inflicted heavy casualties. The discovery of huge caches of skulls and bones served to justify a particularly ruthless campaign which gave little quarter and devastated villages and fields. In October, within a few months of its outbreak, the revolt had been suppressed. Ten of the leaders were hanged and many more sold into slavery.[62]

The mobilization of such a large army to subdue the Xiximes had cost the crown three times the amount spent in the Acaxee war. Officials were determined to secure the sierras of Topia and San Andrés to allow a resumption of silver mining and assure safe passage over the Topia road, which linked Sinaloa and Durango. While Xiximes from seventy-five rancherías were being resettled in five pueblos, several Jesuits were accompanied by soldiers from Sinaloa into the Sierra de Cariatapa in the northwest corner of Acaxee territory. This area along the Río Humaya had not been contacted by Jesuits; thus it served as refuge for Acaxee rebels who had fled there in 1604.[63] New discoveries of silver there served as the impetus for resettlement in mission villages where labor could be mobilized. Xiximes who bordered Tepehuanes northeast of Durango were also contacted for the first time.[64]

Spaniards attempted to secure stability through a mixture of coercion and persuasion. Demographic shifts that narrowed the great gap between the few hundred Spaniards and the many thousands of Indians had improved the invaders' strategic position, but they were still vulnerable. The garrison at San Hipólito was reinforced with additional soldiers and a fort; soldiers patrolled the area to back up the Jesuit campaigns to get Indians to plant and live in the new villages. Force alone was not the solution to keeping Indians in missions, since it could also prompt them to flee to inaccessible areas. Part of the solution was to co-opt Indians with gifts, especially of food, which was in scarce supply after the revolts. More than ever aware of the need to disenfranchise the old Indian leadership, Jesuits redoubled their efforts to assure a loyal cadre of officials. More seminaries were established to train handpicked youths for these jobs. The missionaries also dug in for a long siege with those "emissaries of the devil," the former shamans. Holy day fiestas and processions were employed to compete with the Indian ceremonies, which continued at less frequent intervals at night and away from the villages. And Jesuits vied with Indian healers and curing practices. Even though European methods of bleeding, purging, and inducing sweats were not much more medically efficacious than the native sucking and blowing rituals, when their ministrations saved a life the padres exploited the incident with great drama, affirming that their "magic" was the more powerful.[65]

While an uneasy truce prevailed west of the continental divide, Spanish intrusions accelerated to the east. Even before the revolts, the Topia mines were close to exhausting their higher-quality surface ores (which helps explain the push to exploit other silver deposits—for example, at Cariatapa—after 1610). The disruptions and suspensions caused by the fighting at the turn of the century sealed the shift in production to Guanacevi in Tepehuan territory.[66] In the late sixteenth century, imported labor supplied the needs of the Guanacevi mines, but by the middle of the first decade of the seventeenth, a severe labor shortage was reported there.[67] Jesuits, who had been ministering to the Indian population in Guanacevi since 1597, established a mission nearby at San Ignacio del Zape in 1602. From this site and the already established missions of Santiago Papasquiaro and Santa Catalina, increasing numbers of laborers were recruited to cut wood, make charcoal, and work in the mines themselves. In fact, Spanish miners and vecinos/landholding residents from Guanaceví provided gifts of seed, tools, and animals to entice the Indians to settle in Zape.[68] Other Tepehuanes were lured to Indé. Whenever possible, Tepehuan children were interned in rudimentary mission seminaries, where they were taught Christian precepts in their native languages.[69]

Using another time-honored "civilizing" strategy, officials recruited families of Mexican and Tarascan Indians, who were transported to the north. There they settled in barrios of the Tepehuan missions, providing assistance in catechism and in the construction of churches and irrigation ditches. These acculturated Indians also established a *cofradía*, or religious confraternity dedicated to the cult of a saint. Indian cofradías, American variants of a Mediterranean institution, had become more common in New Spain after the 1570s among central Mexican groups who built up cofradía assets in cash and livestock and exercised some autonomy in controlling these resources. These early Indian brotherhoods in Nueva Vizcaya were not intended for the recently converted Indian neophytes who were neither sufficiently acculturated nor subjugated. Jesuit domination of mission resources also inhibited the development of cofradías.[70]

Smallpox continued to claim Tepehuanes in the severe epidemics of 1602 and 1607, which most heavily affected children but also adults who had escaped the 1597 outbreak.[71] Shamans maintained that disease was brought by the padres in the food they gave the Indians. Among mission Tepehuanes, familiar rituals coexisted clandestinely with Christian. The uncertainty about which gods were more powerful seemed to argue for covering all the bases. Some Tepehuanes reportedly administered the Christian rite of baptism to the dying when the Jesuits could not get there in time. Jesuit concern with saving souls from eternal damnation motivated them to delegate this practice to Indians (a last resort sanctioned by the Church), despite the high probability that the exercise of this prerogative might blur the distinctions between cleric and layperson for neophytes.[72] Some of the padres saw signs that the Indians were becoming more accommodated to the changes. They noted that Tepehuanes were particularly attracted to the Holy Week festivities, where they performed native dances in the church patios. Nonetheless, at night and away from the missions, ritual drinking followed these celebrations. Attacks by Tepehuanes on Acaxee and Tarahumara neighbors had diminished. Their corn was eagerly bought up by traders supplying the mines, at one-fifth the cost of importing it.[73] Payment was rendered in blankets and clothing. Corn supplied by Indians (mostly unconverted ones or *gentiles*) was crucial to the survival of Spanish Nueva Vizcaya in the early conquest period.

Between 1607 and 1612, Jesuits cautiously moved north into the Sierra de Ocotlán, where they oversaw the construction of a large irrigation ditch in the San Pablo valley. Near Spanish settlements and mines at Indé, Jesuits ministered to Tepehuan mine workers, and they agreed to establish another mission at Tizonazo.[74] There they would resettle Salinero Indians who had been taken captive in slaving expeditions and warfare waged in the eastern deserts, along with other indigenous groups held in encomienda by powerful local elites. Epidemic disease struck again in 1610 (smallpox) and 1612 (perhaps typhus and/or dysentery). Seemingly more severe among Xiximes, the Acaxees and Tepehuanes were also affected, with many deaths reported among the latter. Children constituted more than two-thirds of the victims. Traditional ritual celebrations increased in frequency, and the Jesuits noted more cases of child sacrifice. According to the missionaries' interpretation, Tepehuanes believed that the souls or spirits of children could be substituted for those of dying adults.[75]

In spite of the earlier optimism of some of the Jesuits, by 1614 they were petitioning the governor and the viceroy to establish a presidio in the Tepehuan region.[76] They argued that without force to back them up, they could not carry out their program. It was impossible to exercise control over the Indians unless they could get them out of their rancherías. Only in the mission pueblos could they effectively teach the catechism and enforce monogamous unions. Backsliding among converts was common, because the Jesuits could not keep baptized Indians from contact with gentiles. Indian officials assigned to compel compliance with the rules were ignored. When the padres tried to prevent ceremonies involving drinking parties or break up consensual unions not sanctified by sacrament, they were often physically threatened. Padre Juan del Valle was not only bashed in the head with a bow but he also suffered the indignity of being struck by a woman, whom he characterized as having been irrationally motivated by female rage.[77] The Indians openly made fun of the religious and refused to obey their commands. Taking the argument one step beyond insubordination to the Jesuits, the Jesuit *padre provincial* (superior in Mexico) pointed out to the viceroy that there was no way to compel the Indians to work in the mines. Drought and pests severely damaged the corn harvest in 1615, and increased pilfering of livestock from the slowly growing number of ranches in the area contributed to unrest.

The order's fears began to be confirmed the next year. During Lent (perhaps to repudiate the particular fervor of this momentous Christian season) in 1616, a Tepehuan shaman and Christian apostate[78] known as Quautlatas began preaching to the Indians in the environs of Durango. Calling himself Bishop, he carried an icon resembling a primitive crucifix which he said represented the Son of God. He also carried two letters from God the Father that ordered native peoples[79] to rise up against the Spaniards and eliminate them from their territories. The invaders had stolen their lands, enslaved them, and brought death and destruction. Both civil and religious Spaniards were to be targeted. Tepehuanes were ordered to immediately stop participating in Christian rituals, which only made the priests stronger while weakening and even killing (through baptism) the native inhabitants.

To allay fears of Spanish firepower, Quautlatas promised that Indian warriors killed in battle would be resurrected after seven days and regain their youth. Not only would their lands be restored, they would produce corn and cattle in great abundance. The Indians need not fear Spanish reinforcements because divine providence would intervene to sink the invaders' ships. Tepehuanes who failed to take up arms would be punished by God the Father (also called the Sun God), who would send plagues, famines, and earthquakes. Some witnesses said that they saw the shaman open up the earth to swallow disbelievers. Quautlatas also appointed disciples to carry these messages, which were authenticated in written letters. Talking idols and apparitions began to appear in the area, exhorting the Indians to venerate their former gods and prepare for war. A particularly persistent apparition, appearing over fifty times, was called *tlacatla nextli*/resplendent one. Leaders called for secrecy in planning so as not to alert the Spaniards.[80]

The Jesuits soon reported these "machinations of the devil" to the governor. One of the prophet's emissaries, Don Melchor of Santiago Papasquiaro, was arrested and publicly flogged. Although the Jesuits also passed along rumors of the stockpiling of arrows, Spanish officials were not unduly concerned. Don Melchor and others continued to deliver impassioned entreaties, not only to Tepehuanes but also to Acaxees, Xiximes, Tarahumaras, Conchos and scattered bands to the east and north. They claimed the planned revolt would spread south to Zacatecas and north to New Mexico, and predicted that mestizos and mulattoes (whom they perceived as fellow victims) would join the rebels.

Communication over large distances indicates a sophisticated degree of coordination in planning the revolt. This communication may have been facilitated by the process of tribalization—the aggregation of formerly discrete groups—that conquest and missionization imposed. The tendency of the northern Tepehuanes to make stronger bonds across subgroups and rancherías seems to have accelerated after contact.[81] At least six Tepehuan captains committed squadrons of insurgents to the uprising, which was set for November 1616, after corn could be harvested and stockpiled. The leadership came from converted Indians; among them were cowhands and farmers who worked on Spanish *estancias*/ranches and as Jesuit-appointed officials of the missions.[82] One was Antonio, alguacil of Santa Catalina, who later related how he had been contacted and instructed by Tepehuanes from other pueblos, who told him that their goal was to make another world with only themselves in it.[83] The first targets would be the missions of Zape, Santiago Papasquiaro, and Santa Catalina; from the missions rebels would fan out to attack other targets. At the Zape mission, a huge celebration was planned for November 21, the Feast of the Presentation of the Virgin Mary, and Spaniards were expected to attend from miles around.[84]

The revolt actually began on November 16, when one of the Tepehuan captains named Francisco Gogojito attacked a mule train on the Topia road west of Santa Catalina. Most of the Indians were on foot, armed with bows and arrows; other weapons included clubs and lances. A few Indians rode horses. Within the next few days, the insurgents laid siege to the missions of Santiago Papasquiaro, Santa Catalina, and San Ignacio del Zape, as well as the mines of Guanaceví and surrounding Spanish estancias. In the first few days, more than 200 Spaniards, other non-Indians, and hired Indian laborers were killed. Among them were eight Jesuits, one Franciscan, and one Dominican. The missions were completely destroyed.

This destruction was accompanied by deliberate humiliation of the priests and desecration of religious objects. The Jesuits were mocked with Latin phrases from the mass, stripped of their clothing, then clubbed and hacked to death. Sometimes personal retribution was the motive, as in the case of the Tepehuan cacique who murdered Padre Juan Font, reportedly desiring revenge for the public reprimands and humiliation he had received. Rebels celebrated their victories with mock processions that paraded Indian women dressed as the Virgin Mary, statues, crosses, and other religious ornaments. Desecration of these objects followed: statues were flogged; crucifixes became targets for arrows; vestments were shredded and burned. Revelers spat on images of Christ, hurling epithets of "thief" and "drunk," and they urinated on the host. As they sacked missions and Spanish settlements, the natives killed many of the horses but appropriated mules, cattle, flour, tools, and weapons (explaining the harquebuses, swords, and shields that were later found among the rebels).

Although they killed all non-Indian men among the colonists, the rebels took some black women and *mulatas* as prisoners. These scenes of destruction were capped by ritual feasting and dancing throughout the night. Casks of wine for communion substituted for native intoxicants and allowed a few survivors to escape.[85]

When Governor Gaspar de Alvear received word of the rebellion on November 18, he summoned Tepehuan leaders from villages near Durango. Convinced that their denials of complicity were false, he had 70 of them executed. A Tepehuan attack on Durango, where the Spaniards were mobilizing, was repulsed in late November.[86] Only in December did the governor lead a column to Guanaceví and the hacienda of Sauceda where some Spaniards still held out. Their attackers fled. In pursuit, Spanish soldiers took prisoners, mostly women and children; they also discovered rebel supplies stored in caves. Buildings and ore-crushing plants had been completely destroyed.

Most of the rebels were safely ensconced in mountain hideouts. From camps of several hundred to a thousand people, they conducted occasional raids throughout southern Nueva Vizcaya, seriously disrupting mining, commerce, and agriculture.[87] One of the Jesuits reported in 1617 that a principal Tepehuan leader was a mestizo named Mateo Canelas, the son of a Spanish encomendero and a Tepehuan woman.[88] Spanish inability to put an end to these raids early on allowed Tepehuanes time and reason to attract support in 1617 from other groups, including Acaxees, Xiximes, Tarahumaras, Conchos, and Tobosos. In the Sierra de Cariatapa, an Acaxee cacique was persuaded by Tepehuan arguments that recent comets and unusual storms signaled the end of Spanish domination.[89] He warned that Acaxees who refused to follow him would be struck by disease or swallowed up by earthquakes. Emissaries carried his message to the missions, promising long life, abundant food, and freedom to those who followed him. The recent epidemic of measles that had killed many Indians in the fledgling mission at Teguciapa was cited as proof that the padres had brought pestilence with baptism. Among the cacique's followers were two black captains. Some of the rebels had Spanish harquebuses.[90] One of the main rebel leaders, Gogojito, had taken refuge in Xixime territory to the east and southeast, where he attracted allies who joined the Tepehuanes in fortified camps.[91] In the Valle de San Bartolomé, Conchos were attacking and burning Spanish estancias. Some rebel Conchos from the Franciscan mission of Babonoyaba sought refuge among southern Tarahumaras who were sympathizers of the uprising.[92]

At first Spanish resistance was weak in numbers, but even when more troops were mobilized (after nearly a year), the nature of the fighting—scattered guerrilla attacks—limited their effectiveness. In addition to soldiers and militias from Sinaloa and Zacatecas, Spanish forces included Concho, Lagunero, Acaxee, and Tepehuan allies. Some rebel bands were ferreted out of their hiding places; Gogojito was captured and executed in February 1618 near Guarisamey in Xixime territory.[93] Over time the razing of fields threatened to provoke starvation. Eventually, gifts and promises of amnesty proved to be more practical in ending the rebellion.[94] Offers of material rewards for the heads of slain enemies also netted results. For example, one head could fetch four hatchets, four knives, four hoes, machetes, and cloth.[95]

By the beginning of 1619, many rebels had surrendered and capitulated to resettlement. Among the remaining fugitives were several hundred Tepehuanes who were living north of the Sierra de Ocotlán in Tarahumara territory. The Tarahumaras may have feared these Tepehuanes and been inclined to believe the boast that "a single naked, unarmed Tepehuan could easily turn back ten armed Spaniards."[96] Led by an old warrior named Francisco Tucumudagui, these Tepehuanes continued to assault Spanish settlements and travelers along roads to the south. Taking Concho allies, Governor Alvear entered Tarahumara territory in February 1619. There he met with elders from several Tarahumara rancherías, who promised peace with the Spaniards if they would pardon the Tepehuanes. Some rebel Conchos also pledged to lay down their arms. All were given cloth and other gifts. Then Tucumudagui appeared, offering to resettle his followers in the San Pablo valley. He said that Spanish occupation of traditional Tepehuan lands and their treachery in failing to pay Indian allies had led him to revolt.

The main rebel contingents suspended hostilities by midyear, but not all agreed to come to terms with the Spaniards. Some Tepehuanes fled into the Sierra Tarahumara, others to the southern Xixime area. Resettlement efforts were underway among Tepehuanes, lower Tarahumaras, and Conchos, but they were piecemeal and slow. Not uncommonly, Indians sued for peace to buy time and then reneged on their pledges.[97] Some of the new missions were populated by Indians taken forcibly in chains to the new sites. In other cases, Indians were lured by material gifts. The rebellion was estimated to have cost the Spaniards more than a million pesos, in direct aid and loss of mining revenue. Approximately 300 non-Indians and several thousand Indians lost their lives.[98] Many who were not killed in battle were hanged or sold into slavery.[99]

During and after the rebellion, witnesses gave testimony as to the motivations of the Indians. According to the lieutenant governor of Nueva Vizcaya, Martín de Egurrola, the Indians had intended to kill all Spaniards, starting with the Jesuits and other religious whose bodies were to be dragged through the fields and left to feed the wolves and coyotes. Cases of mistreatment by lay Spaniards also surfaced in testimony.[100] The Jesuits later cited the forced draft labor/*repartimiento* of Tepehuanes in mines and haciendas as a cause.[101] The complaints and goals of the Tepehuan revolt echoed those of the previous uprisings. In fact, the characteristics of all three are striking in their correspondence.

Timing was a key factor. The revolts occurred when one or two generations of men and women were still inculcated with precontact worldviews and experiences. Skilled warriors and shamans continued to provide vigorous leadership based on a precontact vision. In all cases, the revolts were first-generation responses to sustained Spanish penetration, which brought demands for unaccustomed labor service, massive death by disease, forced relocations, and new norms of social organization. These changes were cataclysmic in disrupting the social networks and ritual activities that each of these groups had developed for sustaining life. Divine benevolence required ceremonial observances and food offerings that the Jesuits had prohibited. Combat and demonstrations of bravery in warfare no longer provided the means of acquiring social and political prerogatives. Furthermore, monogamy limited the productive and reproductive capacity of principal males; the particular vulnerability of pregnant women to epidemic disease exacerbated this problem. If it was the case that a yet intact cosmology supplied rationale for the revolt, then combat strategy and tactics could still be provided by experienced warriors, skilled in the use of bow and arrow, lance, and club.

All of the revolts had millenarian aspects even if they were not wholly nativistic and desiring a complete return to the past. Confronted by overwhelmingly oppressive threats, many native peoples contemplated the end of the present world order as the only way out.[102] Shamanic predictions of more death and starvation contributed to a highly paranoid ambience and sense of the urgency of action before it was too late. Perico and Quautlatas promised miraculous deliverance to paradise once the Spaniards were expelled. The gods had given them special powers—for example, the ability to turn humans into animals and to resurrect the dead—which assured the success of the insurrections as well as a post-revolutionary land of plenty. Complementing the proven warriors, the rebel leadership was also composed of prophets, former shamans who could legitimate the fight by imbuing it with a sense of divine will. This factor was extremely important in societies that did not clearly distinguish temporal leadership from divine inspiration.[103] Even though the thin documentation of the Xixime revolt does not reveal many particulars about the leadership, we do know that one of the key figures was described as a god-king.

The changes promised by millenarian redemption did not necessarily mean the obliteration of all alien introductions. In fact, as we have noted, a number of the rebel leaders were either biologically mestizos or culturally *ladino* (Hispanicized or acculturated), and they employed sophisticated knowledge about their oppressors in ways that gave them strategic advantages.[104] In a number of cases, rebels attempted to appropriate some of the signs of authority of their oppressors. Perico not only called himself God and Bishop but also performed imitations of the sacraments. The Acaxee who called himself Santiago testified that he knew that Santiago was the patron and captain of the Spanish soldiers; he may also have seen images of Santiago and his powerful horse.[105] Christian symbols also appear in the Tepehuan revolt: bishop, crucifix, Son of God. In part, the fact that Indians employed these particular titles indicates the effectiveness of the Spaniards in transmitting their codes of authority. Quautlatas distributed letters to his followers as a way of showing that his power came from a higher source. The written word and its ability to communicate and legitimate succinct messages could be a powerful phenomenon in a new arsenal of weapons among peoples who had not previously written their languages. The goal of the rebels was to reverse the world but not necessarily to remake it in exactly the same image it had assumed before. The key was to propitiate the forces beyond human control to assure material survival. In part, this meant the resumption of familiar ceremonies of reciprocity and relations of social exchange—especially ritual drinking parties and polygyny. This is why Jesuits who did not understand the Indians' worldview often reduced the reasons for revolt to a desire to reinstate the conditions for drunkenness and sexual promiscuity. Assuring survival also involved the retention of some aspects of the alien material culture—for example, tools and animals—and of the conquerors' religion with its powerful supernatural forces.

Appropriating emblems of the invasive culture for themselves was one way that Indians could effect a reversal. Another was to destroy signs and surrogates of Spanish authority. Destruction of Spanish living and working spaces was apparent in all of the revolts. Churches and mining equipment were particularly obvious reminders of oppression, but houses were also burned. Although cattle and sheep were often appropriated, the rebels were more likely to kill horses, more closely associated with the conquerors' destructive capabilities. The desecration of churches was particularly virulent, with crosses and hosts special targets. Mockery, as represented by the imitations of religious processions and ceremonies and the wearing of Christian vestments, was another way of reversing things. The supernatural forces that resided in the churches were not as menacing when they could be so easily defamed.

Killing was also a part of these revolts. Effecting a reversal meant expelling all the intruders, civil as well as religious. Since priests were seen as having special shamanic powers, they were deemed especially dangerous adversaries. Missionaries were clearly associated with mortality through the ceremony of baptism, which often preceded the death of those dying from epidemic disease as the missionaries hastened to save their souls. That is why the slayings of priests were particularly cruel and humiliating. But other Spaniards, blacks, and mixed-race individuals also lost their lives; occasionally mulatas and mestizas were taken captive and put to work by the Indian women. The non-Indian death toll was by far the highest in the Tepehuan revolt. In part, this is explained by a greater degree of planning and the coordination in executing the initial sieges. The ability of Tepehuanes to mobilize support over a large region and perpetuate the rebellion is another factor.

Ties of kinship and community were crucial factors in attracting adherents to the revolts. These bonds had been weakened by massive mortality but not totally demolished. At the same time, the heightened vulnerability produced by the deaths of able-bodied warriors made ethnic solidarity ever more urgent to the rebels. They did not hesitate to kill native collaborators or threaten to call down supernatural forces to eliminate them. Betrayers were reported to be swallowed up by sudden openings of deep crevices in the earth. That rivalries and distinctions within groups could severely undermine rebel capacity is quite evident in the case of the Acaxee revolt. In that case, the impetus seems to have come mainly from Sobaibo Acaxees, and they held out the longest while other subgroups decided to cooperate with the Spaniards. Tepehuanes seemed to have the most cohesion, which is surprising since they were the most dispersed of the three groups at contact. Their temporary solidarity owed a great deal to the conquerors' efforts to congregate them. Here the tribalization fostered by Spanish attempts to create larger group entities based on linguistic affinities is a factor. But even the Tepehuanes succumbed piecemeal in the end. Intra- and intergroup rivalries meant that factionalism existed for the enemy to exploit. It is obvious that precontact patterns of warfare played an important role in how enmities and alliances were manipulated by both sides in rebellions, but since we have little understanding of how these had been shifting over time in all these warrior societies, it is difficult to speculate on their specifics.[106]

Spaniards were very adept at this ploy, although in the Acaxee and Xixime cases it slowed their initial responses to insurrection. Given their relative disadvantage in numbers and ability to manage the terrain, the Spaniards' first reaction was to identify potential collaborators and to promise rewards for their cooperation. Negotiations dragged on, and it took time to determine whether assurances of cooperation were sincere. Stalling was frequently related to whether indigenous groups could maintain access to provisions, especially foodstuffs that could keep them physically fit. Access to the corn harvest and to obtaining other plants and animals perpetuated resistance. Precontact warfare almost always followed the gathering or storing of food.[107] When diplomacy ultimately failed, Spaniards made effective use of intergroup antagonism to recruit Indian allies. This time-honored tactic once again proved why vastly outnumbered Spaniards could overcome multitudes. Conversely, factionalism was not as much of a problem for Spaniards, who stuck together under attack. Technology was also an asset for the Europeans. Even in rugged terrain and when forced to wage guerrilla warfare, they had the upper hand in arms and their ability to maintain supply. Many Indians who took refuge in impregnable locations were eventually starved out as Spaniards razed their fields. Indian subsistence patterns in agriculture and hunting and gathering did not lend themselves to the stockpiling of resources and discouraged prolonged conflicts.

In these first-generation revolts, civil and religious authorities largely refrained from blaming each other, finding the devil to be both a logical and convenient scapegoat.[108] The references to mulattoes and mestizos among the rebels indicate that there were cracks in non-Indian solidarity. Mixed-race peoples/*castas* who did join the rebel ranks could provide valuable intelligence. For the most part, however, the outsiders enjoyed a unity based on their inability to share the worldview of the region's inhabitants. Even the Nahuatl and Tarascan-speaking Indians from central Mexico had more in common with and more to gain from Spanish ambitions. After each rebellion, Spanish victory was followed by a mixture of cruel exemplary punishments and the use of gifts to cajole submission. Traditional practices of warfare among the northern Indian groups seemed to be stymied.

Yet the degree to which Spaniards could impose conditions varied, and the process of domination proceeded precariously. The congregation of

Acaxees and Xiximes in towns moved forward slowly on foundations that were extremely shaky, as their participation in the Tepehuan revolt demonstrated. Spaniards, more wary and conversant in Indian languages, contrived to manipulate Indian government. Additional Jesuits arrived in the mission fields, and the non-Indian population grew slowly, by 1620 constituting 2,000 at the most. The "peace" prescribed by Spaniards for the Tepehuanes was far from having been achieved. The "conquerors" still found themselves in a defensive position, exposed to attack not only from beyond the frontier of mission settlements but also from within. From the vast landscape of southern Nueva Vizcaya, Spaniards carved out spaces for themselves, small enclaves where they could gobble resources. They also appropriated slices in time, taking advantage of the slowly evolving conditions that gave them an edge. Until they could dominate the whole, their fortunes depended largely on the intervals in which disaggregation, disease, and continuing intergroup warfare weakened Indian resistance. These physical factors put indigenous peoples at a disadvantage, but in this contested terrain they still had an arsenal of material and moral weapons to keep Spaniards at bay. To understand these, as well as to more thoroughly probe the context for the early interactions with Spaniards that have been highlighted in this chapter, let us take a step back in time and place the focus on the indigenous cultures.

ℰNVIRONMENT AND CULTURE

Sierra and semiarid. Although the ecological panorama of the Nueva Vizcayan heartland is remarkably diverse, the Sierra Madre Occidental and aridity are the dominating features of the physical landscape. The geographical boundaries of this study (see Map 1) loosely circumscribe an area that contained the bulk of the far north's Spanish population and economic activities during most of the colonial period.[1] Spanish settlement came to be concentrated in towns and mining reales which dotted the landscape from the southern boundary at the provincial capital of Guadiana or Durango to the north at San Felipe el Real de Chihuahua. The eastern boundary falls in the very arid highland desert known as the Bolsón de Mapimí and the western edge runs through the western escarpment and precipitous canyons of the Sierra Madre Occidental which extend into present-day Sinaloa. Alluvial basin floors and valleys fed by the streams and rivers which flow down from the sierra as well as grassy steppes punctuated by springs are features of the eastern foothills and upland plateau between Durango and Chihuahua. Many of these areas presented more woodlands to the gaze of Spaniards arriving in the sixteenth century than they do today after years of environmental degradation from mining and grazing in the colonial period. These activities continue today along with lumbering in the sierra.[2]

The Sierra Madre Occidental dictates wide variations in temperature and precipitation in the region. Seventy-five percent of the rain falls during the months of July, August, and September, but annual rainfall varies with altitude. On the Pacific side of the Sierra Madre divide, precipitation in hot canyon bottoms and valley floors can average more than 1,000 mm annually; higher, cooler elevations rising to 3,000 m receive less. In the foothills and plateau to the east of the mountains, annual precipitation averages from 400 to 700 mm, with higher elevations receiving slightly more. The eastern edge of the region, an elevated desert floor with enclosed basins and salt marshes, gets the least precipitation. Throughout the area, summer temperatures are high and therefore diminish moisture efficiency during the rainy months. Although summer droughts are frequent, in nondrought years rains can be torrential, causing waterways to flood. In either case transport is difficult, with excessive precipitation prohibiting river crossings and lack of water making it impossible to travel with animals. Heavy frosts are common in January and February, and a longer winter with snowfall at higher elevations east of the divide limits the growing season to April through October.

Although, as we have seen, early Spanish settlement was determined by the location of silver deposits and water sources, aboriginal patterns are not as easily explained. In fact, a significant controversy continues to cloud our understanding of the prehistoric period. It is clear that trade relations linked Mesoamerica and the Greater Southwest (including northwest Mexico) at least as early as the twelfth century, but the degree to which Mesoamerican sociopolitical organization may have penetrated the region is not well understood. The scant archaeological evidence does reveal the existence of large towns with sedentary agriculture, especially in Sinaloa and Sonora. In northwestern Chihuahua, Paquimé in the Casas Grandes Valley has been more extensively studied. At its peak in the fourteenth century, this trading outpost, probably Mesoamerican, housed over 2,000 people in multistoried apartments and boasted an extensive irrigation system, as well as a ceremonial complex.[3] Trade items included copper, turquoise, shells, salt, pottery, and obsidian.

In spite of the fact that no such complex site has been uncovered in southern Chihuahua or northern Durango, a Mesoamerican group known as the Chalchihuites is thought to have migrated north from Zacatecas by 600 A.D. and to have established several ceremonial and trading centers in the eastern foothills of the Sierra Madre. Some archaeologists have argued that the Chalchihuites culture coexisted with already established Loma San Gabriel peoples, part-time farmers who employed terracing in raising corn, but recent evidence suggests that these were not separate groups. The Chalchihuites exhibited clearly Mesoamerican features, including more elaborate building and ceramic styles, but they seem to have disappeared before 1350.[4] This exit coincides with the conventional hypothesis of archaeologists that in the fourteenth and fifteenth centuries most of the larger settlements of the Mexican northwest collapsed. A few dissenters posit that some of these societies with concentrated and socially stratified populations did not disintegrate until Old World diseases preceded Spanish conquerors up the trading corridors from Mesoamerica in the sixteenth century.[5] The controversies regarding the prehispanic north owe much to the relative paucity of archaeological investigation, especially for the protohistoric period, and to the confusion surrounding the characteristics of so-called chichimecas—a generic Nahuatl term (from Aztec times) that became synonymous with supposedly barbarian, nomadic peoples who originated in the far north and periodically invaded the territories of more "civilized" sedentaries.[6]

This debate concerning the nature of northern societies on the eve of conquest is crucial to our understanding of the nature and size of Indian societies in the region at the time of effective Spanish penetration. If precipitous demographic decline coincided with the European arrival in central Mexico, Spaniards moving northward later in the sixteenth century may have encountered native societies at varying stages of disorienting sociopolitical transformations.[7] The detailed descriptions by seventeenth-century Jesuits of relatively small, dispersed communities and low population densities may have led modern scholars to underestimate population size and misconstrue the nature of sociopolitical organization at the time of contact. In other words, the classic ranchería pattern advanced most persuasively by Edward H. Spicer to characterize the majority of northwestern Indian groups may not have been quite so omnipresent.[8]

According to the standard view of this northern prototype, rancherías were dispersed clusters of population comprising from one to a hundred dwellings, with perhaps an average population of 60–70 people.[9] Their inhabitants cultivated maize, beans, and squash with digging sticks, taking advantage of floodwaters rather than using formal irrigation systems. Agricultural activities were complemented by hunting and gathering, and ranchería locations shifted in accordance with subsistence cycles and climatic conditions. Political organization was decentralized and social stratification minimal. Elders guided the affairs of each ranchería, exercising moral suasion rather than coercion to achieve cooperation. Links between rancherías were largely limited to petty trade and to alliances formed within linguistic groups during frequent periods of intertribal warfare.

Analysis of the limited record affords little more than an educated guess about how the aboriginal societies of this study conformed to this pattern. It suggests that Acaxees and Xiximes exhibited somewhat more complex organizational forms and practiced more formal agriculture, that Tepehuanes and Tarahumaras closely resembled the ranchería pattern

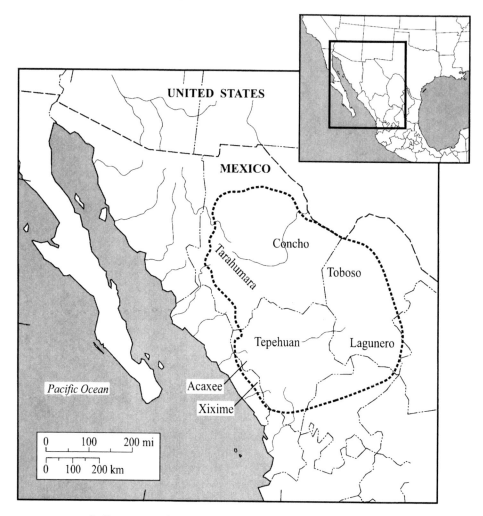

MAP 2. *Indigenous peoples.*

outlined above in that they had more mixed subsistence strategies, and that Conchos subsumed both ranchería and band peoples. All spoke languages of Uto-Aztecan stock, although they were mutually unintelligible. In this chapter, I will draw on the sparse archaeological and ethnological data to highlight cultural characteristics of each group near the time of European contact. In the aftermath of the decline of Mesoamerican centers in the region, these cultures had certainly experienced considerable flux in terms of warfare, migration, subsistence, and probably disease, and they were by no means static when Spaniards arrived. What follows is a somewhat speculative effort to provide a comparative overview of factors that most probably influenced varying patterns and early outcomes of contact with the invaders.

Acaxees and Xiximes occupied the gorges and canyon bottoms of the Sierra Madre in western Durango and eastern Sinaloa. The similarity between their languages (which were closely related to each other) and those of their Cahitan-speaking Sinaloa neighbors led Carl Sauer to suggest that they had migrated from the coastal lowlands.[10] Population estimates are highly speculative, based as they are on random observations by chroniclers of sixteenth-century expeditions and early-seventeenth-century Jesuit counts of souls.[11] Not as dense as the coastal populations, Xiximes and Acaxees nonetheless probably comprised groups of more than 20,000 each.[12] After a devastating epidemic in 1536 obliterated many coastal Sinaloans, some Xiximes moved from the western sierras down toward former Sinaloan territories in the foothills, adjacent to the lowlands along the Río Piaxtla. Most Xiximes and Acaxees remained in the mountains but at lower, warmer elevations in canyons and valleys. These sites were separated by steep canyon walls and high summits, which made communication difficult and hazardous but provided protection from enemies. To travel from one valley to another required great agility in climbing; a few miles distance as the crow flies could mean ten or more times that distance up and down precipitous ravines with hundreds of river crossings. Rope ladders fashioned from vines were used by Indian messengers when communication was urgent.

Among these sierra peoples could be found some apparently defensive settlements—fortified villages at higher elevations with stone and adobe structures—but most people lived dispersed in rancherías along the canyon floors. Where enough sun filtered through the thick pines, they raised corn, beans, squash, cotton, chilies, and fruit (guavas and sapotes) in narrow floodplains. Households (family units) had individual use rights on communal croplands. Slash-and-burn or swidden cultivation also meant frequent rotation or relocation of milpas. In some of the alluvial basin floors of the sierra, corn was planted twice a year and harvested in February and late fall. But the continuous rains from late June to late September could cause floods that inhibited a second planting.[13] The Indians hunted deer, fished in the rivers, and collected honey, wax, and mescal. From the mescal, a type of maguey cactus, the leaves were stripped and the core cooked to yield both food and drink; the process also produced a fiber that could be woven into mats. Native potters used clay deposits from surrounding hills to make ollas and utensils of various kinds.[14] Some of these items were traded to the coast for salt, fish, and shells that were heavily used for adornment by men and women. Through trade they also acquired parrots, which they raised for the feathers needed for their elaborate ceremonies, costumes, and weapons connected with warfare. In terms of both subsistence and trade, the products that could be harvested from the *monte*—wilderness lands of wood and brush—were just as important as those of the milpa.

Both Acaxees and Xiximes were divided into subgroups with distinct names who lived in rancherías and pueblos, not distant from one another as the crow flies but separated by steep canyons and craggy peaks. The rancherías comprised from a handful to a score of dwellings of branches and straw, mud, or occasionally adobe with thatched roofs.[15] The pueblos tended to be located on peaks or defensible outcroppings and contained adobe and stone houses, including at least one larger structure intended for ceremonial use. Ball courts with stone walls were also characteristic of the larger settlements. Residents of neighboring settlements challenged one another to ball games played on a flat sunken court with side walls. The game resembled its Mesoamerican counterpart, being played with a rubbery ball made from tree sap, the size of a head and weighing from two to three pounds. In this case the object of the game (or the target of the ball) is not clear, but the ball could only be passed by hitting it with the shoulders. The elaborate three-day ritual which preceded the game involved dancing and chanting by both women and men to prepare for the match. Probably related to warfare in the pre-Hispanic era, during the early contact period it provided an occasion for gambling. Among the items wagered were objects of clothing, bows, arrows, knives, and even silver.[16] The ball courts certainly suggest that the sierra groups had Mesoamerican affinities or legacies. Another indication is found in the stone altars of the larger settlements. Many of these Mesoamerican characteristics have been corroborated by recent archaeological work at La Mesa de los Tlahuitoles in Durango.[17]

Political organization exhibited some hierarchical elements, or at least there seem to have been different functions distributed among distinct civil, religious, and wartime leaders. Spanish sources indicate that they believed these caciques were heads of lineages or clans. An overlord or petty king is reported to have exercised control over an area that, during warfare at least, transcended single settlements[18] where caciques, war captains, and shamans wielded limited degrees of authority. Bravery in combat conferred status on warriors. Shamans, labeled hechiceros or sorcerers by Spaniards, could summon up supernatural powers which enabled them to manipulate the weather and other features of the natural environment, as well as human behavior and health. Although martial leadership was based on merit, there is some evidence that the office of hechicero was hereditary. All of these men of senior status (*principales*) seem to have enjoyed more economic benefits, possessing more wives and goods than others.[19]

A wide assortment of icons implies a broad pantheon of deities. Most of the images were small, carved pieces of wood or stone in the form of animals (deer, turtles, rabbits, eagles, and other birds) and humans, representing gods of fertility, rain, wind, hail, fire, and sickness. A few more powerful supernaturals were believed to occupy caves. There is some evidence of a supreme deity that may have had a dual character related to sun and moon or wet and dry seasons.[20] Spirits in animal and human form also appeared to Indians, giving them specific commands. Astrological phenomena such as comets and shooting stars were harbingers of bad luck. The dead were buried in caves away from dwellings, along with food and hunting implements.

Communal rituals focused on material survival through warfare and agriculture. Frequent intertribal warfare could take the form of pitched battles or surprise raids. The warriors were skilled in the use of bows and arrows, clubs, and lances. Acaxees and Xiximes (the latter seemingly more bellicose) were aggressive in attacking each other, with the primary intent of acquiring foodstuffs, goods, and women.[21] The assaults tended to be launched just after harvest, when supplies had been stored, warriors were well nourished, and hunting could be forgone for a time. Although not intended as a means of acquiring calories, ritual cannibalism usually followed battles as a part of victory celebrations, which were accompanied by dancing, chanting, drums, and the use of intoxicants (fermented cactus and peyote). Consuming the flesh of slain enemies stewed with corn and beans was believed to impart qualities of courage and daring. We have seen how the Xiximes exaggerated the practice in their attempts to fend off the Jesuits, who did not understand its significance despite its correspondence with the Eucharist. Nor could they find any rationality in another ritual associated with warfare. Among the Xiximes, certain young women were groomed from childhood to bring good fortune during times of warfare. As men went out to do battle, a chaste young maiden was shut up in a cave to fast and pray for their success. If they returned victorious, the maiden was presented with the head or skeleton of a slain warrior which she clothed, fed, and wedded in a ceremonial dance. The rest of the men and women present took their turns dancing with the bones before the ritual feast. Because such relics were powerful forces, Xiximes stored skulls in caves as trophies, and skeletons were suspended from trees to invoke plentiful harvests.[22] Ritual dancing was also associated with agricultural tasks, and fertility rites linked human sexuality and reproductive functions to the fertility of the land. These ritual activities paralleled practices of coastal Sinaloans, suggesting that there was some cultural unity between the groups.[23]

The prominence of warfare seems to have given men more privileged status than women in sierra societies. Timidity and cowardice were construed as female qualities and considered antithetical to male virtues of valor and military prowess. In the seventeenth century, Jesuits reported that Indians in Topia had explained that "the church was like a woman because it had no bow and arrows."[24] In the economic realm, however, there was considerable complementarity in productive activities. Agricultural and gathering tasks were performed by both men and women, while hunting and raiding were the preserve of men. Women were responsible for food preservation and preparation. They wove cloth for mantas, mostly from coarse pita (agave) fiber but also from the cotton cultivated in the warmer elevations, and they made clay pots and baskets. They were also reported to be adept at carrying heavy loads in huge basket frames/*cacastlas* that accommodated provisions and belongings for journeys and migrations. Couples could carry everything they owned, in addition to the smallest children, when they moved. Some women apparently achieved more status than others as shamans, but in general women seemed to have been valued for both their productive capacity and the reproductive function so necessary to survival. Strong affective bonds characterized parent-child relations, and guidance and instruction for children were imparted through oral traditions and example rather than physical punishment.[25]

What are we to make of the few early European observations about women? Some noted that women were remarkably strong and agile in carrying heavy loads through rugged terrain. Does this reflect low status —women as beasts of burden—or female domination of property and living arrangements, including migrations and food distribution?[26] Does the practice of polygyny, the apparent ease with which spouses could be changed, and the active participation of women in drinking rituals indicate male dominance or female freedom in sexual practices? As we have seen, among Xiximes young women who lacked virtue or purity could be held accountable for defeat in warfare and punished by exile or death.[27]

Does this custom imply female centrality in religious beliefs or exploitation? Does the practice of raiding other groups for women signify that they were highly valued for their potential productive and reproductive capacity or that they were simply objects of exploitation for these purposes? Did they serve as prestige items?[28]

Many of the sociocultural characteristics of these groups can never be explained definitively from the meager archaeological and documentary record available to us, but what we do know provides testimony to the capacity of pre-Hispanic Xiximes and Acaxees to organize production and trade and to survive in a relatively inhospitable mountain environment with higher population densities than were achieved under Spanish rule. Their Tepehuan neighbors to the east occupied a more benign habitat, at least for material subsistence.

Tepehuan Indians, the most geographically extended of the sierra groups, have been divided by anthropologists into southern and northern groups who speak different dialects of the Tepehuan language.[29] In the sixteenth century, perhaps 40,000 northern Tepehuanes inhabited the area northwest of the present city of Durango and extending into the upper San Pablo valley of southern Chihuahua.[30] They occupied the eastern foothills of the sierras and the valleys of the Río Nazas headwaters. Today there are approximately 8,000 Tepehuanes living further southwest in upland and canyon rancherías of southeastern Chihuahua, between Guadalupe y Calvo on the south and the Río Verde on the north. These natives, some of whom have mixed with outsiders who have increasingly penetrated the area in the twentieth century, are most probably descendants of Tepehuanes who withdrew from their homeland after the Tepehuan rebellion in the seventeenth century.[31] Jesuits pushed into the fugitive region in the eighteenth century, establishing missions at Baborigame and Navogame with limited success.

The earliest descriptions of Tepehuanes come from Francisco de Ibarra's 1563–1565 expedition. Spaniards noted settlements with adobe and stone houses where Indians raised corn and beans. Nonetheless, Ibarra's chronicler, Baltasar de Obregón, argued that "the chase" was the primary economic activity.[32] Some anthropologists have maintained that the Tepehuanes were the likely heirs of the Loma San Gabriel-Chalchihuites cultures mentioned above, but recent archaeological investigations from the Hervideros Project have reduced the credibility of that assumption and questioned even the nature of Tepehuan agriculture.[33] They were represented as the most bellicose of Nueva Vizcayan agriculturists, and there is some evidence that the continual warfare they waged against Tarahumaras to the north and Acaxees to the west went beyond plunder, becoming attempts to make these groups tributaries.[34] As one elder later explained to a Jesuit missionary, if the Tepehuanes didn't wage war, they had nothing to eat. By the early seventeenth century, descriptions portray Tepehuanes as living in a dispersed, more typically ranchería fashion. One Jesuit reported that they lived in "groups of thirty to forty people, scattered here and there."[35]

The foothills of the eastern sierra and the central plateau occupied by Tepehuanes had higher average elevations than the canyon floors of the western sierra, subjecting them to different climatic conditions in agriculture. The main crops were corn, squash, and beans; maize was harvested only once per year, in the fall, and the ranchería fields were scattered. Winters were longer, and hail and frost (which could be very heavy in January and February) were constant threats to agriculture. Cooler temperatures also prescribed differences in dwellings, which were probably constructed of stone and mud or logs and saplings. A less productive agriculture may have resulted in less concentrated populations than in the case of Acaxees and Xiximes and more reliance on hunting and gathering—Tepehuanes hunted deer, coyotes, rabbits, and other small animals.[36] Tepehuanes were distributed throughout an enormous area, and they apparently mixed subsistence strategies depending upon their locations. In areas north of Durango, they seem to have chosen sites distant from water sources where they practiced dry farming.

Recent research, based on material and linguistic factors, suggests that at about the end of the fifteenth century Tepehuanes split from their Pima relatives in Sonora and moved into the eastern sierra and altiplano regions, where they apparently made use of some vestiges of the former Chalchihuites culture, including burying their dead in spaces under ruined dwellings left by the Chalchihuites.[37] Political organization was probably slightly more decentralized than in the case of the western sierra groups, but expanding warfare in the immediate precontact period may have fostered broader associations. The roles of women conform to the picture sketched above for the other groups. In a Jesuit retelling, one story seems to cast female and male qualities in polar terms. An older woman chose to openly disagree with a group of Tepehuanes who were reacting hostilely to Jesuit overtures, declaring, "Even though I am just a miserable woman, I have the courage and heart to obey the padre."[38]

Some differences between Tepehuanes and their western sierra dwelling counterparts can be seen in religious customs. Although ritual cannibalism of enemy hearts may have been practiced, Jesuits did not report discoveries of huge caches of skulls and bones, where there was such a strong symbolic association between death and fertility, which had so shocked them in the case of the Acaxees and Xiximes. They did find many small fetishes and even a larger stone idol in the form of a column with a human head, called Ubámari. The location of these artifacts west of Zape and in the Sierra de Ocotlán coincided with the ruins of earlier Chalchihuites sites. Whether or not the Tepehuanes appropriated any of these religious artifacts or their significance is not known.[39] One alleged practice of Tepehuanes did occasion the priests' abhorrence: child sacrifice. The Jesuits believed that Tepehuanes engaged in the practice of offering a child to a supernatural spirit as a means of saving the life of a dying adult.[40] They reportedly believed in an afterlife in which one soul could be substituted for another. As the Jesuits (mis)interpreted these beliefs, after death one's soul went to the monte; there a spirit consumed those who had been bad and allowed the good to go on to a better place.[41] A concept of an afterlife is also indicated by native insistence that Christian admonitions about hell were irrelevant, since Tepehuanes were immortal. They also avoided places where people were buried, fearing that the dead would carry them away. When a person died inside his or her house, the dwelling was burned.[42] Like the other groups, Tepehuanes used peyote and fermented mescal in their ceremonies; they may have also organized fiestas in which *tesgüino* or maize beer was consumed. Contemporary Tepehuanes hold such gatherings to ensure good harvests and promote the health of people and animals.[43]

If it is hard to resist the temptation to draw on the ethnographic present to understand the past in the case of the Tepehuanes, it is even more difficult in the case of their northern neighbors, the Tarahumaras. Along with Yaquis, Tarahumaras were the most studied of northern Mexican Indians in the twentieth century.[44] At contact, many of them inhabited the valleys and upland meadows of the eastern Sierra Madre foothills of central Chihuahua; others lived in the higher mountain and canyon country to the west. Today they occupy canyons and high country even further west as a result of deliberate colonial migrations and probably the assimilation of other *serranos*/sierra inhabitants such as Témoris, Tubares, Chínipas, and Guazapares. It is also possible that some of the latter were actually part of the larger Tarahumara ethnic group but had been identified as separate groups by Spanish agents.

The first detailed representations of the Tarahumara come from the early seventeenth century, but more prolonged resistance to outsiders, which for some Tarahumaras has lasted until the present, has left historians a chronologically punctuated series of descriptions of contact peoples. Of all the groups considered here, the Tarahumara, if not unaffected by material changes, best succeeded in perpetuating a worldview which was strongly aboriginal.[45] Because the process of incorporation took so long, population estimates are based on piecemeal guesses, but 100,000 Tarahumaras at contact is probably not an exaggeration.[46] Of the groups discussed so far, they were the most decentralized politically. Rancherías predominated as a settlement pattern; population density was thin, and many Tarahumaras dwelt in caves. Others also lived dispersed along waterways in houses of stone or stick construction. But the houses were so scattered that it was difficult to find "two adjacent dwellings, not separated by leagues."[47] The nuclear family was the basic unit, although an extended family might have separate apartments within caves.[48]

Each ranchería had a headman chosen from among the elders or principales, but decisions were consensual processes undertaken after lengthy discussions among the men. Consultations (or *tlatoles*, as they were called by Spaniards using the Nahuatl word) were also associated with the other groups, but outsiders particularly emphasized them in connection with the Tarahumara. Governance was accomplished without marked hierarchical divisions. Control seems to have been exercised mainly by insistence on conformity to codes of conduct continuously reiterated in the exhortatory speeches or sermons (*pláticas*) of elders. Improper behavior that violated the ponderous emphasis on relations of mutual obligation could elicit the heavy sting of public rebuke and ultimately shunning, tantamount to death in a society based on reciprocity.

Other organizing features of precontact Tarahumara society, including relations with outsiders, economic structures, and division of labor, are not so easily interpreted. Tarahumaras did engage in warfare with the Tepehuanes, but it seems that the latter were most often the aggressors and may have already prompted a Tarahumara tendency to withdraw to the west and north before the Spaniards arrived. There may also have been intratribal warfare among Tarahumaras themselves, and Tobosos from the east also raided Tarahumara settlements. There is some disagreement about whether the Tarahumara practiced the ritual cannibalism described for the other groups. Ceremonies did include dancing with scalps after battles, but we have no descriptions that suggest they consumed flesh.[49] Trade items made of shell suggest that they engaged in long-distance trade; the keen aptitude they demonstrated for trade with Spaniards may have derived from custom. In valleys fed by the Río Conchos, Tarahumaras produced corn and beans with small surpluses, which they stockpiled in stone storehouses of more durable construction than their residences. The substantial contribution of female labor to productive activities impressed several Spanish observers.[50] The transhumance so often associated with the Tarahumaras reflected complementary harvesting of cultigens and of forest resources, but migratory patterns probably became more mixed after the Spanish introduction of sheep.[51]

Ceremonial life, as with the other groups, was dominated by dancing and drinking parties, but in this case we have more detailed descriptions. *Tiswin* (tesgüino) was consumed frequently in celebrations called *tesgüinadas* that occurred around communal projects, including clearing, planting, harvesting, and construction. The primary function of ceremonies and curing rituals was to ensure balance and harmony in the universe by placating supernatural forces. Curing ceremonies by native doctors involved sucking out foreign, harmful objects placed there by sorcerers and blowing their healing breath over bodies. The latter practice probably was related to the Tarahumara concept of the many souls of the body.[52] Contemporary Tarahumara people identify souls with breath and regard them as the repositories of knowledge and behavior. Souls continued to live after one's death, and they tried to get the living to join them. Like the Tepehuanes, Tarahumaras avoided places where people died or were buried.[53]

Concho Indians, who populated an extensive territory—north of the Tarahumaras, east of Tepehuanes and Tarahumaras, and west of hunter/gatherer groups that have been identified as Tobosos, Chizos, Salineros, and Cabezas (among many others)—have generated the least homogeneous descriptions of the nature of their society. Portrayed at times as nomadic and at other times as agriculturalists, it seems most probable that many subgroups of Conchos populated dispersed rancherías, combining farming with hunting and gathering. The degree to which horticulture was practiced varied within the larger generic grouping.[54] Their political organization was probably even more decentralized than that of the Tarahumaras. Franciscans who resettled some of the Conchos in missions in fits and starts left less documentation providing either ethnographic descriptions or successive population estimates.[55] The disaggregation of Conchos appears to have increased over time in the colonial period, partly due to the fact that they were the first group in Nueva Vizcaya intensively subjected by Spaniards to labor service. In addition, they had access on their eastern and northern borders to regions of refuge in the desert and the sierra, where they created shifting alliances with other groups.

Several obstacles make it difficult to classify groups bordering Concho territory on the east—for example, Tobosos, Chizos, Salineros, and Cabezas. Spaniards were apt to apply the label *nación* to seemingly discrete bands[56] that may actually have had affiliations with others. Chantal Cramaussel attributes the confusion to the tendency of ethnohistorians to identify naciones as discrete ethnic groups rather than as subgroupings (probably kin related) of larger entities who were assigned in encomienda to provide labor for a particular Spaniard.[57] At least in the early period, then, Spaniards were subdividing larger ethnic polities into smaller groupings called naciones. This clouds our understanding of the relationship between what Spaniards identified as naciones and the concept of ethnicity, a conundrum which applies to all of the groups studied here. Retroactively, scholars have used linguistic affiliations to define specific ethnic polities. But at what point did peoples speaking the same language or similar dialects began to identify with these classifications? As we shall see, there is considerable evidence to indicate that colonial stresses and new or shifting alliances resulted in the name a people used to identify themselves as a people with a distinct identity.

Whatever their ethnic affiliation, the supposedly band groups rather quickly adopted the horse in the sixteenth century. At the same time that they experienced population loss through disease, they were able to range over more extensive territory to hunt wild animals and feral cattle, affording them considerable freedom from authoritarian impositions. This prompts speculation about whether some of them may have moved from a semisedentary (partially agricultural) to a nomadic-raiding lifestyle in response to Spanish invasion.[58] At least one historian has made a persuasive argument that the Salineros were Tepehuanes (*tepehuanes del desierto*) who followed this strategy to avoid working for Spaniards in the salt pits that supplied Santa Bárbara.[59] Certainly the very arid natural environment east of the Río Florido—that part of the region under study here with the lowest annual precipitation—provides a strong argument for aboriginal nonsedentism, whether it occurred as a result of flight from the invaders or not. They were highly adept at making efficient use of desert resources. In addition to animal proteins obtained from hunting and raiding, these groups derived considerable subsistence (food, clothing, and shelter) from the fruits and fibers of mesquite and cactus plants.[60]

In these more atomized societies, leadership and social standing were heavily determined by hunting skills and bravery in warfare. Clusters of 20 to 50 people—extended kinship groups—lived in mobile bands, deriving subsistence from hunting, gathering, and raiding. War chiefs and shamans provided leadership for discrete situations, offering guidance for battle, subsistence, and ceremonial activities. Ceremonies were similar to the ones described for the more sedentary groups, with rituals related to warfare — ritual cannibalism as well as dancing with heads and booty — occurring more frequently. Shifting interband alliances were common, and they were often cemented through marriage.[61] Although these groups were not as systematically congregated after conquest, they underwent many changes as a result of contact; certainly their presence was heavily felt by Spaniards.

Taken as a whole and considered on a continuum, the indigenous peoples of the Nueva Vizcayan heartland demonstrate a range of cultural and organizational characteristics. Although the variations are not wide, they contain the bases for different patterns of interrelationships with Spaniards and ultimately help to explain different colonial outcomes. In considering these environmental, demographic, organizational, and cosmological factors, we should recognize that no single variable will be deterministic. First, the categories themselves are interrelated; for example, environment will have limiting effects on population density and therefore organization in its political, social, and economic forms. And second, the conditions of Spanish invasion will be diverse in themselves and in their interaction with discrete groups.

Before proceeding, it is important to reiterate that this analysis is based on an imperfect and conjectural view of Indian societies at contact. First of all, how do we define the moment of contact? Does it occur with the invasion of alien microbes or human beings themselves? The interval in Nueva Vizcaya is significant because the former preceded the latter by at least one generation and much more if we are talking about sustained settlement. This situation lends itself to unresolvable uncertainty about the size of contact populations. Archaeology could be of some assistance here, but archaeological investigation and paleopathological studies are sorely lacking for this region. Demographic instability related to warfare, environment, and nutrition undoubtedly characterized Nueva Vizcaya before European invasion, but we have little knowledge of specific migrations and fluctuations.[62] What we know comes largely from a sparse and fragmentary historical record which begins in the later sixteenth century.

These caveats notwithstanding, we can hypothesize about the ways in which certain characteristics of Nueva Vizcayan contact societies might produce diverse outcomes early in the colonial encounter. The interrelationship of physical environment and demography played a crucial role. The most concentrated populations were found in the lower elevations of the western escarpment of the Sierra Madres, home of the Acaxees and Xiximes. Despite the rugged mountain terrain, double cropping in valleys and on canyon floors produced higher yields, capable of sustaining larger discrete clusters. Greater population concentration helps to account for the more hierarchical political organization that seemed to characterize this area. Endemic warfare also had demographic causes and effects. Raiding other groups for foodstuffs may have increased as population strained the carrying capacity of the land before contact. Subsequent drastic population decline could explain continued raiding by groups whose ability to produce and reproduce was in crisis. The Spanish introduction of grazing animals and the heavy deforestation that accompanied mining also reduced the subsistence base. Initial population decline was highest in the areas of greatest concentration, affecting first the coastal Sinaloan Indians, whose territories were targets of Spanish slaving expeditions, and then moving into the Acaxee and Xixime areas. Substantial trade between these regions probably carried disease to the western sierras first.

The effects of disease were probably felt at a less accelerated pace on the eastern side, where the population was more dispersed. The aggressions of the reputedly bellicose and perhaps territorially expanding Tepehuanes may have taken on a more urgent character when they experienced the effects of epidemics. Their attacks on Acaxees and Tarahumaras seem to have increased in the early contact period. Tepehuanes pushed northward, and some Tarahumaras began moving west. Thus the ripple effects of death by disease were felt in northern Durango and southern Chihuahua before Spaniards began to conquer the area in the last half of the sixteenth century.

Other Spanish introductions caused shifts and displacements as well. Eastern groups, whether aboriginally nonsedentary or not, adopted the horse and preyed upon the feral cattle that were a legacy of the Coronado expedition. Some Conchos remained in their rancherías along the Río Florido, while others moved northward. Further dislocations ensued when Spaniards actually began to settle southern Nueva Vizcaya, as we noted in the previous chapter. Where Spaniards found silver and denser populations in the proximity—for example, Xiximes and Acaxees—Indian populations underwent earlier decline and were less likely to recover. Even the more dispersed Tepehuanes, Tarahumaras, and Conchos suffered high death rates when they remained in the region of heaviest Spanish settlement in northeastern Durango and southeastern Chihuahua. On the other hand, these groups had more potential for flight to less accessible, although agriculturally inhospitable, regions.

The picture painted so far emphasizes demography and ecology in explaining cultural evolution. What about the role of material and religious aspects of indigenous societies? The continuum we have sketched in this chapter ranges from a somewhat higher degree of political centralization and hierarchy (and more Mesoamerican features) among Acaxees and Xiximes to successively lesser degrees among Tepehuanes, Tarahumaras, Conchos, and eastern tribes, in that order. Only the latter conform to the nomadic chichimeca stereotype (simplified by Spaniards from the Aztec conception) that is often applied indiscriminately to northern Mexico. The labels themselves were largely a product of Spanish imagination and invention, which linked peaceful Indians with agriculture and bellicosity with hunting and gathering.[63] Although none of these groups had complex systems for shifting resources and surpluses up a hierarchical ladder, primitive accumulation, barter, and some long-distance trade were all present in varying degrees. We have seen in this chapter how the indigenous modes of production and exchange, including frequent warfare, were disrupted by early contact with Spaniards. The relationships between native groups—in particular the internecine warfare of the precontact period—were also altered by the Spanish invasion. Neither bellicosity nor previous patterns of affiliation with outsiders provided the means for achieving more than momentary relief from people who were technologically and culturally a breed apart from anything these Nueva Vizcayan groups had encountered in their historical memory. These factors might have been overcome, but others, like disease and habitat degradation, were more difficult for them to contend with.

Was there something about worldview or religion that afforded some native peoples greater inherent capacity to survive colonialism?[64] Cosmovisions with millenarian overtones that emphasized cyclical destruction and renewal certainly influenced the decisions of the groups that rebelled. But armed resistance alone was not sufficient. To what extent did belief systems provide blueprints that fostered the self-preservation mechanisms of groups? How did colonial impositions themselves shape the process of ethnic identification among linguistically related peoples who had been loosely affiliated and whose previous patterns had included the incorporation of outsiders through raiding and trading? Could the cultural opportunism (borrowings) of these groups and evolving ethnic boundaries counter the disintegrative pressures of disease and coercive labor appropriation? These elements must be correlated with the variable nature of Spanish intrusions in explaining how opportunism was mediated to produce different outcomes across the five groups. To sort through this tapestry of factors in the following chapters, we will examine how its most binding thread—the mission—is interwoven with the world outside it.

THREE

A COUNTERFEIT PEACE, 1620-1690

In the 1620s, for the moment quiescent indigenous peoples in Nueva Vizcaya tolerated the redoubled efforts by Spaniards to assert control. Neither side failed to recognize the fragility of an unwritten truce. Many Indian caciques sued for peace to buy time for regrouping or flight.[1] With their millennial hopes quashed, they had no clear vision of the future. Spaniards did, but they now saw it would be more difficult to impose. The category of "indios de media paz," or half-pacified Indians who had not sufficiently bought into the system, presented a dilemma. These semisedentary groups who practiced some agriculture were considered to have greater potential for reduction than their nomadic counterparts, but Spaniards were divided and unsure about how to deal with their "recalcitrance." Force was not the sole answer, first because Spaniards and their allies were heavily outnumbered. But even when they did have the might in a particular location, labor coercion often resulted in flight to spaces outside of the Spanish sphere. Nor was recompense in material goods attractive to many Indians if contributing to the Spanish market economy took them too far afield of their homelands and traditional subsistence. Although Spanish authorities labeled cultural difference and resistance to subordination as sloth and lethargy, they were well aware of the conundrum and sought to blend sticks and carrots to resolve it throughout the seventeenth century.[2] The Spanish fort or presidio, so often identified, along with the mission, as a primary institution of conquest in the north, has an erratic history. Relatively few presidios, or permanent garrisons, existed in the north before the second half of the seventeenth century, and, until the second half of the eighteenth, the bulk of Spanish force or defense consisted of irregular militias formed by leading citizens and the Indian allies that could be recruited upon short notice, usually members of permanent hacienda workforces.[3]

Following the Tepehuan rebellion, Spaniards enslaved hundreds of Indians who refused to capitulate or violated terms of surrender. Children, as well as women and men, were sold at auctions in Durango and taken in chains to new workplaces. In 1620, Governor Mateo de Vesga resumed the pacification tour begun by former governor Alvear and over the next two years estimated the Indian population of Nueva Vizcaya, including coastal Sinaloa and Parras, at more than 200,000. Some Tepehuanes returned to Santiago Papasquiaro, Santa Catalina, and other villages north of Durango, where they began to reconstruct buildings and plant fields. Nahuatl-speaking Indians from central Mexico continued to demonstrate proper habits by building enclosed houses and deferring to the wishes of the Jesuits.[4] Not all were ready to give in; the caciques around Zape joined forces with Tepehuanes who had taken refuge in the Sierra de Cariatapa under the leadership of a mestizo, Mateo Canelas. Spanish pursuit forced their surrender in 1622. North of the Valle de San Bartolomé, a number of Concho rancherías resisted the customary encomienda roundup for hacienda tasks, but other Conchos allied with Spaniards against them to effect their kinsmen's capture and sale as slaves.[5] The collaborators were rewarded with clothing, iron tools, and cattle.

Gifts continued to buy peace and thwart group cohesion throughout the 1620s and 1630s. Toboso caciques delivered bands of nonsedentary Indians to Atotonilco. This Franciscan mission and its counterpart at San Francisco de los Conchos served as vital labor recruiting stations for grain producers in the Valle de San Bartolomé. Some Indians from the area of salt deposits, called Salineros by Spaniards, returned to the short-lived mission of Tizonazo where Jesuits had resumed their work with resettled Tepehuanes.[6] Missionaries, backed by encomendero recruits and Indian allies from the already established Topia missions, moved into the southern Xixime area, where groups of Tepehuan rebels had taken refuge. They found Tepehuanes who had intermarried with the Xixime subgroups of Hinas and Humes and were tending their milpas, as well as cattle and sheep stolen during the rebellion.[7] Drought made Jesuit offers of seed and livestock attractive to many Xiximes, who agreed to settle in locations along the Río Piaxtla in the 1630s. Epidemics and rebellions had produced disruptions and migrations that resulted in new associations and marriages between groups, as well as changes in familiar patterns of transhumance and subsistence. The prospect of resettlement when accompanied by gift giving may have seemed, if not attractive, at least less foreign in these circumstances.

By the end of the decade, Jesuits had consolidated several thousand remaining Xiximes and Acaxees into eleven mission partidos, units which comprised a head village (cabecera) and attached stations (visitas) where the priest visited once a month.[8] Acaxees living in the missions of Badiraguato, Cariatapa, Tamazula, and Otatitlán worked in Spanish mines and farms in the Valle de Topia and Canelas. Xiximes formed the missions of San Gregorio, Otaez, Los Remedios, Santa Apolonia, San Ignacio, Yamoriba and San Pablo.[9] The latter sites contained Xixime subgroups of Humes and Hinas. The congregation of Indians was not necessarily related to their previous settlement patterns; the determining criterion was relocation near Spanish extractive activities. Otaez was located near Guapijuje, one of the largest settlements of preconquest Xiximes, but this was also the site of a silver mine. Because mining was more important than farming in this serrano region, most of the missions had very little productive land, but they did harvest small amounts of corn and beans and some sugarcane introduced by the Spaniards. In the western sierra, even Spanish landholdings tended to be relatively small, and competition for land around the mining reales was fierce. Trade with the coast supplied the bulk of foodstuffs for Spanish communities.[10] As the Spanish economy evolved slowly on the backs of relocated Xiximes and Acaxees, indigenous communities were further disrupted by smallpox epidemics in the 1620s and 1630s.

The much reduced Acaxee population (under a thousand by 1638) lived in mission villages alongside Spaniards, mulattoes, and *coyotes,* persons of mestizo and Indian ancestry.[11] Close contact and small numbers encouraged racial and cultural mixing. At the level of everyday coping, Indians and black slaves shared secrets for curing various ailments. Spaniards not infrequently sought their services in spite of the belief of some colonists that "Christ had not died to save blacks and barbarians [Indians], but only Spaniards." Itinerant Spanish merchants and cart drivers sought to attract Spanish and Indian women through magical incantations to the devil. In the mining real of San Andrés in 1627, Bartolomé de Salas boasted that he was able to get all the women he wanted by this method.[12] Some Jesuits, now having adopted less confrontational methods to deal with drunkenness and illicit unions, praised the Xiximes' affection for the rosary and images of saints.[13] They also noted the increased devotion to the Virgin in pueblos where cofradías had been established. The existence of these confraternities is perhaps most revealing of the presence of more experienced Christians, whether indigenous or not.[14] More Indians sought baptism (often just before death), and missionary efforts to indoctrinate children appeared to be paying off, if we are to believe the Jesuits' accounts of families divided on the question of conversion.[15]

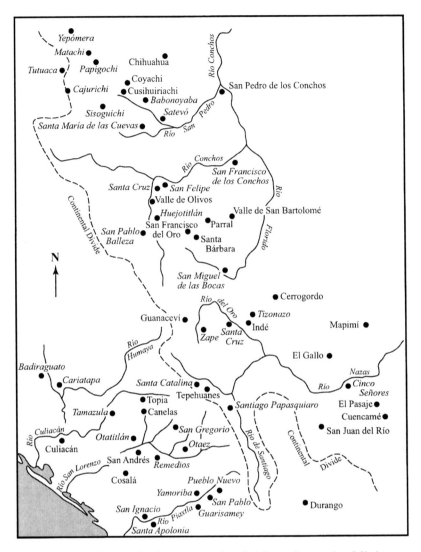

MAP 3. *Nueva Vizcaya in the seventeenth and eighteenth centuries. Mission names in italic type; towns and presidios in roman type.*

New missions had been founded among the Tepehuanes as well. Somewhat belatedly heeding the pleas of the Jesuits to locate a presidio in Tepehuan territory, in 1620 the crown authorized the establishment of the presidio of Tepehuanes adjacent to the Santa Catalina mission. Soldiers were relocated from individual missions to the new presidio, where many acquired land and encomiendas.[16] Progress was slow and padres still feared for their lives, especially in Zape, where Indian archers continued to threaten them and native ritual celebrations provoked Jesuit condemnations of licentiousness and drinking.[17] In nearby Guanaceví, silver discoveries prompted a new flux of immigration. As many as 500 single Spanish men poured into what one Jesuit called "the refuse dump for all of New Spain."[18] Repartimiento provided one source of mine labor, and Tepehuanes were forcibly drafted. These laborers were paid in kind, as were their wives, who received cloth in return for cooking and washing clothes in the mining camps.[19] Jesuits complained they were having little success in forcing Tepehuanes to work in the missions; the only thing that kept the Indians from fleeing was the mission supply of food.[20]

As late as 1638, Jesuits were still dealing with rumors of rebellion in Zape, which had an important preconquest religious site in a nearby cave.[21] Don Pedro, a shaman and brother of the Indian governor, Don Felipe, called on Tepehuanes to expel the Jesuits who had "taken their lands" and other Spaniards who forced them to work in the mines.[22] He was quickly arrested and executed, and the call to revolt went unanswered. There was no question that coercion had been stepped up by the discovery of silver at Parral in 1631.[23] Many entrepreneurs left Guanaceví for Parral, taking with them whatever manpower they could muster. The remaining miners faced an even greater labor shortage than before. Other Spaniards converged on Parral from Santa Bárbara, Indé, and Topia. In less than a year, Parral became the leading population center north of Durango, with 300 vecinos.[24] The governorship of Nueva Vizcaya acquired lucrative possibilities, becoming a more hotly contested prize in the next decades and occasioning frequent vicious and vindictive conflicts between governors and local elites, who were often backed by the Audiencia de Guadalajara (supreme tribunal for the region).[25]

Parral's labor force evolved in the same haphazard manner as its Nueva Vizcayan predecessors. Black slaves, free mulattoes and mestizos, central Mexican, Zacatecan, and Sinaloan Indians with some mining experience, and local native inhabitants came to constitute the partly voluntary, partly coerced labor force. The conventional view holds that the northern mining workforce was made up predominantly of free wage-laborers, who were attracted by pay (both in specie and in coarse woolen cloth), the right to a share of ore (pepena), and exemption from tribute payment. Since northern Indians were already excused from the latter obligation, this would not have provided an incentive for them to work. The lack of precontact precedents in labor service is given as another explanation for the lack of local Indians in the labor force.[26] Recent studies have demonstrated that labor practices were much more eclectic. Certainly much of the agricultural labor force which produced grain and meat for the mining districts was coerced, either through encomienda, repartimiento, or slavery (disguised as naboría).[27] The making of charcoal relied heavily on encomienda and repartimiento laborers. The *carboneros* or charcoal burners for smelting ore were responsible for stripping the oak forests around Santa Bárbara and Parral. Conchos, Tepehuanes, and Sinaloa groups including Mayos comprised their labor gangs.[28] And unskilled labor for the mines themselves came from local Indians, especially Conchos, sometimes voluntary and sometimes coerced. Indians who resisted Spanish attempts to settle them were enslaved after punitive expeditions and sold in the mining centers. Perhaps some were enticed by credit advances,[29] not infrequently unrecouped if we are to believe miners' complaints about the flight of indebted workers. A large number of Indians from Sinaloa and Sonora formed miserable barrios in Parral.[30]

While these groups were being coopted into the labor force, even some Tarahumaras—those Tarahumara whom Padre Juan Font had contacted in the first decade of the seventeenth century—began to settle in missions. Despite the traditional enmity between some groups of Tarahumaras and Tepehuanes, Jesuits convinced a number of Tarahumaras to move to San Pablo, where Jesuits had congregated Tepehuanes and constructed a large acequia in the San Pablo river basin. The Jesuits had assured the Tarahumara that they would be protected from Tepehuan aggression, but by 1626 the padres were complaining that the Tepehuanes retarded the progress of Tarahumara conversion.[31] Sometimes the problem was resolved by separating the groups into different visitas. In the 1620s, other Tarahumaras became the nucleus of San Miguel de las Bocas on the Río Florido, in an area where they had been going to work on Spanish lands.[32] Increased demand for labor in the 1630s provided the impetus for an entrada into an area northeast of Parral inhabited by both Tepehuanes and Tarahumaras.

One of the commanders of the entrada was Lieutenant Governor Francisco Montaño de la Cueva, a tellingly powerful local landowner and Guanaceví miner who already held Indians from the area in encomienda. Reacting to these intrusions and labor coercion, in 1635, Tepehuan Indians attacked the fledgling settlements in San Pablo and San Javier and burned a makeshift church. The leaders were captured and summarily executed by Spanish militias with help from other Tepehuanes and Tarahumaras. After quashing the resistance, the Spanish soldiers from the presidio of

Santa Catalina under Captain Juan de Barraza led a pacification tour, re-settling Tepehuanes and some Tarahumaras in areas of Spanish carbo-neros and ranchos. Aided by caciques willing to cooperate in the reloca-tion effort, Spanish officials and Jesuit padre Juan de Heredia presided over ceremonies in which great fanfare and the firing of harquebuses pre-ceded injunctions to plant fields and build churches.[33]

Governor Francisco Bravo de la Serna met with Jesuits and leading citizens of Parral in 1639 to discuss the feasibility of continuing the entra-das north into Tarahumara country in river valleys fed by the Río Conchos and its tributaries. Most were in agreement that the Tarahumaras were docile in comparison with the Tepehuanes. According to Father Geró-nimo de Figueroa, Tarahumaras could be more easily "Hispanicized"; furthermore, they were productive farmers and their lands contained sil-ver.[34] The Jesuits were encouraged by requests for missions from some Tarahumara elders. It is possible that these leaders were attracted by gifts of blankets and knives, but disease in 1636 may have provided another stimulus. Backed by the entrada of Captain Juan de Barraza, Jesuits estab-lished new missions at San Felipe and Satevó among eastern Tarahumaras. A new mission, San Gerónimo de Huejotitlán, became the cabecera of San Javier. Its founding was inspired by two Indians from Zacatecas who were living among Tepehuanes in this transitional zone. They do-nated land and an outlet for irrigation water/*saca de agua* to the new mis-sion.[35] Franciscans also tried to congregate Tarahumaras at Babonoyaba along with Conchos, but the Tarahumaras protested that the Conchos were taking their women, lands, and maize, and requested Jesuit tutelage (perhaps encouraged by Jesuit promises). In 1640, the governor ordered Tarahumaras removed from the pueblo.[36]

By the mid-1640s, the Jesuit province of Tepehuana and Tarahumara Baja had nine mission districts: Santiago Papasquiaro, Santa Catalina, Zape, Tizonazo, San Miguel de las Bocas, San Pablo, Huejotitlán, San Felipe, and Satevó. Franciscans ministered to Concho doctrinas in the Valle de San Bartolomé and along the southern Río Conchos system at San Francisco de los Conchos and San Pedro de los Conchos. Francis-can missions further north mixed Conchos and Tarahumaras with varying degrees of success. All of these settlements provided repartimiento labor to mines and haciendas; a number of these missions had been founded in areas where Spaniards already held encomiendas.[37] Mission corn and even some wheat were marketed in the Spanish centers of population.[38] Tarahumaras bartered corn to petty traders in grain/*rescatadores* who en-tered their territories.

Although repartimientos from missions continued to grow, encomiendas of Conchos and other ranchería or band groups remained a mainstay of the labor force, as did captives from the slaving expeditions to the north and east of Parral. A number of encomienda Indians had long been incorporated into permanent hacienda workforces, but those who provided seasonal labor became targets for repartimiento. As competition for labor increased, some Spaniards sought legal redress to confirm their grants, but force often proved more expedient. Governor Luis de Valdés not only authorized slaving expeditions but also ignored the petitions of missionaries who wanted soldiers to pursue fugitive Indians. Miners tried to sweeten their repartimiento requests with promises to pay the wives of workers as well. Jesuits complained that labor drafts left missions with only a fraction of their inhabitants, as women and children often accompanied the father. When the latter stayed behind, they could be found away from the mission, collecting seasonal wild food plants, especially the important staple of mescal. Indians who often worked two months for a few lengths of cloth also fled from the mission villages to the wilderness rather than make themselves vulnerable to repartimiento.[39]

Secular officials were more immediately concerned with ensuring labor for mines than in supporting the evangelical endeavor, not only to benefit the crown but also themselves, since many of them invested in mining. And even Jesuit superiors recognized that unless the mission enterprise could serve mining interests, either by congregating laborers or by keeping Indians from disrupting mining operations, the crown would not support it. Perhaps Andrés Pérez de Ribas, who had been a missionary and later superior of the Mexican Jesuit province, had this on his mind as he was preparing a historical sketch of missionary activities for the royal chronicler, Juan Diez de la Calle, around 1643. In a draft of the document where he discussed the difficulties of the conversion endeavor, he crossed out a line stating that Spanish settlers were bad Christians, choosing instead to emphasize how crucial the Jesuit pacification of the Indians was to the production of silver. He also reported that in all of their northern missions the Jesuits had converted more than 200,000 Indians in forty years, but that countless more had died from epidemics than had survived them.[40]

The free-for-all in labor competition provided no panacea for the survivors of disease. Many Indians fled from settled areas and others took up arms.[41] The demand for salt in the silver refining process accelerated attempts to congregate Tobosos and Salineros from the eastern deserts in missions and to use them to extract this resource.[42] Increasing numbers of them, along with Cabezas and Julimes who were also objects of massive slave hunts, joined forces with aggrieved Conchos in 1644 and 1645 to attack Spanish haciendas in the Valle de San Bartolomé and mule trains along the *camino real*/royal road. The leaders were able to attract not only gentiles but also members of the band groups who had been relocated in missions and who worked on haciendas. Some of the latter served as spies, advising their compatriots as to the most propitious circumstances for raiding, and officials claimed that Salinero Indians actually used the Jesuit mission of Tizonazo as a place of refuge after their attacks.[43] A severe peste which lingered in some of the missions for several months in 1645 and 1646 provoked a further exodus from the pueblos, although the Jesuits rarely connected these two occurrences.[44]

Significant numbers of eastern band Indians had become skilled horsemen who were often able to elude Spanish pursuit. In other ways, too, they had learned to emulate the colonizers, as, for example, in the appropriation of new food resources. They substituted beef for game as hunting gave way to raiding and the theft of thousands of head of cattle (many of which were traded to groups in the north). One report noted that a raiding band took time to brew a drink of chocolate after killing a ranch hand. Tobosos and others adopted titles and other symbols of the outsiders' power; leaders sometimes took Spanish names or impersonated Spanish authority figures, or both. One of the Toboso caciques took the name of a Jesuit, Gerónimo Moranta, slain in the Tepehuan rebellion.[45] The responses of these band groups to Spanish intrusion have been characterized by William Griffen as a form of nondirected cultural change in which aspects of Spanish material culture were adopted as mechanisms of survival and adapted to a traditional social system. Warfare probably increased as a means of acquiring new goods, especially in the dry season when wild food sources—e.g., mainstays such as mesquite beans and prickly pears— were scarce, and the hunter-gatherer groupings may have grown in size as the remnants of bands decimated by disease came together to form larger entities. In this milieu, Spaniards increasingly came to associate hunter-gatherers with warriors, implicitly associating the lack of sedentism with barbarity.[46]

As a result of repeated raids and drought conditions, the Franciscan missions of San Francisco de los Conchos, Atotonilco, San Pedro, and San Luis were temporarily abandoned. The Franciscan friars at San Francisco were killed in an attack by various allied bands that included Conchos. Also slain was the "Indian" governor, reportedly the son of a mulatto father and a Concho mother who had cooperated with the Spaniards in labor recruitment. The churches at San Francisco and San Pedro de los Conchos were burned.[47] In the Jesuit mission of Tizonazo, the recently settled 300 families of Cabezas also joined the insurrection. Rebel leaders invoked millenarian hopes and promised resurrection of the dead. Attempts to negotiate with them brought few results until finally several entradas led by Captain Juan de Barraza and supported by Concho and Tepehuan allies, first from his post at Santa Catalina and then from the new presidio of Cerrogordo on the edge of the Bolsón de Mapimí northeast of Tizonazo, forced a number of bands to sue for peace. Although warfare receded, sporadic raids by band groups continued to plague Spanish settlements and livestock for the next several decades.

Padre Nicolás de Zepeda attributed part of the blame for the uprising to the lack of vigorous official efforts to congregate and subdue troublemakers, but he conceded that little could be done with people who were so "inconstant, perverse, ungrateful, beastly, barbarous, obstinate, and without reason, fear, or shame." In short, he viewed them as no different than animals. When a woman who had been convicted as a spy in Tizonazo failed to die after being administered poison, he reasoned it was hardly surprising that people who ingested all manner of vermin and even their own excrement would be unfazed by poison.[48] Zepeda's account as well as others of this period offer tantalizing glimpses of women's roles in these conflicts. Indian women served as spies, messengers, and hostages left with Spaniards by their husbands to ensure the husbands would comply with peace terms. Spanish women also braved uncertainty and peril when they traveled and lived in areas of frequent hostilities. In 1645, Antonia Tremeño, along with her three sons and daughter, was captured by Salineros as she traveled near Mapimí to meet her husband, an immigrant Portuguese freighter. In the days that followed, she was forced to watch as two of her sons were killed. During the next several months she and the daughter were raped, enslaved, and traded by their captors to Tobosos. Eventually her daughter, now pregnant, escaped and made her way to a Spanish hacienda; the Spanish soldiers who attempted to ransom Antonia discovered that she had been killed.[49]

There was no reticence on the part of different Spanish factions in blaming each other for the spreading violence. The hostilities played into the hands of the bishop of Nueva Vizcaya, who hoped to reduce the credibility of the Jesuit endeavor and appropriate mission resources for the diocese. In the mid-1640s, he launched an assault on the Jesuits whose missions, he argued, had failed to subdue the natives. Emulating his mentor, Juan de Palafox y Mendoza, Diego Evía y Valdés became embroiled in a jurisdictional dispute with the order as he attempted to secularize several

Jesuit missions. Unsuccessful in his campaign to force the Jesuits to pay the *diezmo* (state-imposed tithe to support the church) on agricultural produce grown either in the missions or on their haciendas, the bishop tried to bring the missions at Tizonazo and San Miguel de las Bocas under diocesan control. He justified this move by claiming that the Jesuits' coercive attempts to settle Salineros and Cabezas in Tizonazo were the main provocation for the Indian uprising.

The Jesuits responded that the bishop's actions were influenced by his close relationship with Felipe Montaño de la Cueva, a cleric who had purchased land adjacent to the Tizonazo mission visita of Santa Cruz. The mission Indians had brought a lawsuit against Montaño, charging that his livestock were destroying their milpas and that he was planting wheat on mission lands and diverting water from their acequia to irrigate it. In a similar maneuver, the bishop sided with local officials and landowners (of the powerful Urdiñola family) at Parras who wanted access to irrigation water belonging to the Jesuits' Lagunero missions and the vineyards of their colegio. In a fierce battle of wills and retaliatory measures, the bishop was successful in enlisting the aid of two former Nueva Vizcayan governors who owned property near Parras to get the Lagunero missions secularized, although he failed in the case of Tizonazo and Las Bocas.[50]

In a *real cédula*/royal decree of November 1647, the crown cast a wide net of culpability, holding "encomenderos, missionaries, *corregidores, alcaldes mayores* and other ministers" responsible for the oppression of Nueva Vizcayan Indians, while singling out Governor Valdés for harsh treatment and enslavement of Indians.[51] The king's reproach followed upon an investigation by the Audiencia de Guadalajara, whose president wrote to the crown in 1646:

> . . . if they are forced to provide labor to the mines in repartimiento and are not paid; if their corn is acquired by petty grain brokers for practically nothing and resold at exorbitant prices; if these exchanges are directed by unscrupulous local governors, often ethnic outsiders; if their children are sold; if even the Tobosos who have agreed to peace terms are shot in cold blood; then why would the other nations, seeing these excesses and atrocities, not follow suit?[52]

In spite of royal reprimands, a hodgepodge of labor practices mixing coercion and emoluments persisted in the frenzied attempts to expand mining in the region and to supply the mining reales with meat, grain, and fuel. Paying kickbacks to the governor's office and to indigenous labor recruiters became common in the seventeenth century.[53] Elites also expanded their landholdings around Indian pueblos.[54]

These practices and more or less tacit acceptance of them by Jesuits were already deeply entrenched—so much so that Spanish officialdom seemed to take little notice of a proposal sent by a Jesuit missionary in the sierra of San Andrés to the king in 1645. That Padre Nicolás de Barreda proposed an overhaul of the mission system directly to the king, bypassing the order's official chain of command was remarkable enough, but that he professed admiration for Jesuit archenemy Bishop Palafox at the same time is rather astonishing. Barreda criticized the current mission and presidio system as wasteful and ineffective. By creating four huge mission reductions from the more than fifty that existed, he argued, the crown would save over one hundred thousand pesos per year, not only in the savings from mission stipends, but also in presidial salaries. Fewer Jesuits and soldiers would be needed to staff these larger missions, where Indians would be forcibly interned and "domesticated" as farmers, artisans, and tribute payers. Barreda's missive described large migrations of Indians between mission and mining areas. Missions were little more than transitory way stations for mostly defiant and unruly natives. Presidios were useless for curbing disobedience; rather, they offered the opportunity for common soldiers to engage in petty trade, acquire land, and exploit Indian labor. The Spanish system itself, then, fomented anarchy and rebellion. Barreda's autocritique surely rankled his superiors when they got wind of it, and they must have worked to disavow it. Although the plan that he proposed was similar to the Jesuit mission system in Paraguay, with its much larger reductions, such a reform would have upset vested interests beyond the presidios. It would have complicated even further the supply of labor to the dispersed Spanish sites of production in the north.[55] Barreda's report was apparently buried, but the next Jesuit attempts to establish missions proved the wisdom of at least some of this upstart's appraisal.

The Jesuit order began to contemplate the expansion of its Tarahumara mission field at midcentury. Missionaries assessed the pros and cons of such a move, based upon their experiences to date in the Tarahumara Baja. In the missions at San Miguel de las Bocas, San Pablo Balleza, Huejotitlán, San Felipe, and Satevó, barely a decade old, the Jesuits were making some headway. Gift giving and the provision of meat and grains accompanied early efforts to attract converts. The Jesuits were blunt about this time-honored tactic arguing that only with food as bait could they begin to lure Indians to the true faith.[56] Hampered in this goal by several years of drought, missionaries directed the construction of acequias. This enabled them not only to feed the neophytes but also to sell grain to Spanish rescatadores.

Jesuit reports highlighted their efficacious evangelizing tactics. Significant numbers of Tarahumaras participated in the Eucharist and confessed. But they were especially attracted to festive celebrations. Tarahumaras came from afar to celebrate the principal fiestas of the patron saint, Corpus Christi, Holy Week, and Christmas. Eventually the dances, pageantry, and ritual of the Easter celebrations became the most popular festivals, but the *matachines* that are associated with Rarámuri fiestas today may not have been introduced until the eighteenth century. The Jesuit order had a special attachment to the feast of Corpus Christi, and its colorful procession with music and dance was an effective way to engage adults and children.[57] Missionaries also endeavored to acquire paintings and ornaments to decorate their churches and inspire devotion on the part of the Indians. They made specific requests for paintings of saints and the Virgin, as well as silver objects to be supplied from the viceregal capital. Among the artists from central Mexico whose work reached the Tarahumara missions were Cristóbal de Villalpando and Juan Rodríguez Juárez. From mission funds and donations, the Jesuits procured items produced regionally as well as in Mexico City, and mission inventories include sculptures and vases that came from Spain and even Asia via the Philippines. Orders also included canvases and paints for artwork produced locally either by natives or by Indians brought from other regions. It is likely that Tarascan Indians from Michoacán provided expertise for the lovely painted ceiling that still graces Santa María de Cuevas today. Even some ornaments have survived until today, providing evidence that local communities formed strong attachments to them. Missionaries selected specific images and visual representations to convey religious ideas, but we cannot be certain as to how they were perceived by the mission neophytes. As one art historian has noted, Jesuit missionaries often chose scenes from the apostolic endeavors of one of the greatest Jesuit missionaries, Francis Xavier, to grace the walls of their churches and to emphasize the centrality of the missionary vocation to the Society of Jesus.[58]

The fathers believed they were particularly successful in teaching the catechism to children and in using music to animate their participation. Among the musical instruments that were introduced in missions were organs, harps, guitars, lyres, violins, clarions, bassoons, music boxes, and cornets.[59] In time the Tarahumara became very skilled at making violins and guitars. Indigenous instruments such as *chirimías*/reed flutes, drums, and rattles were also incorporated into musical performance. Some adults persisted in conducting ritual ceremonies, perceived by the Jesuits as drunken binges, at ranchería sites.[60] In this milieu of fragmentary transformations, converts, apostates, and unconverted gentiles—never unified tribally—mingled in differing moods of receptivity to the outsiders.

Yet for every Tarahumara convert in 1648, there were perhaps ten gentiles. A substantial number of the latter lived in the fertile Papigochi valley to the northwest of the missionized area. While some of them sought out the Jesuits, traded with Spaniards, and adopted sheep raising, many were resolutely opposed to further Spanish settlement in their lands. As long as Tarahumaras could act independently in trading their corn, beans, chickens, and eggs for Spanish goods, they were willing to interact with buyers who entered their territories. But the Spanish discovery of silver in this area was a red flag to Tarahumaras who had resisted Jesuit overtures. Led by Supichiochiqui (Sopegiosi), Ochavari, and Tepox in 1648, they attacked and razed the most exposed Jesuit mission visita of San Francisco de Borja. Although the rebels were successful in attracting some converted Tarahumaras to their cause, their attempt to destroy the large mission of San Felipe was foiled by loyal Tarahumara converts who warned the priest. It is significant that Tarahumaras were divided among themselves about the threats posed by missions. This discord continued to fester and estrange Tarahumara rancherías until the end of the century.

The attacks prompted Governor Valdés to dispatch Juan de Barraza to put down the rebellion. After seven months, a small Spanish force and hundreds of Indian allies (including Sinaloa Indians drafted from the Parral mines, Conchos, and friendly Tarahumaras) were able to defeat the rebels.[61] Toward the end of the conflict, the newly arrived governor, Diego Guajardo Fajardo, took to the field himself. His reconnaissance produced information that would provoke further conflict. Barraza reported in 1649 that silver was already being mined in the area of conflict. Twenty *cargas* of silver had already been transported to Parral. To encourage exploitation of this resource, Governor Guajardo founded the town of Villa de Aguilar in the Papigochi valley and supported the establishment of a Jesuit mission there. This action cost the governor on two fronts.

First, he incurred the enmity of Bishop Evía y Valdés, who had exercised influence in getting him appointed as governor.[62] The bishop, still embroiled in the attempt to secularize several Jesuit missions, was furious at this betrayal. He had already accused the Jesuits of fomenting the rebellion by exploiting mission Tarahumaras and ordering the execution of Don Marcos, a Tepehuan leader in San Pablo Balleza (a mission of both Tepehuanes and Tarahumaras).[63] Governor Guajardo first asked the bishop to subsidize secular clerics to work in the new Spanish settlement. When he refused, the governor accepted the Jesuits' offer to send Father Cornelio Godínez to Papigochi and for good measure had the bishop placed under arrest. Evía y Valdés responded by excommunicating the governor and attempting to secularize the newly founded Jesuit missions at Huejotitlán and San Felipe. The Jesuits pulled out all the stops to thwart the bishop's attempts to convert missions into parishes. Both parties took their cases to the Council of the Indies in Spain. The claim that secular clerics were too few in number and unprepared in Indian languages tipped the balance in the Jesuits' favor, as it did when the issue of secularization arose periodically thereafter.[64]

A second consequence of the founding of Villa de Aguilar was to aggravate the Tarahumaras, who rebelled again in 1650. After Padre Godínez and two Spaniards were killed in Papigochi, the Spaniards set out in pursuit of more than 2,000 rebels (including some Tepehuanes), but they were deterred by the Indians' use of poisoned arrows. After five months of fighting, some of the insurgents sued for peace so they could return to their rancherías to plant their fields and buy time until they could strike again. As another Jesuit, Jácome Antonio Basilio, prepared to build a new church several leagues from the Villa de Aguilar, he noted that most of the Tarahumaras were harvesting corn in their rancherías and showing little inclination to support the missionary effort.[65] Led by Tepóraca (Teporame) in 1652, they attacked and killed Padre Basilio at the new mission site and burned down the houses of the villa. This third outbreak of rebellion threatened the lower Tarahumara missions, but many of the converts remained loyal and only Satevó was destroyed. Problems with Toboso Indians diverted some of the Spanish troops from the Tarahumara theater, delaying the Spanish counterattack. Eventually Tarahumara allies under Spanish commanders proved to be a key force in putting down the rebellion. The governors of the lower Tarahumara mission pueblos rejected rebel embassies' petitions to join them.[66] The severe epidemic of the previous year may also have weakened the rebel offensive. Once again, many Tarahumaras sued for peace, and the governor accepted their entreaties with the proviso that they turn over Tepóraca to be executed. His lifeless body was left hanging from a tree, whereupon Indian archers showered it with arrows. The Jesuits returned to their already established Tarahumara missions, but for the time being further Spanish incursions into the Papigochi valley came to a halt.[67]

Dealing with enemy Indians on two fronts was hardly practical at this

stage, and the continued depredations of Tobosos and their allies threatened silver mining in Parral. Perceiving that it was best to keep their eyes
on the prize, Spaniards turned their attention to the problem of labor
recruitment and defense of the eastern flank. The necessity of diverting
mine workers to buttress Spanish militias in the previous few years had
proved especially costly due to the extant labor shortage. The situation of
mine laborers was wretched, with most workers living in makeshift huts
and earning meager rations and very little pay. Spanish authorities were
quick to blame each other for the conditions of misery and unrest. For
example, the governor continued his vendetta against the bishop by charging that mercenary clerics in Parral refused to bury indigent miners.[68] At
the same time, he engaged in the sale of Indians taken as prisoners in a
"just war"—along with their wives and children—to local landowners and
miners, in spite of royal prohibitions.[69] And Jesuits responded defensively,
but not without sarcasm, to charges that they exploited Indian labor and
allowed Indians to go naked, arguing that it was "more difficult to get
Indians to wear clothes than to make stones sing."[70]

In another effort to meet the demand for labor, Governor Guajardo
ordered an inspection of the Tepehuan area to determine the number of
able-bodied males in the area. He found that a substantial number of mission Indians had fled to escape service, but many others were working in
Parral or in the Valle de San Bartolomé. Although none of the Indians
assembled by Guajardo in the villages were allowed to complain about the
labor drafts, other resentments and requests could be voiced. In Zape's
visita of San José del Potrero, Pedro, the native governor, charged that
the missionary's livestock were trampling the native fields. Some unconverted Tepehuanes from Ocotlán sought out the expedition and asked to
have lands assigned to them.[71] Mission Indians often provided seasonal
labor on haciendas, while the smaller, permanent labor force was bound to
the hacienda in a variety of legal and illegal ways. Slaving expeditions—
using the pretext that it was legal to capture nonsedentary Indians who
resisted incorporation—continued to commandeer Apaches and Navajos
from New Mexico, Pimas from Sonora, and hunter-gatherers, especially
Tobosos, from the east. Even Christianized Indians in the Valle de San
Bartolomé were kidnapped and sold into slavery in Parral.[72] In some cases,
encomienda Indians had become part of the permanent inventory of haciendas and were rented out to other employers. It was not uncommon for
mayordomos/overseers to profit considerably by keeping the workers' wages
for themselves.[73] At the same time, it was not difficult for some workers
to flee in search of work elsewhere, even after having been extended credit

by the hacendado—aided by both the vast expanses of unsettled territory and the general labor shortage. When they were apprehended, they were sentenced to service in a mine or hacienda of that jurisdiction. Indian vaqueros were especially mobile.[74]

The general instability and volatility of the frontier also made it difficult for Spaniards to keep tabs on Indian workers. Mission Indians who continued to supplement agriculture by gathering mescal and other cactus fruits could be captured and enslaved by nonsedentary raiders, while Indian cowboys were often casualties in livestock raids. A raid by Salinero Indians on the Franciscan pueblo of Atotonilco resulted in many deaths, including whole families who were burned alive.[75] Spanish governors came to recognize the futility of campaigns designed to definitively exterminate the raiding societies, employing instead ad hoc and piecemeal methods of retaliation for specific incidents.

Despite the constant threat of violence, the incentives for silver miners and suppliers of foodstuffs to the mining reales were sufficient to promote the expansion of mines and haciendas in the Parral area in the 1640s and 1650s.[76] But the perpetual encomiendas granted earlier in the century could no longer begin to satisfy work demands. Disputes over labor escalated. Wheat farmers in the Valle de San Bartolomé complained that governors assigned their encomienda Indians in repartimiento to their neighbors. Miners in Parral sought the restoration of encomiendas that had been partitioned into repartimientos for making charcoal and harvesting wheat or appropriated by *alcaldes mayores*/officials for public works projects. Furthermore, Indian wars had resulted in multiplying the number of persons seeking to be rewarded for military service by a grant of encomienda. Single encomiendas were awarded to multiple owners, and even the ensuing lawsuits were not sufficient to deter governors from continuing to grant encomiendas through the 1660s—especially to their favorites.[77] The chaotic mix of free and unfree labor persisted, responding to local precedents and exigencies.[78]

Landholdings—especially livestock haciendas—expanded outside the breadbasket of the Valle de San Bartolomé. Another consequence of the Tarahumara rebellions at midcentury was the threat of famine in Parral, since the bulk of its corn was supplied by Tarahumaras who traded with intermediaries. The scarcity of grain to feed the mine workers also exacerbated the shortage of labor. Hacienda production of grain in the Valle de San Bartolomé only served the needs of Parral for about one-quarter of the year until the late seventeenth century. Expansion of production in San Bartolomé was limited by the general shortage of labor and by depletion of the soil, especially irrigated land.[79] As miners and other Spaniards acquired properties in nearby areas, some mission pueblos began to feel the effects of unfenced cattle encroaching on their milpas. Increasingly, they found their access to irrigation water or floodplains blocked. In addition, wilderness areas used for hunting and gathering were occasionally incorporated for both grazing and charcoal making by Spanish hacendados, who argued that the lands were not being used—read agriculturally—by the Indians. These early—seventeenth century—conflicts over land resulted in part from a growing non-Indian population, but they also reflected the influence exercised by a few powerful landowners.[80]

By 1660, the largest hacendado of all, Valerio Cortés del Rey, had already come to control more than 23,000 acres of grazing land as well as a number of farms. He had arrived in Parral nearly two decades earlier to assume the post of silver assayer.[81] He provided service in the Indian wars, acquired encomiendas, and invested in silver mining in San Francisco del Oro. While serving Governor Francisco Gorráez de Beaumont in the early 1660s, he came to exercise a good deal of political power, acting with virtual impunity in the large expanse of territory he owned along the Río Conchos and several of its tributaries, the most important stock-raising area. His immense holdings in strategic locations permitted him to proclaim himself the "key to the kingdom."

His control of properties and workers fast became a threat to Governor Antonio Oca y Sarmiento when he assumed his post in 1666. In the course of the *residencia*/review of Governor Gorráez' office conducted by Oca y Sarmiento, the new governor leveled a series of charges against Cortés del Rey. He accused him of abusing Indian workers and even of disobedience to the crown.[82] When the governor had Cortés del Rey arrested, the latter's friends in the Audiencia de Guadalajara came to his aid, ultimately succeeding in getting Oca y Sarmiento removed in 1670 through charges that he engaged in illegal commerce in Nueva Vizcaya. A few years later, in 1674, Cortés del Rey was given royal permission to establish an entailed estate/*mayorazgo* which included properties worth nearly three hundred thousand pesos. The family exported sheep and cattle to Zacatecas, Sombrerete, and Guadalajara.[83]

But before he left office, the governor took the side of the Jesuit mission of Satevó in its case against Cortés del Rey. In 1667, Don Pablo, the governor of the pueblo, charged that over the past five years cattle and horses from Cortés del Rey's holdings had wreaked havoc on the milpas of Satevó and its visitas of San Antonio and San Lorenzo. Governor Gorráez, they alleged, had ignored their previous petitions because he was afraid of Cortés del Rey. More recently, sheep from his holdings had not only trampled their fields but also destroyed the monte where they hunted and gathered. Their pueblos, as well as the recently reestablished Franciscan missions of Babonoyaba and Santa Isabel, had suffered serious losses of crops, seed, chickens, and lambs—not to mention the abuse of their women by vaqueros in the employ of Cortés del Rey. All of these missions had been key suppliers of corn and beans as well as small animals to the Parral market. The governor ordered Cortés del Rey to remove his livestock from Indian lands and asked the Audiencia de Guadalajara to determine if reparations should be paid.[84] To strengthen their demands for restitution from Cortés del Rey, the Jesuits reminded the crown of the economic role of missions. They were quick to point out how Cortés del Rey's actions were injurious to a mission system that served the mining economy by supplying foodstuffs and personal service.[85] The foraging of livestock on mission lands raises questions about the extent to which overgrazing had already occurred in the north. Although the year 1665 had brought considerable rains and flooding, the subsequent years were dry, probably reducing pasturage and attracting livestock to watered areas along river courses.

Voicing concerns that differed from the governor's, Juan de Gorozpe y Aguirre, the bishop of Nueva Vizcaya, singled out the pervasive abuse of Indian labor. In a 1669 report to the crown, he detailed the violations of laws regarding encomienda and repartimiento. The queen regent ordered the viceroy and the Audiencia de Guadalajara to investigate these charges in 1670.[86] The audiencia reasoned that "indios de media paz" needed to be compelled to work, but only if they were properly compensated. They should be paid either in specie or in kind; if payment was in kind, commodities should be furnished at the lowest prices. They should only be made to perform a "tolerable" amount of work. The viceroy sent the new governor, Joseph García de Salcedo, a royal order to this effect in December 1670 and charged him with getting more information on labor practices in Nueva Vizcaya. Testimony was taken from leading citizens, all of whom averred that they were not exacting tribute from their encomienda Indians. Ironically, Juan Constantino, a Concho governor, argued that his people would rather pay tribute than be forced to labor under oppressive conditions of physical abuse. When the audiencia lawyer reviewed all of the testimony, he noted that tribute was being levied in the form of personal service and that the practice was illegal. Governor García de Salcedo agreed to enforce the laws and to see that moderation was exercised in labor recruitment. Above all, he concurred, Indians must be paid for the labor.[87]

Renewed royal attention to labor practices signaled the demise of the encomienda in Nueva Vizcaya (after 1672 no new encomiendas were granted), but it also marked the expansion of repartimiento. Labor drafts, of course, fell heavily on the Jesuit and Franciscan missions—the only loci of congregated Indians. As noted above, the missionaries saw this obligation as a necessary concession for ensuring the continuation of a system that would accommodate their evangelical endeavor. But they were engaged in a delicate balancing act—for excessive demands on labor could imperil the existence of missions either by decimating productivity and subsistence or by provoking flight and abandonment.

The interplay of factors that attracted Indians to or distanced them from missions was complex and changed over time. Two of the most attractive inducements were the missions' capacity to provide protection from enemy Indians and to furnish foodstuffs and other commodities (clothing, tools, etc.). As time went on, missionaries complained more frequently that they did not have sufficient resources to feed themselves, much less hand out gifts.[88] Another key was the degree to which missions could serve as a kind of temporary base which allowed indigenous peoples access to their rancherías and wilderness areas for gathering, hunting, and even raising a few of the newly introduced sheep or cattle, as well as for ritual celebrations with intoxicants that facilitated communication with the supernatural.[89] For those who became more thoroughly converted, the missions could provide spiritual consolation and cofradías with material benefits. For those who did not, feast days could be appreciated for the dietary enhancements and escape from work into the pleasurable activities of song and dance.[90]

One of the most oppressive features, surely, was forced labor (either on mission lands or through the furnishing of quotas of workers in repartimiento), but this exploitation of labor had to be weighed against the possibility of enslavement (however illegal) and the degree to which the missionary could serve as a buffer to mitigate abuse. The case of the Tarahumaras poses another scenario. Padre Gabriel del Villar complained in 1664 that it was difficult to keep the Tarahumara in missions when they could go to Parral for two months and earn enough to clothe their families for a year. For the missions to be able to compete, he proposed a system in which the missionaries would become petty traders (although he did not want them to become known as *mercachifles*/peddlers or *pulperos*/storekeepers). If they could exchange salt, soap, needles, thread, hoes, etc. for corn and other commodities, the Indians would be more likely to stay put.[91] Another consideration that cut both ways was disease. Congregation surely enhanced its spread and in some cases reduced the mission population to the point of extinction.[92] On the other hand, priests and the community could also ensure some comforts for the infirm. To the extent that the missions could buffer oppression from other Spaniards without becoming just as oppressive themselves, indigenous peoples might countenance them. Since these factors reflected local conditions, they varied from place to place over time.

A comparative look at the three Jesuit mission areas (Topia, Tepehuana, and lower Tarahumara) and the Franciscan missions in the last third of the seventeenth century is instructive in illustrating the influence of these variables, as well as the amount of time elapsed since contact. The task is partially facilitated by the extensive *visita*/inspection tour undertaken in the late 1670s by the Jesuit Juan Ortiz Zapata, whose task it was to assess the state of the Jesuit missions and count their populations as well as the numbers of nearby vecinos.

By 1690 in Topia, where earlier incidence of disease and exploitation of mining labor had reduced populations of Acaxees and Xiximes by 94 percent since contact, the number of Indians in missions had dwindled significantly. As late as 1662 a particularly virulent epidemic claimed many victims in the space of three days. One Jesuit bemoaned the impossibility of advancing the missions spiritually or economically, comparing the task to that of a galley slave.[93] Others blamed both illness and the lack of progress in conversion on demonic machinations. In 1660, Padre Cristóbal de Robles confronted the devil head-on when he performed an exorcism in San Pedro Guarisamey. A member of the pueblo's local choir had taken ill and, after first losing his voice, was reported to be singing at the top of his lungs in many languages, including Tarascan. Reacting negatively to Father Robles' first attempts to help him, he cried out in agony, enumerating the ills that had befallen him. "The demons have cooked me; they have thrown me to the fire; they have torn me into bits; they have tortured me on a rack of knives." When the Jesuit finally succeeded in exorcising the demons, the unnamed Indian explained how the devil had overpowered him. He had seen a jaguar circling his house, followed by an owl. The owl had entered his mouth, first cutting off his speech and then taking it over. In this case, we can discern evidence of native (Mesoamerican) beliefs regarding shape changing and animal alter egos alongside very Christian images of hell. The coexistence of these ideas was not unusual in central Mexico, where associations between Christian concepts and animals were employed even in the evangelization process.[94] Cultural blending continued in many forms.

The fewer than 2,000 remaining mission Indians were multilingual,

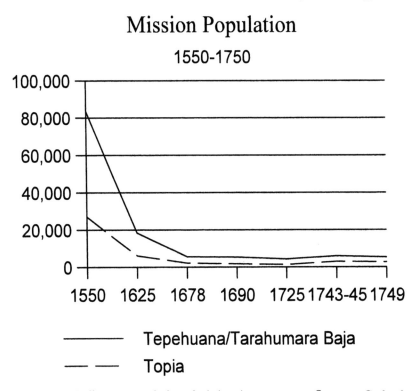

Mission Population
1550-1750

Tepehuana/Tarahumara Baja

Topia

FIGURE I. *Indigenous population of mission sites, 1550–1750*. Sources: *Gerhard, The North Frontier, 170–200; Hackett, Historical Documents, 118–137; AGN, Jesuitas, I-16 and I-17; Ortiz Zapata visita report, DHM, 4-3, 301–419; and mission visita reports, 1685, 1725 (Guendulaín), 1743 (Balthasar), 1751–1753 (Carta) in AGN, AHH, Temp., legs. 79, 277, 279, 1126, 2009; ACD, Varios 1749; Francisco Alvarez report, 1750, AGN, Provincias Internas, 69:4.*

using their native languages, Nahuatl, and Spanish. Jesuits were accused of overworking Indians in meager mission fields, and vecinos violated conditions of repartimiento service by paying workers in glass beads, knives, needles, and ribbons rather than two reales per day.[95] Some of the missions maintained a small indigenous core through migrants from Sinaloa and Sonora (although many of them used these missions as way stations on the journey to mining centers where they sought wage work).[96] But several missions had only a handful of Indian families who engaged in the same subsistence activities as the surrounding non-Indian population—raising a little corn and cotton and producing beeswax and cloth. Where they had once had sizable herds of cattle, these were now scattered and wild. Padre Boltor reported that San Ignacio no longer had its own ranch, although he estimated that there were about 3,000 feral cows in the surrounding area that had been untended for more than fifteen years. The poverty of the Topia missions was widely remarked, and the vecinos were reported to be racially mixed.[97]

The Tepehuan missions had not fared much better. After their fierce rebellion earlier in the century, some Tepehuanes retreated into the isolated barrancas of the most southwestern corner of today's Chihuahua. Others returned to the missions of Santiago Papasquiaro, Santa Catalina, Zape, and San Pablo, where many provided labor to nearby Spanish vecinos. Jesuits not uncommonly sent mission Indians to work as servants in the households of their Spanish friends and relatives, to whom they also ministered.[98] Others were sent to work in the Parral mines. In most of these missions, Indians established cofradías endowed with a few head of cattle. If these confraternities were intended to provide some security in times of trouble, they were not very effective against drought and disease in the 1640s, 1650s, and 1660s. Moreover, the epidemics of 1647 and 1662 were particularly severe. The Jesuits described the terrible plague of the late 1660s, linking the propensity of epidemics to populations weakened by hunger, a condition often resulting from cyclical droughts:

> As its inseparable companion, disease followed hunger, attacking the villages oppressively and without remedy. Wretched and starving, people went from village to village or into the countryside seeking help, finally surrendering their lives to hunger and disease along the royal roads.[99]

Nueva Vizcaya had been temporarily rescued from these miseries at the end of the decade by miraculous appearances of San Francisco Javier, who was selected as the province's patron saint in 1668 by the governor and the bishop. Most of the miracles were connected to Indians and Spaniards cured of the plague. The association was cemented by the painting of Saint Francis in a new chapel dedicated to this saint in 1669. He was depicted as coming from heaven to put an end to the apocalypse.

A high incidence of migration characterized this area even in better times, with Indians leaving their pueblos to fish in the Río Florido and hunt feral cattle in the sierra. In 1690, mission Tepehuanes numbered less than a thousand, a little more than half the number reported by Father Visitor Juan Ortiz Zapata in 1678.[100] Most had small herds of cattle and flocks of sheep; these tended to be somewhat larger in the older missions with more non-Indian inhabitants. In those missions, the Jesuits had purchased irrigable lands beyond the fundo legal of a square league that each pueblo theoretically had a right to possess. From the additional lands, worked in turn by mission Indians, came small yields of corn and wheat. The older missions produced more wheat for sale in Parral and other Spanish towns.[101] Jesuits tended to exercise very strict (though frequently inefficient) control over the disposition of the communal resources in missions, including lands that were part of the fundo legal or belonged to cofradías. Virtually no account books of cofradías or community chests/*cajas de comunidad* have survived for the missions studied here. In the case of the latter, there are only a few allusions to their existence before the mid-eighteenth century.[102]

Interethnic contacts can also be discerned in the more recently established lower Tarahumara missions. But for the most part, these missions were still benefiting from larger indigenous populations (approximately 4,000 total) and the early returns from such enhancements as irrigation and gifts of livestock.[103] As Father Gerónimo de Figueroa noted in 1662, establishing a solid material base in a mission was the surest means of fomenting its spiritual aims.[104] In fact, the lower Tarahumara missions were doing rather well in the material realm. Their fields produced corn and some wheat for the Parral market, enabling the purchase of clothing, beans, and chickens. Many of the Tarahumaras in San Miguel de las Bocas worked on a dozen nearby haciendas and ranches; most owned horses and returned to the mission on feast days. A good number spoke the corrupted form of Nahuatl (*mexicana*) that evolved in the north through contact with Indians from central Mexico. Dozens of Spanish vecinos also attended church at the mission, where mass was celebrated in Tarahumara and Spanish, and they supported it with endowments. A number of them actually resided in the mission, along with mestizos and other mixed groups. At one point, Padre Nicolás de Zepeda counted 300 "vagrant vecinos in the area."[105] In the other, less acculturated lower Tarahumara missions, many Indians confessed annually and celebrated Corpus Christi and Semana Santa.[106] But their resident populations also fluctuated wildly as Indians came and went. Such a high degree of mobility coexisted, seemingly incompatibly, with frequent attacks by band groups on mines, haciendas, and travelers, both Indian and non-Indian. For example, in 1667, Tobosos attacked Padre Rodrigo de Castillo and a group of choirboys as they returned to San Miguel de Bocas from a performance in Tizonazo. All of the Tarahumara boys were killed and the priest subsequently died as a result of his injuries.[107]

Only a few years before, Padre Castillo had reported on the fruits of the conversion efforts in his mission. The children were well versed in the catechism, as they attended classes in the church patio twice daily, and their parents could recite prayers. Apparently the Jesuit was especially prone to use music in his evangelizing endeavors, having the Indians sing *villancicos* or motets after each mass, both in Spanish and in Tarahumara. For Corpus Christi, mission residents decorated the church and its chapels with arches and flowers, and they threw down their mantas to make a carpet for the procession. Father Castillo reported similar reverence during Holy Week, particularly on Palm Sunday. He was especially moved by the Tarahumaras' response to his telling of the appearance of the Virgin of Guadalupe. They enthusiastically took part in the dedication of a painting of the Virgin that he ordered shipped from Mexico City; in the Jesuit's telling, the Tarahumaras' passionate interest derived from the story that Guadalupe had made herself known to an Indian.[108]

Toward the end of the seventeenth century, the lower Tarahumara missions were all part of the local agricultural and mining economy. Reputedly, the wealthiest among them was Huejotitlán, with its plentiful fields and many head of livestock; its multiethnic population included Tarahumaras, Tepehuanes, and even some Apaches. It was also designated as the regional seminary where selected Indian children were sent from surrounding missions to receive special instruction in the catechism, music, reading and writing, and trades such as smithing and carpentry. These mission-seminaries/*colegios incoados* were entitled to own additional properties to support their educational endeavors.[109]

Santa María de las Cuevas and Satevó were surrounded by extensive ranchlands owned by Valerio Cortés del Rey. The powerful landowner employed Spanish overseers for his cattle operations, mestizos and mulatto slaves as cowboys, and a wide array of indigenous peoples as herders and servants. The missions, especially Satevó, also had sizable cattle operations, fed by shipments of yearlings from the Jesuits' Sonoran missions. Some of these young bulls and heifers were sold directly to hacendados in the Parral area at five pesos each, but others were fattened on mission lands and sold in the Parral market.[110] Mission residents included not only neophyte Christians but also unconverted Tarahumaras and mestizos and mulatto outsiders. There was a good deal of interaction among these different ethnic groups, brought together by occasional fiestas, amorous relationships, and folk-curing practices.[111] Other Tarahumara missions were just beginning to feel pressures on land. For example, despite testimony from Tarahumara officials and Padres Gabriel del Villar and Francisco de Valdés that the natives had been using specific pieces of land and springs for growing corn and wheat, the governor awarded arable tracts from the missions of San Felipe and Santa Cruz to Captain Diego de Quiroz in 1675. In 1678, these missions were surrounded by seven livestock estancias.[112]

Spaniards often had the advantage in these cases, not just because they controlled decision-making. Movement of Tarahumaras in and out of missions was still closely associated with older patterns of transhumance, although the introduction of sheep and goats added a new variation. Traditionally, the Tarahumaras were residentially mobile in order to take advantage of different resources and subsistence strategies. They commonly cultivated corn in several locations and moved between them during the growing season. Rock shelters and caves were used before the Spaniards arrived, but their use was modified with the introduction of animals. This is a case in which Spanish material introductions worked against the permanent reduction of indigenous peoples in pueblos, partially because they provided a new incentive to preserve old patterns.[113] Traditional ceremonial gatherings, organized around sharing work at clusters of dispersed rancherías, also encouraged mobility. By the same token, Tarahumaras could be enticed back to the missions for religious fiestas. Their migrational flexibility also lent itself to stints of paid labor outside of missions. But it also explains how they could be perceived in such antithetical categories as recalcitrant and collaborative.

Encouraged by the latter tendency, the Jesuits once again moved into the upper Tarahumara area to the west after a junta of civilian and military notables, appointed by Governor José García de Salcedo, deemed the entrada feasible in 1673. Within a few years, the Jesuits moved deep into the valley, contacting several thousand Tarahumaras. By 1680, there were six Jesuits working there in a score of missions and visitas. A number of churches had been built—some of straw and others of adobe.[114] Over 6,000 head of cattle were sent from Sonora to the new missions in the Tarahumara Alta and neighboring Chínipas in 1682.[115] In the 1680s, silver began to be mined in Tarahumara country at Coyachi and Cusihuiriachi. In the beginning, some Tarahumaras went to work there voluntarily, in the same tradition as those Tarahumaras who sought seasonal wage labor on Spanish haciendas to obtain cloth and tools. As the influx of outsiders into the Sierra Tarahumara increased, however, so did the potential for conflict.

The mission frontier also expanded into other areas through the efforts of the Franciscans. Their missions present a peculiar scenario—that of foundings and refoundings, primarily among the less sedentary Conchos in areas most exposed to enemy Indians. From the Concho missions along the northeastern flank that served as a buffer against the nomadic peoples to the east, in the 1660s Franciscans pressed toward the west and north, establishing missions like Santa María Nativitas Bachíniva, which blended Conchos and Tarahumaras. They also contacted Tarahumaras in the Papigochi valley from their missions farther north in the Casas Grandes area. Subsequently this brought them into conflict with the Jesuits, when the latter penetrated the western Tarahumara, but the Jesuits eventually succeeded in getting monopoly control there.[116] Encouraged by Nueva Vizcayan officials who wanted to work salt deposits in the area around Casas Grandes, the Franciscans congregated Concho and Suma Indians at Namiquipa, San Antonio, El Torreón, Las Carretas, and Janos. These northern outposts were particularly vulnerable to raiders and uprisings in 1667, 1684, and the 1690s.[117]

The eastern Concho missions were also unstable, subject to heavy labor drafts and frequent raiding. In the 1670s the Franciscans succeeded in getting royal officials to remove several hundred Conchos from farms in the Valle de San Bartolomé. These were Indians whose encomienda service had been tantamount to slavery. The repatriation breathed new life into the mission of San Francisco de los Conchos in 1677, and probably served the labor needs of expanding Spanish ranches in the areas of the Río Conchos and Río San Pedro.[118] But volatility tended to characterize the demography of most Franciscan missions in the last decades of the seventeenth century. Since the Franciscans ministered to the least sedentary groups in Nueva Vizcaya and Coahuila, they were at a greater disadvantage in trying to keep their charges in the missions. Other difficulties derived from congregating different ethnic groups or bands in the same mission, where they often fought among themselves.[119] This was also the case of the Jesuit mission of Tizonazo, whose original Tepehuan inhabitants had been decimated earlier in the century; after midcentury Tizonazo informally became the correctional facility for eastern nomadic Indians captured in warfare. The Jesuit mission of Cinco Señores was founded in 1692 for much the same purpose. Its core population consisted of indigenous raiders emanating from the Bolsón de Mapimí who had been captured and interned at the presidio of Pasaje.[120]

Demographic instability and frequent movements in and out of Jesuit and Franciscan missions were noted by Bishop Bartolomé de Escanuela in 1681: "Today there are very few Indians in these villages. . . . Instead, there are Spaniards, mestizos, mulattoes, black slaves, free servants, and workers in growing numbers."[121] Perhaps the volatility of the area can most graphically be conveyed by the story of Antonia de Soto, a mulata slave from Durango.[122] After first confessing her story to a Jesuit priest in May 1691, Antonia, about twenty years of age, turned herself in to the Inquisition agent in Parral. Over the next two years, on several occasions, she supplied further testimony about her activities during the previous six years. Her travels had taken her as far south as Veracruz and back again to the northern frontier.

Her odyssey began when she escaped from her master in the city of Durango, fleeing with a Tepehuan laborer named Matías de Rentería, also in his employ. They made their way first to Parral. There Antonia was aided by a mestiza nicknamed Juana Golpazos, who gave her lily-like flowers called *cacomites* to conceal under the clothing over her breasts, which she said made her unrecognizable to the overseer who had been sent to fetch her back to Durango. From Parral, Antonia and Matías fled with their magical herbs and flowers to Cusihuiriachi, where a flood of new immigrants had recently arrived to exploit newly discovered silver. On the way there, Matías introduced Antonia to a new form of magic spell, induced by peyote. In her mind-altering visions, Antonia witnessed the skillful maneuvers of Matías as he successfully subdued a charging bull. Both learned to dance, taught by a beguiling woman who accompanied them on her guitar. As she recalled the dream state induced by the peyote mixture that the two imbibed on Sundays, Antonia remembered also seeing many serpents, closely followed by an image of a very handsome man she assumed to be the devil, who appeared out of nowhere and promised her freedom if she would join him.

In their travels, Antonia and Matías stopped in the Jesuit mission of San Miguel de las Bocas, where Matías had Tepehuan kin. The presence of a mulata slave in an Indian mission went unremarked, not surprising in this area of considerable Spanish and mixed-race inhabitants. Yet it was there that Antonia experienced a remarkable transformation as she continued to experiment with flowering herbs and miraculous stones. She now made a pact with the devil. Her unholy bargain transformed her into a skilled horseman and bullfighter. She donned men's clothing and imagined a new, powerful life. One of the first signs of her newly acquired muscle was her ability to fight off an assault by Matías, whom she nearly killed by beating him with a cattle prod. Despite this quarrel, they apparently reconciled and set off once again. In the next few years, the two found employment as cowboys on cattle ranches in northern Durango, where they worked with other indigenous and mixed-race peoples. At one point, Antonia hired on as a porter for a mule train that carried silver through Guanajuato to Veracruz, where it was to be shipped to Spain. Returning with another muleteer, she passed through San Luis Potosí, eventually arriving back in the familiar territory of northern Durango.[123]

Throughout these travels, she continued to rub flowers and rosettes over her body and to use particular arrangements of magical stones and incantations to call forth the devil. He usually appeared in the form of a white man, but sometimes she could only hear him speaking to her and once he materialized as a growling bear. Most often he came on horseback carrying a machete. In these encounters he spoke to her and empowered her to gamble, to break horses, and to fight bulls and even men. On one occasion in the mining camp of Urique in western Chihuahua, Antonia and three companions overpowered a mule train, killed three men, and made off with part of the silver shipment. When one of her accomplices stole her silver-laden saddlebags, she pursued and killed him. Later, in the midst of a heated argument, she killed a coworker in Sinaloa. She had become more than just a man; now she was a violent bandit.

Eventually the harrowing experiences took their toll, at least on her conscience, and Antonia decided to give up her life as a swashbuckler. She made her confession to Padre Tomás de Guadalajara in Parral, asking for forgiveness. He replied, telling her that she would have to go before the Inquisition before he could give absolution. After hearing her testimony, the Inquisition agent reported the incident to his superiors in Mexico City, asking how to proceed. Over the next two years, Antonia supplied further testimony to various interrogators. During this time, she was returned to her master, who lost no time in selling her to a military officer. In the frontier milieu,[124] perhaps it was believed that a soldier could exercise more control over such a brazen troublemaker. Antonia's story comes to an abrupt end for us when the Inquisition decided in July 1693 that she was sufficiently repentant to be absolved under ecclesiastical jurisdiction. The Inquisition then ordered her case to be transferred to a civil court.

Antonia's tale reveals a good deal about freedom of movement and violence in this northern area, where conditions of social and political instability prevailed. We see the camaraderie of men as they gambled and caroused, and how easily they seemed to resort to violence.[125] What the story suggests about gender is fascinating. Antonia clearly believed that she would have many more advantages if she could behave like a man; furthermore, she could only exercise male prowess through witchcraft. Resort to petty witchcraft was not uncommon in colonial Spanish America, and this kind of magic seems to have been most commonly practiced by women of lower social status. We know of many cases that involve sorcery for healing, love magic, and protection from abusive relationships. Here the folk practices of diverse racial groups often intersected and brought Indians, mestizos, mulattoes, and Spaniards into close contact.[126] In this case, Antonia was introduced to magic by the Indian Matías and the mestiza Juana Golpazos. She gave magic charms to other transients she met in her travels, among them an Apache Indian and a mulatto slave. The Inquisition asked her quite direct questions about these associations, revealing official concern about the ways in which a popular subculture could undermine royal authority.

It appears that the Spanish crown's attempts to limit geographic mobility and ethnic mixing, especially in less populated northern areas, were not very effective. Some scholars have argued that in areas of greater interethnic mixing and more mobile populations, witchcraft and pacts with the devil were more common.[127] Antonia's case offers a startling illustration of how the practical use of supernatural or divine power could be perceived as destabilizing. The devil in this case was a white man, not the black demon described by the Jesuits in the early rebellion. How frequently was the devil invoked by women and men to try to subvert social hierarchies? Certainly the authorities blamed unrest on the machinations of the devil.

As economic incentives and migratory strategies brought different groups into contact with each other, transactions were sometimes voluntary and peaceful, but more often they had a volatile character predicated on Spanish coercion and the refusals of subordinates. In the face of a relatively unorganized but persistent Spanish urge to imperialism, lower-status groups resisted in myriad ways. Folk remedies and petty witchcraft as responses to disease, privation, and loss were continuous throughout the colonial period. Migration was also pervasive as a resistance strategy. The ever-present labor shortage fostered the unauthorized movement of Indians, who in some circumstances were able to demand higher pay.[128] A mixture of persuasion and brute force continued to be practiced on the most directly defiant indigenous peoples. Yet, as the last years of the seventeenth century later demonstrated, their inconformity did not collapse altogether, even in the midst of demographic and subsistence crises. Opportunistic responses at this stage were still playing out in the face of unpredictable outcomes.

FOUR

CRISES OF THE 1690S
Rebellion, Famine, and Disease

Not a few observers attributed heightened Indian aggression in the 1680s to the successful ouster of Spaniards from New Mexico after the Pueblos rebelled at the beginning of the decade. There is evidence that the Nueva Vizcayan groups not only were aware of the Pueblos' feat but also were in contact with them. Some historians have referred to this period of unrest as the Great Southwestern Revolt or the Great Northern Revolt, because aggressive tactics by indigenous peoples escalated over the larger "borderlands" region. Increased raiding by nomadic groups and outright rebellion from peoples who had been settled in missions were, in part, responses to drought, famine, and disease episodes in the 1670s and 1680s. Furthermore, where mission Indians revolted we can see reactions to the directed cultural changes that Spaniards had tried to impose, but the degree to which the European presence in North America (Spanish and French) affected longstanding trading and raiding patterns of Plains and Greater Southwestern (or Northern) Indians also needs to be considered in understanding this period of conflict.[1]

Continued unrest and the always implicit threat to mining prompted royal orders to establish presidios at El Gallo, Cuencamé, San Francisco de los Conchos, and Casas Grandes to protect shipments of silver and other merchandise transported by oxcart and mule trains along the camino real.[2] Perhaps emboldened by the Pueblos' success, Tobosos, Cabezas, Chisos, Baborigames, Cocoyomes, and other eastern band groups confederated under the leadership of Don Francisco Tecolote, who brandished a silver bastón as a symbol of his authority. Employing an extensive network of spies in Spanish households and missions, the insurgents wreaked havoc on haciendas, stealing supplies and taking Indian captives. The tendency of the Spaniards to subsume all hostile groups under the Toboso umbrella persisted, making it difficult to determine exactly who they were. When raiders were captured, they usually feigned peaceful surrender, only to take up arms again as soon as possible.[3] In 1690, a new mission, Cinco Señores, was founded on the eastern flank of the Tepehuan missions near Cuencamé. Its purpose was to congregate band groups, including Baborigames who pledged to aid the Spaniards in campaigns against Tobosos and others in return for land, tools, seed, and animals.[4]

Indian hostilities were not the Spaniards' only concern. Mining revenues were down, as the richer veins in Parral had played out, and both flooding and the price of mercury (for processing silver) inhibited further exploitation of these mines. Governor Lope de Sierra Osorio reported in 1678 that Parral's economy was on the verge of collapse.[5] A decade later Governor Juan Isidro de Pardiñas echoed the negative sentiment, claiming that mines were not being worked efficiently. And now there was a new worry. Frenchmen were in Texas, trading metal tools and clothing for food and horses and stirring up Indians with stories that the Spanish were planning to attack and kill them.[6]

While campaigns against groups who raided from the Bolsón de Mapimí occupied the attention of the Spanish military authorities, the Jesuits worried about the challenges to their fledgling endeavor in the upper Tarahumara mission rectorate. They had been aided in their entradas by converted Tarahumaras who recognized the leadership of Don Pablo, designated by the Spaniards as "general of the Tarahumaras," a fictive military chiefdom. After several years, however, dissident Tarahumaras led by Corosia, the unconverted cacique of Cajurichi, began to spread unrest. Their tactics provide an interesting window into the multiplicity of indigenous reactions to and alliances with different Spanish invaders. Corosia operated out of the western Tarahumara and had established peaceful relations with the alcalde mayor of Ostimuri in Sonora, perhaps having worked in the mines there. But in 1681 the Jesuits reported that Corosia had begun to visit the sites of recently established Jesuit missions (Guadalupe, Santa Ana, Matachi, and Papigochi), bringing in his entourage about 70 armed Tarahumaras. He timed his arrivals to coincide with Jesuit absences and said he came on the orders of Don Pablo. He also claimed to have a letter from the Spanish governor containing "divine" instructions which ordered the Indians to stop attending mass and living in the mission pueblo. They were to resume their previous ceremonial activities and, above all, to maintain a united but clandestine front against the padres.

What is interesting to observe here is that the agitators were trying to play upon the discontent of neophytes but at the same time invoking the power of both Tarahumara and Spanish civil authorities to legitimize their claims. The effectiveness of these tactics, according to the Jesuits, was demonstrated by the increased movement out of missions and the frequent threats against missionaries' lives—and this despite continued Jesuit gift giving. Subsidized in part by the viceroy, the Jesuits imported several thousand head of cattle from their Sonora missions throughout the decade of the 1680s. A good number of these were pilfered by the Indians. Some Tarahumaras stated openly that the Jesuits were to blame for Spanish exploitation, having paved the way for it. Why shouldn't the Indians "defend themselves like men, rather than acquiesce like women?"[7]

Another interesting aspect of the Tarahumara strategy was based on their recognition that Spanish civil and religious authorities were not always in accord. For much of their first century in Nueva Vizcaya, the Jesuits had readily curried the favor of the provincial governors, who frequently sided with them in their disputes with the bishops. Thus they had been able to avoid most diocesan efforts to secularize missions or even supervise their activities.[8] The last clash of the seventeenth century produced similar results. In a dispute that began in 1681, Bishop Bartolomé García de Escanuela, a Franciscan, was unsuccessful in asserting his episcopal right of visitation. Nor did he prevail in supporting the Franciscan claims to jurisdiction in western Tarahumara territory.[9] Jesuit superiors were generally very adept at maneuvering, using political connections and money to fight their battles in court, although they complained that the administration of the New World tended to be so inconsistent as to make their manipulations difficult:

> [T]he administration of the Indies is extremely variable and doubly so in this kingdom [Nueva Vizcaya]. Lately the governors pay little attention to laws and decrees; each one governs to his taste, looking for laws that suit him and forgetting the ones that do not.[10]

Their concern was well founded in the case of Governor Juan Isidro de Pardiñas, who occupied his post in 1688. More significantly, the enmity that developed between the Jesuits and the governor was not lost on the indigenous groups and arguably made them more willing to resist the Jesuits. As the various Spanish agents competed for their labor, insubordination escalated in the late 1680s.

The missionaries had been dealing with Tarahumaras for more than fifty years, but their experiences and ethnographic descriptions reflect many incongruities. Virtually all mention the Tarahumaras' penchant for bartering. "For a needle, an Indian will give two hens; for a knife, two ewes or a lamb; for some glass beads, a parcel of land; and for a length of cloth, a horse." So wrote Padre Juan Ratkay in 1681 of his initial impressions.[11] Two years later he could still report favorably on Tarahumara trading acumen, their generally good health (which he attributed to eating mostly grains and little meat and to physical exercise), and their basic honesty. At the same time, he characterized them as lazy because their consumerist instincts were not sufficiently developed, and as lascivious, incestuous, given to drunkenness, and rebellious.

Jesuit commentaries from the 1680s concurred in their main concern about the lack of discipline in Tarahumara society. The tesgüinadas where Tarahumaras gathered to share communal tasks and then celebrate were not even the most glaring manifestation of the problem, although they were seen as the source of adultery, homicide, and incest. Since establishing a chain of authority was a key principle of mission orderliness, Tarahumara political organization proved inordinately vexing to Spanish "civilizers" because it was so atomized. Although the Jesuits named a hierarchy of village officials to replace the loose, decentralized government by elders and war leaders of rancherías, the fathers complained that

> the governors and principals, who are usually the most ladino in buying and selling in the name of the others, are more like brokers than governors or captains. In most cases, they simply make suggestions, and everyone does what he wants. Thus it is not enough to reduce the principales, but rather each individual in particular. . . . When the governor orders them to undertake any task, only love, not fear or punishment, will make them do it.[12]

At first the Tarahumara mission Indians were inclined to take what benefits they could see as compatible with their lives and to ignore other aspects of Spanish civilization (much as the Tepehuanes had done earlier).[13] The hoes, axes, knives, plows, cloth (even sheep to make their own woolen cloth), livestock manure, and new food sources were accepted eagerly and considerably changed their material culture. The Tarahumaras went to the mission to celebrate fiestas and transact business, but most refused to build houses in the village or store their grain there. Nor were they active participants in constructing churches or digging the irrigation ditches that watered the mission lands.[14] The fact that many farmed

widely scattered plots (due to the scarcity of arable land and to a bilat-
eral inheritance system) discouraged congregation. More than in the case
of the Tepehuanes, the local environment was an especially conspicuous
modifier of the Spanish blueprint. The acceptances of material goods and
the small concessions of public compliance with ritual aspects of the mission program were matched by withdrawal, evasion, deceit, dissimula-
tion, feigned ignorance, and slander. Ranchería Indians would give the
Jesuits permission to enter, but they would be conveniently absent when
the priests arrived or ask them to come back later. Father Joseph Neumann was most struck by what he described as their unparalleled mastery
in camouflaging their true intentions.[15] Many stubbornly refused to engage the missionaries in dialogue; others simply stated they wanted to go
to hell. They easily ignored Jesuit admonitions to attend mass and requests
for firewood and other necessities. Taking a slightly more aggressive tack,
some insulted the Jesuits behind their backs or in asides, such as the one
reported by Fathers Tardá and Guadalajara: "¿Adónde vienes, padre Cor-
nudo?" ("Where are you going, Father Cuckhold?") Rather than being
a virtue, celibacy was interpreted as a sign of impotence and a failure to
contribute to the reproduction of the community. A few tried to provoke the padres to prove their might, throwing rocks and on one occasion
wounding a priest with an arrow.[16]

The imperviousness of the adults fueled missionary resolve to win the
hearts and minds of the children, an already time-honored conversion tactic. Jesuits concentrated their efforts on periodically boarding youth in
the churches for prolonged catechism lessons. The fathers were also determined to remedy what they perceived as parents' failure to adequately
discipline their children.[17] Adapting the model employed in customary
public sermons by elders, designed to transmit advice about good conduct, Jesuits used the repetitious format of catechism to inculcate their
moral precepts.[18]

The Tarahumara strategy of ignoring those aspects of the Spanish program they found incompatible worked relatively well at first, but silver
strikes in the Tarahumara country (Coyachi in 1683 and Cusihuiriachi in
1686), with hundreds of Spanish miners and other entrepreneurs entering the region, made passive resistance more difficult. The labor needs of
the new mines converted surrounding Tarahumara and Concho rancherías into prime targets for labor brokers, who pressed Indians into service
in mines and cutting wood for charcoal, even though royal officials cau-
tioned against forcing neophytes and the unconverted to labor in repartimiento. Spanish livestock became a serious threat to Indian milpas in the

areas closest to mines. Indians in the new Chínipas missions adjacent to the Tarahumaras complained that the Jesuits had entered their lands in order to turn them over to the Spaniards.[19]

Where the resettlement program of the missionaries was successful, it was inevitably accompanied by epidemic disease,[20] and continued high mortality reinforced negative perceptions of outsiders by the Tarahumaras. Death practices at the time of contact indicate that Tarahumaras feared the dead; they abandoned the houses where people died.[21] Today they believe that the dead pressure the living to join them, and death rituals are crucial for obviating that threat.[22] With their population reduced by at least 30 percent from the time of the first Spanish entradas a half century earlier,[23] the Tarahumaras must have been disquieted by the disruption of reassuring ritual activity. Jesuits, on the other hand, could take comfort in recording the baptisms of dying infants and adults. Their work had purpose, even if the Tarahumaras would not embrace the basic Christian concepts of repentance, salvation, and eternal damnation.[24]

Turning to the less abstract, missionaries stepped up the pressure for Indians to conform at least to basic Spanish norms of urban living, monogamy, and industry. They tried to quell the "love of liberty" epitomized by isolated dwellings, sexual license, and lack of interest in work. The dissent of specialists trying to preserve indigenous rituals earned the punishments reserved for witches: public whippings, condemnation to hard labor and, less frequently, death.[25] Even backsliding converts could be publicly shamed, an experience which was particularly humiliating for Tarahumaras, who avoided confrontation and seldom raised their voices while with one another.[26] They were not accustomed to public shows of denigration and scorn.

Some did find solace in the utopian aspects of millenarian thought. Tardá and Guadalajara recalled the old woman who declared that if all the Spaniards were killed, the Tarahumaras would have an abundance of food: "[E]ven the pines would bear squash and corn."[27] Father Joseph Neumann, missionary at Sisoguichi, reported on the activities of a messianic leader who urged his compatriots to rebel, promising that any Tarahumaras who were killed by Spaniards would be resurrected in three days.[28] The urge to resist grew stronger as Spanish demands for labor penetrated even more deeply into the northwestern corner of Tarahumara territory, as well as into the lands of the neighboring Conchos. Even the offer of pay was not enough to attract Indians who had no interest in the Spaniards' pursuits. It was simple, according to Francisco, a Concho Indian who explained, "All we want is to live like we used to."[29]

Undeterred by the recalcitrance of the Conchos, Tarahumaras, and other groups who inhabited the isolated area around the northwestern mission visita of Naguérachi, Father Diego Ortiz de Foronda threatened to call in force against those Indians who refused to settle in the village and contribute labor to the mission. In response, several Indians pelted him with rocks, leaving his face bruised and bloody.[30] According to the Jesuits, such behavior was promoted by the new governor, who encouraged Indians to take complaints against the padres to local secular officials and frequently supported them. They contended that Pardiñas' strategy was to try to lure Indians from the missions with offers of pay to work in the mines that he so diligently promoted during his tenure. He allegedly also undermined the missionaries' authority by sending officials to the villages to read dispatches and orders addressed to both the Indians and the Jesuits; the fathers argued the Indians took this to mean that the Jesuits were on an equal footing with them.[31] Whether from lack of respect for the Jesuits or the realization that the Spaniards were divided among themselves, many Tarahumaras and Conchos stepped up their evasive tactics, refusing to work in the missions. They also became more daring in pilfering cattle and other mission resources. Reacting to repeated warnings from both Jesuits and Spanish officials in the field, in March Governor Pardiñas met with leading military and civil officials in Parral to discuss the extent of the threat and the resources that could be devoted to quelling it.[32]

Tensions had already reached the boiling point in the mission district of Yepómera where the visita at Naguérachi was located. Father Ortiz had hired some Concho Indians (whose territory bordered the Tarahumaras' on the north) to make bricks for building a reservoir for irrigation, promising to pay them with one or two head of cattle. They claimed that when they completed the work, he reneged and paid them nothing. After consulting among themselves, in compensation they took two of his mules. Several Tarahumaras dispatched in pursuit by Father Ortiz apprehended the Concho men and several women. The missionary sent the men to be punished by Spanish officials in Cusihuiriachi and kept the women at the mission. One of the Conchos escaped and made his way to Naguérachi, where resentment against the priest was strong and where conspiratorial talk about rebellion had a responsive audience.[33] In late March, Indians attacked the mission of Yepómera and killed Father Ortiz de Foronda, along with two other Spaniards.[34]

Living in the rugged terrain of the northwestern corner of Tarahumara territory, the Indians of Naguérachi had a good deal of concourse with neighboring Conchos, Pimas, and Jovas. This area of the headwaters of the Río Yaqui attracted Indians trying to avoid Spanish encroachments from both the western and eastern slopes of the sierras. Various bands of Conchos had rebelled a number of times in the seventeenth century; eventually many had been forcibly settled near the presidio of San Francisco de los Conchos just northeast of Parral and served as auxiliary troops.[35] The Conchos around Casas Grandes and Namiquipa were not as compliant. Some had intermarried with the Tarahumaras and Pimas of the surrounding area. (In fact, there seems to have been a marked incidence of Tarahumara-Pima intermixing among rebels.) The Conchos were particularly aggrieved over the excessive labor repartimientos organized in their pueblos for the mines of Cusihuiriachi and in late March had killed their own governor, who was notorious for cooperating with the Spaniards in organizing the labor drafts.[36] Conchos living in Naguérachi encouraged the Tarahumaras to avenge Father Ortiz's insult to their brethren. Several Tarahumaras needed little urging. Among them was Bernardo, a former official in Yepómera, whom the missionary had flogged for failing to attend mass, and his son, who had also been whipped and had his head shaved publicly.[37] When the rebels reached Yepómera, about half of its inhabitants (widely dispersed along the river valley) supported them in killing the priest and burning the church. According to one witness, the women of the village entreated the rebels to spare the Jesuit's life, but the warriors—who perceived mercy as cowardice—were not receptive.[38] Nor did they seem inclined to listen to women in matters of warfare. Some Tarahumara rebels reportedly taunted compatriots who refused to join them, "asking them if the Spaniards were their husbands."[39]

The rebellion spread rapidly, attracting adherents among Tarahumaras, Conchos, Pimas, Tepehuanes, Guazapares, Chínipas, and many band groups, constituting several thousand insurgents (although they did not all operate together at any one time or place). The bulk of the fighting took place in the Sierra Tarahumara, where most of the new, primitively constructed missions were torched, forcing the Jesuits to flee. Nearly all escaped with their lives; the exception was Father Manuel Sánchez from the mission of Tutuaca. Knowing that the Spaniards were not well provisioned in the first place, rebels deliberately killed Spanish horses and livestock wherever they could. Many of the rebel commanders were former warriors who had earned respect for their fighting skills. Because of their roles in dealing with outsiders, they were often an early point of contact between their rancherías and the Jesuits. Early encounters also included conversations between the fathers and men who had achieved social prestige through their talents as good speakers or curers. Although none of these individuals had the power to coerce others, the Jesuits perceived them as political leaders and frequently named them to the new offices of mission government.

The main Spanish fighting force of a few hundred was constituted by presidial soldiers from Casas Grandes and San Francisco de los Conchos and militia officers hastily drafted from the ranks of the Spanish citizens, as well as all mestizos, mulattoes, and free blacks that could be mustered.[40] Most of their support, however, came from Indian allies—not only from Tepehuanes[41] and Conchos, but also from Tarahumaras themselves. Just as in the previous rebellions, precontact patterns of social organization and warfare obstructed indigenous unity, notwithstanding the rebels' slaying of Indians who refused to join their ranks.[42] There were no pitched battles in this warfare; the Spaniards and their allies had to wage a war of attrition against small contingents of rebels. Spanish officials also employed Tarahumara spies to infiltrate enemy camps to assassinate Indian leaders, offering them a hundred pesos for each slain warrior.[43]

Like the Indians, the Spaniards saw the advantage in depriving their enemies of supplies, and they made a systematic attempt to destroy Indian fields and burn huts in rebel territory. At the same time, Spaniards made some efforts to protect the fields and reward the exertions of their Indian allies. They also moved quickly to requisition and store provisions to feed the troops.[44] As they forced the surrender of pockets of rebels in July and August, the Spanish commanders offered amnesty to Indians who would resettle in missions. In the beginning rebel leaders feigned acceptance of the peace initiative to buy time, but as supplies dwindled a growing number of Tarahumaras acquiesced, at least until they could reorganize a means of subsistence. Rebel fighters captured after the amnesty were hanged on the gallows constructed at Papigochi, headquarters of the Spanish forces and located in the heart of Tarahumara country. Ceremonies of repossession were carried out at most of the mission sites in early 1691, with loyal Tarahumaras being entrusted with staffs of office and given the charge of ending the "pagan" community drinking festivals that missionaries perceived as *borracheras* or drunken orgies.[45] Resettled Indians were required to build houses in the mission pueblos and to police their environs to protect livestock. Captain Juan Fernández de Retana was given the task of patrolling the Sierra Tarahumara to check on compliance, and his reports indicate the persistence of considerable unrest and evasion. Tarahumaras and other sierra groups were biding their time.[46]

The Jesuits, of course, wished to rebuild their missions, but they did not want to do so with insolent converts. For the missionaries, the victory had not been decisive enough to assure either their own safety or the genuine submission of the Indians. They alleged that Governor Pardiñas had not been sufficiently severe in punishing the Tarahumaras and refused to certify that the rebellion had actually been crushed. And they continued to report signs of turmoil.[47] Some of the main instigators had been caught (in most cases by Tarahumaras themselves), executed, and had their heads placed on pikes in the villages. The governor had called off the pursuit of the remaining rebel leaders who had gone into hiding; worse still, he refused to support Jesuit demands for the creation of a presidio in Tarahumara country.[48]

The governor reciprocated with a series of charges against the Jesuits, alleging that their treatment of the Indians and exploitation of Indian labor were the principal causes of the revolt. They should be more moderate and not threaten Indians with soldiers.[49] The Jesuits responded forcefully to these charges and at the same time acted in two ways to discredit his allegations. On one front, they sent Father Tomás de Guadalajara to Mexico City to plead their cause to the viceroy; on another they brought charges against the governor before the Inquisition (in its capacity of ensuring religious orthodoxy). The specific charges consisted of comments Pardiñas had allegedly made to various Spanish vecinos presumed to show that the governor had overstepped his authority in both the temporal and spiritual realms of government. The fathers were particularly scandalized by his accusations that they all cohabited with women and by the manner in which he had publicly incited Indians against them by undermining their prestige. Instead of responding decisively to put an end to the sinful behaviors of indigenous peoples who had been congregated in missions, Pardiñas was reported to have stated: "Since the Indians are by nature aggressive, what difference does it make if they get drunk?"[50]

It is clear that rebel grievances were directed at both the secular and ecclesiastical arms of Spanish control and that there had been intermittent parleys between Indian groups throughout the previous decade in which armed resistance was contemplated. There is considerable evidence that a rebellion was being planned to begin after the harvest in the summer of 1690, but that the incident at Naguérachi had launched it prematurely.[51] Among the complaints that emerged from the investigations during and after the rebellion were grievances over forced labor in missions and mines, as well as damage to Indian lands by Spanish cattle and horses.[52] The missionaries were perceived by many as simply the advance agents of the Spaniards who had been sent to trick them with gifts and false promises. Among mission Tarahumaras, treatment of the padres during the rebellion was mixed. Two Jesuits lost their lives and were mutilated by their assassins; their habits and other religious objects were desecrated in ceremonies intended to parody and palliate the power of the new religion. Yet other Jesuits were warned of impending attacks, giving them time to flee to safety. Indigenous awareness of divisions within the Spanish ranks may have encouraged insubordination, but rebels had no intention of collaborating with either sphere—temporal or religious—of Spanish administration.

Governor Pardiñas had not been able to devote full attention to the Tarahumara situation, as attacks by eastern band groups continued throughout 1691 and into 1692, until epidemics of smallpox and measles slowed their pace. The smallpox epidemic of late 1692 and early 1693 was followed by measles; the effect was devastating to the entire region, as these diseases preyed upon a hungry indigenous population whose fields had been destroyed in the combat. Spanish officials reported that some villages were completely depopulated and in others as many as two-thirds of the residents had died. The governor estimated that one-third of the total Indian population of Nueva Vizcaya had perished, a grim illustration of the particularly lethal effects of piggybacking epidemics.[53] The death rate was also high among non-Indian mestizos and mulattoes working on haciendas.[54]

Rebellion and disease exacerbated the chronic labor shortage in mining areas. Miners at the new site of Urique encountered difficulties when the local official refused to honor labor repartimientos approved by the governor. Some simply took Indians captive, stole their sheep, and forced the Indians to work for them.[55] For many Spaniards, the threat of rebellion did not deter their efforts to appropriate labor by whatever means they could—especially from the older Tarahumara and Tepehuan missions. Indians in the longer established missions like Huejotitlán and San Pablo complained that the missionaries were too exacting; their gifts of grain and clothing no longer compensated for the rigors of the mission regime. Indian fiscales whose duties included administering punishment increasingly refused to carry out the missionaries' orders to flog the disobedient.[56] Tarahumaras were also being sent from the newer missions like Santa Cruz and Cuevas to work in the Valle de San Bartolomé.

Pardiñas was replaced as governor in 1693 by Gabriel de Castillo, formerly alcalde mayor of Puebla. The new governor faced what he perceived as a dire situation: many Indians had died from diseases; others were still at war; and the costs of pacification (resettling Indians with provisions and paying soldiers and their allies) greatly exceeded royal allocations. A severe drought in 1693–1694 further diminished local stores of corn and wheat, producing famine in many areas. Even when repartimientos could be mustered, there was not enough grain to feed the workers. Mining was also retarded by the scarcity of mercury. Furthermore, officials feared that authorizing new mining claims would result in abuse of Indian laborers at a time when rumors of renewed insurrection were still rife.[57] Castillo's requests for more money and presidios coincided with a military inspection undertaken by Joseph Francisco Marín as part of the review of Pardiñas' conduct in office. The assessments of these two officials differed as to the gravity of the situation, but they were in agreement that the operation of the presidios needed to be more efficient.[58]

In their communications with military officials, Jesuits continued to report that they had received warnings from friendly Tarahumaras that Conchos and Tarahumaras from the area around Naguérachi were storing poisoned arrows and supplies to prepare for another revolt intended to wipe out all the Spaniards in the Cusihuiriachi and Casas Grandes areas, including the missionaries. The Jesuits believed that a series of strange natural occurrences in 1696 had either caused or were omens of further unrest; these included an earthquake, a comet, rapidly rising rivers, and church bells that rang by themselves. Governor Castillo was more sympathetic than his predecessor to Jesuit entreaties, and early in 1697 he ordered Captain Retana to reconnoiter the region and punish anyone trying to incite rebellion.[59] Once again the center of the alleged conspiracy was the northwest corner of the Sierra Tarahumara, where mission fugitives from a variety of indigenous groups (Tarahumaras, Pimas, Jovas, Opatas, Tubares, and Conchos) could take refuge but still have concourse with mission Indians as well as Janos, Jocomes, and Apaches from the north. For several years, nonconformist leaders had been recruiting sympathizers who were convinced that their survival depended on the annihilation of the Spaniards. In fact, they used the argument that Retana had been sent to exterminate them.

Efforts to rekindle the revolt may have been delayed by the high incidence of mortality after the 1693 epidemic, but many of the victims were children rather than men of warrior age. Some of the perpetrators of the earlier troubles who had never been apprehended were among the new insurgents, as were the sons and brothers of a number of Tarahumaras who had been executed as rebels or sorcerers. If avenging the deaths of their kin united some Tarahumaras, others were more susceptible to Retana's efforts to break their solidarity. Through Indians appointed by the Spaniards as military chieftains over all the Tarahumaras, Retana recruited several hundred Indian allies from most of the reestablished missions, as well as some unconverted Tarahumaras, and supplied them with scarce flour and beef. By April a number of the insurrection's leaders had been apprehended and sentenced to death. Others were sent into exile near the presidio of San Francisco de los Conchos, and lesser offenders were flogged. Those prisoners receiving death sentences were shot and their heads placed on pikes in front of the church at Papigochi as a warning.[60]

Despite the lesson, the rebellion spread from May through August of 1697. In fact, the harsh punishments seem to have convinced many Indians that there could be no safety in cooperating with the Spaniards. Once again, Spanish troops from several northern presidios could do little damage to Indians who had retreated to their nearly impenetrable rocky peaks, where women rained rocks down on attackers as their spouses showered them with poisoned arrows.[61] Nonetheless, the Spaniards were able to inflict extensive damage on corn and beans ready for harvest in August and September. Still, their mobility from the headquarters at Papigochi was restricted by lack of arms and supplies and also because they suspected the loyalty of the Tarahumaras of this central mission and could not leave it undefended. As a result, other missions were left without much protection and eventually a dozen of their still primitively constructed churches were burned (in most cases with complicity from their inhabitants), although all of the Jesuits escaped unharmed.[62] In most cases, the padres were warned by their parishioners. According to Father Neumann, the rebels feared the consequences of killing the priests, having heard the widely circulated story that the Jesuits killed in 1690 often appeared in the wilderness and chased the Tarahumaras they found there. As in the earlier rebellion, many Indian governors, alcaldes, and other officials were implicated in the planning and execution of the revolt, further evidence that the Jesuits had identified respected or at least authoritative native leaders.[63] Also charged with kindling the flames were several Indian *hechiceras*/female shamans; at least one was summarily executed and her head mounted on a lance. A single woman traveling in the company of warriors was automatically assumed to be a sorceress.[64]

In October, having been instructed by the viceroy, who was receiving civilian reports from Nueva Vizcaya highly critical of the conduct of the war, veteran missionary Tomás de Guadalajara undertook a peace mission.[65] Rebel followers were promised amnesty if they would return to the missions. Although in several instances Indians pretended to accept the offer, it was overwhelmingly rejected. Reinforced by Toboso, Concho, and

Tarahumara allies (from Franciscan and Jesuit missions), Retana and the other presidial captains resumed aggressive pursuit of the rebels, many of whom were now suffering from scarcity of food and water. Only in January of 1698 could the Spaniards claim to have suppressed the revolt, after a year of warfare and starvation for many of the native fighters. Most of the leaders still remained at large and were not captured until later in the year.[66] In June the Tarahumara prisoners, who had been exiled to the Conchos presidio where they were given plots of land and provisions, fled with the intention of returning to the sierra. Most were apprehended, and 17 men received the death sentence from the governor.[67] The harsh measures implemented throughout the second phase of the revolt—especially the summary imposition of the death penalty for hundreds of rebels—provoked an investigation into the actions of both the governor and General Retana. Although he died before it was completed, evidence was gathered as part of the residencia of Governor del Castillo. In the end, the judicial proceeding absolved both of any wrongdoing in the Tarahumara war, attributing the blame to the natives' malevolence. As many as 10,000 Indians participated in the intermittent and scattered fighting; perhaps 400 Spaniards and Indian allies lost their lives while the death toll among the rebels was much higher.[68]

According to the final assessments of the Tarahumaras who had remained loyal to the Spaniards, the revolt that began somewhat haphazardly in 1690 had not been completely suppressed in 1691 as Governor Pardiñas had alleged. Its ashes continued to smolder until the outbreak in 1697. For this reason they agreed with Spanish officials that extreme measures had been necessary to extinguish the conflagration.[69] But had resistance really been suppressed, even in 1698? Certainly the grievances that precipitated revolt had not been eliminated. Indian testimonies touch on the motivations both implicitly and explicitly. Cumulatively they refer (often obliquely) to the appropriation of their lands and labor by Spaniards, the deprivations and abuses of the missionary regime, the denigration of native leaders, and the disruption of harmony in their social structure and belief systems. Occasionally (and frequently under torture) prisoners volunteered that they rebelled to expel all the Spaniards and that they intended to wage a war of extermination against them. They recounted what one of the leaders, Posilegui, a mulatto from Naguérachi, had counseled them: "Leave the missions because the fathers' teachings are wrong."[70] Posilegui claimed to have a true father advising him in the sierra and promised that the rebels would receive aid from other mulattoes and from Frenchmen known to be in the vicinity of the Texas Gulf

Coast. From Conchos and other Indian allies who ranged between the sierra and the plains of the Rio Grande, the rebels would have known about the French efforts in Texas. Spaniards may have been putting words into the rebels' mouths, since Retana himself had been sent with Indian allies to the Rio Grande in 1688–1689 to investigate the intrusions of the French who were trading with Indians in Texas.[71]

Spanish officials, of course, were constrained to record Indian testimonies in a vernacular that excised cultural nuance. Literal transcriptions could be the most damning. When rebels stated that they wanted "liberty" to live as they pleased, Spaniards saw a kind of pathological disorder. Yet in the words of one of the Tarahumara rebels, "they were not men if they constructed houses" in pueblos and lived under the supervision of a missionary. Their insistence on "having many women" could only be interpreted by Spaniards as a perversion of Christian monogamy, not as an integral part of a different social system. To the modern eye, the testimonies reveal other features of kin-related organization and solidarity. Many captured rebels stated quite explicitly that their actions were necessary to exact revenge for wrongs done to their kin. And a major grievance of the rebels concerned the prohibition of tesgüinadas—those ritual celebrations organized to acquire supernatural favor in agriculture and warfare.

The suppression of the 1690s rebellions did not resolve these enormous cultural gaps. But warfare did prompt regroupings on both sides. The power struggles between the governor and the Jesuits at the beginning of the decade may have encouraged indigenous defiance; certainly the missionaries believed that Pardiñas had publicly demeaned their authority. This discord was supplanted at mid-decade by a more harmonious relationship between missionary, soldier, and magistrate, one that inflicted fierce punishments on indigenous peoples, afflicted once again by disease and famine. Spanish civilians cooperated in this alliance when forced to do so by official mandate or immediate threat, but their main concern was to keep their economic pursuits alive—a conundrum, since their need for labor was a key catalyst of the revolts.

In contrast, there were more divisions within indigenous society. In the case of the two largest groups of rebels, the Tarahumaras and the Conchos, not all their compatriots joined the fighting; in fact some became auxiliaries to the Spanish troops. This is not surprising, given a historical lack of political unity or supratribal organization. While the midcentury Tarahumara rebellions had been fought almost exclusively by non-Christians reacting to civil intrusions in their territory, the 1690s rebellions attracted both gentiles and apostates, together constituting probably less than half of the entire population. Some commonalities can be seen among the rebels who were interrogated. They had been mobile in pursuing both subsistence and refuge, and they had been willing to make warring and marital alliances with other sierra groups. Ritual dances with scalps and traditional drinking parties characterized their preparations for battle, indicating retention of precontact beliefs. Ritual specialists who did not participate in the fighting accompanied rebel contingents. Rebel leaders were men who had earned respect from their followers for their fighting prowess. Many rebel leaders were related through kinship, and a number of them reported having relatives who had been abused or punished by Spaniards, both civilians and missionaries. On the other hand, a good many converts remained loyal to the missionaries, and even a few gentiles aided the Spanish cause. The latter were accused by the rebels of being cowardly and effeminate. Whatever their motivations, they must have seen their existence as linked with the Spaniards, for good or for bad.

As noted in the first chapter, the intermediaries who emerged under the conditions of conquest were characterized both pejoratively as traitors and collaborators, and positively as cultural brokers who could mediate impositions and exploitation to a certain degree.[72] In societies where marked levels of hierarchy and social strata did not exist before contact, where minimal political authority and social prestige were based on oratorical ability and exemplary living, and where relations of obligation involved reciprocity, it was inordinately difficult for go-betweens to obey their conquerors without disrupting traditional social practices and exchanges. The fact that a number of rebel leaders were governors and alcaldes who had been removed from their posts by padres provides evidence that the imposed Tarahumara hierarchy was not very successful at this balancing act. Other Tarahumaras who had been punished for witchcraft, bigamy, and drunkenness also took an active role in the fighting.

As sites for planning revolt and for resisting it, missions had once again served as places where the old and the new intermingled, producing uneven results. Although the crown would have deemed it an exaggeration when the Jesuits argued that "in these lands the king has a presidio in every padre,"[73] royal officials still regarded the missions as a fundamental prop in conquest of the north. Once again Spaniards attempted to resettle Indians whose family bonds were newly shattered and whose numbers were further diminished by disease and starvation. The Jesuits, reacting to official pressures, did not attempt to reestablish the mission visitas northwest of Yepómera, where the conspiracies had found the most adherents.

Fluctuating mission populations continued to be the norm in Tarahumara territory as people moved in and out of the pueblos to tend dispersed milpas, harvest wild fruits, follow their herds, hunt, barter, and provide labor service. If anything, the decade of rebellion, epidemic, drought, and hunger had proved the utility of complementary and mobile subsistence strategies through which Indians had access to "starvation" foods in the monte. At the same time, the turn of the century was a critical juncture for those Tarahumaras who could not accept Spanish tutelage. Significant numbers retreated further into the Sierra Madre to multiethnic regions of refuge and reconstitution that were tacitly accepted as such even by the Jesuits, who did not follow them there.

Royal officials renewed their efforts to shore up the supravillage military office of native captain-general established for the Tarahumaras. Since no such office had existed before contact among the highly disaggregated Tarahumaras, the extent to which these Indian officials could command respect or impose authority is unclear. They seemed to have more influence among the more established missions of the Tarahumara Baja, where they also were rewarded by access to land and livestock, indicating that the Spaniards were more successful at co-optation as time went on. Even in the upper Tarahumara where many of the older leaders had been killed, new blood, potentially more malleable, ascended to leadership.[74]

Spaniards had survived another crisis, but unrest and uncertainty were pervasive and there was a general scarcity of provisions in the province. Retana urged the Jesuits and surrounding vecinos to keep their livestock from damaging Indian crops, and royal officials urged moderation in labor recruitment and treatment of the natives.[75] Despite the high death toll in the 1692–1693 epidemics, Indians still outnumbered Spaniards in Nueva Vizcaya by as much as ten to one at the turn of the century. But the ratio was much different in the missions of southern Chihuahua, northern Durango, and eastern Sinaloa, where the surrounding non-Indian population in specific locales surpassed that of the Indians. As the Jesuits tried to rebuild the upper Tarahumara missions, they could take some comfort from the fact that the lower Tarahumara had remained fairly tranquil during the fighting, although significant numbers of Tarahumaras had left those missions to join the rebels.[76] The missions in the lower Tarahumara and in the Tepehuan area had suffered population losses, but some still produced extra grain, including wheat, for sale. Jesuit visitors reported that despite the depletion of seed grains and animals that resulted from the drought, most of the missions had sufficient assets to cover debts they incurred in resuming the production of grain and livestock.[77] That situation changed in the next few decades, as the missions tried to withstand new burdens and demands. These trials were heavy ones for the indigenous populations, whose mechanisms for reproducing cultural forms and ethnic distinctiveness were losing ground.

FIVE

DEFIANCE AND DEFERENCE IN TRANSITIONAL SPACES, 1700–1730S

The 1690s rebellions were the last of the pan-village, first-generation revolts in Nueva Vizcaya. More localized revolts and sporadic raiding continued in the eighteenth century, but virtually no indigenous peoples believed that the Spaniards would withdraw. Stratagems for dealing with this circumstance were varied. Just as flight to remote areas not coveted by Spaniards had been the choice of some Tepehuanes after their great rebellion, considerable numbers of Tarahumaras followed this option at the close of the century, establishing new rancherías and sometimes finding shelter among other sierra groups like Pimas. Many of those who remained in the mission areas continued to flout the Jesuits' dictates. Their lack of obedience, coupled with the constant movement in and out of missions, fanned the missionaries' fears about possible uprisings as they imagined witchcraft all around them.[1] Looking for other measures to bring stability to the frontier, at least as early as 1693, the crown had urged the formation of colonies in Nueva Vizcaya composed of transplanted vagabonds and criminals from more settled areas. Local officials were appalled, believing that such a measure could only add to unrest and impermanence.[2] In the local milieu, the tendency on the part of both Spaniards and Indians was to answer violence with violence in relentless cycles of raids and offensives. As seminomadic groups found subsistence and profit in acquiring horses and mules, raiding escalated along the camino real between Mexico City and New Mexico that carried the main trade goods. In turn, Spanish strikes in the Bolsón de Mapimí yielded captives for reduction. In 1705 Cabeza and Babosariguame (probably Baborigame) Indians were settled at the mission of Cinco Señores in an effort to make them farmers instead of hunters. But missions themselves were targets of raids.

What did all this instability mean for the region's inhabitants, native or otherwise? This chapter will look more closely at how ethnicity was being redefined in the missions in the early eighteenth century as outside pressures on land and labor and ecological constraints escalated. A blow-by-blow sequential account allows us to see the complexity of the multiplying effects of these transformations. The first three decades of the new century were a period of transition in which the mounting Spanish presence in a highly volatile frontier situation was not yet dominating. If anything, the invaders' more determined struggles to impose their will resulted in more chaos than order.

In 1715, veteran missionary Tomás de Guadalajara reflected upon the conditions at his mission of Huejotitlán. "In these mountains of the older Tepehuan and Tarahumara missions, we are experiencing extreme necessity. In part this is due to the relentless battery of these frontiers, to the point that the villagers have barely enough to survive, but it is also because of the continuous labor drafts and the mustering of Indian fighters to take part in the campaigns against enemies." The missionary stipends, he maintained, were sometimes the only source of subsistence for the Indians.[3] Yet fears of rebellion did little to diminish the fierce competition for resources that characterized Nueva Vizcaya in the early eighteenth century.[4] Both the randomness of Spanish administration in the north and the long distances between frontier outposts and central authorities in Mexico City and Guadalajara fostered a capricious environment in which elites vied to monopolize assets and administrators argued over the extent of their powers.

Nowhere was this more evident than in the labor market, where the mix of free and unfree labor persisted with fresh twists and turns. In 1699 a number of Concho families took advantage of Franciscan attempts to revitalize the mission at San Pedro de los Conchos. They asked to be relocated to the mission from the haciendas in the Valle de San Bartolomé, where they had been working for more than fifteen years. The landowners contended that the Indians had never lived in San Pedro. Their argument that they constituted a pueblo was merely a ruse to get them out of their labor obligations.[5] Even though missions served to congregate manpower, at least these Conchos perceived them as affording more freedoms than confinement on haciendas.

In other situations, Indians had less recourse. In the western sierras of San Andrés and Topia, the Jesuits were ineffective in their attempts to protect the relatively small numbers of remaining Indians from demands for labor in the few still producing mines. In 1707 Juan Salvador Esquer, owner of the silver refinery of Los Molinos, petitioned the alcalde mayor of San Andrés for repartimiento labor. He wanted 12 laborers from the mission of Remedios to serve in monthly rotations. The Indians, backed by the missionary, protested and took their case to the Audiencia de Guadalajara, arguing that they could not meet the demands of these *tandas*/periodic labor rotations and still maintain their fields. In the past, excessive labor requirements had caused them to lose their crops, resulting in hunger and starvation for their families. Furthermore, they had to travel over a hundred miles with insufficient provisions to get to the mine and to cross rivers when the waters were high. They complained also of the change in climate, from the warm canyon bottoms to the high altitude and cold water of the often flooded mine. When Juan Gutiérrez, the alcalde mayor, heeded their pleas and refused to grant the miner's request, Esquer took his case to the governor, attempting to refute all of the indigenous complaints.

Esquer may not have succeeded in convincing Governor José Fernández de Córdoba of his benevolence to the Indians, but other ploys were more effective. First he alleged that the labor of Remedios' Indians was misspent because all they produced was corn and sugarcane—certainly inconsequential in comparison to the value of silver. Moreover, Esquer provided the history of his wife's family's service to the crown. These illustrious forebears had participated in the initial entrada into the sierra, they had helped to put down the Acaxee and Xixime rebellions, and they had suffered considerable losses in the process. In granting Esquer's request, the governor cited both of these arguments, demonstrating that lineage and military service still carried a good deal of weight on this frontier.[6]

The escalating battle for resources that characterized the turn of the century can also be seen in land tenure. It was not until the eighteenth century that demographic patterns—a slowing of indigenous rates of decline and the growth of the non-Indian population—produced especially intense conflicts over land acquisition and ownership. In the midst of subsistence crises, labor shortages, rebellions, and the decline in silver output, landowning elites themselves had suffered reversals in the period between 1690 and 1710. Although a good part of the early settler oligarchy in the region endured, some sources indicate marked fluctuation in landownership, and the Cortés del Rey *mayorazgo* (now owned by Valerio's son Juan) required large loans to remain intact. As the growing mining communities at San Felipe and Santa Eulalia provided markets for agricultural products, enterprising entrepreneurs expanded their acquisitions.[7]

Competition for land with reliable water sources became particularly acute and made mission lands more coveted.[8] Over time, Jesuits had acquired properties (by purchase and donation) beyond the original *fundo legal*, both to get access to water sources and to expand pasturelands. In these cases, they were usually careful to obtain titles, but frequently drylands were not registered, making them more vulnerable to encroachment.[9] The loss of parcels of mission lands occurred first where the absolute numbers of mission residents were low and where the surrounding non-Indian population had longer roots. This pattern characterized Santa Catalina de Tepehuanes, located next to one of the region's oldest presidios, in Santiago Papasquiaro in a valley increasingly populated by non-Indians, and in Topia, where many non-Indians had taken up the farming of corn and sugarcane and stock raising on smallholdings when the mines played out in the seventeenth century. In these cases, we can find evidence that deforestation from mining and overgrazing had severely disrupted indigenous patterns of subsistence and ways of husbanding local natural resources.[10]

Nor were these losses confined to the oldest missions. In San Miguel de las Bocas, where both the non-Indian and Indian populations had been growing, disputes over land and water escalated. In 1699 Martín Pacheco donated part of a *sitio de ganado mayor*, a land measure of about 4,335 acres, with a water outlet on the Río Florido, to accommodate Tarahumaras congregated in the mission after the rebellion. Pacheco's sons subsequently began to cultivate a part of these lands, which had never been registered to the mission, diverting acequia water from the Indians' corn. The Pachecos then sold the disputed lands as part of their estate in 1711.[11] Even more recently established Tarahumara missions like Satevó saw common lands nibbled away by the expanding pastures of sheep and cattle raisers.[12] In a protracted dispute between the Franciscan mission of San Francisco de los Conchos and an adjacent wheat farm owned by a succession of officers from the nearby presidio, the village was awarded only a small piece of the land in contention and had to allow the landowner access to the water at night and on religious holidays. The residents, who had been forcibly located there after defeats in warfare and rebellions in the seventeenth century—Tobosos, Tarahumaras, and Indians from a variety of eastern bands—ended up with insufficient water for their fields as more and more of the scarce liquid was diverted to the farm's mill.[13] In another case, the village of Huejotitlán lost some of its farmland to vecinos in 1710 and again in 1720, even though former missionaries had registered the right to use water on these lands.[14] There was also a marked correlation between frequency of land disputes and high numbers of Indians being supplied in repartimiento, perhaps because depopulated missions could not keep their lands under cultivation. Or it may also have been that landowners were beginning to make calculated attempts to deprive Indians of a subsistence base in order to assure their dependence on outside work.

Cultural differences over attitudes toward land became even more pronounced. Spaniards laid claims to *tierras baldías* or "empty lands." If soils were not tilled, fenced, or grazing livestock, they were considered unproductive. But Indian communities saw them as integral parts of their subsistence because they supplied game and edible plants, firewood, charcoal, pasture, thatch, and clay. As a food source, the monte was indispensable where arable lands were scarce. The synergy of longstanding subsistence strategies and the ingenuity of indigenous peoples in managing wilderness spaces were lost on Spaniards, who conceived of property in very different ways. It is also true that their cultural blindness served their covetous and monopolizing proclivities. For even when Indians actually farmed the lands and produced a surplus, Spanish officials involved in commerce worried that they might sell grain independently.[15]

The situation of the Topia missions was the most dire. Outsiders continued to acquire small parcels of land adjacent to missions. Some smallholders like the Mesa family assembled enough tracts near the missions of Remedios and Otatitlán to graze cattle in the rough terrain of canyons and hills. Growing numbers of non-Indians drained labor out of missions through official repartimientos and unlawful coercion.[16] At the same time, more and more smallholders and itinerant merchants took up residence in mission villages. The general poverty of the region was widely remarked. By the early eighteenth century, mining had been reduced to a few small enterprises, and the rugged topography and poor soils made even stock raising a marginal economic activity. The reports imply growing environmental degradation. Writing from San Ignacio de Piaxtla in 1712, Padre Juan Boltor marveled that after decades of poverty, isolation, and marginal harvests he could still chew the occasional jerky and coarse tortillas. As another missionary remarked, "What we have in abundance is need; our excess is in poverty."[17]

Pressures on missions were not confined to encroachments by secular society, as seen in the renewed attempts by the diocesan clergy to regulate them. In 1701 Bishop Manuel de Escalante moved to force the missions to pay the tithe on their produce. The Jesuits reacted strongly in a petition to the king, contending that missions were different from the colegios, which did have to pay. Mission corn and livestock, they argued, were intended to support the Indians, the missionaries, the upkeep of the church, and religious festivals. Moreover, they helped the padres to feed the sick and to provision the Indians who served as allies to Spanish troops. Horses and mules had to be maintained in order to receive supplies and provide conveyance for the missionaries. The Jesuits threatened to abandon the missions if they were forced to pay the tithe. This ploy got the attention of several presidial captains, who wrote to the viceroy that the loss of Jesuit experience and knowledge of Indian languages would provoke the natives to rebel.[18]

The soldiers also knew, as did many civil officials, that Indian allies from settled pueblos were crucial for military operations against Indian opponents. Local elites who were also militia captains had long maintained their autonomy from governing officials and their properties with the aid of private armies constituted by encomienda Indians and other retainers. In 1704 military advisers to the viceroy emphasized the important role that Conchos, Tarahumaras, and Tobosos had played in previous campaigns. They also identified certain southern Tepehuan pueblos and missions of Tepehuanes and Tarahumaras that furnished mining and agricultural labor as well as military service, noting that it was important that these warrior allies continue to draw satisfactory recompense.[19] The need to protect silver shipments and other convoys, as well as travelers, along the camino real prompted a number of experiments to modify or reinforce presidios. The location of the presidio at Santa Catalina was no longer deemed strategically advantageous. In fact, it had been poorly provisioned for many years and lacked uniforms, arms, and horses. The garrison was suppressed in 1713 and moved to Mapimí, where its troops could be deployed more effectively against eastern raiders.[20] Another proposal was to create buffer settlements of mission Indians, to be formed by moving Tarahumara families from Las Bocas and Tizonazo to the sites of haciendas that had been abandoned in the face of continuous raiding. Indians from Cinco Señores were regularly used to protect convoys of goods between the presidios of Gallo and Cerrogordo. In return, these Baborigames and Coahuileños demanded tools and other provisions for their fledgling settlement.[21]

The most serious catalyst for change in the north, however, came with the intensive exploitation of silver that had been discovered nearly a half century earlier near today's Chihuahua City. In the succeeding decades, Spanish landowning families from Parral, San Bartolomé, and Cusihuiriachi,[22] as well as Jesuit and Franciscan missions, had established footholds in the areas north of the Río Conchos, making silver mining feasible by the first decade of the eighteenth century. The mines at Santa

Eulalia and San Francisco de Cuéllar (which later became San Felipe el Real de Chihuahua) intensified demands for labor by the second decade of the eighteenth century.[23] The arrival of Governor Manuel San Juan y Santa Cruz in 1714 marked a turning point in Chihuahua's economic evolution.[24] San Juan, who already had commercial interests in Chihuahua and who took up residence there rather than in Parral, was determined to implement changes to make mining and commerce more productive, not only for the benefit of the crown but also for himself. He faced two seemingly insurmountable problems: labor shortages and indigenous raiding. The governor determined early on that he must find a way to organize and allocate labor in a more efficient manner, but he also recognized he had to walk a tightrope between conflicting interests. In October 1714 he received a royal cédula of 1713 from the viceroy, the Duque de Linares, stating that recently converted Indians should not be compelled to provide labor against their will. Several months later he received petitions from a number of Concho Indian governors that the natives be repatriated to Franciscan missions from their status of virtual peonage in the haciendas of the Valle de San Bartolomé.

The outcry from elites who were highly dependent upon this permanent labor force was immediate.[25] Even though previous governors had authorized repartimiento drafts of Tarahumara Indians for the farms of San Bartolomé, leading citizens argued that they had never constituted a reliable source because they came to work against their will and refused to remain longer than twenty-four days. In fact, many fled before that time was up. In the previous harvest, only half of the Indians solicited in repartimiento had actually been delivered. Yet even in sufficient numbers these labor drafts could not meet all their needs because only the permanent labor force was skilled in the necessary agricultural techniques. In addition, the permanent labor force was necessary in order to be able to defend against enemy raids. And finally, they argued that the Indians' spiritual needs were being served by the local priests. Governor San Juan continued to hear representations from both sides of this dispute, as well as from other sources. Bishop Pedro de Tapis complained to the king in 1715 that the governor and alcaldes mayores collected "kickbacks" for each Indian delivered in repartimiento.[26] Franciscans even accused Jesuits of taking payments from landowners for Indian laborers.[27] The mud-slinging between religious orders did not disguise the fact that both Jesuit and Franciscan missions were key sources of mining labor.

The controversy convinced the governor that a special visita should be undertaken to locate and count indigenous manpower, to identify landed, mining, and commercial properties, and to take a census of vecinos and allies who could be mustered to fight. He named a number of lieutenants to assume these tasks.[28] A new mandate intruded in 1715 when the viceroy ordered the governor to sponsor the founding of several Franciscan missions north of Chihuahua near the Junta de los Ríos among a variety of groups, including Conchos, Coyames, Cholomes, and Julimes. The task was undertaken by Indian captains who demanded the same pay as their presidial counterparts.[29] San Juan saw this as an opportunity to congregate labor for the new mines, and he also supported the founding of the Jesuit mission of Chinarras, which was even closer to the mining camps, to congregate Conchos, Tobosos, Chinarras, and others. This new labor source had the potential to replace the Conchos who had been repatriated to missions from the Valle de San Bartolomé (where San Juan also owned property). To meet the labor needs of San Bartolomé's hacendados, he increased the number of repartimientos of Tepehuanes and Tarahumaras. But a smallpox epidemic in 1718 seriously retarded his efforts at reorganizing the labor pool. The newly congregated groups of Indians, such as those at Chinarras, had their first exposure to the disease. "The Chinarras were horrorstruck by the smallpox epidemic; since they had never before experienced this disaster they fled from each other—husbands from wives, children from parents."[30]

While indigenous peoples struggled to fight off epidemics and regain their numbers, the non-Indian population continued to grow. More and more outsiders actually took up residence in the missions, and interethnic marriages became common.[31] In 1718, Governor San Juan issued a decree calling for stiff fines to be levied against "Spaniards, blacks, mestizos, mulattoes, coyotes, and other castas" whose presence in Indian communities was destabilizing. Specifically he referred to the growing numbers of outsiders who introduced gambling and alcoholic beverages into the villages and took advantage of Indians through trickery and questionable bartering practices, sometimes draining families of even the seed for the next season's planting. He specifically targeted rescatadores, middlemen who bought up market commodities and then resold them at a profit.[32]

The threats posed by the growth of the non-Indian population prompted some missionaries to take proactive measures. In several cases, missions moved to assure titles to lands that were not part of the fundo legal. San Juan, a visita pueblo of San Ignacio de Piaxtla (whose Spanish population was fast growing), paid a fee to have the lands of its cofradía measured and the title regularized.[33] But the pressures on mission properties and land did not abate. Especially vulnerable were fields that had not been planted for some time because they were susceptible to enemy raids. Spaniards were often successful in arguing that these were legitimately vacant lands, and they frequently used legal chicanery to get title histories interpreted in their favor. This was the case in Huejotitlán, where the Indian officials' claims to several parcels of land were rejected in favor of a Spanish landowner who argued they were part of his *merced*/land grant.[34]

Beginning with the governorship of Manuel San Juan, there had been a steady escalation in the number of repartimientos from Indian villages, but during the tenure of Governor Joseph López de Carvajal (1723–1727), repartimiento drafts took an even greater toll on Tarahumara pueblos. Some of the missions must have been virtually depopulated of able-bodied males during peak harvest periods. The largest percentage of labor drafts during this period supplied agricultural labor for the sowing, weeding, or harvesting of wheat (and some corn), but workers were also sent to silver mines (including Parral, which had expanded production after a decline at the turn of the century) to help drain shafts or cut wood for the smelting process. About half of the drafts conformed to the regulation that workers stay no longer than a month at a time, but the rest ranged from two months to more than a year.[35]

Complaints from the mission pueblos reached Spanish officials through letters from Jesuits and Franciscans and from Indian delegations. In some cases, Indians actively resisted the drafts, claiming that they forfeited their own fields when so many residents were forced to leave a village at the same time. As a result, Indian governors and other officials in Santiago Papasquiaro and its visita of Atotonilco were punished for refusing to send laborers. During the scuffle that ensued when the alcalde mayor and three Spaniards tried to arrest him, the governor of Atotonilco refused to surrender his bastón. In these refusals, Indians cited Spanish law to justify their actions.[36] In Bocas, Tepehuanes and Tarahumaras refused to comply with the drafts, arguing that they were working voluntarily on nearby haciendas in order to stay closer to home where they could defend against Indian attacks.[37] Indians also protested having to travel long distances in hazardous conditions (sometimes as far as 80 leagues); for example, returning to their villages during the rainy season meant that they risked drowning at river crossings.[38]

The missionary at Santiago Papasquiaro, Pedro de Hualde, complained to the governor in 1722 that whole families were being taken arbitrarily from the mission to work in the Chihuahua mines, at a distance far greater than the prescribed 10 leagues. During Semana Santa, recruiters had used coercion to obtain 30 workers. In the investigation that followed, Governor Carvajal determined that the alcalde mayor of the Valle de Santiago Papasquiaro had been complicit in the schemes of labor recruiters, earning kickbacks. The Indians (and their wives and children) were kept on the job for months at a time and were seldom paid. They were not able to plant their own fields. Young children were assigned in labor gangs to cut wood. In a revealing twist, the investigation also gave the Indians an opportunity to voice their protests about mission life at Santiago Papasquiaro and to elaborate on the ways in which they were being exploited. In addition to working on communal lands that supported the upkeep of the mission, they provided labor on additional lands of Padre Hualde. In their eyes, in terms of ownership, the legal distinction between communal lands and others acquired by the missionaries was a farce. The padre controlled all the resources necessary for production, including both land and labor. Mission Indians were required to carry mail, make adobes, tend cattle, and perform numerous other tasks without recompense; children summoned to catechism usually ended up weeding in the missionary's fields. When adults disobeyed, Padre Hualde had them flogged. For many, it was preferable to work outside the mission because it was the only way to meet subsistence needs of food and clothing. Tepehuanes also reported that the missionary and the alcalde mayor fought over which of them had the power to appoint Indian officials in the mission village.

After hearing arguments from all the parties, Governor Carvajal ruled that the Indians should fulfill their obligations of observing mass, catechism, and other divine offices. They should provide labor service on the mission lands, firewood for the missionary, and wine, wax, and oil for the church. If they performed additional services, the missionary was required to pay them. The mission residents were also admonished to plant their fields, live in adobe houses, and remain in the village except when they were working for outsiders. As for the vecinos, they were required to get permission from the alcalde mayor to draft Indians to work (only those over sixteen were eligible), and their service was not to exceed one month. Some of the wives could travel with the men to cook for them, but others were to stay in the village to tend the children. Their cumulative pay was not to exceed twelve pesos, because they would be likely to lose or squander it and not return home. Indian officials were not to allow racially mixed mulattoes and coyotes in the pueblos. Spaniards and itinerant merchants could stay for no more than three days, and any attempts to take advantage of the Indians were to be reported to the alcalde mayor.[39]

This case illustrates another early eighteenth-century shift: the increased authority of lesser officials over missions in terms of allocation of labor and settlement of land disputes. This trend was abetted by on-going quarrels among various Nueva Vizcayan officials and the Audiencia de Guadalajara over geographic and functional jurisdictions. Changing practices engendered the kind of legal confusion that made it more difficult for indigenous peoples to seek redress, although occasionally (and usually with the support of the missionary) they did send delegations to make representations to the provincial governor, the audiencia, or even the viceroy himself. Perhaps the most contested function had to do with the recruitment of workers. Governor Carvajal explicitly granted the authority to draft labor to alcaldes mayores, arguing this was necessary because of the distance from the provincial capital. He was less clear about who should oversee the annual village elections, specifying only that the officials selected be the most seasoned and reasonable men. Subsequently the Jesuits reacted vociferously to a ruling by Governor Juan José Vertiz y Ontañón that candidates for office should present themselves to the governor without approval of the missionary. They argued that the Nueva Vizcayan governor would have no way of ascertaining who was qualified without their intervention; furthermore, some Indians would have to travel 70 leagues to reach the provincial capital. As the eighteenth century progressed, protests over the naming of outsiders (often mulattoes) to the post of Indian governor became more frequent, and the Jesuits found their ability to manipulate elections more circumscribed.[40]

The regional representatives of Spanish land judges appointed by the Audiencia de Guadalajara also became more active in measuring the boundaries of mission lands. The increased interest of Spaniards in land-ownership prompted the renewal of *composiciones* (fees paid to confirm or regularize land tenure). The practice had been suspended during the crisis years of the 1690s, but it was resumed in earnest in the 1720s. Governor Carvajal noted in 1724 that land and water titles had never been properly archived, and we know that missions did not have written titles to their original holdings. Even titles to additional lands were often lost or misplaced.[41]

This created a situation that was scarcely favorable for the native inhabitants. According to the Indians of Santiago Papasquiaro, the land subdelegate for Chihuahua (and a large landowner), Juan de Arispaco-chaga, had removed the stone markers that identified the boundaries of the mission and assigned them only a half league of land (rather than the customary square league). When the Indians protested to Governor Martín de Alday, he ordered the judge to issue title to the entire league.

Arispacochaga did not comply and awarded pieces of land long claimed by the community to surrounding vecinos. According to the Indian inhabitants of the visita pueblos of San Nicolás and San Andrés Atotonilco, they had been losing lands to vecinos for some time; they were now so crowded by them that they could not raise any livestock at all.[42] In some cases, missions had sold part of their holdings to pay off debts, but most of the instances involved appropriation by non-Indians of lands not being cultivated at a particular moment. In one such case, additional ranchlands of the mission of Santa Catalina that had been acquired by Padre Pedro de Retes had to be rented to outsiders because, although in the seventeenth century the mission had sold wheat to presidio and mining centers, the numbers of Indians had dwindled so drastically that there was not enough manpower to do more than tend to the immediate needs of the missionary. Almost all of the mission Indians worked on surrounding haciendas.[43]

The need for water continued to provoke conflict, especially in semi-desert areas. The mission of Cinco Señores fought with ranchers over access to waters of the Río Nazas. The vecinos diverted more and more water from the pueblo, and their cattle encroached on Indian fields. The missionary, Juan Antonio de Aragón, was concerned about the stability of this more recently founded mission that had been created to congregate former nomads and raiders from various Indian groups, including Babosariguames (or Baborigames—probably nonsedentary Tepehuanes), along with Tarahumara rebels captured in the 1690s. They not only raised corn and wheat but also provided soldier escorts to protect shipments along the camino real. The padre urged the Indian governor, Bartolomé Sánchez, to take the village's complaints to the alcalde mayor of Cuencamé and to request that their lands be surveyed and water rights confirmed. The Indians also asked that compensation be paid for damage to their crops. As Spanish officials stalled and the case dragged on, Father Aragón's fears were confirmed: the new converts abandoned the village and sought subsistence in the surrounding wilderness. Governor Carvajal intervened several months later because of the security risk posed by the flight of these nomads and their potential for raiding. After the lands were surveyed and markers placed, the Indians returned to the village. Both the mission and the vecinos had the right to divert river water, and a system was worked out for taking turns to it.[44]

The changing mission milieu is very evident in the reports written by Juan de Guendulaín, the Jesuit visitor to all northern missions in 1725.[45] They are filled with references to Tepehuanes and Tarahumaras working

outside their pueblos in agriculture and mining. They also note the growing presence of outsiders in the missions. All of the Tepehuan mission
Indians were ladino, or Spanish-speaking, and the number of full-blooded
Tepehuanes continued to drop. In the older Tarahumara missions, the
men were bilingual, but the women still confessed only in Tarahumara.
Everywhere lands and livestock were dwindling—even in the most productive missions like Huejotitlán and San Pablo, where early missionaries had purchased additional lands. Although mining claims sometimes
encroached on their lands,[46] the newer Tarahumara missions with larger
populations and more distance from Spanish settlements fared better and
produced more. Many of these Tarahumaras made use of their ranchería
locations and were far less acculturated in language and religion. While
the picture painted by Father Guendulaín provides many subtle clues
about cultural mixing, co-optation, and resistance in the missions, a more
direct and biting assessment was provided by General Pedro de Rivera,
who was inspecting presidios on the northern frontier at about the same
time. He was struck by the restraint and flexibility shown by the Jesuits
in dealing with the "reprehensible" and insubordinate behavior of their
charges in the Tepehuan and lower Tarahumara villages.[47]

Local Spanish officials were less concerned with these interactions as
they sought to appropriate mission manpower. In the first third of the
eighteenth century, significant realignments took place around the labor
issue. Although repartimiento drafts had always been oppressive, in the
seventeenth century they had not threatened the complete dissolution of
missions; the system that evolved had allowed the Jesuits to participate in
an unwritten compact that permitted agricultural elites and missionaries
to share local labor for primarily seasonal purposes. The chaos and population decline of the 1690s had shattered this haphazardly constructed
system, provoking more conflict between missions and Spanish elites. In
the eighteenth century, Nueva Vizcayan governors and local elites made
concerted and continued efforts to assess the available manpower and to
more systematically mobilize draft labor. They were most successful in the
eastern Tarahumara, where missions still periodically attracted ranchería
Indians who renewed the labor pool. In the older mission areas, native
population recovery proceeded too slowly to meet labor demands, especially as the numbers of non-Indians continued to expand. The racially
mixed population included and absorbed some indigenous peoples, but
the big jump in non-Indian numbers was attributable to newcomers. If
native numbers were starting to rebound in the eighteenth century, they
took a harsh blow in the severe measles epidemic of 1728.

In that year, Governor Ignacio Francisco de Barrutia reported to the king that agriculture had been seriously set back by the additional drop in numbers of field hands; these deaths from disease had come on top of drought conditions. The death toll was substantial, and those who survived had a long and painful convalescence. Tarahumara missions were especially hard hit. Barrutia was particularly concerned that mines continue to receive priority in meeting their labor needs. Following in the steps of his eighteenth-century predecessors, he sought the solution by first counting the numbers of able-bodied Indian workers available for repartimiento, and he also recommended impressing vagrants into labor service. He lamented that mining production was down and that new silver strikes, such as the one near Indé, could not be satisfactorily exploited, not only because of the labor shortage but also because many mines were vulnerable to Indian attack.[48]

The governor was alarmed by the very high degree of mobility exercised by indigenous peoples on the frontier, not only because it inhibited officials' ability to control labor, but also because it fostered biological and cultural mixing that could thwart social controls on behavior. Certainly the demands of the Spanish regime on local populations were in large measure responsible for migrations. The most common were those in which Indians left the missions to work in silver mines, on haciendas, in domestic service, and as ethnic soldiers. In many cases, these were forced journeys out of missions, the result of frequent repartimiento drafts. But in others, they were deliberate migratory strategies for acquiring material goods, marriage partners, or freedom from oppressive, demanding missionaries.[49] In the countryside, mission Indians who were herders came in contact with Indian and mixed-race cowboys and herders on Spanish ranches, sometimes sharing camaraderie, food, and drink around the campfire. Occasional visits to kin in rancherías exposed them not only to unconverted members of their own groups but also to renegade non-Indians fleeing Spanish justice. On haciendas, mission Indians mingled with mixed-race peoples and occasionally had sexual relations with mulatto slaves. In mining reales, mission Indians socialized with Indians from other northern regions, as well as mixed-race workers. Magical remedies for attracting women, concocted from chameleons, toads, plants, semen, and other body fluids, were readily available.[50] Many sought out healers when they were ailing. Curanderos like Mateo de la Cruz, a Sonoran Indian living in Babonoyaba, used popular techniques to concentrate the illness in the body and extract it through hollow reeds. Mateo also used his breath to alleviate sickness. These activities might have escaped the notice of the authorities if he had not also employed sacred objects like altar cloths and crucifixes in his ceremonies. In 1705, he was sentenced to two hundred lashes, hard labor in the mines, and relocation in the Franciscan mission of Atotonilco.[51]

Increasingly, peoples of different backgrounds gambled and caroused together, enjoying the pleasures of cockfighting and other pastimes. Governor Barrutia attributed to these peregrinations and interethnic contacts a growing incidence of raiding, livestock theft, and highway robbery. In 1729 he issued an ordinance designed to curb the travel that promoted social intercourse and vagabondage in rural areas. Indians who traveled from their pueblos without written authorization from the alcalde mayor, missionary, or Indian governor could be shot if found in hostile territory.[52] Livestock theft and pilfering became so pervasive in the Jesuit and Franciscan areas closest to Chihuahua that Joseph de Berroterán, captain of the presidio of Conchos, set up headquarters in Papigochi for a month in 1729 to investigate their causes and apprehend thieves. One explanation was that the drought had produced widespread hunger; others argued that the missions had been ruined by the racially mixed outsiders who had moved in. Berroterán exiled some of the culprits to the presidio, where they were given plots of land, but many of the Tarahumaras fled back to their homelands. The captain reasoned that it would be better to discipline them in the missions, but the Jesuits, less assured of their authority, were reluctant to inflict punishments without the forceful presence of soldiers.[53] Nicolás de la Cruz, Indian governor of the Franciscan mission of San Andrés, complained that the missionary was extorting money and labor from his Concho charges. He argued that they were not able to tend their fields and, for eight months of the year, they had nothing to eat, forcing them to pilfer from nearby haciendas.[54]

The Tarahumaras presented an enigma to the Spaniards. Bishop Pedro Tapis was impressed with the devotion they demonstrated in a choral musical performance at the mission of Satevó in 1715, complete with bassoon, chirimías, harps, violin, and organ. Pedro de Rivera viewed them as disrespectful but highly industrious. They applied themselves diligently, no matter whether the task was building churches or working in the fields. In the winter, they often went voluntarily to work on haciendas and in mines. Rivera downplayed Jesuit reports, intended to support their request for a presidio, that Tarahumaras were still inclined to rebel or that some of them joined forces with Apaches in raiding.[55] Jesuits also characterized Tarahumaras in contradictory ways. They could be found working at every conceivable task, as farmhands, woodcutters, charcoal makers,

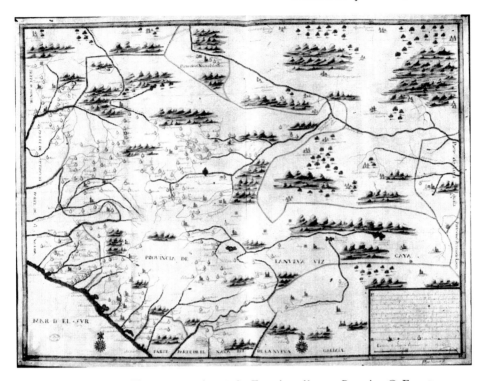

MAP 4. *Nueva Vizcaya around 1726, by Francisco Alvarez Barreiro.* © *España, Ministerio de Educación, Cultura y Deporte. Archivo General de Indias, M.P., 121, Mapa de Nueva Vizcaya, 1726.*

cooks, cowboys, muleteers, artisans, and miners. Padre Ignacio Javier de Estrada opined that without them there would be no silver in Chihuahua but at the same time labeled them as depraved and lazy.[56] These conflicting appraisals are an indication not only of the convoluted labor scene but also of the complexity of Tarahumara interactions with others.

By the 1720s, the Chihuahua mines had made San Felipe el Real de Chihuahua the most important commercial and mining center in the north, controlling even the New Mexico trade.[57] The *corregidor* of Chihuahua became an important official, second only to the Nueva Vizcayan governor. Chihuahua merchants imported a wide variety of foodstuffs and luxury goods, and for the first time since the establishment of missions, they were able to sell goods for less than it cost the Jesuits to buy them in Mexico City and ship them.[58] In the 1720s and 1730s, powerful miners like former governor Manuel San Juan y Santa Cruz consolidated their mining, agricultural, and commercial enterprises, squeezing out smaller competitors and attempting to dominate and discipline their workforce.[59] Repartimiento drafts supplied some of the mine labor, but most of the work was done by Indians and castas who were attracted by two incentives. One was the pepena, or portion of ore mined that they were allowed to keep and sell; the other was a cash or merchandise (probably the most common) advance. According to the missionaries, Tarahumaras were drawn by both sources. When powerful miners, led by San Juan, moved to eliminate the pepena, some of the missionaries believed the measure would make the Tarahumaras more vulnerable to overtures from Apaches and others to take up raiding. Although some Tarahumaras did resort to raiding for subsistence, many more of them continued to work for non-Indians outside their pueblos, occasioning Padre Ignacio Javier de Estrada to remark that the contact was resulting in a whitening of the Indians.[60]

Patterns of cultural adaptation became more conspicuous in the mission pueblos themselves. In the older Tepehuan and Topia missions, ethnic and cultural mixing made it difficult to distinguish Indians from castas. Although cofradías had existed in some mission pueblos since the seventeenth century, by 1730 they no longer necessarily segregated Indians and non-Indians. According to some observers, these confraternities were little more than an excuse for their members to sponsor wild and wasteful fiestas.[61] Although authorities attempted to curb the number of religious holidays and celebrations in Indian towns, these fiestas continued to be an important means of keeping resources within the community as well as of exercising spirituality in blended or layered forms. By using cofradía resources to support fiestas, Indians were able to profit from their own labor more directly than they could from the labor invested in mission fields. For more recently converted Tarahumaras, the Christian festivals may have provided the means to honor the deities that sustained them, reciprocating through food offerings.[62] The outer trappings were Christian but they had local meanings that were connected to older practices aimed at ensuring unity and balance in their universe. Over time, fiestas came to reinforce pueblo political organization and the legitimacy of officials whose roles had evolved beyond the confines of missionary controls.[63]

Another change is reflected in more frequent mentions of casas de comunidad in the documents. They seem not to have been common until communities had become more culturally Hispanicized and missionaries exercised less complete control of community affairs. In central and southern Mexico, community houses accommodated the cajas de comunidad (where the pueblo's income from agriculture and other assets were stored), the election of pueblo officials, and travelers.[64] Because the Jesuits had been able to exercise such tight control over mission finances and the election of officials, there had been little need for a community meeting place outside the church or the missionaries' quarters. Jesuits had believed their dominion over space to be vital to the Hispanicization program. "Proper" outsiders like visiting bishops and civilian dignitaries were accommodated in the Jesuits' houses, part of the church complex. Orthodoxy in sanctioned fiestas could be more easily monitored in church patios; nonsanctioned activities like tesgüinadas took place in rancherías or other clandestine spaces.[65] Such spatial and spiritual dichotomies were becoming eroded. Another sign of acculturation is that surnames began to be recorded for some indigenous officials. Most Indians were labeled as ladino, and where Indian languages were still spoken the most common was an altered form of Nahuatl, referred to here as *mexicana* or *mexicana mazorral*.

As different ethnic groups came together, they developed a mix of practices that began to define a popular culture, shared especially by people of lower status and means. Interethnic violence did not disappear, but people of different ethnicity did form fluid communities of interest. In work situations and chance settings, mission Indians and nonlocal groups like Apaches and Sonoras, mulattoes, and mestizos came together to share magical remedies for overcoming hardship and curing. Among them were the ingestion of various potions, fasting, elimination of salt from the diet, and the use of herbs and hallucinogens like peyote. Missionaries also despaired of the illicit affairs that resulted from too much freedom to mingle.[66] Civil authorities tended to ignore such liaisons and they dismissed much of the magical practice as insignificant (for example, reports of little birds that brought messages from the supernatural), but along with the priests they did become more concerned in cases where individuals admitted to making pacts with the devil or using herbal remedies to provoke abortions.[67]

The psychological freedom and intermittent material advantages afforded by these associations and liaisons served as a pull factor, drawing Indians out of missions where life could be more closely monitored. At the same time, other factors reduced the material attractions and security of the missions. As their workforces and productivity dwindled, frequently the only source of support came in the annual shipments of goods the Jesuits ordered from Mexico City. The orders (*memorias*) were filled at the Jesuit Colegio de San Andrés and discounted from the royal treasury stipends for missions.[68] These utilitarian items and even some frills had always been vital complements to mission production. Most foodstuffs consumed in the missions were those that could be produced on-site, such as corn, wheat, meat, fruits, and vegetables. But some particularly desired consumables were either unavailable or too expensive locally. One of these was chocolate, the most sought after luxury since it provided the means to entertain travelers and other guests, as well as to reward loyal service from subordinates.[69] Tobacco was another of these handouts, as was sugar for those missions that did not produce it. Missionaries also ordered spices including cloves, cinnamon, saffron, cumin, nutmeg, and pepper. Some of the spices also had medicinal uses, and other remedies were also solicited from the capital, for example, treacle, myrrh, camphor, and smelling salts. The missionaries were often called upon to serve as healers, but they were also aware of the therapeutic effects of many native remedies that they sent to Mexico City for study.[70] Medicine and health care were primitive when they existed. The Hospital de San Juan de Dios was established in Parral in the late seventeenth century to care for Indian and mixed-race mine laborers, but it was poorly endowed.[71]

Memorias also sought a variety of items for religious purposes: theological writings, rosaries, medals, images, paintings, baptismal fonts, altar curtains, chalices, incense burners, stamped paper, almanacs, oil, wax, and clerical vestments. More numerous were items of everyday use such as gunpowder, knives, axes and other tools, harnesses, spurs, kitchen utensils, cord, needles, thread, yarn, shoes, stockings, hats, and even pairs of glasses. Many of these were ordered in bulk and were dispensed to mission residents in varying amounts, depending upon their status or labor contribution. The greater part of the supplies consisted of finished blankets and varying grades of cloth: sackcloth, burlap, course agave cloth, canvas, flannel, printed cotton, linen, taffeta, and silk. The gift giving of the missionaries had always been a hook for attracting converts, but in the eighteenth century the Jesuits were desperately employing these doles to keep missions from becoming completely depopulated. Preferred recipients were mission laborers, widows, and children in catechism classes. When annual supplies did not arrive (an increasingly frequent occurrence), activities in the missions were seriously curtailed.[72]

Even though they were not linked directly to the support of the missions, the Jesuit colegios in Durango and Parral owned ranches and farms that produced livestock and grains. At times, they furnished some of their produce to missions being founded, but their profits were intended primarily to support their own educational and religious activities. Some wealthy criollo children received their secondary education at the Colegio de Durango, but many vecinos of means sent their children to Mexico City.[73] Colegios hosted regional gatherings of missionaries who met annually to assess progress, and they provided an urban respite for isolated rural priests. The Colegio de Parral was never quite solvent; its landholdings, which were rented to Spaniards, experienced considerable mismanagement. Conflicts with neighbors, improper maintenance of acequias, and Indian raids plagued its several haciendas. The Jesuits attributed part of the problem to the general decline in mining after the late seventeenth century.

Problems of productivity and lawsuits also retarded the progress of the other regional colegios. Yields of grain and livestock at the Hacienda de la Punta, owned by the longer established Colegio de Durango, declined in the eighteenth century. The newer Colegio de Chihuahua did not fare any better. Founded only in the second decade of the eighteenth century, it was endowed by local elites like José de Zubiate, Juan Antonio Trasviña y Retes, and Manuel San Juan, but the Jesuits found that they did not have sufficient capital to get a significant return on their investments, prompting them to enter lawsuits with the heirs of the original donors. The colegios were ill equipped to bail out the missions whose herds and fields were languishing. In the struggle to dominate regional resources, secular forces had the Jesuits in Nueva Vizcaya at a definite disadvantage by the 1730s.[74]

Although criticisms of a reputed Jesuit monopoly on commerce in the missions were not new, they intensified in the eighteenth century. Franciscans and others had accused Jesuit missionaries of using their annual supplies to create and stock mission stores. The intent of the Jesuit hierarchy was for the missionaries to distribute cloth and other items to all of the Indians, but certainly the Jesuits also manipulated their allocations, favoring indigenous officials and workers who did their bidding. In some areas, the Jesuits adopted a practice common to the south, that of obliging Indians to spin wool and produce cloth.[75]

Another charge focused upon the degree to which the Jesuits dominated production and sales of surplus in the missions. It is clear that they did control the properties they acquired beyond the fundo legal; by the eighteenth century, these were often rented to outsiders, apparently because the missionaries felt they could get a greater return on them. In the 1730s, Jesuits and Indians from the Satevó and Papigochi mission areas of the Tarahumara were supplying substantial amounts of corn and some wheat to the granary in Chihuahua.[76] How much of this production was controlled by the missionaries is not clear. Throughout the mission areas, many variables intervened to determine mission production, for example, the quality of mission soils, availability of manpower, extent and nature of items produced, the degree of authority exercised by the padre, and the willingness of Indians to comply. In some cases and increasingly as time went on, the missionary was not able to force his charges to provide for the church and its upkeep. Even when Indians did furnish a quota of corn or other commodity, the Jesuits still had to contend with civil officials and diocesan authorities who demanded that the natives be paid for their labor. On lands intended for their own subsistence, Indians could and did produce some surpluses, especially in corn, and we know that individuals sold their produce in Spanish settlements. They also contracted petty debts.[77] But the most common transaction by the eighteenth century was the practice of *rescate*, in which middlemen or regraters entered missions to buy corn at low prices (mostly through barter) and then resold it at higher prices in towns.

Periodically Jesuits and royal officials called for investigations of the practice. An illustrative example of the tangled politics of rescate comes to us through a contentious suit initiated in 1734 by Padre Bernardo de Garfías, the local visitor of the newer Tarahumara missions.[78] The missionary directed his complaints against Antonio Morales, the owner of a mule train who resided in Celaya, arguing that he was trading homemade wine for Tarahumara corn. This violated laws that prohibited the sale of alcohol to Indians. Moreover, the missionary contended that the presence of such traders in the villages was a pernicious influence, as Indians vacated their homes to provide lodging for these outsiders and women became their sexual prey. When the alcalde mayor of Cusihuiriachi (alleged by the muleteer to be in league with the priest) issued a decree expelling Morales from the mission of Papigochi and establishing fines and jail time for such transactions, a number of local citizens and traders appealed to Governor Vertiz y Ontañón. They argued that the practice of rescate had been going on for decades as an integral part of supplying urban markets. It was not prejudicial to the Indians, who benefited from the acquisition of subsistence commodities such as blankets and clothing. The merchants glossed over the fact that a principal trade item was alcohol, noting simply that it was common practice. In fact, they argued, it was better for outsiders to come into the missions to barter for surpluses than for the Indians to have to transport them to towns and then find buyers. Furthermore, the natives allegedly squandered the earnings on drunken orgies when they were in the Spanish centers.

These civilians contended that the Jesuits only objected to rescate because it limited their monopoly, arguing that the missionaries were either petty merchants themselves or in league with other middlemen who bartered with Indians. In this case, they said, Father Garfías was protecting Miguel de Migura, the husband of his niece, who had a store in Papigochi. As the case unfolded, further revelations discredited the behavior of Migura and his wife (both alleged to be adulterers and vice-ridden), and they were expelled from the mission. According to some of the leading citizens of Cusihuiriachi, Jesuit monopolies on local commerce were only one example of injury to the regional economy. They testified that the Jesuits had become increasingly autocratic and mutinous in refusing to fulfill the labor drafts required by the authorities: "[T]hey wish to exercise despotic domination and control over the miserable Indians who serve them as if they were their slaves."[79]

Crown officials were less concerned with injury to Indians than with the degree to which the middlemen could hoard or interfere with the supply of grain to the towns. Although precipitation had increased slightly in the early 1730s, a severe drought struck Nueva Vizcaya from 1737 to 1740 and prompted Governor Juan Bautista de Belaunzarán to prohibit rescate altogether. The public good, defined largely in terms of being able to supply the mining centers, was damaged by these middlemen who "buy grain and seed at low prices and turn around to sell them at high prices." In late 1739, as the province was gripped by famine, he forbade the export of all grain and seeds from Nueva Vizcaya and ordered the inventory and impoundment of all corn and wheat available for sale. Even when supplies could be found, transportation and distribution posed serious problems because of the lack of pasture for pack animals. Stores were low everywhere, especially in the Tepehuan and lower Tarahumara missions where some landowners let Indians come into their fields after harvest to glean the leftovers.[80]

The drought coincided with a brutal epidemic of matlazahuatl that spread rapidly throughout Nueva Vizcaya in 1738 and 1739.[81] Historians have not been in agreement in identifying this particular outbreak, which was first labeled as typhus. Several recent studies have connected it with bubonic plague.[82] Non-Indians including adults were affected by the disease, but death tolls in Indian villages were proportionally greater in mission areas of Nueva Vizcaya and seem to have run about three times higher than those of the measles epidemic of the previous decade. It is also instructive to compare the deaths from the two-year period of this epidemic (1738–1739) with the previous and subsequent two years: the death rate was five times higher in San Pablo Balleza during the period of the epidemic and eight times greater in Santiago Papasquiaro. In Papasquiaro, the missionary set up a makeshift hospital in the church to treat the dying, but the primarily herbal treatments and bleeding were not effective.[83] In both of these missions, more adults succumbed than children, and the epidemic wiped out the Indian leadership in Balleza. If the subsistence crises of the 1690s had constituted the first major impediment to the recuperation of indigenous populations that seems to have begun in the last quarter of the seventeenth century in eastern Nueva Vizcaya, the very high Indian mortality of the late 1730s proved to be the decisive blow. In 1730, after the inspection by Pedro de Rivera, royal officials estimated that the non-Indian population of Nueva Vizcaya was approximately three-fourths that of the indigenous groups. The parity between Indians and others apparently achieved between 1725 and 1740 was a direct consequence of the epidemic.[84]

The further reduced Indian population exacerbated the labor shortage and provoked new conflicts over who had the right to assign Indians in repartimiento. In 1738 Manuel Sánchez Durán, the corregidor of Chihuahua, complained to the audiencia that his power to allocate labor in his jurisdiction had been usurped by Governor Juan José Vertiz y Ontañón. The viceroy ruled that the corregidor had this right and that it should not be impeded by the governor.[85] Subsequently, in 1740, Governor Belaunzarán argued that the labor market was completely chaotic and inefficient because the governor's faculty (sanctioned by law and custom) to distribute repartimientos had been appropriated by myriad petty officials working with Indian governors. Only by centralizing the distribution could labor needs, especially in the mines, be met without extreme prejudice to the Indians and the region's economy.[86] There is no doubt that repartimiento drafts were excessive, a fact that prompted gentiles from the Sierra de Tabahueto to the southwest, who had been congregated in Zape for only a short time, to refuse to work in mines; eventually they fled the missions.[87]

The governor had no shortage of complaints from the missionaries about the abuses in the labor system.[88] The Jesuits had long recognized that Indians had to provide some labor for the public welfare and that missions could not be completely self-sufficient in the unregulated Nueva Vizcayan economy that depended in part upon mission labor and production of grains. They believed that their cooperation in the system was necessary to maintain the official support of the mission endeavor, but, paradoxically, over the long term their collaboration carried the seeds of destruction for missions. By 1740, deterioration reached a critical point

Population in Mission Areas
1550-1800

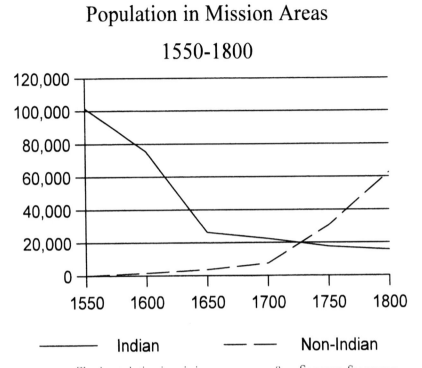

FIGURE 2. *Total population in mission areas, 1550–1800.* Sources: *See sources for Figure 1; Balthasar visita report, 1743; ACD, Varios 1749; AGI, Guadalajara 137; AGN, Jesuitas, I-7, 1753; censuses of 1777–1778 in AGD, cajón 9, and AHP, r. 1787b, fr. 1378–1385; Durango intendancy censuses, 1790, AGN, Historia 522, and 1803, AGN, AHH, leg. 917, exp. 2.*

and the Jesuits found the labor situation to be intolerable. The labor drafts were extracting unprecedented numbers of workers (as much as twenty times the prescribed 4 percent of a pueblo) and forcing them to travel much farther than the stipulated 10 leagues (sometimes as much as 60 leagues). They were paid in kind but in overvalued commodities. Their own fields were jeopardized by prolonged and frequent absences. While they were away, they did not receive religious instruction, and they were exposed to all manner of vices. The Jesuits alleged that their employers even urged them to abandon the missions and disobey their priests. Spaniards paid kickbacks to Indian governors and other labor recruiters, but these emoluments were deducted from the Indians' pay, as were the costs of burial should the worker die far from home. Most laborers took their families along with them, and even the children were forced to work.

In the older Tepehuan missions, Spanish vecinos far outnumbered Indians and controlled local affairs despite the fiction of a set of Indian officials.[89] The very small numbers of Indians remaining in the pueblos of former Xixime territory provoked a reorganization of missions and visitas to consolidate the few assets they still held. Death tolls had been high in former Acaxee lands, virtually depopulating some mission visitas and reducing others to a handful of families.[90]

On top of all of these difficulties, an ominous change at the end of the decade set in motion a series of events that would deal another blow to missions. In 1738 the Juez Privativo de Tierras of the Audiencia de Guadalajara appointed Don Manuel Güemes as superintendent of lands for Nueva Vizcaya.[91] Güemes was an officer of the municipal council/*cabildo* of Chihuahua and, according to the Jesuits, a member of an elite clique of Basques and other Spaniards from the Santander region/*montañeses* who had close economic ties. In supporting their attempts to expand their landholdings, his actions markedly transfigured the prevailing parameters of land tenure in ways that made mission lands less viable. Güemes challenged the status quo by recognizing only a half league of land as the fundo legal of a mission. In order to regularize title to lands beyond the half league, missions were ordered to pay the *composición*/land title fee; the alternative was to submit them for auction. This affront to the Jesuits demanded redress in the Audiencia de Guadalajara. In 1742 a royal cédula reaffirmed the square league, but it did not exempt additional lands acquired by the mission or the Jesuits from composición. The missionaries felt compelled to pay the fees even in cases where lands were not productive in order to provide buffers between mission and vecino lands.[92]

Even the upholding of the league standard was in some ways a pyrrhic victory for the Jesuits. In the interim period before the decision of the audiencia, there was a rush by vecinos to legitimate tenuous claims to land they alleged to possess, often at the expense of mission properties. Two of the most productive missions in the Tarahumara Baja, Satevó and Santa María de las Cuevas, lost both pasture and plowlands. A contingent of Indian officials from Satevó's visita of Santa Ana de la Joya, headed by its governor, Fabián Juan, was unsuccessful in convincing the land judge that wooded lands were essential to the subsistence of the village. It was more important that Cristóbal Marqués be able to cut down the trees there to make charcoal for the mines. Thus the woods were declared empty, unimproved lands and auctioned to Marqués. It is interesting to note that Satevó's missionary, Pedro de Estrada, and a *defensor de indios*/Indian advocate were also present at the surveying of the lands claimed by Marqués. The record tells us that Estrada advocated forcefully for the Tarahumaras, but it is silent about the role of the defender, Ignacio García Carnero. Although the office of *defensor* or *protector de indios* had been established early in the Spanish colonies, these officials were rarely appointed in the early years of missions because the Jesuits used their power to preempt them. The naming of defensores became more common in the eighteenth century as the missionaries' absolute authority was increasingly challenged. In this case, the Spanish defender, García Carnero, was a resident of Satevó. It had become so commonplace to have non-Indians living in missions that it scarcely mattered that one of the duties of the protector was to bar racial outsiders from native villages. Furthermore, when García Carnero had to leave suddenly for Chihuahua, he was replaced by Juan González, a charcoal manufacturer whose impartiality could scarcely be assured. The Jesuits charged that the Indian defenders routinely used their position to acquire land and labor.[93]

Huejotitlán and Bocas, the missions suffering the most from heavy repartimientos, also had lands stripped away. Access to water was a predominant factor in these cases.[94] The proximity of all of these missions to the growing market of Chihuahua made them more vulnerable to labor and land pressures. The zeal shown by the Jesuits in defending properties varied considerably. Some chose not to fight what they saw as inevitable and argued that declining populations in missions meant that they needed less land.[95] On the other hand, Jesuits closest to Sinaloa called upon the new governor, Agustín de Vildósola, to help defend lands of San Juan (a visita of San Ignacio de Piaxtla) against the machinations of unscrupulous Spaniards.[96]

The period between the 1690s epidemics and the matlazahuatl of the late 1730s was a time of marked demographic change in Nueva Vizcaya. The post-rebellion movement of considerable numbers of Tarahumaras into remote areas of the sierra, the decline in mission Indian population, and fluid migration patterns, both voluntary and involuntary, were causes and results of heightened and unremitting practices of labor coercion and the manipulation of land law and practices to appropriate mission lands and water sources. The two disease episodes bracketed this turmoil, with the latter nearly sounding a death knell for missions that could no longer be restocked with new recruits to replace those who died or left. As many of the latter increased their contacts with non-Indians, mestizaje that was both cultural and biological increased. In and around the older missions, grazing and the cutting of trees for building, firewood, and charcoal brought alterations in the physical environment and severely limited, not only hunting, but also the traditionally fail-safe means of riding out famine and scarcity: the collection of mescal and other edible plants. Removal of vegetative cover and native attempts to plant milpas on marginal, steep hillsides caused irreversible erosion and flooding. In the worst scenarios, natives vied with poor non-Indians living in and near the missions for meager resources. With increasing frequency, indigenous rebelliousness and strategies were stymied by the irreversible alteration of the physical environment, low natural reproductivity after disease episodes, and the unremitting, if often haphazard, coercion that the conquerors were able to bring to bear.

As royal officials surveyed the damage caused by the recent epidemic and famine, they began to propose measures to assure that they would be prepared for future emergencies. Natural disasters like drought and its less frequent antitheses, hail and flooding, were thought to be divinely ordained and unpreventable, but officials argued that some rationality could be introduced to alleviate their worst effects. On the one hand, they alleged that fairness to Indians was paramount: labor drafts had to be rotated so that Indian communities had enough labor to produce their own foodstuffs. But they were also concerned that the dwindling Indian population was even less able to meet labor needs, especially in the mines. Could they make "vagrant" and "useless" mestizos and mulattoes pay tribute? What were the merits and disadvantages of allowing non-Indians in mission villages? Was it true that the most "civilized" Indians were those who lived in close proximity to Spaniards? These questions permeated every level of Spanish administration, from the local to the peninsular.[97]

SIX

JESUITS TAKE STOCK
Cosmic Intent and Local Coincidence

The subsistence crises and continued demographic transformations of the 1730s and 1740s coincided with philosophical and practical shifts in the Spanish administration of the New World. As the eighteenth century progressed, the new dynasty of Bourbons stepped up attempts to extract more resources from the colonies through a series of economic and administrative reforms. Bourbon regalism sought especially to take back some of the power and prerogatives ceded to the religious arm of the state. The crown undertook a number of measures to limit the influence and assets of the Catholic Church in its many branches, but the Jesuits, perceived to monopolize wealth and to be too independent and foreign, were singled out as a major obstacle to royal ambitions. This resulted in their expulsion from Spain's domains later, in 1767, but signs of hostility were in evidence much earlier. During the third and fourth decades of the eighteenth century, Jesuits on the mission frontier encountered an increasingly antagonistic climate at the local and metropolitan levels. To what extent did their changing status vis-à-vis the state touch the indigenous lives we have been trying to reconstruct? Although I have deliberately sought to mute and cross-question the preponderant textual voice of the Jesuits, I would now like to move it to center stage to see what its superfluity might reveal. Here, then, is a view from the top.

As we have seen, charges by secular and religious authorities that missions represented opulent sources of Jesuit wealth and that the missionaries exploited Indian labor for their own benefit did not originate in the eighteenth century.[1] But the allegations did take a new tack. The concerns expressed by colonial bureaucrats at midcentury, considerably before the implementation of the main body of Bourbon "reforms," testify to the influence of Enlightenment thought in eighteenth-century Spain, especially in the formulation of ideas for more efficient administrative practices. In addition to the perception that the vast properties accumulated by Jesuits in New Spain were not benefiting the crown directly, officials viewed the missions as a hindrance to the goal of making Indians productive contributors to the economy. It would still take some time before policymakers could see their way clear to completely dispensing with the reliance on Jesuits to congregate Indians in northern missions, but their criticisms of the order became more frequent.

Early troubles in the north emanated from Jesuit conflicts with governors of the newly established province of Sinaloa and Sonora in the 1730s and 1740s who were trying to reduce mission control over land and labor. Governor Manuel Bernal de Huidobro, in particular, sided with Spanish vecinos and entertained the complaints of Yaquis in Jesuit missions. The Jesuits challenged him in a lawsuit; their antagonism, combined with his inept handling of other rebellions, eventually resulted in his removal. Rather than actively encouraging Indians to flout Jesuit authority as the governors had done in Sonora, Nueva Vizcayan officials took a more subtle approach, directing the Jesuits to pay Indians for mission labor and curbing their ability to name Indian officials.[2] The missionaries responded that Indian labor in the missions was destined for the communal good; furthermore, since they did not receive fees for sacraments as parish priests did, they were entitled to Indian labor for work on the churches.[3]

At the same time, the bishop of Durango, Martín Elizacoechea, while praising the Jesuits' overall missionary endeavor, pointed out to the viceroy that their missions were understaffed and that the order received more royal stipends for missions than it had missionaries.[4] Both charges contained elements of truth. Many of the missions had visitas located at such distances from the cabecera that the padre rarely managed even a monthly trip to them, and during the rainy season visits were less frequent or impossible. The second allegation, while true, could be accounted for, because when a mission post fell vacant the nearest missionary provided services until a replacement could be found. Even though one Jesuit could not effectively administer two mission districts at once, it was argued that the stipend provided material and spiritual necessities for the mission residents.[5] Nonetheless, officials of the royal treasury in Mexico City began to require that the Jesuits submit to more rigorous reporting procedures in order to receive the mission subsidies. They were expected to furnish annual reports that specified the names of the missionaries and their locations, rather than the customary list of mission names.[6]

In Rome the Jesuit general, Francisco Retz, monitored reports concerning these outside pressures on the mission system. He was also aware of the shortage of missionaries in New Spain—in 1740, there were 112 missionaries in the field for approximately 300 pueblos (including visitas). Very frequently mission posts that became vacant had to be temporarily filled by the closest missionary, but the replacement was often located too far away to be able to visit. If the Jesuits could scarcely minister to the missions already established, how could they expand the mission frontier northward? Retz moved to deal with these pressures, directing the head of the Mexican province to call a junta of ranking Jesuits to decide which missions could be secularized, or relinquished to the bishop of Durango for conversion to diocesan parishes.[7] This action was a marked departure from Jesuit policy that had heretofore emphasized active resistance to diocesan control or monitoring.[8] But confronted with the pressures of an expanding Spanish society on the mission system and a heightened ideological opposition to the order, the highest Jesuit officials found themselves in an uncharacteristically defensive position. Padre Retz believed it imperative to voluntarily transfer some missions in order to demonstrate the good faith of the Society of Jesus, to deal with the shortage of missionaries inhibiting further expansion, and to eliminate some of the legal disputes over land and labor. Thus the Jesuits would be rid of the obligation of having to defend themselves in court and elsewhere from charges that missionaries were no more than "businessmen, miners, and smugglers." After consultations with experienced and trusted advisers, the Jesuit head of the Mexican province, Cristóbal Escobar y Llamas, instructed Padre Juan Antonio Balthasar to explore the question of which missions might be most appropriate for secularization as part of his general visitation of 1743–1745.[9]

This Jesuit initiative came none too soon, as a number of Bourbon officials in New Spain began in the 1740s to formulate in earnest proposals for profound alterations that would give the crown more control over its northern regions. Particularly outspoken in criticizing missions, the Marqués de Altamira, *auditor de guerra* or chief administrative officer of the viceroy on matters of defense, argued that the crown should provide economic incentives to spur colonization of the frontier by non-Indians. He speculated that the 8 million pesos spent on Nueva Vizcayan presidios in the last century would have been more profitably employed to subsidize Spanish settlement. Whereas soldiers were often troublemakers, civilian colonists would provide a better example. And, rather than continue to channel funds into the missionary enterprise, he proposed that the missions established in the seventeenth century be secularized.[10] Somewhat ironically, at the same time Altamira contemplated the advantages of secularization, the king reiterated a call for the Jesuits to direct the Spanish expansion into Alta California through the lands of the Moquis (Hopis).[11] This coincidence provided the Jesuits a timely opportunity. In November 1745 Padre Escobar y Llamas responded to the king's cédula with a lengthy discussion of the problems and costs of such an endeavor as well as how these might be resolved.[12]

> These difficulties have persuaded me that in order to comply with our duty, it would be expedient for us to give up some of our missions and to turn their administration over to the Bishop of Durango, since today that bishopric has competent clergy without clerical posts. This transfer would accommodate them, and the Society would be able to provide able subjects . . . for new conversions.[13]

In this less than straightforward maneuver, Escobar made a fait accompli look like a sacrificial accommodation to royal desires. These missions fit the criteria he had directed Jesuit visitor Balthasar to look for. They were located in areas of considerable non-Indian settlement and they had small, relatively acculturated populations. Taking Balthasar's astutely crafted reports from the inspection of these areas between 1743 and 1745 as our main focal point, let us look at how local history and global forces intersected at midcentury.

After first visiting the Jesuit Colegio de Durango and the Jesuit residence in Parras (Coahuila) in April and early May 1743, Balthasar proceeded to the easternmost and also the newest of the missions of the Tepehuana province (see Map 3).[14] Cinco Señores (present-day Nazas) was located on the Río Nazas, 53 leagues northwest of Durango. Founded only at the turn of the eighteenth century as a site for congregating disparate groups subdued by force, Cinco Señores lacked cultural unity and internal coherence from the beginning. Its residents included Baborigames (probably nonsedentary Tepehuanes), Tarahumaras, and several other band groups. The mission's lands were never clearly delineated, and frequent conflicts over water with the surrounding non-Indian population, including Spanish, mestizo, and mulatto families from the nearby presidio of Pasaje, hampered economic development.[15] Although the mission had a small vineyard and ranch, it possessed title to neither. Low productivity had forced missionaries to borrow periodically, and Balthasar totaled its debts at over four thousand pesos, by far the largest of any mission. Its population had fluctuated wildly, reaching several hundred in 1729 and declining to about 60 residents in the 1740s. The missionary ministered to a non-Indian population that was ten times larger. The location of the mission on the camino real and the heavy use of its inhabitants as auxiliary troops for escorting silver shipments encouraged transience, as had previous patterns of complementary hunting and gathering. To keep Indians working on mission lands, the Jesuits had been forced to pay them, and Balthasar determined that the product was not equal to the labor costs.[16] Even when the residents made use of the mission's arid lands for their milpas, their access to diversion weirs on the Río Nazas was not assured.[17] Many hired themselves out to neighboring ranchers, and their routine contact with the mixed-race population resulted in a growing incidence of petty witchcraft, according to Padre Juan Ramírez.[18]

From Cinco Señores, Balthasar traveled 53 leagues west to the oldest Tepehuan mission, Santiago Papasquiaro. Thirty leagues north of Durango on the Río Santiago, the mission was situated in a rolling valley surrounded by low hills. It had two visita pueblos, San Andrés de Atotonilco and San Nicolás, farther upstream. In the seventeenth century the missions had acquired additional land by purchase and donation, enabling them to produce and sell wheat, corn, and fruit to surrounding Spanish settlements in northern Durango. Santiago Papasquiaro also had its own flour mill.[19] In addition to the attrition resulting from epidemics, parish death registers record frequent slayings of villagers, especially in the countryside, in Indian raids or assaults. Although the indigenous population of Santiago Papasquiaro and its two visita pueblos had begun to recuperate in the eighteenth century, as we saw in the previous chapter the 1739 epidemic of matlazahuatl cut it by more than one-half, to about fifty families (perhaps 200 people) compared to more than 1,500 vecinos in the valley. The reduced numbers of Tepehuanes who married within their own ethnic groups resulted in the frequent marriage of cousins. The presence of non-Indians (especially mestizos and coyotes) in the parish registers increased markedly after 1690, and many infants baptized were the offspring resulting from marriages of castas with Indians.[20]

The Jesuits had always attended the spiritual needs of the entire population, and they were delegated by the bishop to collect tithe revenue from Spaniards. They also collected fees for sacraments from the non-Indian population. A number of these vecinos owned houses in the missions that were built ostensibly for use during religious fiestas. The social and economic relationships with vecinos were more frequent and extensive in more settled areas, and Jesuit contact with non-Indians occasionally inspired charges of inappropriate behavior. Padre Pedro de Hualde had been removed from the mission in the 1730s because of rumors of a sexual liaison with a Spanish woman. Hualde had strong local ties to Nueva Vizcaya; two of his nieces were married to presidial captains. He argued that he had been framed by vecinos who hoped to be rid of his attempts to reduce the flow of Indian labor out of the missions.[21]

By the eighteenth century, so many Tepehuanes were being drafted into repartimiento that missionaries were paying them three reales a day (more than the two reales paid for draft labor) to work in the fields and tend cattle. A vineyard and orchard provided small surpluses for sale.[22] Nonetheless, many Tepehuanes chose to seek work outside, sometimes as far away as Chihuahua. A good number worked for vecinos on small to midsized ranchos adjacent to the mission.[23] In the 1740s the alcalde mayor of the Valle de Santiago Papasquiaro and one of its largest hacendados, Joseph García y Escontria, was able to circumvent an order from the Audiencia de Guadalajara that he moderate the excessive repartimientos he was appropriating for his own Hacienda de Ramos. He also arrested as vagabonds a number of Indians using wilderness areas away from the mission to cut firewood and collect wild fruits. About this time, the visita of San Nicolás claimed to have lost all of its lands to the Nevares family.[24]

Nearby Santa Catalina mission had even fewer Tepehuanes in residence. The mission lay in a narrow valley on one bank of the Río Santa Catalina opposite the old presidio of Tepehuanes, now inhabited by small farmers and ranchers. The mission itself had fewer than 30 residents. In a historical sketch of the mission, Padre Pedro Retes chronicled its demographic decline. He argued that disease had greatly reduced the population of Tepehuanes in the seventeenth century; numbers were further diminished by eighteenth-century epidemics of smallpox and matlazahuatl. Retes also attributed Indian population decline to death at the hands of hostile Indians and to frequent dispersals of Tepehuanes into mountain refuges or to work for Spaniards. Parish registers in the 1720s and 1730s reported that many Tepehuanes were working on surrounding haciendas, along with Apache and other servants. Santa Catalina had produced wheat, corn, and cattle for the Parral market in the seventeenth century, but by the eighteenth the mission boasted only small plots of corn and beans for subsistence. Mission milpas and cattle were mostly tended by children and non-Indians, who also had their own small properties nearby.[25] Padre Retes described the mixed-race vecinos who had been associating freely with the Indians over a long period:

Most of their property is in the form of livestock, like cattle, some mares, horses, pack mules, very few sheep. Many of them live by taking their mule trains (of six to twelve mules) to the mining towns, principally Chihuahua, where they cut firewood and make charcoal in the surrounding hills to supply the mines. Sometimes they are absent for months, sometimes a year, while their families suffer at home. The little silver they earn rarely suffices to meet expenses, and some return home owing more than when they left. Those who are here when the rains start (they do not irrigate), and who have land and oxen, plant corn and beans. In some years, like the last two, the fruits of the harvest are so meager that they do not provide for the whole year. A few of them travel to the hot country [coastal Sinaloa] to get salt, *panocha* [brown sugar cakes], fish, and fruits, which they bring back to sell in the Real del Oro and other towns, usually at low prices. If one of their mules dies, they lose more than they can earn. Very few of them, especially mulattoes or coyotes, like to work for someone else. There are some who do not provide for their families but only feed themselves by appearing at a neighbor's home at mealtime, and who spend much of the day drinking. . . . Most of the vecinos are in debt.[26]

From Santa Catalina, Balthasar set out for the mission of Nuestra Señora del Zape, situated on a branch of the Río Nazas in small valley at the foothills of the sierra. A hot spring in the middle of the pueblo purportedly had shown healing qualities from the time of the Tepehuan rebellion (of which Zape was the center).[27] In Zape, as in the other missions visited by Balthasar, the Indians all spoke Spanish. The agricultural productivity of the mission was limited by high altitude; early frost threatened both staple crops and orchards. Whereas missions at lower elevations could get more than one corn crop per year, Zape was fortunate to harvest enough from one planting to last half the year. In addition, demands for labor in the nearby mines of Guanaceví also constrained mission production, as did the migrations of Indians to other mining reales farther north. Barely 80 people lived in the mission by the middle of the eighteenth century; San José del Potrero, the former visita of the mission, had been incorporated into the cabecera.[28]

From Zape, the father visitor traveled to the mission of San José del Tizonazo, arriving first at its visita of Santa Cruz. Tizonazo, on the other side of the Río Nazas near the real de minas of Indé, had been founded to congregate hostile Salineros (perhaps nonsedentary Tepehuanes) in the middle third of the seventeenth century. Subsequently, the mission housed other groups, including Yaquis who came to work in the mines. The populations of both Tizonazo and Santa Cruz were in flux throughout their history. They reached a nadir in the 1690s and then began to grow with occasional influxes from other groups, but racial mixing and the in-migration of outsiders meant that by the mid-eighteenth century mulattoes and mestizos outnumbered the indigenous inhabitants. Santa Cruz exceeded Tizonazo in population and had its own cofradía, which had received an endowment in 1716 from Antonio Arispacochaga, for whom many Indians worked. The highly acculturated residents complained that they needed their own priest because it was difficult for the missionary to cross the river to minister to their needs. Both missions, especially Santa Cruz, had experienced heavy labor drafts and encroachments on their lands. In the eighteenth century the Jesuits resorted to advancing credit to Indians and castas to keep them from seeking work outside. This use of debt as a device to prevent mobility is comparable to forms of debt peonage that evolved in northern haciendas, and in both cases the degree to which they were effective in binding workers to the hacienda or mission varied according to the labor market and degree of force that could be exerted.[29]

After surveying the five missions of the Tepehuan province, Balthasar was convinced that ceding them to the bishop would not provoke indigenous unrest, since there were so few Indians left in them. The next several missions, located in the transitional zone straddling Tepehuan and Tarahumara territories, had larger Indian populations, but they were also surrounded by substantial numbers of vecinos. The first of these, located on the banks of the Río Florido northwest of Tizonazo, was San Miguel de las Bocas (today Villa Ocampo). Las Bocas took its name from the large hills surrounding the mission on the east and south. The visita of San Gabriel was located across the river a few miles to the west. The mission's fields and ranch had been productive in its early history, but Spanish haciendas and ranches proliferated in the middle of the seventeenth century to supply the mines at nearby Parral, drawing off labor, both voluntary and involuntary. In the eighteenth century, mission lands, including some irrigated fields, became a target. In 1725 Visitor Juan Guendulaín noted that Spanish haciendas had swallowed up almost all of the lands of San Gabriel and that vecinos outnumbered the mission's mixed Tarahumara and non-Indian population. A local agent of the Inquisition labeled the mix of landowners and mixed-race servants who lived in the mission's environs an uncouth lot, prone to gossip and scandalous behavior.[30] By midcentury, Father Joseph Calderón's pastoral duties outside the mission kept him away for long periods, causing the mission to decline in numbers and productivity. Overwhelmed by repartimiento demands from surrounding haciendas, including the vast Hacienda de Sextín and other properties of Juan de Arispacochaga, the remaining Indians (less than a hundred families) alleged they would actually be better off as salaried peons.[31] Making light of their grievances, Padre Calderón quipped that no overseer would tolerate them. Hostile sentiments were apparently mutual, as the mission residents asked for the padre's removal. His reputation for being harsh and surly was so widespread that the rectorate's supervisor, Pedro de Retes, encountered vigorous protests when he attempted to reassign Calderón to, in turn, Cinco Señores, Santa Cruz, Satevó, Huejotitlán, and Cariatapa.[32]

Northwest of Las Bocas, Tarahumaras and Tepehuanes made up the mission district of San Pablo Balleza. San Pablo was predominantly Tepehuan with a few Tarahumara families; its visita of San Juan was Tepehuan, while the visita of San Mateo was Tarahumara. Located in a valley of the lower mountain ranges at the junction of the Río Conchos and Río Agujas, San Pablo had been an important supplier of grain and cattle to Parral and other Spanish towns in the seventeenth century. But the mission lost pasture and irrigated cropland in the eighteenth century, and repartimiento drafts sent many natives to Chihuahua's mines and surrounding haciendas.[33] The indigenous population was periodically replenished by the arrival of Tarahumaras, who made the missions part of their migration and complementary subsistence strategies. But the non-Indian population in the Valle de Olivos had also been increasing, and the mission was in debt to several vecinos.[34]

Some miles further up the valley was the cabecera of San Gerónimo de Huejotitlán, whose residents were Tepehuanes. Only two or three of the total population of 150 residents were reputed to be descended from the first Tepehuan converts; the rest had immigrated later from various places. The mission was located along an arroyo lined by willow trees (from which it took its name). The three visita pueblos of Guadalupe, San Ignacio, and San Javier were Tarahumara. All four villages had irrigated fields, some of which had been acquired by purchase and were registered along with their irrigation rights.[35] The mission had the status of a regional seminary dedicated to training Indian children, which entitled it to own additional properties, and it did produce wheat, corn, and livestock for the market well into the eighteenth century. Father Benito Rinaldini's garden boasted cabbage, beets, spinach, and lettuce. The repartimiento drafts, however, were unyielding. By midcentury, the labor exodus had become so serious that most families did not have enough corn and beans to last the year, wheat yields were low, and the mission's livestock had been depleted by neglect and theft. Huejotitlán was still one of the most prosperous missions, but its assets were considerably reduced and worn. The once fine mission library had fallen into ruin.[36]

Visitor Balthasar continued on to the Tarahumara mission of Santa Cruz (today Valle de Rosario) and its visitas on the Río Conchos. San Felipe had been the head mission, but easier access from Parral to Santa Cruz resulted in the downgrading of San Felipe to visita in the late seventeenth century. Two other visitas, San Nicolás de la Hoya and San Joseph Salto de Agua, were located to the north. In the late seventeenth and early eighteenth centuries, the mission produced surplus amounts of corn and beans in irrigated fields and its ranches stocked several hundred head of cattle. Father Balthasar was struck by the size and architectural beauty of the church at Santa Cruz, located on a mesa above the river. Its grandeur, however, was not matched in the material realm; the building itself had put the mission in debt.[37] By the 1740s repartimiento drafts were so continuous that influxes of new Tarahumara residents did not compensate for the population decline, and production had fallen. Here, as in the other missions of the Valle de los Olivos, non-Indians in the surrounding area outnumbered the natives in the 1740s.[38]

The last two missions visited by Balthasar in the Tarahumara Baja were the last that had been founded and the closest to Chihuahua. Santa María de las Cuevas had moved from visita to mission status in the last decade of the seventeenth century. Located in a mountain valley along an arroyo of the Río San Pedro, additional lands for Las Cuevas purchased by the Jesuits produced corn, beans, and some wheat. Several of these parcels (some of them irrigated) had been purchased from indigenous neighbors (including one female) at various times in the eighteenth century. Such references to the private ownership of land by Indians in this report of land transactions for Santa María de las Cuevas raise questions about patterns of land tenure in mission areas. Because the indigenous sellers are not identified by name or ethnicity in the documents, we have few clues as to their status or how they came to possess land in the first place. It would be particularly instructive to know the circumstances of the Indian woman who sold her parcel to the mission, in terms of what it might tell us about inheritance. Were the sellers Tarahumaras, converted or gentiles? Did they also have usufruct rights to the original mission lands? Were they outsiders, perhaps Tlaxcalans? Although Indian communal lands could not in theory be alienated, individuals had access to specific plots that they passed on to their children. Nueva Vizcayan mission lands were not formally subdivided or allocated to individual ownership before the late eighteenth century, but from this case we might infer that their usufruct by particular households was recognized and could provide the basis for occasional sale of alienation of lands before that time. Or it may suggest that the more ladino Indians who often accompanied the founding of new missions received private allotments of land in the mission environs.[39]

Whatever the circumstances of land tenure at midcentury, Las Cuevas was not producing any surpluses. Furthermore, the elevated levels of repartimiento as well as substantial numbers of Tarahumaras who sought work in Chihuahua and Cusihuiriachi inhibited the formation of stable communities in Las Cuevas and its visitas of Santa Rosalía and San Lorenzo (today Belisario Domínguez), which were located even closer to the mining centers. Balthasar also commented on the number of Tarahumaras who were absent for long periods, hunting and gathering to supplement short supplies of foodstuffs. Once a large supplier of beef to the mining markets, Las Cuevas did not have title to ranchlands by the 1740s, although it used some pastures that were part of the Cortés del Rey mayorazgo. It was also hard hit by eighteenth-century epidemics.[40]

To the east of Las Cuevas on the Río San Pedro was the mission of San Francisco Xavier de Satevó, with its visita of Santa Ana de la Joya. Here also the Jesuits had made substantial investments in livestock to sell in the nearby markets; they also had a mill and vineyard, in addition to irrigated fields. The once large cattle herds, numbering over a thousand head in the seventeenth century, had dwindled to less than half their former total. Satevó had many of the same demographic and labor patterns as Las Cuevas because of its location so near Chihuahua, but it had also experienced multiple encroachments on its lands. Cattle from the Hacienda de Conchos, part of the Cortés del Rey holdings, had inflicted grave damage on Tarahumara fields in the seventeenth century; in the eighteenth the threats came from other vecinos, whose attempts to obtain some of Satevó's lands were abetted by the land judge. In Satevó as in the other lower Tarahumara pueblos, Balthasar noted, the mission environs contained more non-Indians than natives and the missionary did not preach in Tarahumara.[41]

As he reflected upon the inspection of the Tepehuan and Tarahumara Baja missions from the Jesuit Colegio de Chihuahua, language ability was one of the concerns the father visitor had about mission personnel. He admonished several of the Jesuits to apply themselves to the task of learning the Tarahumara language.[42] Even though most Tarahumaras who had been in missions for a generation understood Spanish, they did not use it among themselves, nor did they like to use it for confession. According to the missionaries, women were less likely to confess at all, for reasons that we can only speculate upon. Language may well have been a barrier, because Tarahumara women tended to have less contact with Spaniards than the men, for both cultural and economic reasons, and were less likely to be in situations where they would require Spanish. Also, more rigid taboos regarding female contact with outsiders, especially men, may have made it more troublesome for Tarahumara women to be alone with clerics, especially when confessing sexual "sins" as they were defined by the church.

Ultimately, however, Balthasar's main concern was that except in the few cases where Tarahumaras had been more recently recruited, the Tepehuana and Tarahumara Baja missions were not very Indian. The decline in Indianness of the pueblos themselves was complemented by the continued growth of the Spanish and mixed-race populations surrounding the missions. The economic disintegration of the missions stemmed not only from outside pressures on their human and other resources, but also from administrative ineptitude and mismanagement by many of the missionaries. Virtually all the missions owed more than they took in. Communal solidarity would have been hard to maintain under these circumstances, but Jesuit paternalism made it even more difficult. Administration and resources were concentrated in missionary hands, and the fathers continued to manipulate the elections of Indian officials. They almost always represented the natives in judicial battles, and they made legal representations in the names of the principales. They controlled all of the economic assets of the missions, including those of the cofradías that existed. Under these circumstances, indigenous peoples were likely to take part in religious celebrations that involved feasting, because they provided at least one way to get access to mission surpluses. Their idea of the common good was more than the upkeep of the church and the opportunity to go to mass, even as many became more devoted to these sacred spaces and their icons. In a situation where the original notions of reciprocity had been weakened, missions had also been unable to sustain the early gift-giving that accompanied their founding. Without compensatory benefits, Indians increasingly demanded pay in specie for their labor in missions. As the eighteenth century progressed, the Jesuits adopted the practice already in use in their northern haciendas of paying mission laborers six pesos per month plus rations of meat and corn.[43]

It was more than a year after Balthasar first toured the upper Tarahumara and Sonora before he undertook the final leg of his inspection, returning to the province where he had served as a missionary in the 1720s. He was not surprised to find that the Topia missions were prime candidates for secularization, but he was dismayed to see the extent of their deterioration.[44] Indian population decline had come early to this region as a result of disease and forced labor in silver mines, and the population was very mixed well before the eighteenth century. Nearly all the missions were located in poor agricultural areas, either at higher mountain elevations or in deep and narrow canyon bottoms. His first stop was San Juan de Badiraguato, located in the western piedmont of the Sierra Madre Occidental (in today's Sinaloa), north of Culiacán. Formerly an area of Acaxees, by the 1740s the pueblo looked very mestizo. The preponderance of mixed-race peoples had been noted by Jesuit visitors since the late seventeenth century. In the cabecera and its three visitas of San Francisco de Alicamac, Tres Reyes de Conimeto, and Santa Cruz, a count taken in 1740 found a total of 66 people. By the time Balthasar arrived, Conimeto had been disbanded, but the other pueblos had received new Mayo migrants from the valleys of the Río Fuerte and Río Mayo to the west in northern Sinaloa and southern Sonora. When mixed-race inhabitants were counted, the total population rose to 285.[45] The mission owned very few animals, not even oxen for plowing, but had several parcels of cropland, although none was irrigated. Here, as in the other warm lowland areas, there were occasional fields of sugarcane. Some of the mission's inhabitants worked for vecinos who struggled for a living in the canyon bottoms and slowly expanded their marginal landholdings from the 1740s on. Other Badiraguato residents collected beeswax and honey to sell, while some hunted for and collected mescal and other wild plants. In the eighteenth century, the Jesuits who staffed this mission spent time away from the pueblos ministering to the vecinos of San Benito.[46]

Northeast of Badiraguato, the mission of San Ignacio de Cariatapa and its five visitas stretched along nearly 30 leagues of the Río Humaya, which twists and turns through canyon bottomlands. Atotonilco, now a visita, had been the original cabecera, but it was virtually depopulated by disease by the late seventeenth century. The other visitas of Santiago Morirato, San Pedro de Huatenipa, San Ignacio de Bamupa, and Soyatitlán had small populations of Acaxees and other groups from Sinaloa who spoke Cahitan languages, trying to cultivate corn on scarce plots of arable land alongside their mestizo neighbors. The mission also cultivated sugarcane, but it was seriously in debt. Cariatapa had been without a resident missionary on a number of occasions in the eighteenth century, bringing about a marked drop in the number of livestock. Few families actually lived in the missions for long periods, as they combined gathering with crop growing. The majority of mission inhabitants provided repartimiento labor for sugar-growing vecinos. In the eighteenth century, some Acaxees who had escaped resettlement in missions after their early-seventeenth-century rebellion were rounded up from their locations in the mountains and taken to Cariatapa, but the only Indian language spoken there was mexicana.[47]

Further south and east (in present-day western Durango), San Ignacio de Tamazula and several visitas stretched along the canyon bottom of the Río Tamazula. Several leagues away through the Topia pass was the mining camp of Canelas. The Tamazula valley had more arable land than the average western sierra mission and had attracted a sizable vecino population of smallholders who made their living from small ranches, cane fields, and orchards. After the mines of Topia and Sianori played out in the seventeenth century, the mission markets were restricted. In the eighteenth century, two visitas were abandoned and their lands taken over by Spaniards. Vecinos also acquired other parcels of mission land, apparently with the collusion of the missionary, Francisco Javier de Lora. In 1744 he supported the claims of two Spaniards (one of whom was his compadre) over those of the pueblo to lands that had been measured in 1738 and declared *realengas*/property of the crown when the Jesuits did not pay the fee to regularize their possession. Balthasar found in 1745 that Tamazula had no properties registered in its name. A few goats were all that remained of the livestock. The cofradía of the pueblo had been gifted a silver mine nearby in Zapotlán, but the mine was leased to a Spaniard and produced no income for the mission.[48]

The dwindling indigenous population of the mission rarely resided within it, mixing freely with the surrounding, mostly mixed-race population. Sometimes they worked voluntarily for their neighbors, but many were drafted into repartimiento. When they were not in labor service, some collected beeswax to sell. Vecinos, predominantly mulattoes and mestizos, raised a few cattle and a little sugarcane. They also collected honey and wax to sell or trade. A few muleteers among them periodically made the journey to the coast to market the meager produce and to buy salt, which they transported over the mountains, along with citrus fruits and panocha from the lowland valleys, to sell in Parral and other towns.[49]

Still further south stretched the four missions located in former Xixime territory; all bordered on the Río de los Remedios and its tributaries. The first of these was Alaya and its visita of Otatitlán. For a time in the seventeenth century, the mission district had two other pueblos and profitably raised sugarcane and livestock, but diseases took their toll. Depopulated areas were taken over by a growing non-Indian population in the late seventeenth century; the latter outnumbered the Indians by more than two to one. The few remaining natives were hard hit by the measles epidemic of 1728. By the 1740s the mission produced very little and was heavily indebted to vecinos.[50] It continued to lose croplands, retaining only some parcels without irrigation and a small ranch. The vecinos were largely poor farmers ministered to by the Jesuits.[51]

The situation was much the same at San Ildefonso de los Remedios, located to the southeast. Population had declined in the mission and its visita of Santa Catalina, due largely to heavy repartimiento demands. Production suffered not only because of the labor drain but also because of the mission's inhospitable location. The area was so hilly and truncated by ravines that level tracts were rare and no one irrigated.[52] The few Indians who actually resided in the mission did not look much different from their neighbors:

> The vecinos, like the Indians, live by their own labor; their milpas rarely yield more than four to six *almudes* [1 almud = 4.1 qt.] of corn, not even enough to meet costs . . . they also eat wild foods and occasionally butcher a cow, although it is difficult to raise cattle because they are easy prey for mountain lions and other wild beasts.[53]

Both Indian and non-Indian women raised a little cotton to make cloth. Some vecinos owned small mule trains for the coastal trade, although their profits allegedly were barely enough to compensate their efforts. When the church in Remedios burned down in 1741, a full rebuilding effort failed because not even the vecinos who attended services there were able to contribute to the costs.[54]

Northeast of Remedios and the mining real of San Andrés was the mission of San Gregorio. In the early seventeenth century San Gregorio and its three visitas raised cattle, corn, wheat, and sugarcane for sale to the mines. By the mid-eighteenth century it had only one visita, San Gerónimo Soibupa. Between the two pueblos there was a total of fifty families, many of whom lived outside the mission and subsisted by hunting and gathering. Like the mission residents, mixed-race vecinos supplemented their small plots of corn, planted on rocky mountain slopes, with game and wild fruits. Some of them had a few cows and goats, raised a bit of sugarcane, and maintained small orchards.[55]

In Santa María de Otaez to the southeast, equivalent numbers of Indian and non-Indian families eked out a meager existence in a high mountain meadow on the Río de los Presidios. In the seventeenth century the mission and its visita of Santiago Borozi had helped supply the presidio of San Hipólito and the silver mines at Guapijuje. The decline in silver production and infertile soils contributed to impoverishing the mission, along with epidemic disease and repartimiento drafts. In 1740 only seven Indians were reported to be living in the mission. As mixed-race *lobos* and coyotes moved in, the population rose slightly; they planted a little corn in small mountain clearings and collected beeswax and honey. The non-Indian vecinos engaged in similar pursuits, in addition to growing some sugarcane and tending orchards of apples, pears, and figs. Father Manuel Ignacio Cartagena described the vecinos in 1749: "[T]hey all claim to be Spaniards, but it would be difficult to find one who truly is."[56]

The Jesuits' southernmost partidos in Topia were initially comprised of related groups of Xixime, Hume, and Hina Indians. San Ignacio de Piaxtla (in present-day Sinaloa) was the mission located farthest to the southwest, in the foothills of the sierras. At various times, it had visitas at San Agustín, San Gerónimo de Ahoya, and San Juan. In the seventeenth century, it produced sugarcane, processed it with a small horse-driven mill, and sold it to towns and mines of southern Sinaloa, but a century later it produced meager amounts of corn, beans, sugarcane, and cotton. Only a few cattle grazed on its ranch, which at one time had accommodated 2,000 head. At mid-eighteenth century, mission residents were ethnically mixed and eked out a living from a variety of subsistence strategies. Most owned one or two animals, and a few were tanners.[57]

The mission and the surrounding area were administered ecclesiastically by the Jesuits until the growing non-Indian population was deemed to be large enough to merit the founding of a parish in San Francisco Javier de Cabazán in 1739. Father Marcelo de León vigorously resisted the loss of parishioners and encouraged them to continue attending mass at the mission. They were inclined to oblige, since the missionary's fees were lower than the rates established by the diocese. The ensuing dispute between the padre and the cathedral chapter in Durango revealed the missionary's close ties with vecinos. In this case, the few Indians left in the mission claimed that he had ignored their spiritual needs for years, rarely offering mass and failing to baptize dying children. They also charged that Padre Marcelo sold them items he received from Mexico City at exaggerated prices.[58] The question of whether the Jesuits should receive fees for sacraments performed for non-Indians continued to be contentious, and there was increasing criticism of the practice from secular priests whose numbers were growing. Jesuit superiors recommended using the fees to buy ornaments and furnishings for the churches.[59]

The native leadership in the visita of Ahoya seems to have recognized that the pueblo could not depend on the padre to guide or protect them. Perhaps through their dealings with Father Marcelo or other litigious neighbors, they became more informed of their legal rights, but their actions seem to be an anomaly in the context of the missions studied here. In 1744, through a non-Indian intermediary, they asked the alcalde mayor of San Joseph de Copala to measure their lands.

> We, Don Manuel Vicente, governor and captain general of the pueblo of San Jerónimo de Ahoya, which belongs to the mission of San Ignacio, Sebastián Ignacio, alcalde, other principales, and the rest of the community . . . considering that our pueblo does not have the title and grant that the king our savior bestows on all Indians who live in pueblos, ask that you come to our pueblo to take the measurements in the four cardinal directions.[60]

The transactions that accompanied this request provide insight into the changing demographic and economic situation of the area. The Indians were all ladino; they spoke Spanish and Nahuatl. The measurements were carried out with considerable difficulty because of the mountainous terrain. Most of the land was declared unfit for agriculture, as there were only a few flat areas other than in the center of the pueblo. The bulk of farming was done along several arroyos that cut through deep ravines. The Indians also asked for adjacent empty lands to be measured, but it would be seven years before they could afford to pay the fees to get title to the extra parcels.[61] Their initiative provides an early indication among the missions of a considerable degree of autonomy from the Jesuit father.

A few leagues upriver from San Ignacio, the mission of Santa Apolonia was situated in a mountain canyon. After declining in population throughout the seventeenth century, it experienced some growth in the eighteenth when San Juan, a visita of San Ignacio, was reassigned to it. In the 1740s just under 300 people lived in the two pueblos, where they planted corn and collected honey and wax.[62] The last two and most isolated Topia missions, Yamoriba and San Pablo, had recently undergone reorganization and been relocated in ostensibly more favorable agricultural locations. Yamoriba reportedly had no level lands at all, although its visita, San Bartolomé Humacen, had milpas of corn and orchards of oranges, lemons, apples, and pomegranates. After their population declined to less than 50 residents, both pueblos were abandoned and their inhabitants moved upriver to San Pedro Guarisamey, a visita of San Pablo. San Pablo and its other visita, Santa Lucía, were reconstituted to the east in Pueblo Nuevo, once the site of a mine and Franciscan mission.[63]

During the reorganization, civil authorities ran into resistance, first from the Christianized Xiximes of the two missions who argued that they were being forced to abandon their fields and orchards only because they were located too far from the mission churches. In spite of the distances, they asserted, they still traveled to the missions for feast days and Holy Week. Resistance to the relocation efforts also came from some unconverted Xiximes whom authorities tried to dislodge from their remote canyon rancherías. Further unrest ensued in 1744 from several natives of San Pedro, who protested when their visita became a head mission; they asked to be settled at the site of the mission's ranch, San Luis. Padre Cartagena blamed all of the unrest on native witchcraft and the use of peyote; he believed that he had barely survived a death spell cast on him by the mother of a girl he had punished for incest. He also reported that much of the sorcery was practiced by Indian women in the places where they gathered wild plants. Their spells were aimed at preventing crops from growing in the mission, and even Padre Cartagena believed that they had been effective in changing the course of the river to the detriment of mission production.

Balthasar encountered a more tranquil scene when he arrived, but the mission was still very poor and had less than 200 inhabitants. Mission residents and vecinos shared a cofradía, but its assets were regulated by the missionary.[64] The area did not prosper until the end of the eighteenth century, when a silver strike generated a small fortune for Basque miner Juan José Zambrano.

Pueblo Nuevo, upriver in a mountain canyon, already had a substantial vecino population of mestizos and mulattoes at midcentury. Alongside the native residents, they cultivated small plots of corn, tended a few livestock, and cared for their citrus groves. The mission had two small ranches, one of them dedicated to the support of a cofradía, but neither property possessed a title. A number of vecinos took advantage of the location midway between Durango and the coastal plain, maintaining small pack trains for transporting goods. Even the missionary, Fernando Caamaño, was involved in petty commerce, earning a rebuke from his superiors.[65]

Balthasar had no doubt that the situation of the Topia missions was dire. In one respect it was similar to the missions of Tepehuana, where Indian populations were being swamped by non-Indians. But the economic conditions were far worse here in the western sierras. Mining had come earlier to this region and had declined more rapidly. During a period of seventy to eighty years, missions were founded but then precipitously depopulated by a convergence of heavy labor demands, epidemic disease, and warfare. At the close of the mining heyday, a much reduced Indian population shared the meager resources of the steep western escarpment of the Sierra Madre Occidental with the Spaniards, mestizos, and mulattoes who elected to remain. The productive land, consisting of a relatively few flat spaces and alluvial valleys that were spaced far apart in steep canyon bottoms, became the primary means of survival for many indigenous peoples and outsiders, who came to look more and more like each other. A few miners and cattle ranchers managed to accumulate more resources, but their activities did not fuel the local economy. In between these strata were the itinerant, predominantly mixed-race merchants and muleteers who traded between the Sinaloa coast and the central plateau on the other side of the sierras. Although the trade items had changed somewhat, colonial Indian and mestizo traders followed indigenous trans-sierra routes. On the coast they obtained salt and fish. From their own canyons came beeswax, honey, fruit, and sugarcane. These items were carried down the eastern slopes of the Sierra Madre to Spanish towns and mines. There the muleteers traded for cloth and luxury items shipped from Mexico City via the camino real.[66]

The Topia road was an important trade route, but it was not one that was easily traversed. Travel was extremely laborious—as Balthasar put it, "intolerable for mules and men."[67] Isolation often meant privation, and the acquisition of sufficient food could be a struggle even for the missionaries. They frequently borrowed from wealthy vecinos in Durango to acquire supplies.[68] Topia missionaries actually received a kind of hardship pay from the crown; an extra fifty pesos was added to their stipend. So it is little wonder that the missionaries were tormented when their supplies did not arrive regularly and that some less scrupulous padres engaged in petty trade. Their requisitions were more detailed and specific than those of their counterparts on the other side of the mountains. And they ordered enormous quantities of chocolate (cacao)—double the amount of the Tepehuana missionaries. The modern-day observer is piqued by curiosity: how could a missionary use 250 pounds of cacao annually? For one thing, the cup of chocolate was both an important symbol of hospitality in a culture of deprivation and a stimulus for socializing with non-Indian

guests and wayfarers. From the perspective of the missionary whose calling was no longer rewarding, it provided a means for fraternizing with
vecinos as well as an escape from drudgery and stagnation. Faced with the
penury of the Topia missions, many of the Jesuits reportedly paid more
attention to the spiritual and temporal affairs of the non-Indians that surrounded them.

Other circumstances troubled Father Balthasar. The shortage of missionaries was exacerbated by the extent to which many were ill-suited
for the job. Jesuit training, however rigorous, did not automatically prepare missionaries for their multiple duties as catechists, farmers, healers,
and administrators. Balthasar ventured his own opinion that the qualities
that made a good spiritual adviser proved antithetical to those which produced a competent administrator or fiscal agent.[69] Physically, the churches
were badly deteriorated in many cases; bare adobe walls crumbled and
leaky towers fell as mission revenues declined. The missionaries no longer
kept the required financial account books.[70] And allegations regarding
the sexual improprieties of missionaries, including solicitation in the con-
fessional, were not uncommon. In one case, Padre Felipe Calderón had
the temerity to accuse a Spanish woman with whom he admitted having
sexual relations of seducing him and rendering him impotent and ill
through multiple incidents of witchcraft.[71]

The personnel situation in Topia was especially unsettling. Four of the
eleven missionaries of the Tepehuana and Tarahumara Baja province were
in extremely poor health and would die within the year; several others
died in the ensuing five years. In the eighteenth century frequent vacan-
cies commonly forced missionaries to do double duty in an area where
travel was extremely difficult. Most of the missionaries were not up to
the task. The one exception was Padre Mateo Sánchez, seventy-five years
old in 1745. He lived to be eighty-six, and when he got too old to ride
his mule he walked to his visitas. But his constitution was unparalleled
in Topia. Padre Sánchez's virtues were not matched by most of his con-
temporaries, either in the spiritual or material realm. Many of them had a
long history of conflict with secular authorities.[72] The general poverty of
the missions did not encourage the padres to apply themselves to temporal affairs, and most avoided keeping even rudimentary accounts.[73] A few
were more enterprising, but their activities did not accrue to the benefit
of the missions. Alcoholism and depression made some of the padres unfit to serve, but there was little possibility of replacing them. And in one
case, a Jesuit visitor decided not to move an incompetent missionary to
another site, "because Padre Cardáveras is too foolish and simpleminded.

At least they already know this where he is now, so it's best not to let it be known elsewhere."[74]

Father Balthasar also reported that most missionaries had less than harmonious relationships with their charges. Given the very paternalistic nature of the interactions and the use of corporal punishment to discipline, it is not surprising that indigenous peoples commonly regarded the missionaries as harsh and unsympathetic. In the cases where they were well regarded, Balthasar noted that they were rarely obeyed. Missionary views of Indians tended to be even more disparaging, arising out of the frustration they felt at what they perceived as native intransigence and incapacity to change. The adjectives used to describe them could also be read counterfactually from the resistance perspective to reveal manifestations of the weapons of the weak described by James Scott. Indians who engaged in foot-dragging and work slowdowns were "lazy and slothful." When they left the missions to engage in the supplementary economic activities of hunting and gathering, they were "vagrant and idle." False deference was interpreted as "insolence," just as other psychological defenses such as gossip and slander were "audacious and impudent." Acts of sabotage were "negligent and careless." Pilfering to get their due was unmitigated "thievery." Assertive behavior was "stubbornness." The persistence of autochthonous practices was "devious." Eighteenth-century missionaries were not sanguine about the possibility of altering these "inherent" personality traits. The best they could hope for was to assume the role of the parent coping with a disobedient child. One Jesuit, describing the Topia missions, put it this way:

> The Indians of the sierra are predominantly ladinos—lazy, impertinent, and badly influenced by Spaniards. They barely attend to the needs of their missions, planting three or four almudes of corn, and this only in some missions. . . . In sum, they are without shame, without fear, and without respect. We have learned from experience that the only way to live with them is to expect nothing.[75]

The visita of Juan Antonio Balthasar—a snapshot in time—amply demonstrates the demoralization of the missionary enterprise in these areas. Its sources varied from mission to mission, based on differing combinations of factors, including demography, natural resources, labor needs, markets, and missionary zeal. But in no case did a mission community correspond to either a Jesuit or secular ideal. They were not self-sufficient and disciplined, nor were they closed to pernicious influences from outside or productively integrated into a taxable regional economy. Their ethnic composition was mixed, with Indianness on the wane at least biologically if not culturally. In this continuum, ways of claiming indigenous space persisted, albeit in different modes. At one end, the ladino officials of San Gerónimo de Ahoya chose recourse to Spanish law to protect their lands; at the other, indigenous women in San Pedro called upon magic to subvert the disassembling of their natural and supernatural worlds. Now, at a crucial juncture, these assorted processes of ethnogenesis and ethnic/cultural absorption at different stages intersected with changing local and imperial Spanish strategies. The denouement is the story of the next two chapters.

SEVEN

"STUCK TOGETHER WITH PINS"
The Unraveling of the Mission Fabric

Taking the matlazahuatl epidemic of the late 1730s as the immediate catalyst, it is useful to analyze how this spark interacted with other short- and long-term processes to hasten social, economic, and ethnic changes. High death rates among the laboring population threatened economic enterprise in the sparsely populated north. In order to overcome the labor shortage, repartimiento demands escalated. In the older missions where proximity to a growing non-Indian population had already altered or arrested indigenous population recovery, the heavy exaction of labor could easily produce economic stagnation. The permanent exodus of some Indian laborers also retarded population recovery in the missions (see Figure 1). This trajectory coincided with loss of mission lands to the expanding Spanish population. Without sufficient land and labor, missions were hard put to produce enough to pay their expenses and sometimes even to provide subsistence for their inhabitants. The need to find or renew other subsistence strategies fueled another impetus for flight from the missions.

The scenario described so far gives preference to local exigencies as the main motors, but imperial policies were crowding onto the stage. For one thing, the dislocations and shortages of foodstuffs resulting from the epidemic prompted higher authorities to investigate the scene more closely. Of paramount concern was the slowing of the Chihuahua mining bonanza which coincided with the crisis of subsistence and epidemic.[1] A series of exchanges between the king and the Audiencia de Guadalajara between 1739 and 1742 tried to assess the extent of potential losses in mining revenue from Nueva Vizcaya and tribute from Nueva Galicia. Officials recognized the changing ethnic composition of the north and discussed the possibility of levying tribute on mixed-race peoples. Another proposal concerned the laws barring Spaniards from living in Indian pueblos, especially in the frontier areas where natives still struggled against incorporation. Rather than isolate indigenous peoples, officials suggested, would it not be more effective for Spaniards to instruct them in proper habits through daily interaction?[2]

As the more affluent local elites stepped up the pressure on the missions in the 1740s, local administrators endeavored to resolve the chronic shortages of labor and supplies in the province. As they had done since the mid-seventeenth century, despite the progressive depopulation in the Nueva Vizcayan missions, the Jesuits displayed pragmatism in dealing with the repartimiento drafts. They still supported them in principle, but at the same time they insisted that the drafts should conform to the laws that regulated them. Their arguments were persuasive to at least one official, although he was mostly concerned with the ways in which missions were important in the provision of labor. In 1744 the corregidor of Chihuahua and acting governor of Nueva Vizcaya, Silvestre de Soto y Troncoso, drew upon their criticisms to describe a deleterious cycle to the viceroy.[3]

He argued that repartimiento was still indispensable to the economic health of the province, but that the system must be made more efficient. The regulation limiting the number of Indians that could be removed from a pueblo at any given time was so impractical it was ignored to the point that villages were being completely depopulated. This meant that mission fields were neglected. Without hope of subsistence at home, repartimiento workers tended to loiter in Spanish towns, mines, and haciendas. The missionaries were left with missions in name only; the few Indians who did return were forced to seek provisions in the wilds, where they could do as they pleased. This inspired disobedience and unrest. Another shortcoming of the repartimiento system could be found in the ways workers were abused by their employers. They were forced to travel long distances, not paid for travel time, and made to work more than the specified number of days. Not only were they paid in commodities rather than specie, but the payment was issued in the form of scrip that could only be redeemed in Parral or Chihuahua. In these urban areas, they were exposed to the petty machinations and immoral behavior of castas.[4]

Soto y Troncoso then made several recommendations. Royal officials should oversee the establishment of *siembras de comunidad* in each pueblo. These communal plantings would be done on suitable plots measured and formally allotted from the village's half league of land. Here we see that

Soto's suggestions were very much related to the functioning of pueblos de indios in the center and south of New Spain. Each village, he also maintained, should have a school with a maestro/teacher paid out of communal funds. Further, vagrant Indians should be settled in the appropriate pueblos, and no employer should have Indians in his service without official authorization. The quota of repartimiento laborers should be changed from 4 percent to one-third, with workers rotated each month under the supervision of an Indian captain or principal. The remaining two-thirds would be required to work on the communal plots. Indian officials and missionaries would submit to the governor annual reports on the state of the community and the numbers of able-bodied men. Finally, presidial captains who were named as Indian protectors or defenders should be prevented from abusing their authority by appropriating Indian labor for their own landholdings.

The acting governor, who had formulated his analysis partly on the basis of Jesuit petitions, as well as on his knowledge of the functioning of Indian pueblos elsewhere, sent a copy of these recommendations to Balthasar and suggested that Jesuit officials in Mexico City might want to respond or consult with the viceroy about them. Father Balthasar received the suggestions with mixed feelings. On the one hand, they aimed to stem the destruction of Indian communities resulting from excessive labor drafts. But they also moved in the direction of transferring control of the Indians away from the missionaries, and they sanctioned the ambitious enclosures being approved by the *juez medidor de tierras* using the half-league standard. The Jesuits were being forced to pay fees to hold on to often marginally productive mission ranches and wilderness areas.[5]

Some of the missionaries saw more harm than benefit in the recommendations, arguing that lands that had been used or improved by Indians should not legally be subject to any form of taxation. In this interpretation, these were lands belonging to Indians "from time immemorial" that had been ceded to the Jesuits for the benefit of the community. Furthermore, it was not the presidial captains who abused the position of protector of Indians, but rather the private citizens who obliged Indians to pay them commodity tribute in corn, chickens, and sheep. Balthasar, concerned about the antagonistic climate, believed that the order should try to accommodate official requests whenever possible; at the same time he endorsed the Jesuits' legal efforts to fight the land surveys.[6] Disquieted after their protracted legal battles with Sonoran governor Manuel Bernal Huidobro, other Jesuit voices agreed that it would be sensible to avoid direct confrontations with local elites.[7] Prudence was indicated at least until the order played its trump card: the offer to secularize some of its missions.

The formal proposal was sent to the king on November 30, 1745, by the Mexican provincial head, Cristóbal Escobar y Llamas.[8] In it he offered to cede to the bishop of Durango the twenty-two mission partidos of Topia and Tepehuana/Tarahumara Baja to enable the Society of Jesus to undertake the expansion of missions into California. These missions had been chosen, he argued, because they were located near parishes, towns, mining reales, and caminos reales. Moreover they were closest to the seat of the bishopric of Durango, and he had already broached the possibility of a transfer to the diocese with Bishop Elizacoechea the previous June. Because he was preparing to leave for his new post in Michoacán, the bishop deferred consideration of the matter to his successor. The new bishop, Pedro Anselmo Sánchez de Tagle, did not arrive until 1747, and the king did not accept the Jesuits' offer until the end of that year.[9] Even then the transfer of the missions was not completed until 1755. But the forces that had set secularization in motion much earlier on inexorably.

In October 1746, Viceroy Revillagigedo issued an order that attempted to rationalize the administration of the troubled northern provinces.[10] In it, he reiterated the charges of the corregidor of Chihuahua and noted that the fees of the Indian governor, serving as middleman, were being deducted from the worker's meager pay rather than being paid by the landowner or miner. His decree incorporated the recommendations of the corregidor almost verbatim. All Indian missions in Nueva Vizcaya and Sinaloa should receive confirmation of title to 600 *varas* (a half league) of land with sufficient cropland, water, and pastures. These lands should be divided fairly among the inhabitants under the supervision of the missionary. Each pueblo should have a school for Indians to learn Spanish from a maestro paid from community assets. Missionaries and Indian officials were responsible for keeping natives in the pueblos. They should make annual counts of the population, and they were to organize fit males into three labor gangs. Only with authorization from the governor of Nueva Vizcaya could miners or landowners receive workers, and the missionary was to be notified of the repartimiento orders. At no time could a village have more than one-third of the able-bodied males drafted, and only for a month at a time. To ensure fair treatment, the workers would be accompanied by a paid Indian overseer. Under this system, the Indians theoretically would work a total of four months per year, spaced at intervals of every three months. No village could be left with less than twenty workers at any given time—apparently the minimum number considered necessary for cultivating crops and caring for animals. Travel days had to be paid, and no worker was to travel farther than 10 leagues from home. The viceroy's decree also authorized local officials to draft vagrant non-Indians, whom he saw as *forasteros*/outsiders, into labor service.

The viceregal order contained conflicting messages about the role of missions. On the one hand, it sanctioned the idea that Indians needed missionary oversight and protection: "[B]ecause of the Indians' ignorance, lack of intelligence, cowardice, and misery, they are easily prone to embrace anything that is prejudicial and noxious to them." Insofar as congregation served the purpose of organizing a labor pool and avoiding vagrancy in the unsettled conditions of the north, imperial and local authorities wanted to use missionaries to keep Indians in missions. In fact, they criticized the missionaries' use of Indians to travel on mission business—for example, in transporting mail and supplies—because it frequently led to conflicts with vecinos.[11] On the other hand, the 1746 order contained elements that weakened missionary control over mission resources and production, especially the provisions specifying employment of a maestro and assigning the proceeds from communal plantings to secular ends. The latter was certainly a step toward implementing more formal taxation in lieu of tribute. And it was complemented by a second decree that forbade missionaries from intervening in elections or removing elected officials, arrogating that power to civil authorities.[12]

In accordance with the latter tack, the Marqués de Altamira, the viceroy's auditor de guerra, continued to push for the secularization of all the northern missions: "[I]n conformity with the law, these could have long since become parishes in which the Indians would pay not only ecclesiastical fees for services (thus saving the costs to His Majesty's treasury), but also tribute. . . ." For the marqués, it was patently clear that isolating Indians in missions had been counterproductive, "for they only understand what they see with their eyes."[13] What he apparently did not realize was that the very integration he proposed was already a fait accompli in Topia, although the result was not auspicious for his prophesied outcome in terms of productivity. But his relative by marriage and the new bishop of Durango, Sánchez de Tagle, was about to find out.[14] As soon as he arrived at his post, he was faced with the daunting task of filling a number of vacant parishes, giving him pause about the possibility of taking over new ones. He quickly got an inkling of the general poverty of Topia, and he decided to seek information directly from both missionaries and secular clergy in all of the areas proposed for secularization.[15] The answers to his seven-point questionnaire were sobering and revealed the general outlines of the history of Topia.

As we have seen, epidemic diseases and harsh forced labor in mines had combined earlier in Topia to produce severe Indian population decline. Profitable silver mining itself played out before the end of the seventeenth century, also slowing migration of non-Indians to the area. Economic viability came to depend almost solely on the region's location between the Sinaloan coast and the Chihuahuan altiplano. Petty traders made annual trips, plodding the Topia road and its transversals, plying their own meager stock of beeswax and honey, as well as expediting the exchange of the commodities originating in the two flanks. Pueblo Nuevo, the mission closest to Durango, had a number of mixed-race petty traders who raised mules for sale in Durango.

For the most part, however, the agricultural potential of Topia was limited, since nearly all the missions had been positioned to serve mining areas. Although most were located in valleys and canyon bottoms below mining reales, agriculture was difficult to sustain along the narrow ribbons of floodplain that wound through the rugged mountains. Soils were poor and flatlands were in scarce supply. Where they could be found, non-Indians came to control them in the first half of the eighteenth century.[16] Very few of them, however, managed to amass large holdings that could be classified as haciendas. If a landowner possessed more than ten sitios de ganado mayor, it was most likely that they were not contiguous parcels. Most landholdings were little more than small plots, very small farms of several *caballerías* of land (105 acres each) suitable for planting corn, sugarcane, and fruit orchards, or modest ranchos composed of from one to a few sitios that supported small herds of cattle or flocks of sheep. For the most part, these were worked by their owners, who could barely afford to feed and clothe their families. As an indicator of the poverty of the average vecino, the missionary in Remedios noted that most women passed their entire lives with only one *rebozo*/shawl, one pair of stockings, and one pair of shoes for outings—and these were usually passed on to their heirs.[17]

Where Indians remained in missions, they planted very little. Some worked for nearby vecinos in repartimiento or voluntarily; in either case they earned a pittance. But by 1750 a large majority of the reduced number of Indians named on mission registers, probably less than 2,000 in all of Topia, lived most of the year in scattered rancherías away from the villages. The Indians of Badiraguato were reported to subsist almost entirely on cactus and forest products: "Nearly all have houses in the pueblos, but few live in them . . . because they consider their true home to be the woods and canyons where they take their wives and children to gather wild fruits, honey, and beeswax. . . . Their fugitive life is abetted by the facility with which they can get odd jobs from vecinos."[18] Some of the missions were virtually depopulated except on feast days when Indians returned to share in communal assets that by this time consisted almost solely of a few head of cattle.

In Topia, these community resources were rarely utilized as assets for an official cofradía, but they functioned in much the same way, providing the means for a less formal devotion to the Virgin through which the members took turns in sponsoring religious celebrations. If the mission had communal fields, they were rented to outsiders or tilled by paid workers and sufficed only for the paltry maintenance of the missionary and church. In some missions, the demographic void was filled by mixed-race peoples who often had consanguineal ties with the Indians.[19] Where non-Indians predominated in a mission, formal cofradías with constitutions existed. The majority of mixed-race peoples were classified as mulattoes and lobos, reflecting the persistent legacy of African American slaves brought to work in the mines as well as mestizaje.

In the mission of San Gregorio, its visita of Suibupa, and eight ranchos, non-Indians outnumbered Indians by two to one, and castas constituted more than three-fourths of the non-Indian total.[20] This swamping of the Indian population was well advanced throughout most of the Topia area; in the few cases where natives still outnumbered outsiders, the non-Indian population had a higher birthrate and soon surpassed them.[21] This was the case to the south and nearer the coast in San Ignacio de Piaxtla. In the cabecera, two visita pueblos, and thirteen ranchos, Indians were still the majority, but they increasingly sought subsistence in the monte and avoided mestizaje for a while longer. By 1749 they had virtually abandoned the cabecera to a majority population of non-Indians. Of the faster-growing non-Indian population, just under one-fifth were Spanish. The other four-fifths were classified by the missionary as mixed-race mestizos, coyotes, lobos, and mulattoes, with the latter group constituting about 45 percent of the total. Approximately half of the non-Indians tended to choose marriage partners from the same racial grouping; among those who did not, more than half of the men contracted marriage with lighter-skinned women.[22]

In 1749 the missionary in San Ignacio, Marcelo de León, described his mission in terms that echoed other Jesuits in Topia, but his report provides interesting detail that helps us to visualize the setting. Only three houses in the cabecera were made of adobes; the rest were mud and wattle constructions with thatched roofs.

> Most are so small that it is difficult to figure out how they can accommodate families, dogs, cats, and chickens. When we have to travel to visit the sick, we almost always have to return home immediately, because in most of the ranches there is no room to spend the night nor can the families feed us. So we have to let the old women apply their remedies or the ones we prescribe; sometimes we send medicines or food. The paths to the ranches are narrow and full of thorny underbrush that tears our clothes. We get stung by wasps and bitten by fleas. . . . The women aid their husbands in many tasks; they also make clothes and blankets for their families and for sale. . . . Some help with the weeding; others milk cows when they have them and make cheese. By selling this or that they can pay for some of the things they need to buy, always at high prices. Almost everyone plants a little corn; a few even manage some beans and cotton. But usually the harvests are barely enough to maintain their families. Most years the crops are lost to drought and families sustain themselves on wild fruits and roots. Livestock die for lack of pasture, or they are not healthy enough to suckle their young and are easy prey for mountain lions and wolves.[23]

Father Marcelo's comments are particularly revealing about gender roles, indicating that women were vitally involved in a variety of economic activities. By this time, the role of healer had come to be largely filled by women. The missionary went on to describe the ways in which local officials schemed to get their pound of flesh from vecinos living in such miserable conditions. The Indians were even poorer, he argued, trying to subsist on what they could harvest from their fields and backcountry areas. Worse still, they were allegedly capricious in religious matters. "Even though they have been exposed to Christian beliefs for a long time, there is still a great deal to fear from them. Their faith seems to be stuck together with pins," and could unravel on a moment's notice.[24]

This judgment was vigorously contradicted by complaints to Jesuit and civil officials from Indian governors who spoke in the name of the común (community) of San Ignacio and Santa Apolonia missions and their visitas and claimed that Padre Marcelo had ignored their spiritual needs for years, failing to minister to the sick and the dying. He allegedly sold cloth, tools, and rosaries from his annual supply requisition at prices that were double those of Durango or Chihuahua, where charges were already higher than in Mexico City. They also denounced his appointment of a free mulatto, Miguel de Figueroa, as administrator of the mission's properties and livestock, charging that the overseer did not employ resources for the common good.[25] Although missionary supplies had always been distributed unequally and with strings attached (as rewards to compliant Indian officials or recompense for Indian labor), the illegal, outright forced sale of these items at inflated prices confirmed the shaky character of the Topia mission enterprise, if not the venality of some unscrupulous Jesuits. Father Marcelo had also been successful in getting the local Spanish official removed, so that for several years he was the only local source of judicial recourse. The complaints of the mission residents describe a situation very similar to the *repartimientos de mercancías* or *efectos*/forced sale of merchandise common in central and southern Mexico, where alcaldes mayores forcibly sold commodities at artificially high prices to Indians in their jurisdictions.[26]

Ethnic transformations and economic decline had been features of the Topia missions for generations, but they were exacerbated in 1748 and 1749 by a protracted drought.[27] Production of corn dropped even more precipitously because very few missions had irrigation ditches, and the scarcity of pastures resulted in the continued dwindling of livestock. The link between acculturation in missions and poverty is particularly striking in the case of Topia. Some of the more enterprising missionaries sought creative but illegal solutions in trying to profit from mission stores and engaging in commerce. Others bet on horse races, turned their residences into inns for pay, or engaged directly in silver mining. Vecinos charged that some of them fathered children, and secular priests clashed with the missionaries in trying to collect fees for sacraments in Otatitlán, Otaez, Badiraguato, and San Ignacio.[28] In these areas and others where missionaries served the non-Indian population, parishioners did not have to pay the prescribed rates for sacramental services; in fact they often compensated the missionaries in commodities of little value. Chagrined at the prospect of having to pay in specie, petty traders in the vicinity of the Remedios mission wrote to the bishop that they would never be able to support a parish priest, arguing that they, like the Indians, subsisted on natural vegetation and roots during part of the year.[29]

It is little wonder, then, that the bishop showed reluctance to receive the Topia missions. Their counterparts in the Tepehuana and Tarahumara Baja province looked more appealing, but they were not without problems either. The decline in the Indian population of the Tepehuan missions was well advanced. At the same time, the Tarahumara Baja was still getting new recruits, helping to fill ubiquitous repartimiento demands but also buttressing resistance to conversion. Pressures on Jesuit mission lands closest to Chihuahua escalated as the juez medidor de tierras, Manuel de Güemes, and members of the Chihuahua cabildo manipulated the adjudication of titles.[30] San Antonio de Chuviscar and other Franciscan missions along the Conchos drainages also lost lands while their inhabitants were away, forced to work on surrounding farms and charcoal-making haciendas. The latter blocks of woodland were carved out of the Indians' monte, further reducing their possibilities for subsistence.[31]

Even in the barren eastern deserts, Spaniards expanded their cattle ranches where they could get access to waters of the Río Nazas. The mission of Cinco Señores had lands on both sides of the river at this site on the presidial corridor. In order to defray the huge debts incurred by the mission in building irrigation canals and grain storage bins to boost productivity, in 1743 Visitor Balthasar had proposed the sale of a small ranch on the bank of the river opposite the improvements. The reduced Indian population of the mission—approximately sixteen families—protested the pending sale, sending their complaints in a petition to the viceroy.[32] Already surrounded by several hundred vecinos, the Indians (a mixture of different band groups, Tepehuanes, and Tarahumaras) feared further encroachments and loss of access to irrigation water. They also complained that Padre Juan Ramírez was arbitrary in imposing his choices for officers of the pueblo, rather than respecting the community's right to elect them. The Jesuits responded that they would give the *ranchito* (of about 200 acres) to the Indians if they would assume responsibility for the mission's debts, help rebuild the church, and agree to a rotation system for sharing water with neighbors. It is interesting to note the Indians' resort to judicial recourse here, as well as the Jesuits' attempted dismissal of their complaints as those of petty and lazy natives inclined to robbery and flight. The situation was complicated by the fact that Padre Ramírez was reported by his superiors to be mentally unstable.[33] The practical problem for the Jesuits was to find a purchaser who could pay in cash. The prime potential buyer was the captain of the presidio of El Gallo, who owned adjacent lands, but he could only offer a payment plan.[34] The matter remained unresolved for the next few years as the Jesuits continued to entreat surrounding landowners to contribute to the building of a new church.[35]

The oldest Tepehuan missions, located in today's northwestern Durango in the Río Papasquiaro and Río Tepehuanes valleys, were also surrounded by growing numbers of vecinos.[36] In Santiago Papasquiaro and

Santa Catalina, the remaining Indians were being paid to work on communal lands that produced corn, wheat, beans, and chile. In these most acculturated missions, there were several cofradías, two for Indians and two for vecinos. In terms of assets there was little to distinguish between them. They had small herds of cattle, as well as cash earned by the members in their frequent trips to Spanish towns to beg for alms. Here the Tepehuanes had mastered a way to keep some of their resources out of Jesuit control. These assets were sufficient to meet the expenses of the annual saint's day celebration, as well as to fund feasting on Corpus Christi and Holy Thursday. The cofradías themselves had patron saints and resources dedicated to their fiestas: San Ignacio de Loyola in the cabecera of Santiago Papasquiaro, and Ecce Homo and the Señor de la Columna in the visitas of San Nicolás and Atotonilco. These fiestas were an important integrative force in missions beset by so many extractive pressures. They tended to draw back the many mission Indians who were drained off periodically by repartimiento drafts or seasonal and other labor on the expanding lands of the Hacienda de Ramos.

In Santiago Papasquiaro, of 92 Indian heads of household, four-fifths were engaged in agriculture. They had their own milpas on which they produced mostly corn; only about 10 percent of these farmers also raised some wheat. Approximately 9 percent owned a few animals, primarily sheep. The non-Indians outnumbered the Indians by more than two to one, but they were a modest lot in economic terms. Sixty percent of them possessed no land of their own; of the 40 percent who did, two-thirds had only a few acres. Slightly larger holdings, small farms or ranchos, belonged to the other third. Only 6 percent of vecino landowners owned estancias larger than half of a sitio. Using livestock to measure assets produces a similar picture, as 60 percent of the vecinos had none. Of the 40 percent who owned animals, three-quarters had only a few horses, mules, or cows, 13 percent possessed cattle herds of 50 to 100, 7.5 percent owned over 100 head, and 4.5 percent boasted a packtrain. Padre Ríos reported that landless and indebted vecinos routinely left the valley to work in mining or in the manufacture of charcoal for the smelting process.[37]

In nearby Santa Catalina, only fifteen Indian families remained, most of them scattered throughout the surrounding hills and engaged in harvesting and roasting mescal cactus—a time-honored survival tactic in times of drought with a coveted food source. In 1749 Padre Pedro de Retes commented that the vecinos were heavily indebted and that a third of them owned no land.[38] Although he enumerated 54 percent of the non-Indian population as Spanish, he stated that very few of them were completely "untainted" by race mixture. Nonetheless, they must have met some somatic norm for whiteness, as he broke down the other 46 percent into the categories of mestizo (18 percent), mulatto (13 percent), coyote (11 percent), and lobo (4 percent). He also observed that there were still fourteen Spanish families who owned a total of 45 slaves. Retes' comments on racial status, taken together with those of other missionaries who accorded the matter any specificity, give us pause to ponder the question of the idiosyncratic differences among Jesuits in assigning racial categories and how these might have been blanched over time. If the category of Spaniard could include mixed-race peoples, what did a mixed-race label signify? Did it denote lesser acculturation, insufficient piety, a distinctive cultural configuration, a lower social standing, fewer material assets? One suspects that in varying combinations all of these figured into a missionary's perception and designation of ethnicity.

Except in the case of elite Spaniards who owned expanding haciendas, the labels must have involved subtle distinctions among mission residents and vecinos who functioned in the more localized economic venues. Father Retes noted that agriculture was a principal source of subsistence for vecinos, but because of cyclical (and current) drought, only those with irrigated fields were able to reap profitable harvests.

> Most of the vecinos make their living by either going themselves or sending their sons with their packtrains, consisting of six to ten or twelve mules, to the mining towns, principally Chihuahua, where they cut wood in the surrounding wooded hills and make charcoal to sell. They do this for several months or a year while their families suffer privations. . . . The money they earn is rarely enough to pay their debts and clothe their families. . . . A few go to the coastal lowlands to get salt, sugar, fish, and other fruits and foodstuffs to take to the Real del Oro and other places to sell . . . but the prices they can get are rarely enough to cover their expenses.

Padre Retes was particularly critical of the mulattoes and coyotes who were not inclined to work, charging that they mostly made a habit of hanging around the corrals of their more affluent neighbors, where they would get drunk and then show up at someone else's house at mealtime. Exceedingly cynical after a quarter century in missions, he also charged that the resources dedicated to cofradía fiestas were used mostly for food and alcohol rather than for the adornment of the church. The eighteenth-century evolution of the mission of Santa Catalina is shadowy. In this valley, surrounded by oak and pine forests, the families of the now defunct presidio located across the river from the mission had expanded and acquired land. The Jesuits themselves had come into possession of a large cattle ranch, comprised of 56 sitios de ganado mayor and tended by hired cowboys. Serving as the local visitor of Tepehuan missions throughout much of his missionary tenure, Father Retes was often absent from his own pueblo. His record keeping was less than complete for Santa Catalina, making it difficult to track the population shifts that left the mission with so few Indian families by midcentury.[39]

In Zape and Tizonazo, the missionaries reported little productivity and considerable theft of mission supplies. Celebrations of saints' days drew Indians who were mostly absent to the missions. Tizonazo's visita of Santa Cruz had healthy cofradía assets, but its livestock were vulnerable to the pilfering of Yaquis living in two nearby rancherías. The transplanted Yaquis were also alleged to steal corn from nearby Spanish farms as they rotated in and out of these sites between their homeland in Sonora and the Chihuahua mines.[40] In both missions, the numbers of Tepehuanes continued to decline. The older Tepehuan missions had become less Indian and Tepehuan was no longer spoken in them (although most Indians spoke a Nahuatl patois). The majority of Indians and mixed-race vecinos were poor, but some of them (fewer Indians than mestizos) had managed to accumulate enough capital to rise above the others on the economic scale. Far above them were the hacendados, who stepped up efforts after mid-eighteenth century to extend their holdings adjacent to missions, for example, in the haciendas of Canutillo and Cerrogordo.[41]

North of the Tepehuan area Tarahumaras continued to be recruited periodically to missions, keeping them afloat and, of even greater consequence for Spanish enterprise, providing a steady supply of repartimiento workers, especially for agriculture.[42] San Miguel de las Bocas had customarily furnished labor to the Spanish haciendas of Santa Catalina and Tascate since the seventeenth century. Fluent in Spanish, most of the men were reputed to be cowboys or skilled horsemen who rode their mounts to job sites outside the mission. Others tended the mission ranch and its 300 head of cattle. As in the Tepehuan case, the little corn harvested tended to last less than half of the year, spurring an exodus in January from mission to rancherías, where the hunting and gathering mode intervened for nominal mission residents. Substantial numbers of vecinos regularly attended church at the mission.[43]

Farther north, there were over a thousand Tarahumaras and Tepehuanes in the missions of Huejotitlán and San Pablo. In 1749 Father Benito

Rinaldini described the mission, visitas, and rancherías of Huejotitlán, reporting that the Indians had little property beyond modest numbers of livestock:

> Some, not all, have one or two animals; each of twelve families owns about 20 cattle and some horses; and there are fifteen families who have flocks of sheep, but none over 50 head. One family has a string of pack mules. Most everyone subsists on the corn and beans from their harvests, but these stores are rarely enough for the whole year, so they supplement them with mescal cactus and wild fruits, as well as fruit from their orchards. They also receive foodstuffs when they work in the Spanish haciendas and farms where they are sent by the governors of Nueva Vizcaya. When they are not away in labor drafts, which consume a considerable part of the year, they are in their pueblos and rancherías, where they have their own governors, fiscales, and other officials. . . . They come to the cabecera for feast days or when they are called. Only in Huejotitlán are there Tepehuanes, but both Tepehuan men and women speak Spanish. The visita pueblos are Tarahumara; in these, all of the men and some women are conversant in Spanish. But the ranchería dwellers use their native Tarahumara tongue.[44]

Rinaldini was an experienced missionary, known for his language expertise and especially for his grammar of the Tepehuan language. His sketch at midcentury of the state of Huejotitlán and San Pablo (which he was administering temporarily) is a good index of the continuum of acculturation that characterized the Jesuit province of Tepehuana and Tarahumara Baja. As we have seen, the oldest Tepehuan missions were the most ladino and mestizo. In the missions that mixed the two Indian groups, there were still some Tepehuanes in the cabeceras, and their numbers were being steadily augmented by mixed-race outsiders.[45] But when the visitas and rancherías of recent converts are included in the total mission count, Tarahumaras outnumbered Tepehuanes by about four to one. The missionary's remarks distinguish the ranchería dwellers as sierra peoples whose mixed subsistence strategies were still more integrated than those of the pueblo dwellers, where hunting and gathering had become an increasingly collateral form of subsistence. His comments also demonstrate that some of the villagers, including the governing officials, had more resources than others. Although the indigenous societies had never been completely egalitarian, social divisions became more pronounced as acculturation progressed.

According to Father Rinaldini, the labor drafts from all of the Tarahumara missions were destined primarily for agriculture in the proliferating haciendas of San Joseph de la Ciénaga, a factor which resulted in a perennial scarcity of grain in the missions. The communal fields were planted only when the Jesuits paid the workers.

> These circumstances mean that the Indians are often left without enough to eat, because the labor drafts are so continuous and numerous at precisely the time for planting and preparing the fields. . . . All this has led to the present situation, in which the missions are short of resources and lack the decency they used to enjoy.

Over time the stores of seed had diminished, and periodic droughts were a problem for most of the Indians who did not irrigate. The fact that landowners paid them in overvalued goods meant that they could not bank resources for the future. The situation described by Rinaldini for Huejotitlán and San Pablo also applied to the mission of Santa Cruz, to the north on the Río Conchos, except that conditions there were even worse according to Padre Cristóbal Moreno. There Tarahumaras worked on nearby landholdings, including the Hacienda de Cieneguilla and ranches owned by the Quintana, Quesada, Talamantes, and Ochoa families, but many were sent even farther away—sometimes more than a hundred miles—to become debt peons or accumulate credits in hacienda account books.[46]

Because they were closest to Chihuahua, the Tarahumara missions of Santa María de las Cuevas and Satevó experienced heavy labor drafts to support mining. Las Cuevas was the most populous of the Tarahumara Baja missions, with Santa Cruz second and Satevó third in numbers. All of them continued to receive groups of unconverted Tarahumaras, thus maintaining a sizable labor reserve. Nonetheless, the measles epidemic of 1748 resulted in a drop at all three missions, with only Satevó recovering by 1753 through additional recruits.[47] Some of the Indians in Las Cuevas worked for Spaniards who rented mission lands to cut wood and make charcoal.[48] But most traveled to Chihuahua on foot with their wives and children because they had no horses or mules. Some carried produce to sell, and others worked on the haciendas of the local commercial and mining elites. There was a good deal of movement in and out of the missions, as Tarahumaras mixed subsistence strategies, using the pueblos when it benefited them. In Satevó the Indians were absent most of the time even though they had homes in the missions, which ranged from relatively finished houses near the church to more rustic dwellings spread out along

TABLE 2. POPULATION FLUCTUATIONS IN THREE TARAHUMARA
MISSIONS, 1743–1753

	1743	*1749*	*1753*
Las Cuevas	1,776	1,210	642
Santa Cruz	981	857	562
Satevó	667	609	850

Sources: See sources for Figure 1.

the river for several miles. One was reported to own a small flock of sheep, and five had a few cows. Most subsisted on small plots of corn, the small animals they hunted, and the mescal they collected when they were not performing labor service in Chihuahua. Small amounts of mission produce were taken to market in the mining real.[49]

In these northernmost missions of the Tarahumara Baja, the Tarahumaras were taught the catechism in their own language, but Padre Calderón was of the opinion that they neither understood nor accepted it. Practically none took communion, and none of the Tarahumara missions had formal cofradías for Indians, although there was one in Santa Cruz for Spaniards. However, in all the missions some properties were informally dedicated to the support of religious celebrations, but only under the strict supervision of the missionary. One padre noted that the Tarahumaras rarely contributed the fruits of their individual labor to support religious fiestas; the exception was All Souls' Day or Day of the Dead, when maize was offered. This solitary practice in regard to Christian holidays may have had some relationship to food offerings that accompanied Tarahumara death rituals.[50] Control of nonsanctioned rituals was more difficult, since the potential danger of so many neophytes coming into contact with practitioners of petty witchcraft outside the missions was an ever-present reality in the less regulated frontier spaces of the north.[51]

Although it is possible to debate whether or not the viceregal order of 1746 was intended to bolster or dismantle the mission system, the question is largely irrelevant, as local exigencies played the deciding roles. The heavy demand for labor led local officials and property owners to circumvent the orders of Nueva Vizcayan governors, which virtually nullified the regulations on the size and frequency of repartimiento drafts. Jesuits pressed for adherence to the viceregal order of 1746, citing multiple abuses. Not only were Indians deprived of their pay in specie, but employers deducted from their wages the fees for labor recruiters as well as burial costs for fellow workers who perished on the job. They were alleged by the Jesuits to receive no religious instruction. To the contrary, they were educated in all manner of sin and crime, including drunkenness, sexual deviance, and gambling. Indian governors were duped into collaborating with venal labor recruiters. In 1750 Governor Juan Francisco de la Puerta y Barrera reported to the king that he could do nothing to enforce the law, and that even the corregidor of Chihuahua disobeyed it.[52] The worst excesses were in the Tarahumara Baja, where Indians were being drafted willy-nilly to work in Chihuahua.[53]

At the same time, missionaries were less than zealous in protesting encroachments on mission lands. Father Rinaldini charged in 1749 that some of his fellow Jesuits in the Tarahumara acted complicitly in deals with Spaniards (with whom they frequently had close social relationships) that allowed these outsiders to acquire mission property. The pressures on land intensified at midcentury as the downturn in silver mining prompted elites, a number of whom had initiated their economic activities in the area as landholders, to diversify or enlarge their holdings. Even though the Jesuits had won a suit in the Audiencia de Guadalajara in 1748 that reaffirmed the right of each mission to possess a square league of land, most of the missionaries tacitly accepted the local judges' limit of a half league. At the same time, Jesuits continued to lose control over community harvests to local officials.[54]

Drought conditions in the late 1740s and early 1750s further diminished mission revenues and subsistence. Seed was in short supply and in 1749 the price of a *fanega* (1.5 bushels) of maize in Chihuahua jumped from three to thirteen pesos. Some observers estimated that half of the livestock in the Durango area perished during that year and the next.[55] The drought also stimulated an increase in Apache raids on livestock, forcing them to forage further south, and retarded the supply of beef products to Chihuahua.[56] We have noted cycles of drought in Nueva Vizcaya from the beginning of Jesuit occupation: 1600-1610, 1615, 1630s, 1640s, 1650s, 1660s, 1690s, 1720s, 1737-1740, and 1748-1753. There is dendrochronological evidence that indicates increasing climatic variability in areas of northwestern Mexico and the southwestern United States in the period from 1670 to 1750.[57] But we also know that droughts affected the region before the Spaniards arrived with their livestock. Therefore it is difficult to assess the degree to which droughts may have been caused or aggravated by the influence of Old World invaders. The proliferation of livestock in the seventeenth and eighteenth centuries would have reduced vegetation cover over time. We can only guess at the extent and wonder whether the complaints from mission villagers about the destruction caused by the foraging of vecino livestock on their land may have signaled increasing desertification. The growing numbers of haciendas de carbón for the Chihuahua mines in the eighteenth century contributed to deforestation in climatic conditions of low annual rainfall. The destruction of natural grasses and woody vegetation cover in dry areas can affect the temperature of topsoils and the humidity of the air. It is probable that these processes advanced desertification in some areas of the north, making it more difficult for people to weather the normal cycles of drought. Surely they diminished the supply of edible wild plants. Even if we weigh the potential benefits of the introduction of livestock for native peoples as sources of food, clothing, and fertilizer, we cannot ignore the likelihood that substantial environmental degradation resulted from the new practices.

The effects of the midcentury drought received extensive comment from officials and clergy. Hunger forced people to scavenge in the countryside. According to the bishop of Durango, in addition to roots, cactus fruits, plant leaves, and grasses, they also ate the toasted hides of dead cattle. He himself claimed to have gone months without either a piece of bread or meat having passed his lips, subsisting mainly on milk. Weakened by hunger, many people succumbed to an epidemic of influenza or croup.[58]

The period from the late 1730s to the early 1750s exhibited chronic features that were scarcely new in the history of Nueva Vizcaya, but it was punctuated at both ends by fierce episodes of disease and drought that disrupted the life cycles of humans, other animals, and plants. These disasters accelerated the transition from Indian mission to mixed parish, not only by impeding Indian population recovery, but also by rousing Spaniards to rationalize chaotic relations of production and exchange. As local and viceregal officials made greater efforts to sort out the unruly frontier, to ensure a labor supply for productive enterprises, to account for changing demographic ratios, and to rein in the all-too-independent Jesuits, they piggybacked on transformations in the human and natural environments. As James C. Scott has suggested, early modern states were keen to implement standardizing processes to be able to get a better read on their subjects for taxation and other purposes. On the Nueva Vizcayan frontier, efforts to measure were in rudimentary stages, but they were beginning to make the region more legible.[59] A midcentury report by the captain of the Conchos presidio, José de Berroterán, provided a detailed list of settlements in Nueva Vizcaya, arranged by category. Although the number of haciendas had doubled since the beginning of the century, Jesuit and Franciscan missions still outnumbered Spanish towns and presidios by more than four to one.[60] But this ratio changed as the growing non-Indian population surpassed the numbers of natives. This transformation at midcentury was a crucial watershed in the evolving processes of absorption (cultural and biological) and ethnogenesis. Let us see how it interacted with the more aggressive policies of the Bourbons in the (re)construction of ethnic and cultural identities.

EIGHT

RENDERING UNTO CAESAR AT THE CROSSROADS OF ETHNICITY AND IDENTITY

In turns prompted and impeded by crisis and uncertainty, the secularization process stumbled forward. This chapter examines its unfolding from various official and local levels, with an eye to capturing its ethnic and cultural denouement. Support for secularization was given a strong philosophical boost from the viceregal and imperial levels, but local officials were no less enthusiastic for more practical reasons. They expected direct material payoffs in access to labor and land. Diocesan officials, on the other hand, were not at all sure that the church could profit despite the potential to accumulate money from fees. Nor were the Jesuits certain they had chosen the right path, especially when they could not get a guarantee that the missionary stipends would be reallocated to staff mission expansion into Alta California. For the local non-Indian residents and vecino population, there were pluses and minuses to consider. The poorer among them would lose their access to the free administration of sacraments, while the hacendados might encounter fewer obstacles to expanding their landholdings. Finally, most of the indigenous peoples could expect few benefits from the change of overseers. Where the missionaries had served to mitigate abuses, Indians would lose protection; potentially they would also become subject to commodity tribute and ecclesiastical fees, in addition to labor requirements. Nevertheless, a privileged few who had acquired more resources under Jesuit tutelage might be able to expand their assets with less scrutiny. In the free-for-all competition unleashed by secularization, labor would be the crucial factor. José Rafael Rodríguez Gallardo, royal visitor to the north, recognized this quite explicitly in his 1750 report on Sinaloa and Sonora by suggesting that secularization furnished one avenue for consolidating pueblos and concentrating labor for repartimiento.[1] His views were similar to those of the Marqués de Altamira who was determined to convert Indians into wage laborers, voluntary or not.[2]

The visitor's general criticisms of the mission system as an impediment to settlement and commercial expansion in the north[3] flourished in a general context in which royal officials sought to curb ecclesiastical power in temporal matters.[4] In central and southern Mexico, secularization of doctrinas (parishes staffed by regular clergy of the orders) increased markedly in the first half of the 1750s, in tandem with decrees from the king in 1749 and 1753 to transfer Indian parishes to the secular clergy. These mandates were attenuated somewhat in subsequent edicts that called for secularization only when a post was vacated and stipulated that local officials could make exceptions in cases where there were no replacements, for example, in remote provinces.[5]

While the Jesuits had already felt some hostility in the 1740s, the climate became more unfriendly in the 1750s, as Juan Antonio Balthasar noted in his correspondence with the Jesuit general in Rome. Balthasar had become concerned that mission stipends had not always been administered either efficiently or legitimately, and he proposed a number of administrative and accounting reforms to rectify the situation. The crown, he realized, was promoting secularization to bring an end to direct monetary subsidies. At the same time he worried about the waning enthusiasm for the missions within the order itself: "If the truth be known, many of the [royal] complaints have a basis in fact. . . . there are very few missionaries who are highly motivated." No longer could apostolic zeal be invoked as the raison d'être of the Society of Jesus in Mexico.[6]

As the authorities in Mexico City pushed the secularization of the Nueva Vizcayan missions forward, the people on the ground launched a protest. As early as 1749, Santiago Papasquiaro, the oldest Tepehuan mission, sent a delegation to the viceroy to protest the transfer. These native officials argued that removal of the Jesuits would be disastrous. For years their "beloved" padres had ministered to their spiritual and physical needs, feeding and clothing them. If they could not even support themselves, then how could they pay fees for services and provide the living of a priest? The viceroy assured the Tepehuan governor and other members of the delegation that the bishop would replace the missionary with a priest who would see to their needs as well as protect them from abuse by vecinos and local officials.[7] Because the Papasquiaro valley had a sizable vecino community of modest means, some officials alleged that the vecinos had actually put the Indians up to the protest because they wanted their exemption from ecclesiastical taxes to continue. By 1751 the surrounding population had increased to number over 2,000 communicants; many of them were impoverished migrants who had been attracted during periods of drought by the relative abundance and water sources of the valley. Furthermore, the missionary, Padre Antonio de los Ríos, had been generous in aiding the poor, liberally using his stipend from the crown to distribute goods.[8] As word of the impending transfer of missions spread, Tepehuanes and Tarahumaras in other villages began to consider the consequences. Jointly (*de mancomún*) they appealed to the bishop, claiming that they would not be able to support the expense of secular clerics. Their preference was to have the Jesuits remain because, they argued fervently, the padres had saved their forebears from eternal damnation and captivity by the devil ("del captiverio de Satanás"). If this were not possible, then the bishop must protect them from the rapacity of new priests and prevail on the governor to reduce the labor drafts.[9]

Efforts by the viceroy and the bishop to mollify the petitioners did not have the desired effect of quieting them, as they directed a new complaint to the viceroy in late 1752, after having received no response from the governor of Nueva Vizcaya whom they had petitioned earlier in the year. The governor, principales, and commoners of Santiago Papasquiaro now turned their attention to stemming outsider infiltration into the village itself. After the Tepehuan rebellion, their ancestors had gradually allowed some hacendados to build small houses in the pueblo for use during religious celebrations like Holy Week. Although these structures were not intended to be permanent, over time some vecino families had come to occupy them perpetually or to rent them out to merchants and other non-natives for long periods of time. Outsiders also violated the law by selling alcohol to the Indians. Ranches and farms adjacent to the mission had expanded onto village lands. The Tepehuanes of Santiago Papasquiaro asked the viceroy to prohibit the building of new houses in the pueblo and to limit the use of the homes already established to the original vecino families at fiesta times. The outsiders should make contributions to the celebrations and stay no more than eight days at a time. The viceroy ordered an investigation of these claims, to be undertaken by the captain of the new mobile squadron of soldiers.[10] The seemingly new awareness on the part of the villagers of their rights—especially their manipulation of the concept of the común or community assets and prerogatives—aroused suspicion on the part of the authorities.

Father Agustín Carta, the Jesuit visitor general assigned to inspect the missions in 1751 and attend to the logistics of the transfer, had no doubt as to the extent of acculturation in many of the villages when he reported to the head of the province: "[C]alling them missions does not disguise the fact that they are really parishes."[11] Shocked by the poverty of the majority of the missions chosen for secularization, he took up the task of negotiating the material terms of the transfer with Bishop Sánchez de Tagle. The missionaries had already been ordered by superiors in Mexico City to liquidate mission debts by selling assets. Father Carta found that the realization of this directive had been thwarted by several factors. The protracted drought had both diminished mission resources and limited the number of prospective buyers.[12] More problematic was the confusion over categories of assets. Who actually owned mission properties, buildings, furnishings, livestock, and grain? As we have seen, the communal claim to a half league of land rested simply on the right of possession (*derecho posesorio* or *tierra por razón de pueblo*), since the original allotments of mission lands were not recorded. Over time, additional properties had been acquired by the Jesuits (through purchase and donation); in some missions, cofradías came into possession of small ranches, sometimes donated by vecinos or other Indians. Church ornaments and furnishings had been supplied initially by the crown and the Jesuit order; over time the Jesuits, vecinos, and Indians had added others. Indian labor had contributed to the assets acquired by the missionaries. Did all the properties belong to the church or to the community? What things could the Jesuits sell or take when they left?

Disagreement over the answers to these questions proved to be one of the sticking points that delayed the secularization process for nearly two years, as diocesan and Jesuit authorities looked for precedents that might maximize their economic advantage. Never mind that "the Indians deemed everything in the missions to be theirs," as Father Carta noted.[13] He also observed that they were particularly attached to the church ornaments, like statues of their patron saints. After protracted negotiation, it was resolved that the Jesuits would discharge any mission debts that existed through the sale of grain, livestock, or land that was not part of the fundo legal.[14] If lands or livestock purchased by the Jesuits were left over after settling debts, the Jesuits could keep or sell them. They could also take what animals were necessary to transport themselves and their personal property (clothing and books) to the next post. Everything else, including enough grain to support a parish priest until the next growing season, would remain in the mission. This included church furnishings, household objects, and farm tools and equipment. The reckoning of mission accounts finally began in 1753. Even by pooling their assets, the Topia missionaries were barely able to satisfy their creditors. But from the Tepehuan and Tarahumara Baja missions, the Jesuits were able to send several hundred head of cattle to their colegios in Durango, Parral, and Chihuahua. A number of small ranches were transferred to colegios, and the large grazing tract near Santa Catalina was sold.[15]

The negotiations over these matters had confirmed the bishop's fears that the diocese was acquiring a liability. So he was not too disquieted by the Jesuits' attempt to delay the transfer until they received assurances that these stipends would be reassigned to found missions in Alta California. When this was not forthcoming, the order took advantage of the recent Pima Indian uprising in Sonora to raise the specter of possible Indian insurrection in the areas to be transferred. Despite these machinations, in early January 1753 viceregal officials determined to proceed. Neither the Jesuits nor the bishop dared refuse.[16]

As both sides prepared to execute the transfer formally, Sánchez de Tagle advised the secular clerics named to the new parishes (eight in Tepehuana/Tarahumara Baja and six in Topia) how to proceed. The parish boundaries had been drawn wherever possible to include Spanish settlements with vecinos who would be able to pay fees and other ecclesiastical taxes. The bishop reiterated his determination regarding mission properties and explained that the clerics would need to subsist on mission produce and sacramental fees collected from vecinos until they could gradually begin to charge fees or otherwise extract resources from the Indians. The key was to get the natives to work their fields. This would be a difficult task, he argued, because the Indians were naturally lazy and duplicitous; the priests would need to coax their new parishioners so as to avoid riots and flight from the missions.[17]

The Jesuit surrender of the missions began in August 1753 after rains had begun to end the drought. Ironically, the only unrest that erupted during the transfer came at the very beginning, in the oldest of the missions. Once again the protest came from Santiago Papasquiaro, where the Tepehuanes were not intimidated by the ceremonial spectacle that had been devised by the authorities to effect the transfer from Jesuit to secular authority. Present were the bishop's representative, Bachiller Don Juan Joseph de Ochoa y Herive, the new cleric assigned to the pueblo, Felipe de León y Muñoz, Jesuit visitor Carta, the missionary Antonio de los Ríos, and the alcalde mayor of the Valle de Santiago Papasquiaro. Padre Carta later reported that as these dignitaries gathered in front of the church, men and women, young and old, began to wail and shout that they did not want a new priest. They begged the authorities to let Padre de los Ríos stay. The protest went on for three days, during which the new cura was sent off to wait at a nearby ranch and Father Carta attempted to negotiate with the Tepehuan governor and his lieutenants, whom he later characterized as "shameless and obstinate." Fearing that their discontent could spread to other missions, the visitor worked with Padre de los Ríos to reassure them that they would be well treated under the new arrangement. He sweetened the bargain by giving them 50 head of cattle for fiestas that he had planned to send to the Colegio de Durango's Hacienda de la Punta. In his letter to Father Balthasar, Carta professed befuddlement over the "cantankerous" behavior of these "most domesticated, pious, devoted souls who showed such adoration for novenas, processions, mass, and even confession."[18] To the modern observer, the answer to the father visitor's conundrum seems rather plain: they had embraced the Spanish system to advance their concerns and needs.[19] Acculturated and probably sincerely Christian, these Tepehuanes shrewdly stepped into the brokering space being vacated by the missionary.

Father Carta was sufficiently concerned to request from the governor of Nueva Vizcaya a soldier escort to accompany them as they completed the circuit of the Tepehuan and lower Tarahumara missions. There were no more incidents, however. The narrative report that recorded the acts of each transfer, as the officials traveled from one mission to the next, revealed some interesting fiscal facts that had not appeared in the account books kept (often casually) in the missions. Against the rules of the order, some missionaries had loaned money rather liberally to vecinos and more affluent Indians. For example, in Tizonazo parishioners owed over a thousand pesos, and the Indian governor of San Ignacio, a visita of Huejotitlán, gave land to the Jesuits in repayment of a loan.[20] The last Tarahumara Baja mission, Satevó, was turned over to the diocese uneventfully on October 8, 1753. The transfer of the Topia missions was begun a month later, in Pueblo Nuevo, and was completed at the beginning of 1754. Indebtedness there had been reconciled by virtually stripping the missions of assets. In the rugged terrain of the eastern sierra, the arable lands that remained as part of the fundo legal would become the focus of protracted disputes. Here the diocese was forced to provide stipends for most of the new curacies because the income from non-Indian parishioners was inadequate to support them.[21]

Governor Mateo Antonio de Mendoza reported to the king in May 1754 that the missions had been successfully turned over to the diocesan clergy, despite fears of unrest. A few months later, Viceroy Revillagigedo referred to this accomplishment in his instructions to his successor. The key to "civilizing" Indians in the north was to integrate them with Spaniards. If they had not been isolated in missions for so long, they would have been disciplined and subordinated much earlier.[22] The viceroy had taken his cues from financial and military advisers who had been pressing to end the mission and presidio drain on viceregal resources, contemplating the secularization of all the Jesuit and Franciscan missions in the north. In February 1753, five presidios in eastern Nueva Vizcaya—Mapimí, El Gallo, Cerrogordo, Valle de San Bartolomé, and San Francisco de los Conchos—were abolished, to be replaced by one mobile squadron.[23]

To what extent did secularization have the desired effect of making the Indians more exploitable? Living in close proximity to Spaniards did not of course necessarily make indigenous peoples more subservient, as the community of Santiago Papasquiaro was about to prove once again. Bishop Sánchez de Tagle believed that the village's first delegation to the viceroy had been motivated by the vecinos and that the Jesuits had encouraged the second. The Tepehuan protest at the time of secularization had garnered some rewards, but not enough to keep them from appealing to the viceroy again in 1754.[24]

On this occasion, three village officials, Lorenzo Madueño, Cristóbal de Estrada, and Tomás Basilio de la Cruz, solicited the return of the former missionary, Antonio de los Ríos, who was now serving in the Jesuit residence at Parras. Claiming that they had not heard one sermon preached in Santiago Papasquiaro since the padre left, they offered to provide land to found a colegio so that he could come back. They claimed that he had treated them with charity for over twenty years and was still sending aid to widows and orphans in the village. This was a far cry from the beatings they were getting from the new priest. The viceroy responded that he would direct the bishop to look into the situation and rectify any wrongdoing. His letter to the bishop, however, reveals that he was not convinced of the Indians' sincerity or forthrightness. In his probing to discern a hidden agenda, he argued that even under Jesuit tutelage Nueva Vizcayan indigenous groups had demonstrated twisted and depraved intentions. Yet he dismissed the possibility that the Jesuits were behind their machinations, attributing this instead to the pernicious influence of vecinos. He was most suspicious of the Tepehuanes' offer to found a colegio. How could they afford this now, when they had purported only a short time before to be too poor to support a priest?[25] Nonetheless, he urged the bishop to investigate their claims.

Diocesan officials sought information from the alcalde mayor of the Valle de Santiago Papasquiaro, Joaquín de Echeverría. A native of the valley, Echeverría responded that the strongest impulse for the latest petition had probably come from poor vecinos who had also benefited from the charity and gift giving of Padre de los Ríos. The main issue was not spiritual relief, because the parish priest had actually hired an Augustinian friar to preach in the village. The alcalde mayor did not believe that the Tepehuanes even with support from the vecinos could support a colegio, since they had to work on their own plots six days a week just to maintain themselves. He deemed the Indians to be sincere in seeking the temporal assistance that the Jesuits had provided but the secular clerics could not. He surmised (seemingly ingenuously) that another reason for the petition was that the padre had been at least partially effective in limiting the repartimiento drafts from the village.[26] Despite the alcalde mayor's surprisingly judicious assessment, the bishop decided to ignore the Tepehuan complaints, arguing that the small number of Indian families rendered the situation inconsequential. Most of the pueblo's residents were Spaniards, mestizos, and mulattoes, and there was no shortage of space for vecino ranchers to build their townhouses in the villages. Bishop Sánchez de Tagle was more inclined to see the hand of Padre de los Ríos in all of this; the quick and dirty solution would be to get the Jesuit posted far away from Santiago Papasquiaro.[27]

In the aftermath of secularization, the Tepehuanes were more inclined to make use of Spanish structures to protect themselves. Since the seventeenth-century rebellions, the Spaniards had endeavored to assign native military leaders who were loyal to the Spaniards to carry out periodic inspections of the Tepehuan and Tarahumara countryside. This was part of the overall Spanish strategy of trying to impose a manipulable centralized hierarchy where none had existed before. In the eighteenth century, a Tarahumara "governor-general" came to dominate this function for the entire region. This scheme enjoyed limited success during the mission period, but efforts to tribalize seem to have born fruit later, aiding the small surviving indigenous populations of the new parishes to act in concert. In 1754 Tepehuanes from several villages (the former missions and two remaining Tepehuan missions of Navogame and Baborigame) demanded their own governor-general, arguing that they were not well served by the Tarahumaras. As the Spanish saw it, neither were the Tarahumaras fond of their former enemies: "It is a rare and stoic Tarahumara who will tolerate the indolence of the Tepehuanes."[28] Two jurisdictions were constituted, but the Tepehuanes were not happy with the choice of Tepehuan general. In November they petitioned the viceroy to substitute Marcos de la Cruz for Don Diego de Ardiola, who was not a native. "He is mulatto and not of Tepehuan origin. We are not Spaniards but of Tepehuan and Xixime lineages."[29] The use of *linaje* here is new. The other official position that had authority over the entire Tepehuan group was the *protector de indios de la nación tepehuana*. This office had metamorphosed unevenly in northern Mexico. While it became an avenue for legal redress in New Mexico, especially regarding land claims, in Nueva Vizcaya the protector was associated, at least until the late eighteenth century, with a military function: assuring that indigenous peoples were peacefully settled in villages. That is why the office was usually exercised by presidial captains, who used its power to keep Indians in compliance with Spanish demands and even to appropriate Indian labor and lands for themselves.[30] The Tepehuanes did not use this official to broker their legal representations to the viceroy.

Although the Tepehuan indigenous communities—especially Santiago Papasquiaro—were undeniably more prompt and vocal in articulating their concerns about the damage that secularization could bring, Indians in the other new parishes soon experienced the intense competition for their labor and land that was unleashed by the process. This was especially true in the old Tarahumara Baja missions. Only two weeks after Satevó was turned over to the parish priest, Miguel Fernández de Sierra, local officials called for implementation of the 1746 viceregal order that mandated the establishment of siembras de comunidad.[31] The corregidor of Chihuahua had attempted to impose the law even while Satevó was still a mission, but Padre Lázaro Franco was successful in getting the order suspended until the secularization process was completed. He was aware of the damage that had already been done to nearby Franciscan missions when the corregidor of Chihuahua, Antonio Gutiérrez de Noriega, sent his lieutenants in 1752 to implement it in Santa Isabel, Guadalupe, and Chuviscar. The corregidor reported to the viceroy in July that although the Franciscans had rich fields in these missions, the Concho Indians were not receiving any benefits. They were actually seeking repartimiento service, he said, because this was the only way to assure their subsistence.[32]

But the Franciscan response indicates that this situation was a result of the disruptions provoked by the corregidor's actions. First he had pressured the Franciscans to secularize the missions; when they resisted, he appointed overseers to direct communal plantings and allocate repartimientos. The activities of these mayordomos immediately provoked a series of conflicts. Which of the lands customarily used by the mission Indians would be incorporated in their half-league allotment? The answer was almost always the tracts with the poorest access to water. In Santa Isabel, the governor, Don Lucas Ceballos, was forced to assign the best parcels to several members of the overseer's family. Francisco Jaques and his brothers also allowed their cattle to graze freely on the pastures of the Chuviscar mission. They inflated the rolls of available workers to be able to draft more than half of the able-bodied men from the villages at a time, a lucrative endeavor since they received a kickback from the Spanish employers for each Indian supplied. They forced some of the workers from the Guadalupe mission to travel through hostile Indian areas. Most of the drafts lasted for well over the prescribed month.[33]

Jaques had also been imposing onerous labor requirements on the Jesuit mission of Satevó, but he was only able to effect changes in land tenure after the mission became a parish. His first action was to assign lands that the priest had earmarked for his upkeep to a maestro appointed to teach Spanish and other basics. Jaques also allotted irrigable lands and the flour mill to the communal holdings, evoking another protest from the parish priest as he saw his subsistence base shrink. The priest argued that without the mill and sufficient cropland he could not support his relatives.[34] Attempts to negotiate this conflict ensued in a series of communications between ecclesiastical and civilian personnel, who ignored or omitted comment by the indigenous communities. The corregidor argued that he could not disregard royal provisions for communal plantings, but he offered to allow the parish priest one-third of the proceeds from the production of the communal lands.[35] The bishop replied that this amount would be insufficient to support parish priests, who were not allowed to charge fees for sacraments in the new parishes. He charged that the corregidor's assistants would be the main beneficiaries of village resources, abusing both the Indians and the priests. The prelate discounted the corregidor's examples of successfully functioning communal distributions in Franciscan missions where maestros had been placed. These were not comparable, he argued, since the friars were receiving stipends.

Through several more rounds of information gathering and veiled threats, it became clear that not everyone could have his need (or greed) satisfied. The bishop finally conceded that priests were going to have to receive some funds from the diocesan tithe as a direct subsidy, but not before he made several efforts to intimidate the corregidor by reminding him of his duty to serve the general good and avoid unrest. By giving too much land to his lieutenants and the maestros and by exacting heavy repartimiento drafts, he said, the corregidor was provoking discontent and unrest in the villages. The Indians might react aggressively, and the parish priests would be ill equipped to quell trouble, since their authority was already being undermined by the corregidor. The bishop could not promise that the priests would be willing to stay in the villages, and he vowed he would hold the civil official responsible if they should leave. This prophecy proved true within a few years in a number of the new parishes, where curas were not able to derive the income they deemed to be sufficient either through the direct acquisition of landed property or by charging fees.[36] And it had not been easy to find enough clerics to fill the new posts in the first place, since the relatively smaller number of priests in the north sought the more coveted posts in urban and mining areas.[37]

Undaunted by the bishop's admonitions, in June 1755 the *justicia mayor/* chief magistrate of Ciénaga de los Olivos, another area of former Tarahumara missions, called for the implementation of the 1746 viceregal order.[38] Diego de Mendía ordered that siembras de comunidad be established in Santa Cruz, Santa María de las Cuevas, and Huejotitlán, once again threatening the livelihood of the parish priests, who proceeded to pepper the bishop with requests to intervene. They had already been trying for nearly two years to survive without sufficient income because they purported to realize how crucial it was to show compassion to the Indians by not charging fees. They estimated that the fees paid by vecinos covered only about a third of their costs; it was imperative that they have access to some of the village lands. Finally, they argued that where the practice of communal plantings had been implemented, Indians had suffered aggravations from vecinos, frequently prompting them to flee.[39]

On this occasion, the bishop decided to take the case to the governor of Nueva Vizcaya, Antonio de Mendoza. Having determined that it was futile to try to stop the actions of local officials in relation to the siembras de comunidad, he attacked them from a different angle by citing their egregious violations of the laws regarding the distribution and functioning of repartimientos. Local officials drafted far more than the one-third of workers allowed to leave the village at one time, and they let their employers keep them for months at a time. Sometimes there were no Indians in the towns at all. The natives could not plant their own fields, nor were they receiving religious instruction. Bishop Sánchez de Tagle went on to address the problem of subsistence for the priests and asked the governor to contribute stipends for them.[40]

More aggressive measures by local officials also characterized other areas of the Sierra Tarahumara where Jesuits remained in control of missions. The missionaries frequently protested interference from civil authorities in the selection of Indian governors and in the distribution of the profits from the común. Nor were the missionaries being given sufficient backup to make Indian officials enforce prohibitions against gambling, drinking, and unauthorized ritual celebrations. The Jesuits also complained that repartimiento drafts were escalating to unconscionable proportions, making new Tarahumara conversions difficult. "The older gentiles refuse baptism on the pretext of their advanced age arguing that they are no longer capable of hard labor, while the younger ones try to avoid settlement in missions by promising to be baptized when they are old."[41]

Although secularization in the Tepehuana and Tarahumara Baja province made Indian lands more vulnerable to encroachments from outsiders, the main initial threat was the increase in number and frequency of repartimientos. In Topia, the relatively small indigenous population also faced labor demands, but the most serious challenges for the reduced native communities that remained had to do with land. As we have seen, the topography of most of the missions severely limited the extent of lands suitable for cultivation or even grazing. Many of the missions had steadily lost land since the end of the mining boom in the seventeenth century. And since virtually none of the villages held title to the fundo legal but rather claimed the land through customary rights of possession (*derecho posesorio de buena fe*), it was not difficult for the larger vecino population to get access to it once the Jesuits were gone. The most common device for acquiring land was to claim that it was vacant or not being used. Because hunting and gathering activities were common in this mountainous area, it was not unusual for Indians to be away from their plots of land rather frequently. In the absence of a missionary who was familiar with these patterns, it was less troublesome for outsiders to lay claims on plots of land or for poor neighbors to squat on them. Vecinos quickly came to control cofradía livestock and small ranches where they existed. But most of the vecinos were needy themselves, explaining why several of the new parishes (Pueblo Nuevo, Guarisamey, and Otaez) had to receive a supplementary stipend from the bishop.[42]

The diocese of Durango had been ill equipped both financially and in terms of personnel to take on its new responsibilities. Most of the new priests had never participated in competitions for vacant parochial benefices, having served as unbeneficed assistants to curas.[43] Very few of the new priests had administered rural or Indian parishes, although two of them, Miguel Cano in Guarisamey and Juan Delgado in Santa Cruz, were reported by the bishop to be indigenous themselves (*de calidad indio*). Cano ministered to about 200 Indians of Xixime and Tepehuan descent in an area removed from Spanish towns. Delgado was placed in Santa Cruz, where the Tarahumaras numbered over 600. Whatever his specific ethnic background, Delgado was not well regarded by his charges, who in 1756 accused him of mistreating them and charging fees. In the Tarahumara parishes, priests were somewhat startled to discover that the Indians were not sufficiently prepared to take communion. In some cases, the clergy worked with the maestros to train the brightest children, who could in turn teach Spanish and catechism in their respective home pueblos. In his report of 1755 on the state of the diocese, Sánchez de Tagle revealed that many of the priests in the new parishes were old or infirm. Not surprisingly, by 1762 two-thirds of the new posts were vacant.[44]

The difficulties in sustaining the new parishes derived in some cases from lack of indigenous cooperation with the curas, but the primary reason was the church's intense competition with vecinos for scarce resources. In 1760 Governor Mendoza sent a list of complaints to Sánchez de Tagle's successor, Bishop Pedro Tamarón y Romeral, blaming the parish priests in the secularized missions for causing unrest by contradicting the orders of civil officials and mistreating Indians. He accused them of forcing the natives to provide personal service, denying them access to water and land, and not giving them enough time to tend their own fields. He singled out Salvador de Ibarguen in Huejotitlán and Joseph de Molinar in San Francisco de los Conchos as particularly exploitative.[45] The complaints of curas about the abusive behavior of local officials were just as frequent, citing their manipulation of Indian governors and demands for personal service. The priests attributed significant absenteeism and flight by Indians to secular officials and vecinos. In Satevó, where the governor denied a request by the justicia mayor, Matías de Dorsal, to furnish servants daily to his house, the official had him flogged.[46]

Increased friction between ecclesiastical and civil officials was only one manifestation of disquiet and ferment. The decade after secularization was also characterized by heightened volatility in population movements, by the escalation of lawsuits over land in the more acculturated areas, and by the increased use of repartimiento in the eastern Tarahumara area, where sizable indigenous populations still existed. The non-Indian population in Nueva Vizcaya grew rapidly after surpassing the indigenous population in numbers at midcentury. While the indigenous population stabilized or declined very slightly in the next fifty years, non-Indians came to outnumber natives by more than two to one (see Figure 2).[47]

The influx of Spaniards and castas into central and western Chihuahua in the 1750s brought heightened pressures to the Tarahumaras in parishes and the missions of the upper or western Tarahumara. Indian labor was in greater demand, and land became more valuable to outsiders. At the same time, increased raiding by Apaches brought another kind of strain, as live-stock belonging to Indian communities was targeted along with the herds of Spanish ranchers.[48] The Tarahumaras tended to practice two kinds of resistance to these threats. They continued to use the time-honored tactics of foot-dragging, pilfering, and frequent absences from their villages, provoking this characterization by Father Blas de la Palma: "after thirty years of administering them, I find them ever more rebellious and disobedient; this is especially the case of young men, who are always running off with women who aren't their wives to get drunk and cause trouble." Another missionary noted that the Tarahumaras didn't seem to care much about Christianity until they were dying, and then they usually asked to confess. He cited the case of one "Chepe Tonto" who was inclined to theft. When he was scolded for "immoral" behavior, he commonly retorted, "Let the devil take me!" But he was apparently ambivalent enough to confess his "sins" on his deathbed.[49]

Reporting on general conditions and the status of Spanish-Indian relations in Nueva Vizcaya in 1762, Captain José de Berroterán judged that the Tepehuan and Tarahumara villages were worse off than they had been thirty years earlier. The escalating Spanish presence had resulted in greater delinquency on the part of the Indians, many of whom were fugitives living in isolated barrancas, from which they staged raids and other criminal activities. The second response, then, was aggression. Berroterán believed that many sedentary Indians were operating under the umbrella of the Apaches with whom they were probably in league.[50] At least some Tarahumaras made common cause with or posed as Apaches in carrying out raids on Spanish haciendas and ranchos and sometimes even the missions themselves. The primary targets for Apaches were horses and mules that could be driven north to New Mexico and Texas to trade for buffalo meat and European goods. Cattle were also stolen, but they were more difficult to move long distances. In smaller numbers, they were more useful prey for those Tarahumaras who could find not-too-distant places of refuge to pasture them or trade them locally with other sierra groups.[51] The raiding could provide goods and certainly a preferable alternative to compliance with the Spaniards' demands for labor.

Access to horses tended to magnify the problem of unauthorized contact between indigenous groups and between Indians and others. But these contacts proliferated in urban areas as well. Yaquis who came from Sonora to work in the mines squatted in areas outside the mining camps, where they traded with other Indians and engaged in other unsupervised behavior that worried authorities (who, at the same time, did not want to impose harsh measures that might result in their flight and loss as a labor source). Repartimiento drafts themselves contributed to migratory patterns that could breed unrest. Labor gangs from the Tarahumara areas mixed with urban workers and drifters. And the desire to avoid unremitting repartimiento service resulted in a high degree of fugitivism.[52]

At the same time, even more outsiders, many of mixed race who declared themselves to be Spaniards in the parish registers, moved into the Tarahumara area to engage in mining and petty trade. Indians frequently complained to the local priest or civil officials that merchants were defrauding them, but such gouging was rarely redressed. In the old mission of San Pablo Balleza, apparently with the connivance of the alcalde mayor, a shady trader made money on the side by prostituting his Spanish wife.[53] Other threats to communities came even more directly in the form of the mayordomos or *caporales*/overseers hired to manage communal agriculture. They were commonly mulattoes or mestizos who clashed with the Indians.[54]

Where indigenous peoples did remain in villages, their lands dwindled. On the eastern borders of the old Tepehuan mission area, cattle ranchers expanded their holdings onto lands claimed by the communities of Tizonazo, Santa Cruz de Tepehuanes, and Cinco Señores. Other landowners expanded their holdings in the Valle de Santiago Papasquiaro.[55] Indians from the villages nearest Chihuahua increasingly rented out their lands. During his episcopal visita of 1765, Bishop Tamarón y Romeral commented that ladino Indians in Topia were continuously engaged in lawsuits with vecinos over scarce, arable land.[56] Two years later, in 1767, the expulsion of the Jesuits opened a new round of land disputes in the lower valleys of the Tarahumara area, as well as around San Felipe el Real de Chihuahua where the order had large ranches.[57]

Bishop Tamarón saw the solution in the disappearance of the Indians. He was frank in his appraisal of ethnicide as the key to peace and prosperity in the north. There were so few Indians left in Topia and Tepehuana and they were such bad workers; better that they should be absorbed into the racially mixed population and become vecinos. That would eliminate such nuisances as the success of the Indians of Santiago Papasquiaro in keeping Spanish vecinos, who outnumbered them by about five to one, from acquiring lots in the town and nearby acreage. His call for mestizaje was unwittingly aided by the parish priest in Santa Catalina, Juan Joseph Romano, who solicited Tepehuan women and fathered children. But the parish records for the 1750s and 1760s indicate that the process was well along by then.[58] The governor of Nueva Vizcaya was inclined to agree with the bishop that, in general, the Tepehuanes were capricious in their natural aversion to Spaniards, as well as in their irrational appetite for liberty. He believed that the Indians had extra lands that could be alienated without prejudice.[59]

Notwithstanding the bishop's desires to make Indians into Spaniards in Tepehuana, the first of the former missions to be officially converted into a Spanish town was in the old Topia province. In 1778 the fundo legal of San Ignacio de Piaxtla was divided into *solares*/lots. Any remaining Indians became tribute payers by fiat. Officials had complained that the non-Indian residents of the town were claiming Indian status to avoid paying taxes. When tribute collection was imposed, they changed their tune, paving the way for the metamorphosis of the pueblo into a Spanish town. The more affluent residents raised livestock and produced some sugar and *chiles negros* on holdings outside of town.[60]

Local authorities did attempt to collect tribute from Indians in San Ignacio's former visita pueblos, but they, along with the few tributary Indians remaining in the other Topia villages, tried to evade this payment. Some hired themselves out to vecinos; others fled to steep ravines where they struggled to plant corn; and several claimed cacique status. This prompted some officials to recommend that they might achieve better results by forcing the Indians to work in repartimiento.[61] Scarcity continued to characterize much of the region, perhaps explaining why a prophet who appeared in the former missions in 1771 attracted the attention of locals. An Indian from Tlaxcala, calling himself José Carlos Quinto, king of the Indians ("rey de los naturales"), attempted to extort money, grain, and horses from the Indian elders of San Juan, Santa Apolonia, and San Gerónimo de Ahoya. He told them that they should disobey repartimiento orders and refuse to allow Spaniards in their villages. Although he apparently touched a chord, if we are to judge by the villagers' favorable reception of this purported king and his entourage, he was quickly apprehended and tried by the authorities.[62] As the Indian population of the former Topia visitas continued to decline, royal officials approved their consolidation into one village.[63]

In the 1770s Apache and other Indian raids multiplied, targeting Spanish haciendas and ranchos and Indian villages as far south as Santiago Papasquiaro. The missions of the upper Tarahumara were particularly easy targets for a number of years after the expulsion of the Jesuits, as royal officials were scarcely able to provide overseers for their former properties. Raiding forced the abandonment of many Franciscan missions. Bachíniva, for example, had only a few Indians who planted in the center of the village to better protect the fields against attacks by Suma and Gileño Apaches, but soils there were being depleted. A 1777 report on Indian hostilities counted 116 abandoned ranches and haciendas in Nueva Vizcaya, nearly all in areas to the west and north of Chihuahua. Although most of the perpetrators were reported to be Apaches, there was evidence of the involvement of other groups, including not only Tarahumaras but also Indians from Tizonazo. At the same time, many Indians from the former missions had become auxiliary troops in the Spanish struggle to subdue the Apaches.[64]

The Franciscans who had taken over the upper Tarahumara missions reported significant instability in the region.

> The Tarahumara move continuously between pueblos and to Spanish haciendas, where they sometimes work for long periods or switch from one to another. They also go to the mining towns, where they receive neither catechism nor holy sacraments, and where they don't have to worry about proper behavior or whether the women they take with them are theirs or others'. . . . And they do all of this simply to enjoy complete freedom.

The Franciscans argued that the Tarahumaras were protected in their mobility by their own governors, Spanish officials, and employers who were benefiting in different ways from their labor, which was poorly paid.[65] Royal officials ordered a military sweep of the area in 1787 to apprehend fugitive Tarahumaras. Some of the 148 captives were returned to their villages; others were incarcerated; and a number were sent in chain gangs to Chihuahua textile shops (*obrajes*) and northern haciendas.[66]

The indigenous population in the pueblos continued to dwindle.[67] But as the non-Indian population expanded and generated more economic enterprise in Nueva Vizcaya in the last quarter of the century, the demand for this shrinking labor pool rose. Repartimiento continued to be a major mechanism for meeting it, even at this late date. In 1777 Governor Felipe Barri tried to halt what he believed to be egregious abuses in the allocation of repartimientos to hacendados and miners by reserving the right to assign them exclusively to himself, on pain of fine of five hundred pesos.[68] Franciscans in the missions nearest Chihuahua reported that the repartimiento drafts were so continuous that these, along with Apache depredations, kept the indigenous Concho and Tarahumara residents from being able to plant their crops. As a result, many of them rented out their lands to vecinos, not only because of their forced absences but also because they lacked oxen and equipment for plowing. In addition, vecinos often got the lion's share of water that was to be distributed to both the pueblo and surrounding farmers. Most of the corn and beans harvested by the Indians was destined for consumption within the pueblo; these commodities were rarely sold in the markets of Chihuahua as they had been earlier. By 1778 there were no siembras de comunidad in the Franciscan pueblos.[69]

In 1790 the crown ordered Diego de Borica to undertake a general visita of the intendancy of Durango (which comprehended the present-day states of Durango and Chihuahua). Of the forty-two pueblos de indios in the intendancy, less than half were former Jesuit mission sites. The visitor found that a majority of Tarahumara and Concho Indians were absent from their pueblos, either working for Spaniards or gathering food. Priests, who were not carrying out their spiritual duties, routinely compelled Indians to work in their fields (land that they had appropriated illegally, according to Borica) and transport goods without compensation. The visitor also discovered that many repartimiento Indians were not being paid by their Spanish employers. Tarahumara Indians were frequently forced to work in Chihuahua obrajes, as well as in the draining of flooded mine shafts in Cusihuiriachi. All of these abuses were attributable, he noted, to the vagabondage of mixed-race workers.[70] In the expanding agricultural and mining economy of Durango and Chihuahua, demographic stability was still an illusion at the end of the eighteenth century.[71] Between midcentury (when the number of non-Indians overtook that of Indians) and 1803, when another census was taken, the overall population quadrupled, but by the last decade of the eighteenth century the indigenous sector had dwindled to less than a third of the total.[72]

In 1792, over half of the Indian parishes of Nueva Vizcaya were without a priest.[73] In a marked departure from the opinion of the first Conde de Revillagigedo to serve as viceroy, the second viceroy Revillagigedo argued in 1793 that the secular clergy had not proved capable administrators of the former missions, although he did believe that good Spanish families could provide a salutary example in Indian pueblos. As supervisors, however, only the clergy belonging to religious orders seemed able to deal with the Indians, who were "fickle, ungrateful, cowardly, vengeful, unambitious, and inclined to idleness and theft."[74] With the benefit of hindsight and from multiple perspectives, a different analysis can be offered.

CONCLUSIONS

The frontier, a recurrent theme in world history, has frequently been featured as the crucible in which the so-called civilized and savage have come into contact, collided, and transformed one another. What is often silenced or simply unchronicled is the mutations they have undergone, which are far more dialogical and complex than most analysts realize (or than historical protagonists may have intended). The theme conventionally advanced by students of premodern societies, and certainly plausible, is that "barbarians" such as Mongols and Goths were absorbed by the civilized centers but infused a kind of ill-defined vigor into the decadent aesthetes of these centers.[1] With the expansion of Europe into the Americas, this truism took a somewhat different form. Europeans could understand and adapt to the sedentary peoples they met and rapidly conquered, as could the sedentary peoples to them. Thus the old relationships between peasants and cities, between tribute payers and consumers of luxury goods, continued under new leadership. Conversely, it has been generally accepted that where Europeans met semisedentaries or nomads, such mutual cultural understandings and recognitions failed on both sides. The early result was endemic warfare. In the long run, the invaded peoples disappeared, were expelled beyond the new frontiers established by the invaders, or were herded onto reservations.

Defiance and Deference has attempted to show that while such a schema may be broadly true, it fails when applied to specific historical and cultural contexts. In Nueva Vizcaya some peoples disappeared early, others survived until somewhat later, and still others stubbornly refuse to succumb even today. In the third quarter of the eighteenth century, the situation of the five groups studied here was very mixed. How, in fact, did they identify and how had they fared through conditions of conquest and colonialism? We have seen that both disease and the heavy demand for labor in a silver-mining economy had the potential to destructure and destroy these indigenous societies. How or why did this potential vary within and between discrete groups? By this time there were only a few thousand people who identified as Acaxee, Xixime, and Concho, and they disappeared as recognized ethnic identities in the nineteenth century. Approximately 3,000 Tepehuanes and Tarahumaras remained in the area of the former Tepehuana/Tarahumara Baja province of the Jesuits, perhaps 4 percent of their sixteenth-century numbers. These communities were already mixed ethnically, but in the nineteenth century most lost their status or identification as Indian pueblos. In addition, there were perhaps 25,000 Tarahumaras and a few thousand Tepehuanes living in western Chihuahua, where some had loose attachments to missions while most lived in dispersed rancherías.

In the nineteenth century, most of the former Tarahumara Alta missions of the Papigochi valley became mestizo communities, but the rancheria peoples and some pueblos preserved their separate ethnicity into the twentieth century, as did Tepehuanes in the corners of southwestern Chihuahua and northwestern Durango. The key to the persistence of these Rarámuri and Odame (as the Tarahumaras and Tepehuanes call themselves today) lies in their retreat from Spanish strongholds to these marginal areas in the Sierra Madre after their seventeenth-century rebellions were suppressed. Relative isolation until the late nineteenth century was crucial to preserving the separate ethnic status (*etnia*) that each has today. Yet these are not the indigenous peoples whose history is detailed in this book.[2] Why did some Tepehuanes and Tarahumaras have the option of isolation while others did not? What colonial factors help to explain the incorporation of the latter into the larger society in the nineteenth century and that of their Acaxee, Xixime, and Concho neighbors even earlier?

Preconquest organizational structure provides some clues, although not in the way that might have been predicted by models mentioned in the introduction. The most sedentary groups, the Acaxees and Xiximes, might have been expected to have had greater potential for maintaining social and economic boundaries against outsiders. Yet they were the first to succumb. Returning to the concept of mediated opportunism, we can see that part of the answer lies in the endemic intertribal warfare that characterized the entire northern region. These groups were the earliest of the groups studied here to be contacted by Spaniards, who were ruthless in their search for laborers to extract the silver they had discovered in the western sierras. Not only were the Acaxees and Xiximes traditional enemies, unlikely to join forces in the face of Spanish intrusions, but the Spaniards had little trouble in recruiting allies from antagonistic groups. And the antagonistic relations among these groups had other negative consequences. Their high, fortress-like structures had proved a powerful deterrent against surrounding indigenous groups with similar weapons and military tactics, but were not very effective against Spanish arms. Even more deadly than Spanish military force was epidemic disease, which affected these groups before it reached those on the other side of the sierra divide. In the Acaxee and Xixime settlements, which were more concentrated and had smaller overall populations than those of their eastern counterparts, smallpox and other diseases spread more rapidly, producing a higher, earlier mortality and probably a greater decimation of native elites.

Coming on top of massive deaths from epidemics, other factors inhibited population recovery of Acaxees and Xiximes. Slaughter in the combat they initiated to resist the Spanish intrusion, the terrible conditions of forced labor, and continued disease cycles reduced their numbers to levels that deterred recuperation in the long run. When the native birth rate rose slightly in the mid-eighteenth century, these groups had already been swamped by outsiders and interracial mixing was well under way. Indigenous peoples had been displaced from their once productive agriculture in warm canyon bottoms to marginal farming areas near the mines. They supplemented the meager produce of their milpas by working in the depressed non-Indian economy and gathering the fruits of the forest. Cofradías and Christian festivals supplanted native ritual, but a few vestiges survived through petty witchcraft. These selective adjustments to an altered physical and cultural environment were not enough, in the case of the Acaxees and Xiximes, for them to overcome the biological or reproductive barriers to recuperation. The early high death tolls resulted from factors both endogenous and exogenous to native societies: warfare and disease. They mediated against a cultural hybridity in which indigenous elements could predominate. Instead, they facilitated the transformation of these Indians into mestizos whose daily lives were not much different from those of their poor Spanish neighbors in a fragile ecosystem disrupted by mining, its decline, and subsequent grazing.

Meanwhile, the more dispersed Conchos in eastern Chihuahua, who were much less cohesive as a social unit, had also been contacted early, but the responses of discrete groups or bands of them were much more mixed than those of the Acaxees and Xiximes. Some fled to the north and east, while others raided and pilfered Spanish livestock in southeast-ern Chihuahua. Yet as a result of Spanish slave-raiding expeditions, some Concho bands became part of the labor force in haciendas and mines. And Concho social organization lent itself to encomienda service when caciques, or seemingly paramount chiefs of smaller groups, served as labor brokers. Over time some Concho groups settled in missions and Spanish centers (where diseases also took their toll) and furnished auxiliary troops to Spaniards, while many others formed shifting relationships with other eastern tribes, often in opposition to the Europeans. These less obliging natives enhanced their mobility by adopting the horse. In the end, neither accommodation nor armed resistance (both of which lacked cohesion and coordination) proved effective against the slow but constant decimating force of Spanish institutions and military power. Within this group, the subsistence strategies chosen in the face of Spanish invasion were the most diverse, primarily because the Concho bands did not perceive themselves as ethnically bound to a larger entity. In the case of the Conchos, this frailty of communal or ritual bonds and broader support networks worked to limit the benefits of their selective and inventive accommodations to colonial intrusion. The Spanish tactic of divide and rule effectively medi-ated against their considerable cultural creativity.

Tepehuanes, between the previous groups on the continuum of popula-tion concentration, proved to be more effective earlier in resisting Spanish intrusions, but even their more serious rebellion of 1616, which counted on substantial cohesiveness and martial ability, could not eject the invaders. With hindsight, we can see that this was a decisive moment for Tepehuan ethnicity, which persisted largely through the peoples who chose and were able to remove themselves from the Spanish orbit by taking their live-stock to remote locations of the Sierra Madre in the southwestern corner of Chihuahua and northwestern Durango. From this moment of destruc-tion, these Tepehuanes worked to rebuild their society by incorporating some elements of Spanish material and religious culture, while at the same time evolving barriers to counter penetration by non-Indians. In this case, as with the Tarahumaras later, we see how the variations within frontier zones could be of immense significance. These groups took advantage of frontier areas that were less occupied by Spaniards than others, primarily because of their unfriendly physical environments and extreme margin-ality to Spanish interests.[3]

Less than 2,000 Tepehuanes remained in the missions of the Spanish heartland after the rebellion, and they continued to succumb to disease and other Spanish pressures over time. The reduced group of Tepehuanes, however, tended to be less accommodating than nearby Tarahumaras, who were more apt to provide voluntary labor service to Spaniards for remuneration in trade goods. Tepehuanes were seen by Spanish officials as leading troublemakers and shirkers because they were so adept at false deference and evasive tactics. They also proved to be the most skilled at using Spanish legal channels to defend their spaces after secularization. This cultural opportunism was supplemented by varied subsistence strategies that increased social differentiation within the mission pueblos. Ironically, these differences, at least in the case of Santiago Papasquiaro, were minimized in the community as it took a corporate stand against encroachments by vecinos in the later eighteenth century.

In a pueblo for which we have no written petitions authored by indigenous peoples before the 1740s, we suddenly find Tepehuanes themselves using Spanish legal instruments. Their abrupt assertion of a sophisticated understanding of corporate forms of redress is not so incongruous when we consider their deeply rooted yet ambivalent relations with missionaries. They had been reasonably successful over time at supplementing their own foot-dragging tactics by using the Jesuits as buffers and brokers in certain situations. Their voices had been muted in the semidespotic missionary regime and mostly kept out of the written record, but their actions had consistently negated any suggestion that they were silent pawns of the system.

In terms of ethnicity and identity, the Tepehuan común was not exclusively Tepehuan but also incorporated other ethnic groups, most notably Xiximes and also mixed-race conjugal partners of the mission Indians. Varied subsistence and resistance strategies had increased both ethnic and social differentiation, but these differences were minimized in the corporate community that identified itself as Indian and Christian. This identity facilitated their ability to take advantage of laws that would hinder further encroachments, not only from elite vecinos, but even from the growing numbers of more marginal non-Indians who did not look so different from themselves. At the same time, the unions between the lower-status groups, still racially different but culturally similar, multiplied and folded outsiders into the corporate community.

In the case of Santiago Papasquiaro these "Indians" successfully maneuvered to control former mission lands and precious water for the next seventy-five years. They also assumed control (without official transfer of title) of an adjacent property to the north called simply the "Hacienda." This farm and mill had been assembled from parcels purchased by or donated to the Jesuits in the late seventeenth century and thus belonged to a class of mission property whose ownership was nebulous. Legal maneuvers in the 1820s by the citizens of the surrounding valley, in a curious twist of history, succeeded in wresting control of the hacienda's irrigated fields and pastures from the "antes llamado indios" (peoples formerly known as Indians).[4] Their victory resulted largely from a quirk of historical memory, the recollection that the Jesuits had been suddenly and forcibly expelled from Santiago Papasquiaro in 1767, rather than having voluntarily ceded the mission to diocesan control in 1753. The truth of the matter is that the Jesuits had the right to freely dispose of the property in 1753, at which time they had allowed the Indians to come into de facto possession of it. But as a result of this historical "misremembering," the "Hacienda" became classified as part of the Jesuit properties/*temporalidades* that had come under the control of the crown and by extension the Mexican state, making it subject to auction. By this time, the Tepehuanes of Santiago Papasquiaro were much more divided by local politics and income disparities. The degree to which villagers identified themselves as culturally indigenous varied widely in Santiago Papasquiaro and other former Tepehuan mission communities, but it is clear that there were far fewer "antes llamado indios."

In the case of the Tarahumaras, their early rebellions also proved to be a watershed in determining ethnicity and identity. Although they had established a pattern of migration toward the west and north even before the arrival of the Spaniards, the events of the 1690s solidified the tendency of some to claim spaces deeper in the sierra and more clearly detached from areas of interethnic and intercultural antagonism. This process did not mean complete isolation, because western Tarahumaras mixed with and incorporated other sierra groups, including Pimas and Guarijíos, in the late seventeenth and early eighteenth centuries. Later they participated in multiethnic raiding bands. At the same time, western Tarahumara ethnogenesis followed a cultural path that increasingly drew moral boundaries between themselves and non-Indian outsiders. New patterns of transhumance that combined agriculture, sheep raising, hunting, and gathering modified gender responsibilities and provided subsistence. The shared cultural memories that evolved in their greater isolation from Spanish society provided moral and social cohesion in the absence of strong communal bonds.

The responses of the eastern Tarahumaras, where Spanish penetration was greater, both in productive enterprises and force, could not be the same, and their options for accommodation and resistance produced different outcomes. Rates of absenteeism were very elevated in the Tarahumara Baja missions, and no doubt some of these fugitive or missing people did opt for more isolated locations, where they could use the resources of the monte. But the majority were drawn or forced into the Spanish-driven economy. Not a few observers noted that Tarahumaras in the eastern localities were often eager to barter their produce or service for Spanish trade goods, perhaps in a variation of precontact trading practices. Many traded and provided labor service in colonial centers where they mixed with other ethnic groups. In the Tarahumara Baja, influxes of ranchería-dwelling migrants periodically inflated mission populations despite epidemic disease. But loyalty to the corporate community was slow in coming. While a sense of Rarámuri identity was evolving in the western areas, the eastern Tarahumaras seem to have continued to exhibit the extreme decentralization that the invasive culture found so frustrating—in the sense that it made it more difficult for the missionaries to impose their rules through all-powerful local leaders.

Although the Jesuits in the Tarahumara Baja had more force to back them up than they did in the Tarahumara Alta, they were still complaining in the 1750s that their conversion efforts had not been very successful except among a few Indians in the cabeceras. It appears that cultural persistence among these eastern Tarahumara was less threatened by missionaries than by their experiences in Spanish work sites and population centers. As their choices in migration and mixed-subsistence strategies became more circumscribed by the growing non-Indian population and the rapid degradation of the pine and oak forests in the middle of the eighteenth century, the eastern Tarahumaras found less psychic and territorial space for developing communal resistance strategies. It is tempting to ask whether their disposition to act independently from one another in exchanges with Spaniards may have contributed to cultural erosion. At any rate, they were more and more drawn into the regional economy, sometimes voluntarily but mostly in forced labor. The missionaries were hardly able to slow their incorporation into the Spanish orbit, and the transfer accelerated markedly when the Jesuits turned the missions over to the diocese.

How, then, do we assess the role of missions in all of these transformations? To what extent did missions skew or refract the forces that we have identified as crucial in the processes of mediated opportunism: on the one hand, the cultural and environmental creativity that indigenous peoples showed in responding to Spanish invasion; on the other, the endemic warfare of the precontact period, the mortality rates produced by disease, and the (in)capacity to adjust to changes that threatened the universe as understood by native peoples?

As this study has demonstrated, missions first and foremost served Spanish interests by congregating previously dispersed populations and making them available for labor and other, lesser services. They also endeavored to answer the call to "civilize" and Christianize by propagating a new set of religious ideals and moral rules about monogamy, marriage, and property. These changes in turn destabilized autochthonous ritual practices designed to foster harmony in relations with supernatural forces and material sustenance. In the process, however, some Indians demonstrated great ingenuity in carving out spaces and benefits for themselves both within and outside the missions. As time went on, some also mixed rather freely with non-Indians in forging new social networks.

Semisedentary and nonsedentary groups used missions very selectively in Nueva Vizcaya. Mission populations were notoriously unstable, as their nominal inhabitants frequently deserted the pueblos to dodge labor regimes imposed by the missionaries. They also continued to use former ranchería locations for hunting and gathering, as well as ritual celebrations. Not only could mission residence be adjusted to suit traditional seasonal migratory patterns in mostly arid lands where gathering was as important as maize agriculture, but transhumance took a new turn with the introduction of sheep, the need for other pastures, and deforestation. Forced labor drafts also stripped mission pueblos, not only of men to work in mines and on haciendas, but also of the women and children who regularly accompanied them. These drafted workers may have left the missions involuntarily, but there were countless other mission Indians who chose to seek work on Spanish haciendas and in mines.

Many native peoples resided in the mission pueblos largely at their convenience. In the early life of the missions, Indians were often attracted to them by the promise of food for subsistence and as places for devising reorganizing strategies in the face of epidemic disease and demographic collapse. Yet nursing and spiritual consolation were not as seductive after epidemics claimed mission converts as well. In this region of intertribal warfare, some groups sought refuge from enemy Indians in the mission pueblos. Gifts of food, clothing, and metal tools also lured Indians, at least at certain times of the year, as did saints' days and other religious holidays accompanied by ritual feasting. Missions also offered opportunities for pilfering supplies and livestock. And there were situations in which nonsedentary Indian raiders who had been congregated in missions after capture continued to raid clandestinely (and in concert with non-mission Indians), using the pueblos as cover. A covert trade in livestock was a permanent feature from the seventeenth century on, but it expanded dramatically in the late eighteenth century.

At the same time, this study has not meant to suggest that none of the Nueva Vizcayan Indians lived permanently in missions. When times were good and crops were plentiful, missions had substantial core populations. Certain individuals acquired special benefits from continuous residence; the Indian officials appointed by the priests had more access to prestige and spoils, and they received kickbacks for supplying workers. Both missionaries and entrepreneurial natives sometimes used missions as petty trading centers, perhaps as substitutes for earlier ports of trade that had brought Indian groups together to barter. Finally, missionaries could sometimes be called upon to defend Indian land use rights in the Spanish legal system, and mission residence meant exemption from tribute. Some of these manipulations allowed indigenous peoples to isolate themselves from outsiders, but the bulk of these patterns brought them into contact with other ethnic groups.

This book has highlighted many types of interethnic activity. Within the mission pueblos themselves a variety of transactions crossed ethnic boundaries. Various kinds of trading activities brought outsiders into the villages. Some of the missions located on the camino real that carried silver to Mexico City, or on the trans-sierra route that linked the central plateau to the Sinaloa coast, hosted intermittent trading and bartering. At least some of these sites may have been precontact port of trade enclaves—neutral zones where different groups carried out trade and sometimes marriage negotiations. Grain brokers came to missions and rancherías to purchase surplus corn. Muleteers delivered annual shipments of supplies to the missions from Mexico City. Spanish and other non-Indian travelers used the missions as way stations on their journeys, places to secure lodging, meals, and the coveted cup of chocolate. Most passed through quickly, but some drifters (of all ethnicities) lingered and rested up, conning the locals and occasionally marrying their daughters. Missions not only served as zones of refuge for groups being persecuted by other Indians, but paradoxically they also provided hiding places for outlaws and vagrants. Despite Spanish legal proscriptions, outsiders increasingly obtained lots in the mission villages and, by the mid-eighteenth century, many of the Nueva Vizcayan mission Indians had rented lands to non-Indians. In the Topia missions straddling the sierra between Durango and Sinaloa, by this date women were weaving cotton cloth at the behest of middlemen. Some enterprising villagers worked as muleteers in the trade that carried wax and honey to the coast, bringing back salt, fish, and other foods. As time went on, Indians frequently complained that the missionaries appointed non-Indians (mestizos and mulattoes) as governors and other village officials.

Religious celebrations also attracted Spanish vecinos from surrounding ranchos and haciendas with no resident priests. Corpus Christi and Semana Santa drew adjacent populations of non-natives to these popular mission fiestas. One of the most lavish was the Feast of the Presentation of the Virgin Mary at Zape, held yearly on November 21. Coincidentally, this area in northwestern Durango still contained some large stone sculptures and other vestiges of Chalchihuites culture, appropriated in different ways by Tepehuanes. By mid-seventeenth century relics connected to older religions had been largely displaced to accommodate cofradía devotions. In missions where outsider presence was greatest, cofradías emerged to support patron saint and other feast-day celebrations. Religious authorities complained that the nominally Catholic cofradías provided a cover for idolatrous practices and deviant behavior. They also fostered absenteeism, as Indians periodically left missions to solicit alms for their cofradías in neighboring Spanish towns.

Different Indian ethnicities also mingled in missions. The earliest ones were founded with the help of Indians from central Mexico (Tlaxcalans and Tarascans) who helped dig acequias, plant milpas, and build churches, thereby providing a "civilized" example for local Indians to emulate. Nahuatl, or some version of it, became a lingua franca in many of the missions. Not all of the Indian outsiders were so acculturated, however; nonsedentary raiders and rebellious neophytes were also deposited in the missions nearest to presidios, where they might be "tamed." And some missions mixed formerly adversarial groups such as Tarahumaras and Tepehuanes or Acaxees and Xiximes.

While the interethnic contacts within missions were myriad, they were even more abundant outside. Some mission converts served as ethnic soldiers, fighting under presidial soldiers against rebellious and hostile natives that included members of their own groups. The most common situations were those in which Indians left the missions to work in silver mines, on haciendas, and in domestic service. In some cases these were forced journeys out of missions, the result of frequent repartimiento drafts. In many others, they were deliberate migratory strategies for acquiring material goods, marriage partners, or freedom from oppressive, demanding missionaries. Missionaries also used Indians as messengers and as transporters of goods. In the countryside, mission Indians who were herders came in contact with Indian and mixed-race cowboys and herders on Spanish ranches, sometimes sharing camaraderie, food, and drink around the campfire. Occasional visits to kin in rancherías exposed them not only to unconverted members of the their own groups but also to renegade non-Indians fleeing Spanish justice. On haciendas, mission Indians mixed with castas both socially and biologically. In mining reales, mission Indians mingled with Indians from other northern regions, as well as mixed-race workers. They gambled and drank together, enjoying the pleasures of cockfighting and other pastimes.

Since most of the these contacts were casual, unsupervised, and usually amicable, they were infrequently documented, but the random references are suggestive. The most frequent glimpses come to us when the associations are classified as aberrant, illegal, or morally reprehensible, as in the case of criminal acts. Typically, we find these interactions in cases of petty witchcraft involving healing, love magic, and protection from abusive relationships. Folk practices of diverse racial groups commonly intersected in the areas of healing and casting spells on enemies or prospective lovers, and brought Indians, mestizos, mulattoes, and Spaniards into close contact. Witchcraft was also employed as a resistance strategy to immoderate demands by ecclesiastical and civil authorities, explaining why Jesuit worries about rebellion in the earlier period were reborn in their allegations of *hechicería*/sorcery in the eighteenth century.

Secularization of the missions only stepped up the process of the fluid migrations between former missions, unacculturated settlements, and Spanish towns, and between regions. Royal officials worried about these peregrinations, attributing to them responsibility for a growing incidence of raiding, livestock theft, and highway robbery. Their reports are replete with standard and exaggerated references to the disruptive and pernicious influence of mestizo and mulatto vagabonds. Ordinances attempted to regulate travel that promoted social intercourse in rural areas, and to control the ethnically heterogeneous working classes of mining towns. While authorities sought to impose social controls on the lower echelons of society, Indian and mixed-race northern migrants commingled with immigrants from the south (e.g., muleteers, itinerant vendors, and artisans) and attempted to forge new social networks. Indian communities increasingly rented out their lands and eventually lost or forfeited their claims to them. Connections with outsiders also brought increasing social differentiation within Indian communities, including changes in women's roles and men's status and wealth. At the same time, the gap between poor

Spaniards, castas, and Indians, on the one hand, and regional, predominantly Spanish merchant-miner-landholder elites, on the other, widened, as the latter tended to consolidate wealth and power and to incorporate Indian lands in the later eighteenth century.

Missions, then, proved to be a critical factor in the interaction between Indians and others, as well as in mediating the diverse indigenous strategies based on cultural and environmental opportunism. Congregation in missions also enhanced the links between deadly microbes and indigenous bodies. Missionization, despite the criticisms of Bourbon officials, surely increased acculturation, itself hardly a peaceful experience. Missions were never completely self-sustaining, as they operated in an economy of labor and monetary exchange. Missionaries were brokers, but their mediation was certainly not intended to preserve indigenous ways, and ultimately they failed to protect Indians from exploitation. In fact, the Jesuits and the Franciscans cooperated in sowing the seeds of their own destruction as missionaries. Where they exercised greater control, the missions declined economically and demographically. Their complicity in supplying repartimiento drafts brought indigenous peoples into closer contact with sectors of society not previously experienced. Migration was largely facilitated by labor demands of agricultural and mining cycles, and some indigenous peoples actually found that conditions outside of missions could be more liberating. Increased intimacy with non-Indians produced interracial unions first in the Spanish population centers, both mines and haciendas. Racial mixing was also advanced at two crucial turning points, the devastating epidemics of the 1690s and the 1730s, which further decimated indigenous populations, leading in each case to even heavier labor demands and the increased immigration of non-Indians into mission pueblos and their environs.

By 1750, less than 8,000 natives remained in the former Jesuit and Franciscan missions of the Nueva Vizcayan heartland, and this number had declined to little more than 5,000 several years later. These Acaxees, Xiximes, Conchos, Tepehuanes, and Tarahumaras were at different stages of material, cultural, and ethnic change at mid-eighteenth century. How they identified themselves in ethnic and cultural terms varied considerably, since the changing demographics of racial mixing could determine ethnic but not cultural labels. Processes of destructuring and marginalization had proceeded furthest in the cases of Acaxees and Xiximes, who engaged in the same occupations as their mostly needy non-Indian neighbors and increasingly mixed with them biologically. Depending upon the choices they had made regarding sedentism, Conchos had become assimilated into other raiding bands or into the agricultural economy that surrounded the few missions in which they had been congregated. While some Tepehuanes were asserting their corporate rights to farm their small plots, many others rented out their lands and went to work for Spanish landowners as permanent and seasonal laborers. The eastern Tarahumaras did the same, but they were not yet completely incorporated into the mining and agricultural economy as a servile labor class. All of these processes were still unfolding at the time of secularization; their outcomes will need to be traced further in order to better understand the decisive role of this frontier region in the processes of economic modernization and social transformation that occurred in Mexico after 1850.

The elements of mediated opportunism developed in this study—the different impacts of conquest, the nature of precontact indigenous warfare and culture, the degree of economic pressures exerted, the ecological environment, comparative demography and epidemiology, and the availability of empty zones too unattractive or difficult for the invaders—combined in more complex patterns than the conventional models posit. Sorted in various combinations, they afford a more nuanced picture of the defiance and deference manifested by culturally diverse native groups in their encounters with Spaniards. This book has presented a composite vista that allows us to look at the complexity of indigenous groups (whose identities, despite the fact that I have assigned them five designations, were in flux before as well as after contact) with the intent of multiplying the perspectives from which we might interpret how social and cultural differentiation occurred within these groups and how multiple associations were created across and outside of them.

So whose story is this? I suspect that today's mestizo community of Santa María de Cuevas, Chihuahua,[5] would find it somewhat surreal. But they would also recognize things that are still part of their lives today: cornfields along the Río San Pedro, cyclical droughts, horse corrals and cow pastures, gatherings in the church patio, the choir singing in the seventeenth-century church with its lovely painted ceiling, and the matachín dancers mixing cultural traditions in the caves from which the community takes part of its name. The migratory strategies of their Tarahumara ancestors and other predecessors would also resonate with most families, except that now their loved ones are working in Paris, Texas, and Phoenix, Arizona, instead of Chihuahua and Cusihuiriachi.

Notes

INTRODUCTION

1. *La Jornada* (Mexico City), June 17, 1994. Although the newspaper used the colonial term "Tarahumara," today this group calls itself "Rarámuri" or "Ralámuli." Except when referring to recent times, I will follow the colonial usage. Translations are mine unless otherwise indicated.

2. The reference to the uprising of the Zapatista National Liberation Army in Chiapas which began January 1, 1994, pointed to the interconnectedness of indigenous problems and needs, as well as strategies for getting their voices heard. Today in 2002, after nearly a decade of drought and hardship in the sierra, negotiations of the Chiapas rebels with the government, and the inauguration of a changed political order, Indian peoples still strive to attain a system that respects pluralism. See, in reference to the Sierra Tarahumara, the editorial by Ricardo Robles, "ABC para otro sexenio," *La Jornada*, January 27, 2001. On March 28, the Zapatistas obtained a hearing before the Mexican Congress to present their arguments for the adoption of a law that would give more autonomy to Indian communities. The law that was eventually passed removed key passages proposed in the indigenous draft to strengthen local community control over natural resources and governance.

3. An early source is Carl Lumholtz, *Unknown Mexico: Explorations in the Sierra Madre and Other Regions, 1890–1898*. Among later works, see William L. Merrill, *Rarámuri Souls: Knowledge and Social Process in Northern Mexico*; John G. Kennedy, *Tarahumara of the Sierra Madre: Beer, Ecology, and Social Organization*; Campbell W. Pennington, *The Tepehuan of Chihuahua: Their Material Culture*; and Guadalupe Sánchez Olmedo, *Etnografía de la Sierra Madre Occidental: tepehuanes y mexicaneros*.

4. For recent summaries and bibliographies of this literature, see the postcontact volumes of *The Cambridge History of the Native Peoples of the Americas*: vol. 1, Bruce G. Trigger and Wilcomb E. Washburn, eds., *North America*; vol. 2, Richard E. W. Adams and Murdo J. MacLeod, eds., *Mesoamerica*; vol. 3, Frank Solomon and Stuart Schwartz, eds., *South America*.

5. For a sample: Charles Gibson, *The Aztecs under Spanish Rule* and *Tlaxcala in the Sixteenth Century;* Murdo J. MacLeod and Robert Wasserstrom, eds., *Spaniards and Indians in Southeastern Mesoamerica: Essays on the History of Ethnic Relations;* Nancy M. Farriss, *Maya Society and Colonial Rule: The Collective Enterprise of Survival;* Grant D. Jones, *Maya Resistance to Spanish Rule: Time and History on a Colonial Frontier;* Kevin Gosner, *Soldiers of the Virgin: The Moral Economy of a Colonial Maya Rebellion;* Robert W. Patch, *Maya and Spaniard in Yucatan, 1648–1812;* William B. Taylor, *Landlord and Peasant in Colonial Oaxaca;* John K. Chance, *Race and Class in Colonial Oaxaca* and *Conquest of the Sierra: Spaniards and Indians in Colonial Oaxaca;* Judith Francis Zeitlin, "Ranchers and Indians in the Southern Isthmus of Tehuantepec: Economic Change and Indigenous Survival in Colonial Mexico," *Hispanic American Historical Review* 69, no. 1 (1989): 23–60; María de los Angeles Romero Frizzi, *El sol y la cruz: indios de Oaxaca colonial;* Ramón Gutiérrez, *When Jesus Came, the Corn Mothers Went Away: Marriage, Sexuality, and Power in New Mexico, 1500–1846;* Karen Spalding, *Huarochirí: An Andean Society under Inca and Spanish Rule;* Steve J. Stern, *Peru's Indian Peoples and the Challenge of Spanish Conquest: Huamanga to 1640;* Ann Wightman, *Indigenous Migration and Social Change: The Forasteros of Cuzco, 1570–1720;* Karen Vieira Powers, *Andean Journeys: Migration, Ethnogenesis, and the State in Colonial Quito;* Susan Ramírez, *The World Upside Down: Cross-Cultural Contact and Conflict in Sixteenth-Century Peru;* Thomas B. Abercrombie, *Pathways of Memory and Power: Ethnicity and History among an Andean People.*

6. Indigenous language sources have been used intensively by Susan Kellogg, *Law and the Transformation of Aztec Culture, 1500–1700;* James Lockhart, *The Nahuas after the Conquest: A Social and Cultural History of the Indians of Central Mexico, Sixteenth through Eighteenth Centuries;* S. L. Cline, *Colonial Culhuacan, 1580–1600: A Social History of an Aztec Town;* Robert Haskett, *Indigenous Rulers: An Ethnohistory of Town Government in Colonial Cuernavaca;* Susan Schroeder, *Chimalpahin and the Kingdom of Chalco;* Rebecca Horn, *Preconquest Coyoacan: Nahua and Spanish Relations in Central Mexico, 1519–1650;* and Matthew Restall, *The Maya World: Yucatec Culture and Society, 1550–1850.*

7. Among the exceptions: Edward H. Spicer, *Cycles of Conquest: The Impact of Spain, Mexico, and the United States on the Indians of the Southwest, 1533–1960* and *The Yaquis: A Cultural History;* William B. Griffen, *Indian Assimilation in the Franciscan Area of Nueva Vizcaya;* Evelyn Hu-Dehart, *Missionaries, Miners, and Indians: Spanish Contact and the Yaqui Nation, 1533–1820;* Ignacio del Río, *Conquista y aculturación en la California jesuítica;* José Cuello, *El norte, el noreste y Saltillo en la historia colonial de México;* Leslie S. Offutt, *Saltillo, 1770–1810: Town and Region in the Mexican North;* David Block, *Mission Culture on the Upper Amazon: Native Tradition, Jesuit Enterprise and Secular Policy in Moxos, 1660–1880;* Cynthia Radding, *Wandering Peoples: Colonialism, Ethnic Spaces, and Ecological Frontiers in Northwestern Mexico, 1700–1850;* James S. Saeger, *The Chaco Mission Frontier: The Guaycuruan Experience;* Barbara Ganson, "The Evueví of Paraguay: Adaptive Strategies and Responses to Colonialism, 1528–1811," *The Americas* 45, no. 4 (1989): 460–488; Kristine Jones, "Comparative

Raiding Economies: North and South" and Mary Karasch, "Interethnic Conflict and Resistance on the Brazilian Frontier of Goiás, 1750–1890," in Guy and Sheridan, eds., *Contested Ground*, 97–134; Cecilia Sheridan Prieto, *Anónimos y desterrados: La contienda por el "sitio que llaman de Quauyla": siglos XVI–XVIII.*

8. The ranchería pattern of settlement characterized many Nueva Vizcayan groups at the time of effective Spanish contact. Living in dispersed settlements of only a few to perhaps several hundred households, ranchería inhabitants cultivated corn, beans, squash, chiles, and cotton. Locations shifted in accordance with seasonal cycles and soil fertility and the need to supplement agriculture with hunting and gathering.

9. Spicer, *Cycles of Conquest*, 8–15. François Chevalier's work (first published in 1952) on the evolution of Mexican latifundia was enormously influential in propagating this view: *Land and Society in Colonial Mexico: The Great Hacienda.*

10. James Lockhart and Stuart B. Schwartz, *Early Latin America: A History of Colonial Spanish America and Brazil*, 31–57. Lockhart develops these ideas more fully in "Receptivity and Resistance," ch. 11 in his *Of Things of the Indies: Essays Old and New in Early Latin American History*, 304–332. For another example pertinent to North America, see Richard White, *The Middle Ground: Indians, Empires, and Republics in the Great Lakes Region, 1650–1815.*

11. Radding, *Wandering Peoples*, 34. See also Charles W. Polzer, S.J., *Rules and Precepts of the Jesuit Missions of Northwestern New Spain*, 3–12, on mission terminology.

12. Hayden White, *Tropics of Discourse: Essays in Cultural Criticism;* Alun Munslow, *Deconstructing History.*

13. "The Promise and Dilemma of Subaltern Studies: Perspectives from Latin American History," *American Historical Review*, 99, no. 5 (1994), 1491–1515.

14. Ranajit Guha, "On Some Aspects of the Historiography of Colonial India," in Guha, ed., *Subaltern Studies*, vol. 1, 1–8; Rosalind O'Hanlon, "Recovering the Subject, *Subaltern Studies* and Theories of Resistance in Colonial South Asia," *Modern Asian Studies* 22, no. 1 (1988): 189–224; Gyan Prakash, "Writing Post-Orientalist Histories of the Third World: Perspectives from Indian Historiography," *Comparative Studies in Society and History* 32, no. 2 (1990): 383–408, and "Subaltern Studies as Postcolonial Criticism," *American Historical Review* 99, no. 5 (1994): 1475–1490.

15. James C. Scott, *Weapons of the Weak: Everyday Forms of Peasant Resistance* and *Domination and the Arts of Resistance: Hidden Transcripts.*

16. Michel Foucault, *The Order of Things: An Archeology of the Human Sciences;* Edward Said, *Orientalism.*

17. Lynn Hunt, ed., *The New Cultural History;* Victoria Bonnell and Lynn Hunt, eds., *Beyond the Cultural Turn: New Directions in the Study of Society and Culture.*

18. See William Sewell, "The Concept(s) of Culture," in Bonnell and Hunt, eds., *Beyond the Cultural Turn*, 35–61, and Eric Van Young, "The New Cultural History Comes to Old Mexico," *Hispanic American Historical Review* 79, no. 2 (1999): 211–247. Van Young argues that "cultural history should actively colonize economic relations."

19. Van Young, "The New Cultural History Comes to Old Mexico," 232–236.

20. See, for example, the use of ethnogenesis by Powers, *Andean Journeys*, and

Radding, *Wandering Peoples*. Also on northern Mexico, see William L. Merrill, "Cultural Creativity and Raiding Bands in Eighteenth-Century Northern New Spain," in Taylor and Pease, G.Y., eds., *Violence, Resistance, and Survival in the Americas*, 124–152.

21. Abercrombie, *Pathways of Memory and Power*, 408–410.

22. Gayatri Spivak has argued that this is impossible in "Can the Subaltern Speak?" in Nelson and Grossberg, eds., *Marxism and the Interpretation of Culture*.

23. Among critiques of the reductive understandings of resistance that result from trying too hard to find agency are Sherry B. Ortner, "Resistance and the Problem of Ethnographic Refusal," *Comparative Studies in Society and History* 37, no. 1 (1995): 173–193; and Michael F. Brown, "On Resisting Resistance," *American Anthropologist* 98 (1996): 729–735. Stuart Hall has suggested that we can see "subalterns" as important even if they are not always agents; "On Postmodernism and Articulation," in Morley and Chen, eds., *Stuart Hall: Critical Dialogues in Cultural Studies*, 140.

24. Griffen refers to changes within northern Mexican societies that occurred as a result of new biotic and cultural conditions as "a kind of environmental opportunism." "Observations on the Limitations of Data on the Ethnohistory of Northern Mexico," in Hers et al., eds., *Nómadas y sedentarios*, 264.

25. Radding, *Wandering Peoples*, 3. See also her "Ecología y cultura en dos fronteras misionales: Sonora (Nueva España) y Chiquitos (Alto Perú) en la época postjesuítica," in Bernardo García Martínez and Alba González Jácome, eds., *Estudios sobre historia y ambiente en América*, vol. 1, 268–285.

26. Radding, "The Colonial Pact and Changing Ethnic Frontiers: Frontiers in Highland Sonora, 1740–1840," in Guy and Sheridan, eds., *Contested Ground*, 52–66.

27. *The Yaquis*. See also Thomas E. Sheridan and Nancy J. Parezo, eds., *Paths of Life: American Indians of the Southwest and Northern Mexico*.

28. Erick Langer and Robert H. Jackson, eds., *The New Latin American Mission History*. In one of the essays, "The Ibero-American Frontier Mission in Native American History," 1–48, David Sweet reassesses Bolton's classic study, "The Mission as a Frontier Institution in the Spanish American Colonies," *American Historical Review* 23, no. 1 (October 1917): 42–61, within a critical postcolonial framework.

29. Robert C. West, *The Mining Community in Northern New Spain: The Parral Mining District* (Berkeley: University of California Press, 1949). The many works of Peter Masten Dunne on the Jesuits stand out in the heroic genre, but other Jesuits and Franciscans wrote in the same vein. Even the work of Herbert E. Bolton contributed to the heroic literature.

30. In addition to works cited in note 7 above, examples can be found in the work of Robert H. Jackson, including *Indian Population Decline: The Missions of Northwestern New Spain, 1687–1840* and (with Edward Castillo) *Indians, Franciscans, and Spanish Colonization: The Impact of the Mission System on California Indians*. See also the various essays in Robert H. Jackson, ed., *New Views of Borderlands History*, including Ross Frank, "Demographic, Economic and Social Change in New Mexico," 41–72. Other relevant works and collections of essays include Ricardo León García, *Misiones jesuitas en la Tarahumara: siglo XVIII*; Jesús F. de la Teja, *San Antonio de Béxar: A Community*

on *New Spain's Northern Frontier;* Langer and Jackson, eds., *The New Latin American Mission History;* Guy and Sheridan, eds., *Contested Ground;* Steven W. Hackel, "Land, Labor, and Production: The Colonial Economy of Spanish and Mexican California," in Ramón A. Gutiérrez and Richard J. Orsi, eds., *Contested Eden: California Before the Gold Rush;* and William L. Merrill, "Cultural Creativity and Raiding Bands in Eighteenth-Century Northern New Spain," in Taylor and Pease, G.Y., eds., *Violence, Resistance, and Survival in the Americas,* 124–142.

31. For example, Guillermo Porras Muñoz, *Iglesia y estado en Nueva Vizcaya, 1562–1821;* Luis Navarro García, *Sonora y Sinaloa en el siglo XVII;* María del Carmen Velázquez, *Establecimiento y pérdida del septentrión de México;* and Oakah L. Jones, Jr., *Nueva Vizcaya: Heartland of the Spanish Frontier.*

32. Cheryl E. Martin, *Governance and Society in Colonial Mexico: Chihuahua in the Eighteenth Century.* Chantal Cramaussel, *Primera página de historia colonial chihuahuense: la provincia de Santa Bárbara en Nueva Vizcaya, 1563–1631,* and "Evolución en las formas de dominio del espacio colonial: las haciendas de la región de Parral," *Encuentro* 20 (1990); Salvador Alvarez, "Tendencias regionales de la propiedad territorial en el norte de la Nueva España: siglos XVII y XVIII," in *Actas del Segundo Congreso de Historia Regional Comparada,* and "Agricultural Colonization and Mining Colonization: The Area of Chihuahua during the First Half of the Eighteenth Century," in Craig and West, eds., *In Quest of Mineral Wealth: Aboriginal and Colonial Mining and Metallurgy in Spanish America,* 171–204. See also Philip Hadley, *Minería y sociedad en el centro minero de Santa Eulalia, Chihuahua, 1709–1750;* and Michael M. Swann, *"Tierra Adentro": Settlement and Society in Colonial Durango* and *Migrants in the Mexican North: Mobility, Economy, and Society in a Colonial World.*

33. For an overview of their vision, see their introduction to Clara Bargellini, ed., *Misiones y presidios de Chihuahua,* 9–17.

34. These are occasionally found in the notarial records of the Archivo de Hidalgo de Parral (AHP) and in the judicial archives of the Audiencia de Guadalajara, Biblioteca Pública de Jalisco, Archivo Judicial de la Audiencia de Nueva Galicia (AJANG).

35. The Archivo General de Indias (AGI) in Seville has such records in its branches of Audiencia de Guadalajara and Patronato, but they are also found in the Archivo General de la Nación (AGN) in Mexico City and in notarial archives.

36. Jesuit records became very scattered after their expulsion from Mexico in 1767. I have located some of them in the AGN's branches of Archivo Histórico de Hacienda (AHH), Jesuitas, Misiones, Historia, and Provincias Internas. They are also found among the Franciscan papers in the Archivo Franciscano of the Biblioteca Nacional (BN-AF) in Mexico City. The Jesuits' own archives in Mexico City (Archivo Histórico de la Provincia de los Jesuitas en México–AHPM) and Rome (Archivum Romanum Societatis Iesu–ARSI) contain valuable materials. Microfilm copies of some of these records are in the Jesuit Historical Institute, Documentary Relations of the Southwest, University of Arizona, and in the library of Saint Louis University. Materials pertaining to Jesuit missions in the AGI were copied in the nineteenth century by Pablo Pastells, S.J., and are available on microfilm in several repositories. Some

Jesuit records ended up in U.S. libraries, most notably in the Nettie Lee Benson Latin American Library at the University of Texas (UTNLB) and the Bancroft Library of the University of California. In addition to those in the Biblioteca Nacional, other Franciscan records exist in various parts of Mexico and the United States. Diocesan records can be found in the Archivo de la Catedral de Durango (ACD); many of these have been copied and are available on microfilm at New Mexico State University. Administrative and military records are located in notarial, regional, national, and Spanish archives.

37. Parish registers have been microfilmed by the Genealogical Society of the Church of Jesus Christ of Latter-day Saints (GS). Some land records are in the Biblioteca Pública de Jalisco, Archivo de Instrumentos Públicos, Tierras y Aguas (AIP-TA). Inquisition records are in the AGN and the Archivo Histórico Nacional (AHN) in Madrid.

38. For example, Sweet, "The Ibero-American Frontier Mission"; Radding, *Wandering Peoples*, xv; and Saeger, *The Chaco Mission Frontier*, xi–xv.

39. *Available Light: Anthropological Reflections on Philosophical Topics*, 82, 102.

1. SPANISH ENTRADAS AND INDIGENOUS RESPONSES IN TOPIA AND TEPEHUANA, 1560–1620

1. Andrés Pérez de Ribas, *Historia de los triunfos de nuestra santa fé entre gentes las más bárbaras y fieras del nuevo orbe*. This, despite the title, is the best ethnographic source for the seventeenth century on a number of the indigenous groups studied here. The most recent editions are a facsimile reprint of the original 1645 edition with notes by Ignacio Guzmán Betancourt and a fine English translation, *History of the Triumphs of Our Holy Faith amongst the Most Barbarous and Fierce Peoples of the New World*, translated by Daniel T. Reff, Maureen Ahern, and Richard K. Danford. I will cite this work by its divisions into books and chapters in order to facilitate access to the various editions. See book 4, ch. 5, and also my tables.

2. Christopher Hill, *The World Turned Upside Down: Radical Ideas during the English Revolution*. Deeds, "Las rebeliones de los tepehuanes y tarahumaras durante el siglo XVII en la Nueva Vizcaya," in Campbell, ed., *El contacto entre los españoles e indígenas en el norte de la Nueva España*, 9–40; and "First Generation Rebellions in Seventeenth-Century Nueva Vizcaya," in Schroeder, ed., *Native Resistance and the Pax Colonial in New Spain*, 1–29. Chapter 2 will highlight the patterns of these Indian groups that were profoundly disrupted.

3. For precursor entradas and campaigns, see Philip Wayne Powell, *Soldiers, Indians, and Silver: The Northward Advance of New Spain, 1550–1600*. It is quite probable that the measles pandemic of 1530–1534 reached the Xiximes and Acaxees from Sinaloa; Daniel T. Reff, *Disease, Depopulation, and Culture Change in Northwestern New Spain, 1518–1764*, 108–111.

4. The Ibarra expedition was chronicled by Baltasar de Obregón in *Historia de*

los descubrimientos antiguos y modernos de la Nueva España (1584), but his geographical references are imprecise. For early settlements and administrative history, see Peter Gerhard, *The North Frontier of New Spain;* Oakah Jones, *Nueva Vizcaya;* J. Lloyd Mecham, *Francisco de Ibarra and Nueva Vizcaya;* and Porras Muñoz, *Iglesia y estado.* Cramaussel, *La provincia de Santa Bárbara,* 60–76, provides a prosopography of early settlers.

5. Cramaussel, *La Provincia de Santa Bárbara,* 38–42, and "Encomiendas, repartimientos y conquista en Nueva Vizcaya," *Actas del Primer Congreso,* 73–92; Deeds, "Rural Work in Nueva Vizcaya: Forms of Labor Coercion on the Periphery," *Hispanic American Historical Review* 69, no. 3 (1989): 424–449; and Silvio Zavala, *Los esclavos indios en la Nueva España,* 184–219; Pérez de Ribas, *Historia de los triunfos,* book 8, ch. 4; Peter Boyd-Bowman, "A Spanish Soldier's Estate in Northern Mexico, 1642," *Hispanic American Historical Review* 53, no. 1 (1973): 95–105.

6. Fragment on the history of Topia missions, anonymous Jesuit, n.d. (eighteenth century), UTNLB, William B. Stephens Collection (WBS), 1744, 471–474.

7. Viceroy to king, October 19, 1577, AGI, Audiencia de México, leg. 20.

8. The terms "peste" (Spanish) and "cocolitzli" (Nahuatl) mean epidemic in the generic sense. Often specific epidemics were not identified in the records. Elsa Malvido Miranda, "El arca de Noé o la caja de Pandora? Suma y recopilación de pandemias, epidemias y endemias en Nueva España, 1519–1810," in *Temas médicos de la Nueva España,* 49–87; for discussions of the 1570s epidemic or pandemic, see Reff, *Disease, Depopulation and Culture Change,* 124–126, and Elsa Malvido Miranda and Carlos Viesca, "La epidemia de cocoliztli en 1576," *Historias* 11 (1985): 27–33, who make a strong case that this was a pandemic of bubonic plague. A recent suggestion that it was a viral hemorrhagic fever similar to hantavirus is weakly supported; see David Stahle, "American Plague," *New Scientist,* December 23, 2000.

9. Diego de Ibarra to king, October 14, 1582, AGI, Audiencia de Guadalajara, leg. 29.

10. Testimony of Capt. Alonso Bello de Montes de Oca, October 22, 1641, in autos/case files on disputes over encomienda ownership, AHP, reel 1657b, frames 820–897.

11. This process has been well studied by Cramaussel: "Encomiendas, repartimientos y conquista en Nueva Vizcaya," *Historias* 25 (1992): 73–92, and "Haciendas y mano de obra en Nueva Vizcaya: el Real de Parral en el siglo XVII," *Trace* 15 (June 1989): 22–30. See also the inclusion of encomienda Indians in a list of property belonging to haciendas and ore-crushing plants in AHP, r. 1652c, fr. 980–982, 1049; and the declaration of Nicolás, August 18, 1694, AGI, Audiencia de Guadalajara, vol. 156, fol. 1172.

12. *Descripción geográfica de los reinos de Nueva Galicia, Nueva Vizcaya y Nuevo León,* 186–200.

13. Information on land grants in BN-AF, caja 11, no. 159. Cramaussel has examined patterns of southern Chihuahuan land tenure in *La provincia de Santa Bárbara,* 63–76, 98–101, and "Evolución en las formas de dominio del espacio colonial." See

also Deeds, "Mission Villages and Agrarian Patterns in a Nueva Vizcaya Heartland, 1600–1750," *Journal of the Southwest* 33, no. 3 (1991): 345–365. The evolution of land tenure in the production of grain and livestock exhibits considerable variations that deviate from the model that Chevalier developed, most appropriately for the Mexican northeast. Agricultural enterprises certainly required periodic infusions of capital from miners and merchants who were interconnected by marriage with the landed oligarchy. Fortunes based purely on agricultural pursuits were rare here as elsewhere; see Eric Van Young, "Mexican Rural History since Chevalier: The History of the Colonial Hacienda," *Latin American Research Review* 18, no. 3 (1983): 17; and Deeds, "Land Tenure Patterns in Northern New Spain," *The Americas*, 41, no. 4 (1985): 446–461.

14. Joseph Arlegui, *Crónica de la provincia de N.S.P.S. Francisco de Zacatecas* (1737), 32–41, 76, 82.

15. Autos on disputes over encomienda ownership, AHP, r. 1657b, fr. 820–897; autos on treatment of Indians in Nueva Vizcaya, 1670, Biblioteca Pública del Estado de Jalisco, Audiencia de la Nueva Galicia (AJANG), Civil, c-12, exp. 2.

16. Testimonio jurídico de las poblaciones . . . , AGN, Historia, vol. 20, exp. 19; carta annua, P. Hernando de Santarén, 1604, ARSI, Mexicana, vol. 14, fol. 381v.

17. Reff, *Disease, Depopulation, and Culture Change;* Jackson, *Indian Population Decline,* 69.

18. Francisco Javier Alegre, S.J., *Historia de la Compañía de Jesús de Nueva España,* ed. Ernest J. Burrus, S.J., and Félix Zubillaga, S.J. On the early history of Jesuits, see also John W. O'Malley, *The First Jesuits,* and Dauril Alden, *The Making of an Enterprise: The Society of Jesus in Portugal, Its Empire, and Beyond, 1540–1750.*

19. James D. Riley, *Haciendas jesuitas en México: la administración de los bienes inmuebles del Colegio Máximo de San Pedro y San Pablo de la Ciudad de México;* and Rutilio González Ortega, "La california de los jesuitas," doctoral thesis.

20. See Peter M. Dunne for heroic accounts of Jesuit evangelization: *Pioneer Black Robes on the West Coast, Pioneer Jesuits in Northern Mexico,* and *Early Jesuit Missions in Tarahumara.* The demographics are derived from the seventeenth-century Jesuit catalogs in the ARSI.

21. Pérez de Ribas, *Historia de los triunfos,* book 10, chs. 2–5; relación que el H. Juan de la Carrera hizo al P. Antonio de Mendoza, 1597, ARSI, Mexicana, vol. 16, fols. 152–157.

22. P. Nicolás de Arnaya to P. Prov. Francisco Baez, February 9, 1601, AGN, Historia, vol. 19, exp. 8.

23. Carta annua, 1597, in Félix Zubillaga, S.J., and Ernest J. Burrus, S.J., eds., *Monumenta mexicana,* vol. 6, doc. 107, 324–341; carta annua, 1598, AGN, Historia, vol. 19, exp. 7.

24. Carta annua, 1596, AGN, Historia, vol. 19, exp. 5.

25. This is one of the factors that inhibits our grasp of the actual numbers of people who died in epidemics. Pérez de Ribas, *Historia de los triunfos,* book 8, ch. 12, observed that the much reduced population of Indians in Topia was pleasing to God because it was Christian. Another Jesuit had a more compassionate interpreta-

tion, arguing that God wished to give the Indians eternal rest from the misery and oppression brought by Spaniards. Francisco de Florencia, *Historia de la provincia de la Compañía de Jesús de Nueva España* (Mexico City: Archivo Literario, 1955), book 4, cap. 11.

26. Viceroy Luis de Velasco to king, México, April 6, 1596, Colección Pablo Pastells, Razón y Fe Library, Madrid (copies in Jesuita Collection, St. Louis University, Jesuit Historical Institute, Tucson, and AHPM, Mexico City), vol. 2, fols. 371–374; cartas annuas, 1596 and 1597, AGN, Historia, vol. 19, exps. 5 and 6; carta annua, Juan Florencio, May 16, 1624, AGN, Misiones, vol. 25, fols. 90–92; historical sketch by P. Pedro Retes, Santa Catalina, June 29, 1745, in Mateu Private Collection (MPC), Barcelona (copy in Jesuit Historical Institute, Tucson). Tlaxcaltecans were present in missions and in mining centers such as Indé.

27. Relación que hizo Hermano Juan de la Carrera, 1597, ARSI, Mexicana, vol. 16, fol. 154v. In the present-day Tepehuan village of Santa María Ocotán, there is a close association between religious purity and cleansing by bathing in the river.

28. For example, the visitas of the Santiago Papasquiaro mission, San Nicolás and Atotonilco, were created from encomiendas in this region that were probably formerly rancherías of Tepehuanes. See report of P. Antonio de los Ríos, Santiago Papasquiaro, July 11, 1749, ACD, Varios, Año 1749.

29. The *bastón de mando* was a Spanish introduction, but one that came to be readily accepted among nonsedentary peoples. See the discussion in Chapter 2 of native political systems. As missions declined in population, the number of official positions also dropped to include the governor, sometimes a lieutenant governor (*teniente*), and an alcalde. The mission regime differed from the system of Indian government in the center-south of Mexico, not only in the names and functions of officials, but especially in the degree of control exerted by the missionary. See Dorothy Tanck de Estrada, *Pueblos de indios y educación en el México colonial, 1750–1821*, 45–56.

30. Report by P. Rodrigo de Cabredo, May 18, 1611, in Thomas H. Naylor and Charles W. Polzer, S.J., eds., *The Presidio and Militia on the Northern Frontier of New Spain, 1570–1700*, 220. In the case of the Xixime "cacique" Don Francisco, his wife also received the title of doña.

31. Petition of Don Bartolomé, principal de San Andrés Atotonilco, November 13, 1720, AGN, Indios, vol. 44, exp. 86. On intermediaries in other areas, see: Powers, *Andean Journeys*, 108–109; Richard White, *The Middle Ground: Indians, Empires and Republics in the Great Lakes Region, 1650–1815*, 177–185, 493–502; Saeger, *The Chaco Mission Frontier*, 120–130.

32. Carta annua, 1606, ARSI, Mexicana, vol. 14, fols. 468v–470; Pérez de Ribas, *Historia de los triunfos*, book 8, ch. 5; book 10, ch. 7. For rules covering the conduct of missionaries, see the Code of 1610 promulgated under Jesuit provincial head Rodrigo de Cabredo, in 1610, translated in Polzer, *Rules and Precepts*, 61–65, and Pérez de Ribas, *Historia de los triunfos*, book 7.

33. The first three tended to be the most commonly celebrated religious fiestas throughout Mexico; Tanck, *Pueblos de indios*, 287–336. The particular Marian devo-

tions of the Jesuits are glossed with bibliographic references in Pilar Gonzalbo Aizpuru, "Las devociones marianas en la vieja provincia de la Compañía de Jesús," in García Ayluardo and Ramos Medina, eds., *Manifestaciones religiosas en el mundo colonial americano*, 253–265.

34. Cuentas de la Real Caja de Durango, May 22, 1599, AGI, Contaduría, vol. 925.

35. Memorial del P. Procurador General Bernardo Rolandegui, ca. 1704, AGN, AHH, Temporalidades (Temp.) leg. 325, exp. 51.

36. P. Juan Font to P. Prov. Ildefonso de Castro, Guadiana, April 22, 1608, in Luis González Rodríguez, ed., *Crónicas de la Sierra Tarahumara*, 178–181.

37. Deeds, "Mission Villages," 360. In the sixteenth century these lands were usually designated as "tierras para vivir y sembrar." The term "fundo legal" appears in the late eighteenth century. Its size varied throughout New Spain, but generally the dimensions were larger in the more arid north, comprising a square league; Tanck, *Pueblos de indios*, 77–79. A real cédula of April 4, 1742, mentions the differences between the jurisdictions of Nueva España and Guadalajara in respect to the land entitlements for Indian pueblos, AGI, Audiencia de Guadalajara, leg. 106. The lack of formal titles later created difficulties for indigenous communities trying to hold onto their lands, as well as for historians who try to explain regional and other discrepancies in the size of the fundo legal; Michael C. Meyer, *Water in the Hispanic Southwest: A Social and Legal History*, 80.

38. P. Juan Antonio Balthasar to P. Prov. Cristóbal Escobar y Llamas, Mexico City, August 15, 1745, AGN, AHH, Temp., leg. 2000, exp. 20; P. Prov. Ignacio Calderón to P. Proc. Pedro Ignacio Altamirano, Mexico City, November 11, 1753, AGN, AHH, Temp., leg. 540, exp. 2. Of the more common 300-peso stipend, 50 pesos were designated for schooling Indian children. Sheridan Prieto reports that the Franciscans in Coahuila eventually received 450 pesos annually, reflecting the greater isolation of their mission outposts, *Anónimos y desterrados*, 187.

39. Carta annua, 1604, ARSI, Mexicana, vol. 14, fol. 376v. As we shall see, the work regimen varied from mission to mission and over time. The annual requests for supplies (memorias) comprise many of the legajos in the Archivo Histórico de Hacienda in the AGN.

40. P. Prov. Rodrigo de Cabredo to viceroy, August 5, 1614, AGN, AHH, Temp., leg. 278, exp. 7.

41. Interethnic relations are highlighted in the case of Ana Romo, Topia, August 1, 1611, AGN, Inquisición, vol. 292, fols. 172–175. The Valle de Topia, where the Franciscans first established a mission, and the real de minas de Topia were located several leagues apart.

42. Since only a few Franciscans remained in Topia, Bishop Mota y Escobar assigned the area to Jesuits, but they declined to take over the real de San Andrés; carta de P. Hernando de Santarén, n.d., AGN, Jesuitas, II-4.

43. Salvador Alvarez, "Chiametla: una provincia olvidada del siglo XVI," *Trace* 22 (1992): 5–23.

44. Testimonio jurídico de las poblaciones y conversiones de los serranos acaxees . . . , AGN, Historia 20, exp. 19. Enslaving of Indians was common in the north until the late seventeenth century based on arguments of "just war," still held to be applicable in the case of "chichimecas." There is evidence that enslavement of descendants of captured chichimecas continued into the eighteenth century; AGN, Indios, vol. 60, exp. 63. Sheridan Prieto provides a summary of viceregal positions on this issue, *Anónimos y desterrados*, 90–98. On the usefulness of performance, see Armando Guevara-Gil and Frank Solomon, "A 'Personal Visit': Colonial Political Ritual and the Making of Indians in the Andes," *Colonial Latin American Review* 3 (1994): 3–36; and Patricia Seed, *Ceremonies of Possession in Europe's Conquest of the New World, 1492–1640*. The casa de comunidad referred to would have followed the procedure for founding pueblos de indios in New Spain, but there is virtually no evidence that they were constructed in missions before the eighteenth century. The reasons are discussed in Chapter 5.

45. Pérez de Ribas, *Historia de los triunfos*, book 9, chs. 1–5. The original version of the flesh-tasting story is in carta annua, 1604, P. Hernando Santarén, ARSI, Mexicana, vol. 14, fol. 384. Peter Hulme elaborated the contemporary literary discourse in *Colonial Encounters, Europe and the Native Caribbean, 1492–1797*, 100–134; see also the discussion by Gananath Obeyesekere, "'British Cannibals,' Contemplation of an Event in the Death and Resurrection of James Cook, Explorer," *Critical Inquiry* 18 (summer 1992): 630–654.

46. P. Nicolás de Arnaya to P. Prov. Francisco Baez, February 9, 1601, *Documentos para la historia de México* (cited as *DHM* with series, volume, and page numbers), 4–3, 61.

47. Pérez de Ribas discusses how this silver was used in betting on ball games, *Historia de los triunfos*, book 8, ch. 3. The custom was established early in the north: Antonio Nakayama, ed., *Relación de Antonio Ruiz: la conquista en el Noroeste*, 72–73.

48. Entrada, 1600, AGN, Historia 20; José Gutiérrez Castillas, *Santarén: conquistador pacífico*, 84.

49. Carta annua, P. Prov. Francisco Báez, April 1602, in Naylor and Polzer, eds., *Presidio*, 154–163.

50. Much of the following account of the Acaxee revolt is taken from these sources: Pérez de Ribas, *Historia de los triunfos*, book 8, chs. 8–10; relación de P. Prov. Francisco Baez, April 1602, and other documents in AGI, Audiencia de Mexico, leg. 1254, published in Naylor and Polzer, eds., *Presidio*, 154–199; Urdiñola to king, Durango, March 31, 1604, in Charles W. Hackett, ed., *Historical Documents Relating to New Mexico, Nueva Vizcaya, and Approaches Thereto, to 1773*, vol. 2, 89–93; and relación del Capitán Juan de Castañeda del castigo de los indios, Durango, April 13, 1604, CP, vol. 4, pp. 9–20. See also Deeds, "Indigenous Rebellions on the Northern Mexican Mission Frontier: From First-Generation to Later Colonial Responses," in Guy and Sheridan, eds., *Contested Ground*, 32–51.

51. See contemporary accounts in n. 50, above, and Francisco Cervantes, *The Devil in the New World: The Impact of Diabolism in New Spain*.

52. Bishop Alonso de la Mota y Escobar to king, March 2, 1602, CP, vol. 3, pp. 133–135; bishop to viceroy (Conde de Monterrey), May 20, 1602, CP, vol. 2, pp. 597–604; relación de P. Diego Ximénez, San Andrés, 1633, AGN, Jesuitas, III-15, exp. 4.

53. Pérez de Ribas, *Historia de los triunfos*, book 8, ch. 11.

54. The characteristics are considered as a whole below and in Deeds, "First Generation Rebellions."

55. Francisco de Urdiñola to king, March 31, 1604, in Hackett, ed., *Historical Documents*, vol. 2, 89–93.

56. Pérez de Ribas, *Historia de los triunfos*, book 8, ch. 6.

57. Pérez de Ribas, *Historia de los triunfos*, book 8, ch. 16. Triennial catalogs of Mexican Jesuits in ARSI, Mexicana, vol. 4, demonstrate the importance they attached to learning the Indian languages. Most learned Nahuatl first in Mexico City and then went on to write grammars and dictionaries in the languages of their missions.

58. See Gutiérrez, *When Jesus Came, the Corn Mothers Went Away*, 75–81, for a discussion of the strains produced when missionaries undermined the authority and roles of parents.

59. Carta annua, 1607, and carta de P. Luis de Ahumada to P. Martín Peláez, November 13, 1608, both in AGN, Historia 19.

60. See the description of Xiximes by P. Diego Ximénez, San Andrés, 1633, AGN, Jesuitas III-15, exp. 4.

61. Pérez de Ribas, *Historia de los triunfos*, book 9, chs. 1–4.

62. Carta annua, 1610, ARSI, Mexicana, vol. 14, fols. 580–584v; relación de la entrada . . . xiximes, 1610, UTNLB-JGI, Varias Relaciones, I-1. (Another version of this report by P. Rodrigo de Cabredo, May 18, 1611, is published in Naylor and Polzer, eds., *Presidio*, 200–244.)

63. Capt. Martín de Olivas to Capt. Diego Martínez de Hurdaide, Topia, May 4, 1613, AGN, Jesuitas II-4, exp. 1; autos sobre Topia, 1609–1614, AGN, Jesuitas II-12, exp. 4.

64. Excerpt from a letter by P. Juan del Valle, in carta annua, P. Juan Font, 1611, in González Rodríguez, ed., *Crónicas*, 168–170.

65. Autos sobre Topia, 1609–1614, AGN, Jesuitas, II-12, exp. 4; Pérez de Ribas, *Historia de los triunfos*, book 9, chs. 8–12.

66. Alvarez, "Chiametla: una provincia olvidada."

67. Mota y Escobar, *Descripción geográfica*, 204.

68. Petitions presented by Guanaceví miners, February 8, 1648, AHP, r. 1648, fr. 188 ff.

69. Debate over the need to teach the Spanish language went on throughout the colonial period, but it was not actually required until the eighteenth century; Tanck, *Pueblos de indios*, 153–214.

70. Carta annua, P. Juan Font, 1611, in González Rodríguez, ed., *Crónicas*, 165–171; carta annua, 1615, ARSI, Mexicana, vol. 15, fols. 26–27v; Pérez de Ribas, *Historia de los triunfos*, book 10, chs. 7, 12. For a recent review of the literature on the evolution of Indian cofradías in Mesoamerica, see Murdo J. MacLeod, "Desde el Mediterráneo

y España hasta la Guatemala indígena: las transformaciones de una institución colonial, la cofradía," in Pastor and Mayer, eds., *Formaciones religiosas en la América colonial*, 203–227.

71. Carta annua, 1607, AGN, Historia 19, exp. 9; carta annua, P. Juan Font, 1608, in González Rodríguez, ed., *Crónicas*, 160–165.

72. Carta annua, P. Juan Font, 1611, in González Rodríguez, ed., *Crónicas*, 165–171; ordenanza de P. Rodrigo de Cabredo, 1610, in Polzer, *Rules and Precepts*, 61–65.

73. Carta annua de 1608, P. Juan Font, in González Rodríguez, ed., *Crónicas*, 160–165; carta annua, 1615, ARSI, Mexicana, vol. 15, fol. 26v.

74. Carta annua de 1610, ARSI, Mexicana, vol. 14, fol. 577; carta annua, P. Juan Font, 1612, in González Rodríguez, ed., *Crónicas*, 171–174; autos of the alcalde mayor of Indé, October 18, 1618, AGN, Historia, vol. 311, fol. 52.

75. Carta annua, P. Juan Font, 1611, in González Rodríguez, ed., *Crónicas*, 186–193; Reff, *Disease, Depopulation, and Culture Change*, 154–155.

76. Request by P. Diego Larios, 1614, and P. Prov. Rodrigo de Cabredo to Viceroy Marqués de Guadalcázar, August 5, 1614; both in AGN, AHH, Temp., leg. 278, exp. 7.

77. Pérez de Ribas, *Historia de los triunfos*, book 10.

78. Carta annua, 1616, AGN, Jesuitas, III-29, exp. 21. One witness, Andrés de Heredia, a Franciscan from Topia, had heard some Indians say that Quautlatas came from New Mexico. Testimony given in the interrogatory administered by P. Francisco de Arista, January 25, 1617, AGN, Historia, vol. 311, fols. 3–46.

79. In one case, an Indian witness used the Nahuatl *macehuales* or commoners to denote those that this god had chosen to favor; testimony given in the interrogatory administered by P. Francisco de Arista, January 25, 1617, AGN, Historia, vol. 311, fols. 3–46. Do these reported letters indicate that the written word had supernatural attributes or that natives quickly learned to take advantage of its practical application? See Peter Wogan, "Perceptions of European Literacy in Early Contact Situations," *Ethnohistory* 41, no. 3 (1994): 407–427.

80. Much of this information on the Tepehuan rebellion comes from the testimony taken by P. Arista in early 1617, AGN, Historia, vol. 311; and in ARSI, Mexicana, vol. 17, fols. 153ff; from Pérez de Ribas, *Historia de los triunfos*, book 10, chs. 17–32; and from relación de lo que sucedió en la Villa de Guadiana del alzamiento de los indios tepehuanes, Durango, November 24, 1616, BN-AF, caja 11, exp. 169. Other interpretations of these sources are found in Dunne, *Pioneer Jesuits in Northern Mexico*, 119–175; Bradley W. Case, "Gods and Demons: Folk Religion in Seventeenth-Century New Spain, 1614–1632," Ph.D. dissertation, 143–257; Reff, "The 'Predicament of Culture' and Spanish Missionary Accounts of the Tepehuan and Pueblo Revolts," *Ethnohistory* 42, no. 1 (1995): 63–90; Deeds, "Indigenous Rebellions"; Charlotte M. Gradie, *The Tepehuan Revolt of 1616: Militarism, Evangelism, and Colonialism in the Seventeenth Century;* and Christophe Giudicelli, "Guerre, identités et métissages aux frontières de l'Empire: la guerre des Tepehuán en Nouvelle Biscaye, 1616–1619" (Ph.D. dissertation, Université de Paris III, 2000).

81. See the discussion of tribalization and ethnic identity in R. Brian Ferguson and Neil L. Whitehead, "The Violent Edge of Empire," in *War in the Tribal Zone.* Southern Tepehuanes were not missionized until later by Franciscans, but there seems to have existed a separation between the two groups even before the rebellion, probably long before Spaniards arrived. Some did, however, participate in the revolt.

82. Testimony of Andrés de Arruez, January 30, 1617, AGN, Historia, vol. 311.

83. Interrogation of Antonio by Gov. Gaspar de Alvear, January 26, 1617, ARSI, Mexicana, vol. 17, fols. 153–154v.

84. Account of the Tepehuan rebellion, May 16, 1618, in Hackett, ed., *Historical Documents,* vol. 2, 100–115.

85. Deeds, "Indigenous Rebellions," 8–10.

86. See Woodrow Borah, "La defensa frontera durante la gran rebelión tepehuana," *Historia Mexicana* 16, no. 1 (1966): 15–29, on the problems of mobilizing.

87. Spanish soldiers reported eight such strongholds in 1618. Relación de lo sucedido en la guerra de Tepehuanes (P. Francisco de Arista), Guadiana, February 1618, AGN, Historia, vol. 311, fols. 47–51.

88. Report of P. Diego de Alejos, Tecussiapa, May 18, 1617, AGN, Archivo Provisional, Misiones, caja 2 (these documents have been moved to Misiones since I first saw them).

89. Ibid.

90. Testimony taken in interrogatory, AGN, Historia, vol. 311, exp. 1.

91. Report of P. Alonso de Valencia, Guatimapé, May 9, 1618, in Naylor and Polzer, eds., *Presidio,* 247–293.

92. Relación de lo sucedido en la jornada que Don Gaspar de Alvear . . . hizo a los tarahumares . . . hecha por el P. Alonso de Valencia, April 1620, UTNLB-JGI, Varias Relaciones, I.

93. Report of P. Valencia in Naylor and Polzer, eds., *Presidio,* 247–293.

94. Report of alcalde mayor of Indé, October 1618, AGN, Historia, vol. 311, f. 52; autos del governador Mateo de Vesga, May 19, 1622, in Hackett, ed., *Historical Documents,* vol. 2, 118–137.

95. Report of P. Valencia, in Naylor and Polzer, eds., *Presidio,* 247–293.

96. Relación de lo sucedido en la jornada que Don Gaspar de Alvear . . . , UTNLB-JGI, Varias Relaciones, I.

97. Autos del governador Mateo de Vesga in Hackett, ed., *Historical Documents,* vol. 2, 118–137.

98. Estimates of Indian deaths range from four to fifteen thousand. The former is given by P. Diego de Medrano to include Indians who died in combat and by starvation and sickness. Relación de P. Diego de Medrano, August 31, 1654, in Naylor and Polzer, eds., *Presidio,* 414. The latter comes from Arlegui, *Crónica,* 199.

99. Zavala, *Los esclavos indios,* 217.

100. Relación que hizo el P. Francisco de Ximénez, San Andrés, 1632, AGN, Jesuitas III-15, exp. 33.

101. Pérez de Ribas to Viceroy Marqués de Cadereyta, September 12, 1638, AGN, AHH, Temp., leg. 2000, exp. 1.

102. See Sylvia Thrupp, *Millennial Dreams in Action*. Different levels or cycles of the universe were common features of indigenous worldviews; Gradie, *The Tepehuan Revolt of 1616*, characterizes the revolt as a nativistic revitalization movement, 167–171.

103. Ranajit Guha, *Elementary Aspects of Peasant Insurgency in Colonial India*, ch. 6.

104. This point is made most forcefully by Christophe Giudicelli, in "El miedo a los monstruos: indios ladinos y mestizos en la guerra de los Tepehuanes de 1616," *Nuevo Mundo: Mundos Nuevos* (France) 1 (2001): 176–190.

105. See William B. Taylor, "Santiago's Horse: Christianity and Colonial Indian Resistance in the Heartland of New Spain," in Taylor and Pease, G.Y., eds., *Violence, Resistance, and Survival in the Americas*.

106. See Chapter 2.

107. Report by P. Rodrigo de Cabredo, May 18, 1611, in Naylor and Polzer, eds., *Presidio*, 223.

108. Reff, "The 'Predicament of Culture.'" Reff talks about the association of the devil with blackness, both in Spanish and Indian imagery; see also carta annua, P. Francisco de Mendoza, Zape, June 6, 1662, AGN, Misiones, vol. 26, fols. 167–171.

2. ENVIRONMENT AND CULTURE

1. I have called this area the heartland ("Mission Villages"), not to be confused with Oakah Jones' characterization (also apt) of the entire province as the heartland of the northern frontier in *Nueva Vizcaya: Heartland of the Spanish Frontier*. This study excludes most of the territory of Sinaloa and Sonora, which was made a separate province in 1733, and the Parras-Saltillo area to the southeast, which eventually became part of Coahuila.

2. Robert West and J. J. Parsons, "The Topia Road: A Trans-Sierran Trail of Colonial Mexico," *Geographical Review* 31 (1941): 406–413; and Chantal Cramaussel, "Transformaciones en el medio ambiente: una laguna desaparecida en el sur del estado de Chihuahua," *Suma* 1 (1989): 5–12. Descriptions of specific geographic locales can be found in Gerhard, *The North Frontier*, 161–243.

3. Charles DiPeso, *Casas Grandes: A Fallen Trading Center of the Gran Chichimeca*.

4. Michael S. Foster and Phil C. Weigand, eds., *The Archaeology of West and Northwest Mexico*. Marie-Areti Hers posits earlier dates for the emergence and decline of the Chalchihuites culture in the northern reaches of Mesoamerica, and she disputes the existence of a separate Loma San Gabriel culture. *Los toltecas en tierras chichimecas*, 183–197; and "¿Existió la cultura Loma de San Gabriel? El caso de Hervideros, Durango," *Anales del Instituto de Investigaciones Estéticas* 60, 33–57.

5. For summaries of this debate, see Carroll L. Riley, *The Frontier People: The Greater Southwest in the Protohistoric Period*; F. Joan Mathien and Randall H. Mc-

Guire, eds., *Ripples in the Chichimec Sea: New Considerations of Southwestern-Meso-amerian Interactions;* and David H. Thomas, ed., *Columbian Consequences*, vol. 1: *Ar-chaeological and Historical Perspectives on the Spanish Borderlands West.*

6. Deeds, "Cómo historiar con poca historia y menos arqueología: clasificación de los acaxees, xiximes, tepehuanes, tarahumaras y conchos," and William B. Griffen, "Observations on the Limitations of Data," both in Hers et al., eds., *Nómadas y seden-tarios.* See also Charlotte M. Gradie, "Discovering the Chichimecas," *The Americas* 51, no. 1 (1994): 67–88.

7. This is the argument advanced by Daniel T. Reff in *Disease, Depopulation, and Culture Change*, especially 89–95.

8. See, for example, Edward H. Spicer, "Northwest Mexico: Introduction," in Wauchope, gen. ed., *Handbook of Middle American Indians*, vol. 8, 777–791.

9. Carta annua, September 23, 1599, Zubillaga and Burrus, eds., *Monumenta mexicana*, 6, doc. 219, 625, suggests this figure for Parras (Coahuila).

10. *The Distribution of Aboriginal Tribes and Languages in Northwestern Mexico*, 15–20. See also Ralph L. Beals, *The Acaxee: A Mountain Tribe of Durango and Sina-loa*, who speculated that these groups made a bridge between southwestern U.S. and Mesoamerican cultures.

11. These sources include Antonio Tello, *Libro segundo de la Crónica miscelánea, en que se trata de la conquista espiritual y temporal de la Santa Provincia de Xalisco en el Nuevo Reino de la Galicia y Nueva Vizcaya y descubrimiento de Nuevo México;* and Obregón, *Historia de los descubrimientos.*

12. Reff, *Disease, Depopulation, and Culture Change*, 205, estimates 21,000 each. The discussions of population in regions inhabited by the two groups in Gerhard, *The North Frontier*, suggests at least that many; 170–171, 208–209, 228–229, 240, 254–255, 260–261. Other evidence comes from Razón y minuta . . . , 1625, in Hackett, ed., *His-torical Documents*, vol. 2, 152–159; and Pérez de Ribas, *Historia de los triunfos*, book 8, ch. 2.

13. The ethnographic information on the Acaxees and Xiximes is synthesized from the following sources: Pérez de Ribas, *Historia de los triunfos*, books 8, 9; Tes-timonio jurídico de las poblaciones y conversiones de los serranos acaxes hechas por el Capitán Diego de Avila y el venerable Padre Hernando de Santarén por el año de 1600, AGN, Historia, vol. 20, exp. 19, fols. 183–294; carta annua, 1602, Misión de la Serranía de Topia y de San Andrés, ARSI, Mexicana, vol. 14, fols. 288v–295; carta annua, P. Hernando de Santarén, 1604, ARSI, Mexicana, vol. 14, fols. 381–388v; rela-ción del Padre Diego Ximénez, San Andrés, 1633, AGN, Jesuitas, III-15, exps. 4, 33; relación topográfica, Tamazula, 1777, BN (Madrid), ms. 2450, fols. 155–159. One of the first descriptions of Topia comes from Obregón, *Historia de los descubrimientos*, 58, who describes at least one fortified pueblo with a fort, stone staircase, and stone walls along with what appears to be a community meeting house of some kind.

14. Medidas . . . de tierras, San Gerónimo de Ajoya, 1744, AIP-TA, libro 37-1, exp. 5.

15. Carta annua, 1602, ARSI, Mexicana 14, fol. 288v.

16. A detailed description of the ball game is provided by P. Hernando de Santarén in the 1604 carta annua, ARSI, Mexicana, vol. 14, fols. 381–388v.

17. José Luis Punzo Díaz, "La mesa de Tlahuitoles en lo alto de la Sierra Madre de Durango" (Thesis: Escuela Nacional de Antropología e Historia, 1999).

18. Spaniards did identify certain individuals as caciques, but when their following is mentioned, it usually does not exceed 40–60 people; see, for example, the Jesuit annual report of 1610, in Naylor and Polzer, eds., *Presidio*, 219. On the other hand, Pérez de Ribas, *Historia de los triunfos*, book 9, ch. 7, mentions a *reyezuelo* (little king) from Guapijuxe who commanded the allegiance of 17 Xixime rancherías during the Xixime rebellion.

19. Pérez de Ribas, *Historia de los triunfos*, book 1, ch. 3.

20. Pérez de Ribas, *Historia de los triunfos*, book 8, ch. 3, reports belief in a god called Meyuncame (he who knows everything) that he equates with the devil. Acaxees call the sun the true god in a report by P. Diego de Alejos, Teguciapa, May 18, 1617, AGN, Archivo Provisional, Misiones, caja 2. See also carta annua, April 12, 1592, in Zubillaga and Burrus, eds., *Monumenta mexicana*, 4, doc. 88, 354–355.

21. Pérez de Ribas, *Historia de los triunfos*, book 2, ch. 1.

22. Relación de la entrada que hizo el gobernador de la Nueva Vizcaya Francisco de Urdiñola a la conquista, castigo y pacificación de los indios llamados xiximes, 1610, UTNLB, JGI, Varias Relaciones, I-1. One Jesuit reported that they believed souls were trapped in the bones. Large caches of bones were stored in caves and in ceremonial structures according to the Jesuits who later endeavored to destroy them: "y tienen guardados los huesos de estos sus enemigos en que idolatran bailándoles y adorando en ellos sus hazañas . . . adoran su valentía en los huesos de los vencidos." The ceremony of the virgin maiden appears in the annual report of 1610, in Naylor and Polzer, eds., *Presidio*, 242–243. If the warriors lost the battle, the *doncella* was blamed and banished. Pérez de Ribas argued that various Sinaloan groups practiced cannibalism as a food source, but there is little corroborating evidence for this; Pérez de Ribas, *Historia de los triunfos*, book 1, ch. 3. Obregón, *Historia de los descubrimientos*, 52, called the western sierra groups "indios caribes," a reference to the supposedly flesh-eating group of Santo Domingo.

23. See, for comparison, Nakayama, ed., *Relación de Antonio Ruiz*.

24. Pérez de Ribas, *Historia de los triunfos*, book 8, ch. 12.

25. Although Jesuit missionaries expressed horror at cases of infanticide, these invariably were linked to the death of the mother in childbirth or other factors which would have inhibited the child's own sustenance or the well-being of the family. See Pérez de Ribas, *Historia de los triunfos*, book 8, ch. 7. Obregón, *Historia de los descubrimientos*, 60, says that when the warriors made peace with the Spaniards, "they brought their women loaded with supplies."

26. See the discussion in Carol Deven, *Countering Colonization: Native American Women in Great Lakes Missions: 1630–1900* (Berkeley: University of California Press,

1992), ch. 1. Jesuits commented on the substantial loads carried by women; carta annua de 1604, P. Hernando de Santarén, ARSI, Mexicana 14, fols. 381–388; carta annua de 1638, Atotonilco and Badiraguato, AGN, Historia, vol. 316, exp. 8.

27. Relación de la entrada . . . a los indios llamados xiximes, 1610, UTNLB-JGI, Varias Relaciones, I-1.

28. One may also speculate about whether this practice was longstanding or a more recent result of the particularly high mortality of pregnant women and infants in epidemics.

29. The southern Tepehuan inhabited parts of Jalisco, Nayarit and Durango. See Carroll L. Riley, "The Southern Tepehuan and the Tepecano," in Robert Wauchope, gen. ed., *Handbook of Middle American Indians*, vol. 8, pt. 2, and Pennington, *The Tepehuan of Chihuahua*, 1–6.

30. Reff, *Disease, Depopulation, and Culture Change*, 205, suggests 21,000. Gerhard, *The North Frontier*, 164, 170–171, gives estimates for the regions inhabited by Tepehuanes that would yield a population closer to 60,000.

31. Contemporary Chihuahua Tepehuanes have been studied by Pennington, *The Tepehuan*.

32. Mecham, *Francisco de Ibarra*, 74, 85, 126.

33. Carroll Riley and H. D. Winters, "The Prehistoric Tepehuan of Mexico," *Southwestern Journal of Anthropology* 19, no. 2 (1963): 177–185. Marie-Areti Hers and her students have made significant progress in revising these older ideas. See especially Fernando Berrojalbiz Cenigaonaindia, "Desentrañando un norte diferente: los tepehuanes prehispánicos del Alto Río Ramos, Durango," in Chantal Cramaussel, ed., *Asentamientos y movimientos de población en la Sierra Tepehuana desde la prehistoria hasta nuestros días.*

34. Carta annua, 1608, in González Rodríguez, ed., *Crónicas*, 160–165. In another account, a very old Tepehuan warrior, Tucumudagui, recounts his exploits in expanding Tepehuan boundaries; Relación de lo sucedido en la jornada que Don Gaspar de Alvear y Salazar . . . hizo a los tarahumares desde los 26 de febrero deste año de 1619 hasta los 20 de abril del dicho año hecha por el padre Alonso de Valencia . . . , UTNLB-JGI, Varias Relaciones I.

35. Pérez de Ribas, *Historia de los triunfos*, book 10, ch. 1. The quote is from P. Martín Peláez, cited in Miguel Vallebueno, "El poblamiento del valle de Santiago Papasquiaro, Durango, hasta 1743," *Transición* 8 (1991): 4.

36. Pennington, *The Tepehuan of Chihuahua*, 130–131; Gov. Rodrigo Río de Loza to king, October 29, 1591, CP, vol. 2, pp. 143–154.

37. Berrojalbiz, "Desentrañando un norte diferente."

38. Pérez de Ribas, *Historia de los triunfos*, book 10, ch. 3.

39. Carta annua, P. Juan Font, 1607, in González Rodríguez, ed., *Crónicas*, 156–158. In a letter of 1612, Font speculates that ancient Mesoamericans had reached this area; ibid., 173–174.

40. Pérez de Ribas, *Historia de los triunfos*, book 10, chs. 6, 35.

41. Carta annua, Juan Font, 1611, González Rodríguez, ed., *Crónicas*, 186–193.

42. Jesuit carta annua, 1597, AGN, Historia, vol. 19, exp. 6; carta annua, 1602, ARSI, Mexicana, vol. 14, fols. 296–297.

43. Campbell W. Pennington, "Northern Tepehuan," in William Sturtevant, gen. ed., *Handbook of North American Indians*, vol. 10, 307.

44. Tarahumaras were of great interest to Carl Lumholtz, *Unknown Mexico,* and to Wendell C. Bennett and Robert M. Zingg, *The Tarahumara: An Indian Tribe of Northern Mexico.* More recent studies include Campbell W. Pennington, *The Tarahumar of Mexico: Their Environment and Material Culture;* John G. Kennedy, *Tarahumara of the Sierra Madre;* and François Lartigue, *Indios y bosques: políticas forestales y comunales en la Sierra Tarahumara.* The best contemporary work is by William L. Merrill; see *Rarámuri Souls,* and "Tarahumara Social Organization, Political Organization and Religion," in Sturtevant, gen. ed., *Handbook of North American Indians,* vol. 10.

45. Although Jesuits provided ethnographic information as early as the first decade of the seventeenth century, some the richest sources come from later in the century when the order renewed its conversion efforts in the upper Tarahumara. Luis González Rodríguez painstakingly sought and reproduced a good deal of the colonial documentation produced by Jesuits; for example, *Tarahumara: la sierra y el hombre, Crónicas,* and *El noroeste novohispano en la época colonial.* Especially helpful are two detailed reports by Jesuits (which were being prepared for publication in English with William Merrill at the time of González Rodríguez' death). One is a report sent by Padres Joseph Tardá and Tomás de Guadalajara to P. Prov. Francisco Ximénez in August 1676 (cited hereafter as Tardá and Guadalajara report). The complete letter was forwarded to Rome (Archivum Romanum Societatis Iesu, Provincia Mexicana 17, 355–392); copies of parts of it are found in AGN, Historia, vol. 19, fols. 259–280; and Misiones, vol. 26, fols. 216–225. Another is the report of P. Juan María Ratkay, Carichi, March 20, 1683 (hereafter cited as Ratkay report); I have seen only the translation from the Latin in the University of California Bancroft Library, Bolton Collection, Mexicana 17. For analysis of non-Christian and Christian elements in Rarámuri religion, see William L. Merrill, "God's Saviours in the Sierra Madre," *Natural History* 93, no. 3 (1983), and "Conversion and Colonialism in Northern Mexico: The Tarahumara Response to the Jesuit Mission Program, 1601–1767," in Hefner, ed., *Conversion to Christianity,* 129–163.

46. Cramaussel, *La provincia de Santa Bárbara,* 87.

47. Testimony of Antonio, governor of Yepómera, Carichi, September 22, 1690, AGI, Patronato, leg. 236, fol. 347.

48. Carta annua, Juan Font, 1611, González Rodríguez, ed., *Crónicas,* 186–193.

49. Testimonies of Hernando and Margarita (Indians from New Mexico), May 22, 1690, AGI, Patronato, leg. 236, fols. 112–120; report of Capt. Juan Fernández de Retana, Bachíniva, September 15, 1697, AGI, Guadalajara, leg. 156, fol. 404.

50. Testimonio de los autos . . . acerca de la entrada de los Padres Gerónimo de Figueroa y Joseph Pascual . . . Tarahumara, June–October 1639, printed in *Textos de la Nueva Vizcaya: Documentos de San Joseph del Parral* (occasional documentary publication of the Universidad Autónoma de Ciudad Juárez) 1, no. 3 (1993): 26–39. An

earlier version appeared in Francisco Orozco y Jiménez, *Colección de documentos inéditos relativos a la Iglesia de Chiapas*, vol. 1, 93–95.

51. Robert J. Hard and William L. Merrill, "Mobile Agriculturalists and the Emergence of Sedentism: Perspectives from Northern Mexico," *American Anthropologist* 94, no. 3 (September 1992): 601–620.

52. See Merrill, *Rarámuri Souls*, passim, which explains the centrality of this concept to the Indians' worldview.

53. Carta annua, Juan Font, 1611, González Rodríguez, ed., *Crónicas*, 186–193, interprets the belief in an afterlife in more simplistic terms.

54. Griffen, "Observations on the Limitations of Data," 257–258, discusses the reasons why the colonial observations on eastern groups are so disparate. See also his *Indian Assimilation;* and Cramaussel, *La Provincia de Santa Bárbara*, 85–87. Conchos and their eastern neighbors have received the most ethnohistorical attention from Griffen, who speculated that Conchos may have been primarily sedentary agriculturalists who later resorted to nomadism to escape exploitation by Spaniards. The claim by Gary C. Anderson in *The Indian Southwest, 1580–1830: Ethnogenesis and Reinvention*, 21, that Conchos and Tobosos were generic terms for a variety of related Jumano bands lacks substantiation, especially since there is little agreement on who the Jumanos were. Nonetheless, he provides useful commentary on the trading complex centered at the junction of the Conchos and Río Grande that was a source of horses and probably involved a number of the groups considered here, 15–60. La Junta was also a region of refuge for raiding bands.

55. In 1622, Franciscans did provide counts of Indians in their missions in the province of Santa Bárbara, but these 1,003 would be only a fraction of the total population (already decimated by disease). See the padrones y minutas in BN-AF, caja 11/171; and Razón y minuta . . . , 1625, in Hackett, ed., *Historical Documents*, vol. 2, 152–159.

56. See Griffen, *Culture Change and Shifting Populations in Central Northern Mexico*, 155–169, for a multitude of groups identified by Spaniards.

57. Chantal Cramaussel, "De cómo los españoles clasificaban a los indios: naciones y encomiendas en la Nueva Vizcaya central," in Hers et al., *Nómadas y sedentarios*, 275–303. Sheridan Prieto, *Anónimos y desterrados*, 67–69, discusses sources that link classification to linguistic characteristics.

58. Griffen, *Culture Change*, 144–152. Despite the negative meaning of the term "raid," I employ it to connote a legitimate means of warfare (resistance) and of material survival. The Tobosos, who later came to represent the stereotypic chichimeca savages, apparently practiced some limited agriculture well into the seventeenth century: Traslado de los autos hechos en razón de la paz que se asentó con los indios de nación tobosos y salineros por el señor maese de campo don Francisco Montaño de la Cueva . . . 1645, AHP, r. 1645a, fr. 227–243.

59. Cramaussel, "De cómo los españoles," and Alvarez, "Agricultores de paz y cazadores-recolectores de guerra: los tobosos de la cuenca del Río Conchos en la Nueva Vizcaya," in Hers et al., eds., *Nómadas y sedentarios*, 305–354.

60. Sheridan Prieto, *Anónimos y desterrados*, 38–39, 53–60; see also her discussion of cultural factors that suggest why a nomadic lifestyle would be preferred to a sedentary one, 45–50.

61. Ibid., p. 66. Autos hechos sobre las invasiones que hacen los indios rebeldes . . . 1690–93, AGN, Provincias Internas, vol. 29: the testimony of Joseph de la Fuente, August 26, 1691, discusses a marriage alliance between Tobosos and Cabezas; see also Griffen, "Southern Periphery: East," vol. 10, 334–340.

62. Ann L. W. Stodder and Debra L. Martin, "Health and Disease in the Southwest before and after Spanish Contact," in John W. Verano and Douglas H. Ubelaker, eds., *Disease and Demography in the Americas*, 55–73.

63. Alvarez, "Agricultores de paz y cazadores-recolectores de guerra," 305–354.

64. Cynthia Radding, "Cultural Boundaries between Adaptation and Defiance: The Mission Communities of Northwestern New Spain," in Nicholas Griffiths and Fernando Cervantes, *Spiritual Encounters*, 116–135.

3. A COUNTERFEIT PEACE, 1620–1690

1. Mateo de Vesga, 1620–22, Hackett, ed., *Historical Documents*, vol. 2, 118–137, and AGI, Audiencia de Guadalajara, leg. 37, exp. 46.

2. Autos concerning treatment of Indians in Nueva Vizcaya, 1670–1671, BPE, AJANG, Civil, caja 12, exp. 2 (157). These resulted from an investigation ordered by the queen, who had received complaints from Bishop Juan de Gorospe y Aguirre about labor and other abuses.

3. This reality accentuates the highly defensive nature of Spanish military activities in the north. Although provincial governors often underwrote sporadic and informal campaigns, with or without the assurance of viceregal funds, the time-tested custom of conquest relied heavily on encomenderos or first settlers to provide their own troops to enforce or maintain the peace. The lack of a consistent military strategy for the north has been described in many studies, including Max L. Moorhead, *The Presidio: Bastion of the Spanish Borderlands;* Guillermo Porras Muñoz, *La frontera con los indios de Nueva Vizcaya en el siglo XVII;* and Naylor and Polzer, eds., *Presidio*. On the private armies of powerful local landowners and miners, see Cramaussel, "El poder de los caudillos en el norte de la Nueva España: Parral, siglo XVII," in Castañeda, ed., *Círculos de poder en la Nueva España*, 39–58. For a recent summary focusing on the northeast, see Sheridan Prieto, *Anónimos y desterrados*, 117 ff.

4. Petition of Don Francisco, gobernador, Santiago Papasquiaro, March 18, 1623, AGN, Jesuitas III-16, exp. 7; carta annua, P. Juan Florencio, May 16, 1624, AGN, Misiones, vol. 25, fols. 90–92.

5. Mateo de Vesga, 1620–22, Hackett, ed., *Historical Documents*, vol. 2, 118–137, and AGI, Audiencia de Guadalajara, leg. 37, exp. 46.

6. Petition of Tobosos, May 7, 1724, Hackett, ed., *Historical Documents*, vol. 2, 136–143; María Teresa Huerta Preciado, *Rebeliones indígenas en el noreste de México en*

la época colonial, 82–83; carta annua, P. Juan Florencio, May 20, 1627, AGN, Misiones, vol. 25, fol. 164. Cramaussel and Alvarez have argued that the Salineros were actually eastern Tepehuanes (see Chapter 2), but in the mid-seventeenth century the Jesuits listed Salinero as one of the Indian languages spoken by the missionary in Tizonazo; Jesuit catalog, 1663, ARSI, Provincia Mexicana, vol. 5, fol. 107.

7. Pérez de Ribas, *Historia de los triunfos,* book 9, chs. 14–21.

8. Polzer, *Rules and Precepts,* explains this organization and the rules upon which it was based.

9. Reports of P. Diego Ximénez, 1632–1633, AGN, Jesuitas, III-15, exps. 4, 33. The early missionaries used the spelling "Santa María Utais," but later we find "Otais," "Otaez," and "Otaes" being used interchangeably. The modern-day spelling is "Otaez."

10. West and Parsons, "The Topia Road," 409–411; case of Diego de Paz Tinoco, March 1627, AGN, Inquisición, vol. 360, pt. 2, fols. 375–383.

11. Puntas de annua de la misión de Atotonilco y Badiraguato, ca. 1638, AGN, Historia, vol. 316, exp. 8, fols. 307–312; report of P. Pedro de Robles, n.d., AGN, AHH, Temp., leg. 279, exp. 47.

12. Inquisition denunciations, Topia and San Andrés, 1627, AGN, Inquisición, vol. 360, fols. 30–39.

13. Carta annua, 1626, AGN, Misiones, vol. 25, fols. 164–165.

14. Carta annua, P. Pedro Gravina, Santa María Utais, March 11, 1629, AGN, Misiones, vol. 25, fols. 241–242.

15. Pérez de Ribas, *Historia de los triunfos,* book 9, chs. 10, 11.

16. Report of Juan de Cervantes Casaús, Parral, October 1654, CP, vol. 8, pp. 499–554.

17. Carta annua, P. Juan Florencio, May 16, 1624, AGN, Misiones, vol. 25, fols. 90–94.

18. ". . . la sentina de la basura de toda la Nueva España," testimony of P. Alberto Clerici, Zape, June 3, 1627, AGN, Inquisición, vol. 360, fol. 30.

19. Petition of Alonso de la Medina, Parral, March 13, 1641, AHP, r. 1648, fr. 12–14.

20. Puntos de annua de la misión de Tepehuana, 1630, AGN, Misiones, vol. 25, fol. 229.

21. Carta annua de P. Francisco de Mendoza, Zape, June 6, 1662, AGN, Misiones, vol. 26, fols. 167–171.

22. P. Gaspar de Contreras to P. Prov. Andrés Pérez, Santiago Papasquiaro, September 13, 1638, AGN, Misiones, vol. 25, fols. 282–283.

23. West, *The Mining Community,* 47–55.

24. Ibid., 13.

25. Información hecha de pedimiento del Sr. Gen. Don Francisco Bravo de la Serna, February 12, 1640, *Textos de la Nueva Vizcaya* 1, no. 3 (1993): 40–44.

26. West, *The Mining Community,* 48; Ignacio del Rio, "Sobre la aparición y desarrollo del trabajo libre asalariado en el norte de Nueva España (siglos XVI y XVII)," in Frost et al., eds., *El trabajo y los trabajadores.* See the list of salaried skilled workers

employed by a Parral miner and rancher: autos de inventario . . . de Pedro Correa, AGN, Inquisición, vol. 602, exp. 6.

27. Cramaussel, *La provincia de Santa Bárbara*, 38–42; Deeds, "Rural Work." Both agriculture and stock raising near the mines were considerably stimulated. In addition to meat, stock raisers also supplied tons of tallow for the candles to light the mines; West, *The Mining Community*, 25.

28. Causa criminal contra Juan indio tepeguan . . . , Parral, November 23, 1636, AHP, r. 636, fr. 629–640.

29. West, *The Mining Community*, 52; autos de inventario y embargo de bienes de Pedro Correa, Hacienda de Chicanaya, June 6, 1667, AGN, Inquisición, vol. 602, exp. 6, fols. 89–91.

30. Petition of Lucas Merino, July 3, 1646; AHP, r. 1648, fr. 54; testimony regarding bigamy of Juan Martín, indio sinaloa, September 1640–May 1643, Archivo Parroquial de Parral, caja 17a, 1–1; charges of Marcos Beltrán, Parral, February 9, 1649, AHP, r. 1649d, fr. 275–281.

31. Carta annua, P. Juan Florencio, San Pablo, 1626, AGN, Misiones, vol. 25, fol. 164; Naylor and Polzer, eds., *Presidio*, 204.

32. Carta annua, P. Juan Florencio, San Pablo, May 30, 1627, AGN, Misiones, vol. 25, fol. 164.

33. Traslado de los autos e información originales hechos en la pacificación y asunto de los indios tepehuanes y tarahumaras de los valles de San Pablo y San Ignacio, October–December 1635, CP, vol. 6, pp. 291–410.

34. Junta testimonies, 1639, in *Textos de la Nueva Vizcaya* 1, no. 3 (1993): 40–44; Gov. Bravo to Viceroy Marqués de Cadereyta, Durango, n.d. 1639, AGN, Jesuitas, I-16, exp. 38.

35. Informe de la situación y estado de Huejotitlán, October 25, 1745, MPC.

36. Petition of Capt. Juan de Barraza, defender of the Tepehuanes and Tarahumaras, Parral, January 4, 1640, AGN, Jesuitas, I-16, exp. 10.

37. See Cramaussel, "De cómo los españoles," 295–297, for a description of what she calls "encomiendas de indios de misión."

38. Correspondence between viceroy and P. Prov. Andrés Pérez de Ribas, August–September 1638, AGN, AHH, Temp., leg. 2009, exp. 1.

39. Petitions for repartimiento labor, 1640s, AHP, r. 1648, fr. 12–16, 23–25, 44, 56–57; report of P. Nicolás de Zepeda to P. Prov. Francisco Calderón, San Miguel de las Bocas, April 28, 1645, AGN, Historia, vol. 19, fols. 121–135.

40. Draft is in BN (Madrid), ms. no. 3000, fols. 238–241.

41. Testimony of Capt. Baltasar de Ontíveros, December 26, 1645, and Sebastián González de Valdez, Parral, July 30, 1646, both in AHP, r. 1648, fr. 25, 44.

42. Relación de méritos y servicios de Gonzalo Gómez de Cervantes, 1650, AGI, Indiferente General, leg. 113; testimonio . . . de la laguna de la sal llamada Sta. María de los Tobosos, September–October 1639, in *Textos de la Nueva Vizcaya* 1, no. 3 (October 1993); encomienda grant to Capt. Diego Romo, February 3, 1648, AHP, r. 1648, fr. 7–8.

43. Medrano report, 1654, in Naylor and Polzer, eds., *Presidios*, 419–421. Tizo-

nazo was alleged to be the "capa con que se entren y disfrazen para hacer mal"; Casaús report, October 1654, CP, vol. 8, pp. 540.

44. P. Zepeda to P. Prov., San Miguel de las Bocas, April 28, 1645, in *DHM*, 4-3, 130; carta annua de 1647, ARSI, Provincia Mexicana, vol. 15, fols. 261–263.

45. P. Zepeda to P. Prov., San Miguel de las Bocas, April 28, 1645, in *DHM*, 4-3, 130; Sheridan Prieto, *Anónimos y desterrados*, 115–116.

46. William Griffen, *Culture Change*, 144–152; investigation of Indian problems by Gov. Enrique Dávila y Pacheco, Parral, October 1654–January 1655, CP, vol. 8, pp. 463–555. See also the discussion by Alvarez, "Agricultores de paz y cazadores-recolectores de guerra."

47. Traslado de los autos hechos en razón de la paz que se asentó con los indios de nación tobosos y salineros por el señor maese de campo don Francisco Montaño de la Cueva . . . 1645, AHP, r. 1645a, fr. 227–243.

48. Reports of P. Zepeda, San Miguel de las Bocas, April–September, 1645, AGN, Historia, vol. 19, fols. 121–166. The poisoning reported by Zepeda would have been most unusual, but it may have been considered a more humane way of executing a woman. Indians themselves used poisoned arrows in their skirmishes with Spaniards.

49. Ibid.; Deeds, "Colonial Chihuahua: Peoples and Frontiers in Flux," in Jackson, ed., *New Views of Borderlands History*, 27–28.

50. Documents concerning the bishop's quarrel with the Jesuits can be found in AGN, Historia, vol. 20, exp. 9; AGN, AHH, Temp.: leg. 2009, exp. 30; leg. 278, exps. 30, 39; leg. 324, exps. 12–14; and leg. 325, exp. 64; P. Zepeda to P. Provincial, San Miguel de las Bocas, April 10, 1652, AGN, Jesuitas, I-17, exp. 38. See also: P. Joseph Pasqual, Parral, July 1649, AHP, r. 1649c, fr. 1412; and Pueblo de Santa Cruz del río de Nazas contra . . . Don Phelipe Montaño de la Cueva, Parral, July 12, 1649, AHP, r. 1653b. Gov. Gaspar de Alvear married the heiress of the Urdiñola fortune, and Gov. Luis de Valdés had property in the Parras area; see David Adams, "The Tlaxcalan Colonies of Spanish Coahuila and Nuevo León: An Aspect of the Settlement of Northern Mexico," Ph.D. dissertation, 267–277.

51. Real cédula to governor of Nueva Vizcaya, November 30, 1647, AHP, r. 1652d.

52. Oidor Pedro Fernández de Baeza to king, August 17, 1646, AGI, Audiencia de Guadalajara, leg. 10.

53. By the mid-eighteenth century, the governor's secretary received from the employer four reales for each Indian delivered; the Indian recruiter got two reales each; Gov. Joseph Carlos de Agüero to viceroy, Durango, July 5, 1767, AGN, Provincias Internas, vol. 94, exp. 2.

54. Autos concerning mine labor, Guanaceví, February 1648, AHP, r. 1648, fr. 188ff; petition of Capt. Juan de Echavarría to Gov. Luis de Valdés, January 4, 1648, AHP, r.1648, fr. 5–6; petition of Sargento Mayor Juan Martín Lineras, Real de San Diego, June 15, 1649, AHP, r. 1649c, fr. 1484; land sales, 1649, in AHP, r. 1649b, fr. 816–819, 824–828.

55. Nicolás de Barreda to king, Sierra de San Andrés, July 5, 1645, CP, vol. 7, pp. 209–248. Cramaussel provides an extended description and analysis of this document in "Un projet de réductions indigènes pour la Nouvelle-Biscaye: L'avis de Nicolas

de Barreda, missionaire jésuite à San Andrés en 1645," in Musset and Calvo, eds., *Des Indes Occidentales à L'Amérique Latine*, 39–54. On the Paraguayan reductions, see Guillermo Furlong Cardiff, *Misiones y sus pueblos de guaraníes*, and Philip Caraman, *Lost Paradise: The Jesuit Republic in South America*.

56. P. Proc. Bernardo Rolandegui to king, 1704, AGN, AHH, Temp. leg. 325, exp. 51.

57. O'Malley, *The First Jesuits*, 156–157. Kristin Dutcher Mann, "Music and Popular Religion in Northern New Spain," *Catholic Southwest* 12 (2001): 7–27, and "The Power of Song in the Missions of Northern New Spain," Ph.D. dissertation.

58. Libro de alajas de la Iglesia de San Gerónimo Huejotitlán, December 27, 1690, AGN, AHH, Temp., leg. 279, exp. 65; P. Domingo de Lizarralde to P. Prov. Diego de Almonacir, Satebó, October 17, 1695, AGN, Jesuitas, I-12, exp. 292. Memoria, Tamazula, 1726, AGN, AHH, Temp., leg. 282, exp. 48; P. Francisco Xavier de Lora to P. Proc. Joseph Ferrer, Tamazula, August 3, 1738, AGN, AHH, Temp., leg. 2017, exp. 3; Clara Bargellini, "At the Center on the Frontier: The Jesuit Tarahumara Missions of New Spain," in Thomas Dacosta Kaufmann, ed., *The Geohistory of Art*. Representations of San Francisco Xavier were present almost universally throughout the missions, along with those of Jesus Christ and the Virgin.

59. P. Bernardo de Treviño to P. Proc. Joseph Ferrer, San Miguel de las Bocas, July 16, 1737, AGN, AHH, Temp., leg. 2017, exp. 3; inventario de las alajas y bienes . . . Satebó, September 1749, AGN, Archivo Provisional, Temp., caja 5.

60. Carta annua de P. Jose Pascual, San Felipe, June 24, 1651, AGN, Jesuitas, III-15, exp. 7; informe del obispo Alonso Franco y Luna, May 12, 1638, ARSI, Provincia Mexicana, vol. 24.

61. Carta annua de P. Jose Pascual, San Felipe, June 24, 1651, AGN, Jesuitas, III-15, exp. 7; varied versions of Pascual's account are also found in AGN, Historia, vol. 19, and *DHM*, 4-3, 179–209. The latter is translated in Thomas E. Sheridan and Thomas H. Naylor, eds., *Rarámuri: A Colonial Chronicle, 1607–1791*, 16–31. See also the report by Juan de Barraza, April 15, 1649, in AGN, Jesuitas, I-12, exp. 253.

62. Expediente sobre los agravios hechos a Luis de Valdés . . . , March 2, 1651, AGI, Audiencia de Guadalajara, vol. 28.

63. P. Joseph Pascual to Bishop, San Felipe, September 6, 1649, AGN, Jesuitas I-17, exp. 60.

64. Gov. Diego Guajardo y Fajardo to king, Parral, April 24, 1652, AGN, Jesuitas I-16, exp. 8. The governor alleged that the bishop had other reasons for his enmity. Guajardo had ordered an investigation of Felipe Montaño's claims to the estate of his uncle, Francisco Montaño de la Cueva, who died intestate, and who had been a mortal enemy of Guajardo. The nephew, a cleric, belonged to the bishop's circle; the governor alleged the two had colluded to acquire the substantial fortune left by Parral's wealthiest miner. Governor to king, Parral, March 9, 1652, CP, vol. 8, pp. 149–155. See also P. Gabriel de Villar to governor, Parral, August 26, 1653, AGN, Jesuitas I-16, exp. 3. Rubén Rocha Ch., *Obispos de la Nueva Vizcaya*, 8. Real acuerdo ordinario to viceroy, Guadalajara, April 27, 1684, AGN, AHH, Temp., leg. 2019, exp. 29.

65. Gen. Juan Fernández de Morales to governor, Villa de Aguilar, June 22, 1650,

CP, vol. 8, pp. 45-48; P. Basilio to P. Prov. Andrés de Rada, Villa de Aguilar, October 10, 1651, AGN, Jesuitas, I-11, exp. 111.

66. Carta annua, 1662, San Miguel de las Bocas, AGN, Misiones, vol. 26, fol. 60.

67. Carta annua, 1651, P. Joseph Pascual, San Felipe, AGN, Jesuitas, III-15, exp. 7.

68. Diputados del Real de Parral contra curas de Parral sobre derechos de naboríos, May 15, 1651, BPE, AJANG, caja 3, exp. 9.

69. Porras Muñoz, *La frontera con los indios*, 514.

70. Apologético defensorio . . . , November 1657, in AGN, Historia, vol. 316.

71. Tepehuan visita, 1651, AHP, r. 1651a, fr. 186-224.

72. Viceroy Duque de Albuquerque to Audiencia de Guadalajara, April 25, 1659, BPE, AJANG, Civil, caja 4-1 (39); petition of Don Gerónimo Francisco, Valle de San Bartolomé, October 27, 1655, AGN, Indios, vol. 18, exp. 255. Charles L. Kenner, *A History of New Mexico–Plains Indian Relations*, 14-18, argues that even Pueblo Indians were sent as slaves to Nueva Vizcaya through the connivance of New Mexican governors. Indian slave trading was a complex business in which Indian groups themselves participated. Salvador Alvarez has argued that the name "Toboso" had become a generic appellation for raiders who used the deserts of the Bolsón de Mapimí as areas of refuge; the continued attribution of unrest to them justified Spanish expeditions against them. "Agricultores de paz y cazadores-recolectores de guerra," 351-354.

73. Criminal case against D. Francisco de Bustamante, Parral, June–July 1652, AHP, r. 1652d, fr. 1736 ff.; sale of hacienda, San Diego de las Minas, August 18, 1655, AHP, r. 1652, fr. 980-982; lease agreements in AHP, 1652c, fr. 1049, and r. 1654d, fr. 913-915.

74. Testimony in the case of Juan, a Concho Indian, Parral, November 29, 1652, AHP, r. 1652d, fr. 1785ff; causa criminal contra Andrés Pérez y otros indios . . . , Parral, June 1660, AHP, r.1660c, fr. 1692-1724.

75. Testimonies before Gov. Enrique de Avila Pacheco, 1653, BN-AF, caja 11, exp. 180; Parroquia de Santiago Papasquiaro, Entierros, 1653, GS, microfilm collection, no. 654992; governor to viceroy, 1659, BPE, AJANG, caja 12, exp. 2-157; autos en razón de haverse retirado indios . . . , 1689, AGN, Provincias Internas, vol. 30, exp. 6.

76. On mining and hacienda production, see the inventory in BN (Madrid), ms. 3047, fol. 120.

77. Petition of Francisco Martínez Orejón, Valle de San Bartolomé, June 6, 1655, AHP, r. 1655b, fr. 640-650; case of Capt. Bernardo Gómez de Montenegro, 1657, AHP, r. 1657b, fr. 820-897; Hackett, ed., *Historical Documents*, vol. 2, 31.

78. Account books, Hacienda de San Juan, Santa Bárbara, 1660, AHP, r. 1668b, fr. 590.

79. Chantal Cramaussel, "Haciendas agrícolas y abasto de granos en el Parral del siglo XVII," in Guedea and Rodríguez O., eds., *Five Centuries of Mexican History/Cinco siglos de historia de México*, vol. 2, 348-353; diputados de Parral . . . escaseses de maíz, 1654, AHP, r. 1654d. See Meyer, *Water in the Hispanic Southwest*, 47-73, on the centrality of water in land tenure. Even grants of pasturelands often included a watering place; West, *The Mining Community*, 59.

80. Declaration of governor of Zape during Tepehuan visita, November 7, 1651, AHP, r. 1651a, fr. 186–204; charges of pueblo of Santa Cruz del Río de Nazas, July 1649, AHP, r. 1653b; registro de un sitio . . . en términos de Huejotitan, 1668–70, AHP, r. 1669a, fr. 282–299. See also Alvarez, "Agricultural Colonization," 179; and Radding, *Wandering Peoples*, 171–207, for comparative context on the occurrence of land disputes in the north.

81. West, *The Mining Community*, 120–121. Louisa Hoberman, *Mexico's Merchant Elite, 1590–1660: Silver, State, and Society*, 83–92, discusses the advantages of the assayer post for acquiring wealth. The extensive pasturelands acquired by Spaniards in the north were relatively undeveloped and completely unfenced; for an analysis of the functioning of these "haciendas trashumantes" or "agostaderos volantes," see Sheridan Prieto, *Anónimos y desterrados*, 109–114.

82. Letters of Gov. Oca y Sarmiento to viceroy (March 12, 1667) and queen (March 19, 1667), Parral, Hackett, ed., *Historical Documents*, vol. 2, 188–195.

83. Francisco R. Almada, *Resumen de historia del estado de Chihuahua*, 73; Keith W. Algier, "Feudalism in New Spain's Northern Frontier: Valle de San Bartolomé," Ph.D. dissertation, 79–100.

84. Documents in this case are found in AHP, r. 1667b, fr. 738–743, and in AGI, Escribanía de Cámara, leg. 396b.

85. Letter of Padres Gerónimo de Figueroa, Gabriel del Villar, Virgilio Maes, and Bernabé de Lozano, to viceroy, January 11, 1669, AGN, Jesuitas, I-16, exp. 17.

86. Real cédula, June 22, 1670, Hackett, ed., *Historical Documents*, vol. 2, 200–201.

87. Autos concerning treatment of Indians in Nueva Vizcaya, Audiencia de Guadalajara, 1670–1672, BPE, AJANG, Civil, caja 8, exp. 111; caja 12, exp. 2. Case of Capt. Pedro Zubia Pacheco, Valle de San Bartolomé, June–July 1674, AHP, r. 1674d, fr. 1970–1999.

88. P. Gerónimo de Figueroa to P. Visitador General, San Pablo, May 9, 1664, ARSI, Provincia Mexicana, vol. 17, fols. 298–300.

89. Carta annua de P. Gerónimo de Figueroa, San Pablo, June 8, 1662, *DHM*, 4-3, 217–222. This point about adaptive responses to (changing) environmental circumstances has been made by other scholars: Sheridan and Naylor, eds., *Rarámuri*, 72; James Saeger, "Another View of the Mission as a Frontier Institution: The Guaycuruan Reductions of Santa Fe," *Hispanic American Historical Review* 65, no. 3 (1985), 493–517; and Radding, *Wandering Peoples*, 142–167.

90. Carta annua de 1646–47, ARSI, Provincia Mexicana, vol. 15, fols. 261–263; inventarios [Tepehuana], 1665–1666, AGN, Jesuitas, II-18.

91. P. Gabriel de Villar to P. Prov. Pedro Antonio Díaz, San Gerónimo, May 20, 1664, AGN, AHH, Temp., leg. 1126, exp. 3. This practice was expressly forbidden by Jesuit rules. Various grades of cotton cloth, flannels, muslin, and coarse woolens from the south were introduced early through distribution by missionaries and as commodity pay for repartimiento service or free wage labor. Although Tarahumara women adapted to the weaving of woolen blankets from the sheep they herded, there was

no local weaving industry until the eighteenth century. Therefore woolen goods were particularly valued.

92. The Jesuits were well aware by this time of the high coincidence between disease and congregation. Carta annua, 1636, AGN, Jesuitas, III-15; and Nicolás de Barreda to king, Sierra de San Andrés, July 5, 1645, AGI, Guadalajara, leg. 68. They also observed that children were highly susceptible, especially the firstborn; puntos de annua, San Pablo, November 14, 1668, AGN, Jesuitas, III-15, exp. 5.

93. Carta annua, P. Francisco de Mendoza, Zape, June 6, 1662, AGN, Misiones, vol. 26, fols. 167–171. P. Ignacio de Medina described the "tan cruel peste" of 1662, to which he also nearly succumbed, in a carta annua, Otais, February 8, 1663, AGN, Misiones, vol. 26, fol. 179. Puntos de annua de la misión de Topia, n.d. [1660s], AGN, Misiones, vol. 26, fol. 190. P. Estevan Alvarez to P. Prov. Andrés de Cobián, San Gregorio, October 20, 1672, AGN, Jesuitas, I-12, exp. 331. From an anonymous Jesuit report of the early 1670s: "Es un reventadero. Es un destierro. Es como remar en galera." AGN, Jesuitas, I-17, exp. 41. Report of P. Joseph López Rendón, Otatitlán, ca. 1690, AGN, AHH, Temp., leg. 279, exp. 44. My population estimates are derived from Gerhard, *The North Frontier*, 170–200; visita counts by P. Juan Ortiz Zapata, 1678, in *DHM*, 4-3, 301–419; and mission reports [1685] in AGN, AHH, Temp., leg. 279, exps. 8, 71, 118, 119.

94. Carta annua de P. Cristóbal de Robles, San Pedro Guarisamey, February 16, 1663, AGN, Misiones, vol. 26, exp. 30. See the discussions of the devil, owls, and nagualism in Louise M. Burkhart, *The Slippery Earth: Nahua-Christian Moral Dialogue in Sixteenth-Century Mexico*, 39–45; and Serge Gruzinski, *Images at War: Mexico from Columbus to Blade Runner, 1492–2019*, 179–180.

95. Testimiento de dos provisiones de la Real Audiencia de Guadalajara, July 18, 1673, AGN, AHH, Temp., leg. 1955, f. 44; Lesley B. Simpson, *The Repartimiento System of Native Labor in New Spain and Guadalajara*, 61; P. Manuel Gutiérrez to P. Provincial, Piaba, April 10, 1681, AGN, AHH, Temp., leg. 278, exp. 39; report of Capt. Tomás de Chaide, Real de Minas de San Andrés, January 7, 1684, AGN, AHH, Temp., leg. 325, exp. 74.

96. Puntos de annua de la misión de Topia, 1663, AGN, Misiones, vol. 26, fols. 190–192.

97. In his visita report of 1678, Ortiz Zapata comments that many estancias belonged to people who were reputed to be Spaniards, *DHM*, 4-3, 307; report of P. Juan Boltor, San Ignacio de Piastla, May 25, 1691, AGN, AHH, Temp., leg. 279, exp. 46; report of P. Martín Martínez de Cantería, San Gregorio, ca. 1690, AGN, AHH, Temp., leg. 279, exp. 41; report of P. Pedro Ignacio Olivas, Yamoriba, December 28, 1690, AGN, AHH, Temp., leg. 279, exp. 39.

98. Instrucción secreta del P. Prov. Hernando Cabrero to P. Vigilio Maes, November 10, 1664, AGN, AHH, Temp., leg. 2009, exp. 48.

99. "Siguió a la hambre como inseparable compañera la peste, picando en los pueblos con rigor y sin remedio, apretaba a los miserables la hambre y saliendo a buscar el remedio de unos pueblos a otros o a los campos, rendían en medio de un camino

real la vida a manos del hambre y de la peste." The quote is from the carta annua of 1668, AGN, Historia 19, fols. 247–261 (reproduced in *DHM*, 4-3, 259). See also: carta annua de 1647, ARSI, Provincia Mexicana, vol. 15, fols. 261–263; report of Francisco Montero, Santiago Papasquiaro, ca. 1650, AGN, Jesuitas, II-4, exp. 29; carta annua, P. Francisco de Mendoza, Zape, June 6, 1662, AGN, Misiones, vol. 27, fols. 167–171; carta annua, Gerónimo de Figueroa, San Pablo, June 8, 1662, *DHM*, 4-3, 217–222; Ortiz Zapata visita report, 1678, *DHM*, 4-3, 301–419. In regard to the relationship between variables in subsistence crises, the missionary's observation is not corroborated by modern research: "there is no inevitable relationship between dearth and pestilence"; Murdo J. MacLeod, "The *Matlazáhuatl* of 1737–8 in Some Villages in the Guadalajara Region," in Robert H. Claxton, ed., *Investigating Natural Hazards in Latin American History*, a special edition of *West Georgia College Studies in the Social Sciences* 25 (1986): 8. See also Enrique Florescano, *Precios del maíz y crisis agrícolas en México, 1708–1810*, 159–172.

100. Declaration of Juana Isabel (tepehuana de San Pablo), January 24, 1692, AGN, Provincias Internas, vol. 29, exp. 5; population estimates are derived from Gerhard, *The North Frontier*, 170–200; Tepehuan visita counts, 1651, AHP, reel 1651a, fr. 186–224; Ortiz Zapata visita report, 1678, *DHM*, 4-3, 301–419; and mission reports (1690–1691) in AGN, AHH, Temp., leg. 279, exps. 65–70, 112–116.

101. Testimonios de todos los papeles, instrumentos y recaudos de las tierras, aguas, casas y huertas que está poseyendo en este pueblo de Santiago Papasquiaro la religión de los misioneros de la compañía de Jesús, July 3, 1721, AGN, Temp., vol. 38, exp. 9, fols. 317–318; Tarahumara visita of Capt. Juan Fernández de Retana, Huejotitlán, January 28, 1693, AGI, Patronato, leg. 236, fol. 840.

102. P. Francisco de Medrano Ibarra to P. Prov. Ambrosio Oddon, Santiago Papasquiaro, March 2, 1691, AGN, AHH, Temp., leg. 279, exp. 116; P. Diego de Poza to P. Proc. Joseph Ferrer, Alaya, July 16, 1736, AGN, AHH, Temp., leg. 2016, exp. 2. Missionaries and natives would later disagree over the ownership of additional lands that had been donated to the mission or purchased with mission income. Mission Indians rarely owned private property, as was common in central Mexico for elite natives, but some were rewarded by the Jesuits with access to larger parcels of land within the mission.

103. Estimates are based on Gerhard, *The North Frontier*, 170–200; Ortiz Zapata visita report, 1678, *DHM*, 4-3, 301–419; and mission reports (1690–1691) in AGN, AHH, Temp. 279. The total Tarahumara population had been estimated by Gov. Diego Guajardo Fajardo in 1649 at 25,000 to 30,000; governor to P. Provincial, Parral, May 11, 1649, AGN, Jesuitas, I-17, exp. 61.

104. "Lo temporal es el fundamento firmísimo y solidento fomento solidísimo para procurar, principiar, promover, asegurar y fixar lo espiritual destos pueblos . . ."; puntas de annua, San Pablo, 1652–62, AGN, Jesuitas, III-15, exp. 26.

105. Catálogo de los pueblos y partidos . . . , San Miguel de las Bocas, ca. 1650, AGN, Jesuitas, I-16, exp. 19; carta annua, San Miguel de las Bocas, 1662, AGN, Misiones, vol. 26, fol. 160; Ortiz Zapata visita report, *DHM*, 4-3, 317; testimony of Juana

de Aguilar, Parral, March 9, 1686, AGN, Inquisición, vol. 1551, part 2, exp. 39, fols. 563–571; report of P. Francisco Xavier de Medrano, Las Bocas, ca. 1690, AGN, AHH, Temp., leg. 279, exp. 69.

106. Memoria de P. Antonio de Herrera, Santa Cruz de Tarahumares, ca. 1690, AGN, AHH, Temp., leg. 279, exp. 115; in a letter to the Padre Provincial, P. Nicolás de Zepeda commented that although many of the local natives could understand the "común y corrumpida mexicana que se usa," it was not possible for the priests to confess them in any other than their native language; AGN, Jesuitas, I-17, exp. 38.

107. An auto de inventario y embargo de bienes de Pedro Correa, vecino de Parral, June 1667, AGN, Inquisición, vol. 602, exp. 6, refers to this incident, as well as other Indian attacks. Dunne, *Jesuit Missions in Tarahumara*, 91, 93.

108. Carta annua, 1662, P. Rodrigo del Castillo, Bocas, AGN, Misiones, vol. 26, exp. 27.

109. Ratkay report, March 20, 1683, UCB-B, Mexicana 17; libro de alajas de . . . Huexotitlan, December 27, 1690, AGN, AHH, Temp., leg. 279, exp. 65; on colegios incoados, see Instrucción secreta del P. Hernando Cabero al P. Vigilio Maes, November 10, 1664, ARSI, Provincia Mexicana, vol. 17, fols. 301–303; and report of P. Prov. Bernardo Pardo, August 14, 1683, UTNLB-WBS, 1747, 1–2. In 1691 there were 40 seminary students in Huejotitlán; P. Francisco de Medrano Ibarra to P. Prov. Ambrosio Oddon, March 2, 1691, AGN, AHH, Temp., leg. 279, exp. 116.

110. Sugerencias de un padre jesuita, ca. 1675, AGN, Jesuitas, I-17, exp. 41; memoria de P. Domingo de Lizarralde, San Francisco Xavier de Satevó, December 26, 1690, AGN, AHH, Temp., leg. 279, exp. 67.

111. Inquisition case against Nicolás de Guzmán, 1673, AGN, Inquisición, vol. 516, exp. 7, fols. 405–451. This story is told in Deeds, "Colonial Chihuahua: Peoples and Frontiers in Flux," 30–31.

112. Land case, Real de Minas de San Diego, June 1674–January 1675, AHP, r. 1671a, fr. 379–395; Ortiz Zapata visita report, *DHM*, 4-3, 319.

113. Pennington, *The Tarahumar*, 17; Kennedy, *Tarahumara of the Sierra Madre*, 1–21. For a complex analysis of residential mobility among contemporary Tarahumaras, see Hard and Merrill, "Mobile Agriculturalists."

114. Almada, *Resumen de historia*, 74; autos sobre la Tarahumara Alta, December 1675–January 1676, AGN, Jesuitas, I-16, exp. 3; testimonio de lo resuelto en la junta . . . de 1681, AGN, Jesuitas, I-11, exp. 1.

115. Luis González, ed., *Crónicas*, 136–138.

116. Carta del P. Tomás de Guadalajara, Matachi, July 20, 1677, AGN, Misiones, vol. 26, fols. 237–238; Fray Antonio de Valdés to P. Comisario General, Parral, June 17, 1677, BN-AF, caja 12, 195.2; P. José Tardá to P. Prov. Bernardo Pardo, Parral, October 8, 1681, AGN, AHH, Temp., leg. 1126, exp. 3.

117. Correspondence of Franciscan superiors with viceroy, 1667–1669, AGN, Historia, vol. 19, fols. 233–246; Arlegui, *Crónica*, 95–101.

118. Fray Antonio de Valdés to P. Comisario General, Parral, April 29, 1677, BN-AF, caja 12, 195.1.

119. Report of Bishop Bartolomé de Escanuela to king, Durango, April 18, 1681, AGI, Audiencia de Guadalajara, leg. 206; Sheridan Prieto, *Anónimos y desterrados,* 149–151.

120. Indios baborigames y cabezas, 1690–1703, AGN, Jesuitas, I-14, fols. 60–75; report of P. Vis. Juan de Guendulaín, May 18, 1725, AGN, AHH, Temp., leg. 2009, exp. 99.

121. Carta of bishop, November 13, 1681, BN-AF, caja 12, 200; reports of Jesuits at Santiago Papasquiaro, Santa Catalina, and Zape, December 1690–February 1691, in AGN, AHH, Temp., leg. 279, exps. 70, 112, 114.

122. Denunciación que contra si hizo Antonia de Soto, mulata esclava de Francisco de Noriega, vecino de la Ciudad de Durango de diferentes hechos con pacto con el demonio, 1691, AGN, Inquisición, vol. 525, exp. 48, fols. 500–520.

123. The extensive freighting business that transported silver and merchandise means that hundreds of mules and carts moved along the caminos reales throughout the winter months (the dry or traveling season); West, *The Mining Community,* 85–91.

124. Little has been written on black slavery in northern Mexico, but there is a good deal of anecdotal evidence on black slaves imported to work at haciendas and mines in the seventeenth century, often as overseers. By the eighteenth century, however, other evidence suggests that African American slaves had become an economic burden to their owners, especially those men who were married to free black women and had families. See the correspondence between Jesuit administrators of the Colegio de Durango and their superiors in Mexico City in the 1730s and 1740s: AGN, Jesuitas, I-17, exps. 239, 240, 245.

125. Various cases involving violent attacks, even between religious, in the mines of Urique, 1693, AGN, Inquisición, vol. 689, exp. 23, fols. 339–346.

126. For other seventeenth-century examples, see AGN, Inquisición, vol. 360, exp. 2; vol. 482, fols. 132–153; vol. 516, exp. 7; vol. 661, exp. 22.

127. Cases against Juan de Ledesma, Parral, 1680, and Bernabé Rodarte, Durango, 1693, AGN, Inquisición, vols. 640, exp. 1, and vol. 689, exp. 20, respectively. Ruth Behar, "Sex and Sin, Witchcraft, and the Devil in Late Colonial Mexico," *American Ethnologist* 14, no. 1 (1987): 34–54; Solange Alberro, *Inquisición y sociedad en México, 1571–1700,* 283–408.

128. P. Tomás de la Jara to P. Prov. Bernardo Pardo, Parras, January 3, 1681, AGN, AHH, Temp., leg. 278, exp. 39.

4. CRISES OF THE 1690S

1. P. Tomás de Guadalajara to P. Prov. Bernardo Pardo, Parral, December 4, 1681, ARSI, Provincia Mexicana, vol. 17, fol. 466. On the "Greater Southwestern" connections, see James F. Brooks, *Captives and Cousins: Slavery, Kinship, and Community in the Southwest Borderlands,* and Anderson, *The Indian Southwest.*

2. Naylor and Polzer, eds., *Presidio,* 548–567 (the garrisons intended for Cuen-

camé and Casas Grandes were actually placed at Pasaje and Janos); Capt. Joseph de Berroterán to viceroy, Presidio de Conchos, April 17, 1748, AGN, Historia, vol. 41, exp. 8, fols. 355–384.

3. Autos sobre las invasiones . . . , 1691–93, AGN, Provincias Internas, vol. 29, exp. 5; autos en razón de haverse retirados los indios cabezas . . . , December 1689, AGN, Provincias Internas, vol. 30, exp. 6.

4. Expediente sobre indios babosarigames y cavesas, 1690–1703, AGN, Jesuitas, 1-14, fols. 60–75.

5. Governor to king, México, September 26, 1678, in Hackett, ed., *Historical Documents*, vol. 2, 210–217; West, *The Mining Community*, 24.

6. Governor to king, Parral, November 21, 1688, and testimonies of Indians, 1688–89, in Hackett, ed., *Historical Documents*, vol. 2, 228–289. These references are to the encounters between groups of Jumanos and others with members of the LaSalle expedition.

7. Letters of P. Nicolás del Prado to P. Vis. Juan Baptista de Anzieta, Guadalupe, December 11, 27, 1681, AGN, Jesuitas, 1-12, exp. 246; P. Joseph Pallares to P. Prov. Bernabé de Soto, Batopilas, April 24, 1689, in González Rodríguez, ed., *Crónicas*, 139–141.

8. See Chapter 3 on Evía y Valdés.

9. Instructions of P. Prov. Tomás de Altamirano, 1680, AGN, AHH, Temp., leg. 282, exp. 21; P. Prov. Luis del Canto to viceroy, ca. 1683; AGN, Jesuitas, leg. 1-17; Ratkay report, March 20, 1683, UCB-B, Mexicana 17; real acuerdo ordinario de Guadalajara to viceroy, April 27, 1684, AGN, AHH, Temp., leg. 2019, exp. 29.

10. P. Francisco de Bañuelos to P. Prov. Ambrosio Oddon, Sinaloa, November 12, 1690, AGN, AHH, Temp., leg. 285.

11. P. Juan Ratkay to P. Nicolás Avancini, February 25, 1681, in Mauro Matthei, ed., *Cartas e informes de misioneros jesuitas extranjeros en Hispanoamérica*, 155–159.

12. Tardá and Guadalajara report, August 15, 1676, ARSI, Provincia Mexicana, fols. 377–378. The mission pueblos were composed of discrete parcialidades identified by their allegiance to specific elders. See, for example, the mention of "los de Yepómera de la parcialidad de un indio viejo llamado Malagara," testimony of Inés, July 8, 1690, AGI, Patronato, leg. 236, fol. 190.

13. Much of the following synthesis comes from the Ratkay and Tardá and Guadalajara reports, which contain valuable ethnographic information.

14. Aclaraciones a las acusaciones del Gobernador Juan Isidro de Pardiñas (draft), n.p., n.d. (1690s), in BN-AF, caja 12, exp. 207; this document has been published in Roberto Ramos, *Historia de la tercera rebelión tarahumara;* Ramos attributes the unsigned draft to P. Tomás de Guadalajara.

15. Joseph Neumann, *Historia de las rebeliones en la Sierra Tarahumara, 1626–1724,* ed. and tr. by Luis González Rodríguez, 33. For a critique of the applicability of James C. Scott's concept of hidden transcripts to contemporary Rarámuri, see Jerome M. Levi, "Hidden Transcripts among the Rarámuri: Culture, Resistance, and Interethnic Relations in Northern Mexico," *American Ethnologist* 26, no. 1 (1999): 90–113.

16. Ibid.; Tardá and Guadalajara report, August 15, 1676, ARSI, Provincia Mexicana, fol. 370. These forms of everyday resistance are examined in Scott, *Weapons of the Weak.*

17. Tardá and Guadalajara report, August 15, 1676, ARSI, Provincia Mexicana: "ni el padre va contra lo que quiere su hijo." There are also reports of parents becoming enraged when corporal punishment was used on their children; visita to Huejotitlán, February 1693, AGI, Patronato 236, fol. 447.

18. Ratkay report, March 20, 1683, UCB-B, Mexicana 17.

19. Mandamiento, 1693, AHP, r. 1693, fr. 13–18. Letter from Francisco Ramírez to governor of Nueva Vizcaya, Bachíniva, May 15, 1690, AGI, Patronato 236, fols. 89–90. Missionary reports, 1690, in AGN, AHH, Temp. leg. 279, exps. 66, 67, 69, 70, 112–115. P. Joseph Pallares to P. Prov. Bernabé de Soto, Batopilas, April 24, 1689; in González Rodríguez, ed., *Crónicas,* 139–142. Parish records from Cusiguiriachi report on the deaths of Indians from surrounding missions: Parroquia de Cusiguiriachi, Entierros, 1690s, GS, no. 162459. Alvarez, "Agricultural Colonization," 180, argues that Spanish hacendados from San Bartolomé and Parral had moved into the region earlier, but that their stability was assured after the mines were developed.

20. See the 1678 visita report of Juan Ortiz Zapata, *DHM,* 4-3, 301–419. As early as 1610, when P. Juan Font began to work with Tarahumaras, the smallpox epidemic of 1610 claimed three-fourths of the children; carta annua, 1611; González Rodríguez, ed., *Crónicas,* 186–193.

21. Carta annua, P. Juan Font, 1611; González Rodríguez, ed., *Crónicas,* 186–193; Ratkay report, March 20, 1683, UCB-B, Mexicana 17.

22. Merrill, *Rarámuri Souls,* 153–182.

23. Peter Gerhard, *The North Mexican Frontier,* 190.

24. Ratkay report, March 20, 1683, UCB-B, Mexicana 17; also see Merrill, "Tarahumara Social Organization, Political Organization, and Religion," 303–304.

25. Letter of P. Diego Ortiz de Foronda to P. Rector, Yepómera, February 22, 1690, and testimony of Gerónimo, governor of Papigochi, May 16, 1690, both in AGI, Patronato, leg. 236, fols. 7, and 84–86, respectively.

26. Tardá and Guadalajara report, August 15, 1676, ARSI, Provincia Mexicana, fols. 376–377.

27. Ibid., fol. 369.

28. For more details, see Neumann, *Historia de las rebeliones;* González Rodríguez, "Testimonios sobre la destrucción de las misiones tarahumares y pimas en 1690," *Estudios de Historia Novohispana* 10 (1991): 189–235; and Deeds, "Indigenous Rebellions," 12–23.

29. Testimony of Francisco, San Antonio de Casas Grandes, March 20, 1690, AGI, Patronato, leg. 236; the long expediente is entitled Nueva Vizcaya 1693. Testimonios de los autos y demás diligencias que el Señor Governador y Capitán General de este Reino formó en la guerra y pacificación de los indios de la nación Taraumara y sus aliados.

30. Declaration of Joseph de Yepómera, Santo Tomás, October 17, 1690, AGI, Patronato, leg. 236, fols. 396–397; declaration of Antonio, governor of Yepómera,

Carichi, September 22, 1690, AGI, Patronato, leg. 236, fol. 347; Jesuit responses to charges of Gov. Pardiñas, ca. 1690, BN-AF, caja 12, 207.

31. Autos sobre unas proposiciones que dijo el Gobernador Juan Isidro de Pardiñas Villar de Francos, Parral, April 16, 1692, AGN, Inquisición, vol. 684, fols. 218–219.

32. Francisco Ramírez de Salazar to governor, Casas Grandes, March 10, 1690, AGI, Patronato, leg. 236, fols. 1–3.

33. Declaration of Nicolás of Yepómera, Naguerachi, July 5, 1690, AGI, Patronato, leg. 236, fol. 187; declaration of Rafael, Papigochi, October 18, 1690, AGI, Patronato 236, fol. 402.

34. P. Francisco Zelada to governor, San Borja, March 30, 1690, AGI, Patronato, leg. 236, fols. 6–7.

35. See Griffen, *Indian Assimilation*, 4–24.

36. Testimony of Concho Indians, Casas Grandes, March 20, 1690, AGI, Patronato, leg. 236, fol. 772.

37. Declaration of Gerónimo, governor of Papigochi, May 16, 1690, AGI, Patronato, leg. 236, fols. 84–86.

38. Declaration of Inés, Naguerachi, July 8, 1690, AGI, Patronato, leg. 236, fols. 189–194.

39. Declaration of Tadeo, Papigochi, May 25, 1697, AGI, Audiencia de Guadalajara, leg. 156, fol. 206.

40. Report of junta of leading citizens of Parral, AGI, Patronato, leg. 236, fols. 20–25.

41. Autos practicados con motivo de dar paz a los indios enemigos, Parral, December 1699, AHP, r. 1699.

42. P. Joseph Neumann to P. Rector Francisco María Piccolo, Sisoguichi, May 16, 1690, AGI, Patronato, leg. 236, fol. 125.

43. Report of Gov. Pardiñas, Papigochi, May 31, 1690, AGI, Patronato, leg. 236, fol. 135.

44. P. Juan María de Salvatierra to governor, Cuiteco, May 19, 1690, AGI, Patronato, leg. 236, fols. 110–111; report of governor, Papigochi, May 28, 1690, AGI, Patronato, leg. 236, fols. 130–131; governor to viceroy, Cusiguiriachi, December 6, 1690, AGI, Patronato, leg. 236, fols. 509–512.

45. Report of Gov. Pardiñas, Tomochi, January 1691, AGI, Patronato, leg. 236, fols. 594–595.

46. Reports from the visita of Juan Fernández de Retana, October 1692–January 1693, AGI, Patronato, leg. 236, fols. 803–831.

47. P. Juan María de Salvatierra to governor, San Javier, December 5, 1692, P. Francisco María Piccolo to governor, Carichi, January 24, 1693, P. Francisco de Velasco to governor, January 30, 1695; all in AGI, Patronato, leg. 236, fols. 823, 808, 855, respectively.

48. Junta of officers, Tomochi, January 17, 1691, AGI, Patronato 236, fols. 592–593.

49. Report of governor on junta in Santo Tomás, October 20, 1690, AGI, Patronato, leg. 236, fols. 428–430.

50. The case presented to the Inquisition by the Jesuits is in AGN, Inquisición,

vol. 684, fols. 215–220: Autos remitidos por el comisario del Parral sobre unas proposiciones que dijo el gobernador . . . , Parral, June 1692.

51. Declaration of Gerónimo, governor of Papigochi, May 16, 1690, AGI, Patronato, leg. 236, fols. 84–86; testimony of Nicolás, Naguerachi, July 5, 1690, AGI, Patronato, leg. 236, fol. 181.

52. Francisco Ramírez Achero to governor, Bachíniva, May 15, 1690, AGI, Patronato, leg. 236, fols. 89–90.

53. Reports of Capt. Martín de Hualde, Cerrogordo, June 19 and December 26, 1692, AGN, Provincias Internas, vol. 29, exp. 5; Capt. Juan Fernández de Retana to governor, San Joseph de Temaichi, December 28, 1692, AGN, Provincias Internas, vol. 29, exp. 5; governor to viceroy, Parral, March 16, 1693, AGI, Patronato 236, fols. 860–861; report of fiscal, Madrid, April 1, 1698, AGI, Audiencia de Guadalajara, leg. 151. P. Neumann reported a triple epidemic of dysentery, smallpox, and a type of bubonic plague; *Historia de las rebeliones*, 67. Burial records from the mission of Santiago Papasquiaro and the parish of Parral corroborate high death rates for Indians, amounting to as much as ten times the average figure; see Parroquia de Santiago Papasquiaro and Parroquia de Parral, Entierros, GS, nos. 654993 and 162562, respectively.

54. Parroquia de Valle Allende, Entierros, 1693, GS, no. 162655.

55. Orden para que trabajen . . . , 1693, AHP, r. 1693, fr. 13–18; declaration of Ramón, Huejotitlán, January 28, 1693, AGI, Patronato, leg. 236, fol. 850; testimonio de los autos que se practicaron sobre las providencias de bastimientos, AHP, r. 1694.

56. Visita de Huejotitlán y San Pablo, January–February 1693, AGI, Patronato, leg. 236, fols. 847–848; see comments on gift giving: P. Joseph Neumann to P. Prov. Ambrosio Oddon, Sisoguichi, February 4, 1690, AGN, Misiones, vol. 26, fols. 311–312.

57. Governor to king, Parral, April 24, 1694, AGI, Audiencia de Guadalajara, leg. 151, exp. 1; autos sobre . . . falta de maiz y trigo, Valle de San Bartolomé, September 1694, AHP, r. 1694a, fr. 48–125; P. Antonio de Gomar to Capt. Juan Fernández de Retana, Santa Teresa, March 23, 1696, AGI, Audiencia de Guadalajara, leg. 156, fol. 1182.

58. The Marín report has been published in Hackett, ed., *Historical Documents*, vol. 2, 365–463; see also the report of the fiscal, which summarizes some of his arguments as well as those of Castillo, April 1696, AGI, Audiencia de Guadalajara, leg. 151, exp. 14.

59. Letters of P. Joseph Neumann to governor, Sisoguichi, December 25, 30, 1696; and governor to Capt. Fernández de Retana, Parral, January 10, 1697, AGI, Audiencia de Guadalajara, leg. 156, fols. 24–25.

60. Declaration of Malagara, Cocomorachi, March 14, 1697, and autos de Retana, April 28, 1697, AGI, Audiencia de Guadalajara, leg. 156, fols. 45–181.

61. P. Antonio de Gomar to Retana, Santa Teresa, July 18, 1697, AGI, Audiencia de Guadalajara, leg. 156, fol. 346.

62. Retana to viceroy, Papigochi, January 8, 1698, AGI, Audiencia de Guadalajara, leg. 156, fols. 605–632.

63. Interrogatories conducted by Retana, April–May 1697, AGI, Audiencia de

Guadalajara, leg. 156, fols. 102–215. In one case, witnesses from Casas Grandes testified that their Indian governor, Juan Corma, had been chosen by the Jesuits despite the fact that he had been evil ever since he was a child; ibid., fols. 216–256.

64. Neumann, *Historia de las rebeliones,* 95; report of Retana, Sisoguichi, June 26, 1697, AGI, Audiencia de Guadalajara 156, fol. 301.

65. Viceroy to P. Guadalajara, July 11, 1697, AGI, Audiencia de Guadalajara, leg. 156, fols. 455–456; autos, fols. 474–492.

66. Autos, Papigochi, May 17, 1698, AGI, Audiencia de Guadalajara, leg. 156, fols. 777–783.

67. Autos, June 1698, AGI, Audiencia de Guadalajara, leg. 156, fols. 795–833.

68. See these documents in AGI, Audiencia de Guadalajara, vol. 156, fols. 835–1199.

69. Testimonies of officials from various Tarahumara pueblos, December 1, 1699, AGI, Audiencia de Guadalajara, leg. 156, fols. 864–882.

70. Declaration of Muñaquiqui, Matachi, April 14, 1697, AGI, Audiencia de Guadalajara, leg. 156, fols. 128–133.

71. Testimony of Indians and Franciscans, La Junta de los Ríos, 1688–89; Hackett, ed., *Historical Documents,* vol. 2, 234–289; Alcalde Mayor Don Manuel de Agramont y Arce to viceroy, April 22, 1693; ibid., vol. 2, 315.

72. Margaret Connell Szasz, *Between Indian and White Worlds: The Cultural Broker;* and Frances Karttunen, *Between Worlds: Interpreters, Guides, and Survivors.* Andean works on the development of the *cacicazgo*/chiefdom also provide insight: Powers, *Andean Journeys,* and Ramírez, *World Upside Down.*

73. Tratado del servicio personal involuntario de los indios . . . , n.p., October 3, 1698, BN-AF, caja 32, 650, fols. 1–42.

74. Report of Rodríguez Gallardo, August 18, 1750, AGN, Provincias Internas, vol. 176, exp. 6.

75. Ibid.

76. P. Sebastián de Aguilar, Catálogo de familias . . . , San Pablo, December 20, 1690, AGN, AHH, Temp., leg. 279, exp. 66.

77. P. Francisco de Medrano Ibarra to P. Prov. Ambrosio Oddon, Santiago Papasquiaro, March 2, 1691, AGN, AHH, Temp., leg. 279, exp. 116.

5. DEFIANCE AND DEFERENCE IN TRANSITIONAL SPACES, 1700–1730S

1. Causa criminal . . . contra Matheo de la Cruz . . . por indicios de hechizero, 1703–1705, AHP, r. 1703, fr. 973–982; autos de guerra y sublevación de la Tarahumara, 1704–1705, AGN, Provincias Internas, vol. 176, exp. 11, fols. 358–406.

2. Viceroy to king, México, February 20, 1706, CP, vol. 23, pp. 203–210.

3. P. Tomás de Guadalajara to P. Proc. Juan de San Martín, Huejotitlán, February 24, 1715, AGN, Jesuitas, IV-7, exp. 22.

4. Report of Junta de Guerra to viceroy, México, August 4, 1704, AGN, Historia, vol. 20, exp. 1.

5. Gestión de D. José Neira y Quiroga . . . February 10, 1699, AHP, r. 1699, fr. 42–49.

6. Hechos para que los indios vayan a trabajar a la hacienda de los Molinos, Topia, July–November 1707, AHP, r. 1709, fr. 4–19, 81–98. In Spanish society, there was a longstanding belief in the contractual basis of obtaining rewards for one's services and the services of one's ancestors to the king. The king or his delegate was obliged to requite these military, ecclesiastical, or administrative services. See Murdo J. MacLeod, "Self-Promotion: The *Relaciones de Méritos y Servicios* and Their Historical and Political Interpretation," *Colonial Latin American Historical Review* 7, no. 1 (1998): 25–42.

7. Deeds, "Mission Villages," 354–356; see title histories in AIP-TA, lib. 28, exps. 75–76, 130–135.

8. See Meyer, *Water in the Hispanic Southwest*, 47–73.

9. Report of P. Francisco Medrano, Santiago Papasquiaro, February 20, 1691, AGN, AHH, Temp., leg. 279, exp. 114; Gen. Juan de Retana to P. Francisco de Bañuelos, San Francisco de Conchos, February 25, 1704, UTNLB-WBS, 66, 3–5.

10. Inventario de temporalidades, Santa Catalina, 1704, AGN, AHH, Temp., leg. 1955; padrón de Santa Catalina, 1707, AHP, r. 1707, fr. 74–81; autos y diligencias . . . pueblo de San Nicolás, Parral, August 1703, AHP, r. 1703, fr. 254–262; land titles and confirmations in AIP-TA, lib. 16, exp. 59; lib. 17, exps. 16, 19, 22; lib. 19, exp. 35; lib. 20, exps. 10, 13; lib. 39, exp. 14. On the effects of deforestation in the mining center of Parral, see Chantal Cramaussel, "Sociedad colonial y depredación ecológica: Parral en el siglo XVII," in Bernardo García Martínez and Alba González Jácome, eds., *Estudios sobre historia y ambiente en América*, vol. I, 92–107.

11. AHP, r. 1700a, fr. 33–38, and r. 1711a, fr. 170–176.

12. Título y confirmación a Don Juan Cortés del Rey, August 14, 1717, AIP-TA, lib. 35, fols. 164–166.

13. Various petitions from the Indian officials of San Francisco de Conchos, 1717–1718, AGN, Indios, vol. 42, exp. 51. Título de merced al Capitán Juan Baptista de Ybabe, November 25, 1719, AIP-TA, lib. 12, exp. 78.

14. Denuncia de tierras, San Jerónimo de Huejotitlán, November 1, 1720, AHP, r. 1720b, fr. 1373–1376; informe de la situación y estado de Huejotitlán, October 25, 1745, MPC.

15. Que los españoles no se introduzcan a los pueblos de indios (order of Gov. San Juan), January 18, 1718, AHP, r. 1718a, fr. 12–17.

16. Report of P. Antonio Marín, ca. 1690, AGN, AHH, Temp., leg. 279, exp. 43; P. Marín to P. Agustín de la Sierra, Utais, June 3, 1707, AGN, Jesuitas, I-12, exp. 245; title disputes, Guapijuxe, 1715–1732, AIP-TA, lib. 36, exp. 5.

17. P. Juan Boltor to P. Proc. Cristóbal de Laris, San Ignacio, April 22, 1712, AGN, Jesuitas, I-14, f. 154; P. Gregorio de Valdés to P. Proc. Juan de Iturberuaga, Humacen, May 16, 1711, AGN, Jesuitas, I-14, fol. 195. These sentiments were echoed

by other Topia missionaries in their requests for supplies. Although it was not uncommon for missionaries to claim privation, this particular mission district was widely acknowledged to be the poorest.

18. Escrito hecho por . . . Manuel de Escalante to Audiencia de Guadalajara, AGN, Jesuitas, I-17; memorial del P. Procurador General Bernardo Rolandegui, ca. 1704, AGN, AHH, Temp., leg. 325, exp. 51; presidial captains to viceroy, Parral, July 28, 1701, AGN, Jesuitas, I-16, exp. 9.

19. Junta de Guerra to viceroy, México, August 4, 1704, AGN, Historia, vol. 20, exp. 1. On the colonial evolution of "ethnic soldiers," see R. Brian Ferguson and Neil L. Whitehead, eds., "The Violent Edge of Empire," in *War in the Tribal Zone.*

20. Report of Capt. Gabriel Mendoza de Tapia, Santiago Papasquiaro, n.d., 1705, CP, vol. 23, p. 105; report of P. Pedro Retes, Santa Catalina, June 29, 1745, MPC.

21. Petition of Indians, Cinco Señores, December 7, 1719, AGN, Indios, vol. 42, exp. 173. Report of Gov. Martín de Alday, September 12, 1721, AHP, r. 1721, fr. 71-73; interrogatory regarding presidios (probably part of Gov. Manuel San Juan's residencia), Parral, February 1724, BN-AF, caja 14, 237; Berroterán's history of presidios to 1748, AGN, Historia, vol. 41, exp. 8; orders of Sargento Antonio de Ribas, November 5, 1737, AGN, General de Parte, vol. 31, exp. 200.

22. Visita de . . . San Francisco de Cuéllar, November–December, 1716, AHP, r. 1716a, fr. 283-307; Alvarez, "Agricultural Colonization," 182-185.

23. Martin, *Governance and Society,* ch. 1.

24. For the most complete biographical sketch to date of San Juan y Santa Cruz, see Catherine Tracy Goode, "Corrupting the Governor: Manuel de San Juan y Santa Cruz and Power in Early Eighteenth-Century Chihuahua," M.A. thesis.

25. Petition of landowners from the Valle de San Bartolomé to governor, August 27, 1715, AHP, r. 1715a, fols. 457-521.

26. Bishop to king, Cusiguiriachi, August 26, 1715, AGI, Audiencia de Guadalajara, leg. 206.

27. Anonymous Franciscan report, n.d., eighteenth century, Thomas Gilcrease Institute (Tulsa, Oklahoma), Hispanic Documents, 176-6.

28. Musters ordered by Gov. Manuel San Juan y Santa Cruz, Parral, January–March 1716, AHP, r. 1716a, fr. 311-365; various visitas, ibid., fr. 283-307. Also autos sobre misiones . . . , 1715, AGN, Historia, vol. 20, exp. 17. Although undertaking inspections of their territories was a charge to all governors, only a few actually carried them out themselves.

29. Various autos, 1716-1718, CP, vol. 24, pp. 120-258; petitions of Antonio de la Cruz, San Antonio de Julimes, October 14, 1715, and August 27, 1718, AGN, Indios, vol. 39, exp. 164, vol. 42, exp. 55.

30. Carta annua, 1719-1720, ARSI, Provincia Mexicana, vol. 18, fols. 22-23. Here is evidence of virgin soil epidemics even in the eighteenth century.

31. Case against Joseph de Lara, Santa Cruz, 1720, AGN, Inquisición, vol. 783, exp. 1; charges against P. Ignacio Xavier de Estrada, San Borja, November 23, 1721, AGN, Inquisición, vol. 789, exp. 28; denunciation by María Josefa de Mesa y Baeza, Valle de Basuchil, April 7, 1733, AGN, Inquisición, vol. 848, fols. 440-444.

32. Que los españoles no se introduzcan a los pueblos de indios, January 18, 1718, Parral, AHP, r. 1718a, fr. 12–17.

33. Juez privativo . . . , July 1720, AIP-TA, lib. 19, exp. 27; land confirmations of Copala, 1721, BPE, AIP-TA, lib. 14, exp. 32.

34. Petition from San Jerónimo de Huejotitlán, November 1, 1720, AHP, r.1720b, fr. 1373–1376.

35. Mandamientos de repartimiento, 1723–1727, AHP, r. 1723d, fr. 2554–2561; autos de la visita que practicó el gobernador . . . 1724, AHP, r. 1724b, fr. 656–687, 731–756; Swann, *Migrants in the Mexican North*, 64.

36. Quejas dadas contra Nicolás de Valenzuela . . . Santiago Papasquiaro, July 18–19, 1720, AHP, r. 1720b, fr. 1360–1367, 1532–1549.

37. Petition of Indians of San Miguel and San Gabriel de las Bocas, May 4, 1722, AGN, Indios, vol. 46, exp. 54, also cited in Simpson, *Repartimiento System*, 39.

38. Petition from Tarahumara Indians, December 1720, AGN, Indios, vol. 44, exp. 97; report of P. Vis. Juan de Guendulaín, Chihuahua, May 18, 1725, AGN, AHH, Temp., leg. 2009, exp. 99.

39. Visita que hizo el gobernador . . . , April 1724, AHP, r. 1722b, fr. 659–687.

40. Decree of Gov. Carvajal, August 7, 1724, AHP, r. 1723b, fr. 608–609; decree of Gov. Vertiz, March 1, 1735, response by P. Bernardo de Garfías, Papigochi, AGN, Jesuitas, I-11; charges of Sonoran governor, Manuel de Huidobro, 1735, BPE, AJANG, Civil, caja 93, exp. 3; P. Marcelo de León to Sargento Mayor Agustín de Vildósola, San Juan, October 20, 1741, BN-AF, caja 38, 840; P. Joaquín Trujillo to P. Vis. Bartolomé Braun, Tutuaca, April 6, 1764, UTNLB-WBS, 66.

41. Autos de entrega, Zape, September 10, 1753, AGI, Audiencia de Guadalajara, leg. 137, fols. 528–533; Bohumil Bad'ura, "Apuntes sobre las composiciones de tierras en Nueva España," *Historia* (Academia Praha) 24 (1984): 214; see also Cramaussel, "Evolución en las formas." Tanck, *Pueblos de indios*, 81, reports an intense period of composiciones in areas further south between 1711 and 1720.

42. Declaration of villagers, April 25, 1724, AHP, r. 1724b, fr. 664–666.

43. Visita to Santa Catalina, AHP, r. 1724b, fr. 673–675; Parroquia de Santa Catalina de Tepehuanes, Entierros, GS, no. 604871.

44. Documents relating to this case are found in AIP-TA, lib. 20, exp. 5; AHP, r. 1727a, fr. 323–357; informe de . . . Pedro de Rivera, November 3, 1728, AGI, Audiencia de Guadalajara, leg. 135, exp. 3; governor to captain of Conchos presidio, February 1, 1729, AGN, Historia, vol. 52, exp. 1. Many title histories indicate water conflicts in the area; e.g., AIP-TA, lib. 19, exp. 17.

45. Reports from the Guendulaín visita are found in AGN, AHH, Temp., leg. 2009, exp. 99, AGN, Jesuitas, II-4, exp. 32, and AGN, Historia, vol. 20, exp. 3.

46. Complaints of pueblo of Carichi, June 28, 1732, AHP, r. 1732, fr. 374–383.

47. Informe de . . . Rivera, AGI, Audiencia de Guadalajara, leg. 135, exp. 3; see also Thomas H. Naylor and Charles W. Polzer, eds., *Pedro de Rivera and the Military Regulations for Northern New Spain, 1724–1729.*

48. Governor to king, Parral, June 4, 1728, AGI, Audiencia de Guadalajara, leg. 110; nómina de los indios . . . , n.d. [1728], AHP, r. 1728a, fr. 157–170; P. Matheo

Sánchez to P. Prov. Andrés Nieto, San Gregorio, August 16, 1728, Archivo Histórico de la Provincia de los Jesuitas en México (AHPM), 1404; P. Constancio Gallarti to P. Proc. José Ferrer, San Felipe el Real, June 30, 1729, AGN, Jesuitas, I-12, exp. 7; P. Balthasar Ravik to P. Prov. Juan Antonio de Oviedo, Sisoguichi, October 17, 1730, AGN, AHH, Temp., leg. 278, exp. 7. See also the drop in tithe income, cuarto cuaderno . . . , 1731, AGI, Audiencia de Guadalajara, leg. 208.

49. P. Lorenzo de Mendibil to P. Cayetano de Lascaiban, Baroyeca, October 31, 1727, AGN, AHH, Temp., leg. 17, exp. 53.

50. Case against Bernabé, aliás Barrabas, mulato hechicero, Parral, 1680–84, AGN, Inquisición, vol. 661, exp. 22. On love magic, see Noemí Quezada, "Cosmovisión, sexualidad e Inquisición," in Quezada et al., eds., *Inquisición novohispana,* vol. 2, 77–86.

51. Causa criminal . . . contra Matheo de la Cruz, Babonoyaba, 1703–5, AHP, r. 1703, fr. 973–982. On the punishment of curanderos, see Noemí Quezada, "The Inquisition's Repression of Curanderos," in Perry and Cruz, eds., *Cultural Encounters,* 37–57.

52. Order of Gov. Ignacio Francisco de Barrutia, June 18, 1729, Parroquia de Santiago Papasquiaro, Informaciones Matrimoniales, GS, no. 658011; P. Balthasar to viceroy, 1754, UTNLB-WBS, 1719.

53. P. Balthasar Ravik to P. Prov. Juan Antonio de Oviedo, Sisoguichi, October 17, 1730, AGN, AHH, Temp., leg. 278, exp. 7.

54. Charges of Indians from San Andrés, San Felipe el Real, December 4, 1731, AHP, r. 1731a, fr. 5–9.

55. Bishop to king, August 1715, AGI, Audiencia de Guadalajara, 206; report of Rivera, August 23, 1730, AGN, Provincias Internas, vol. 69, exp. 4; P. Juan Manuel del Hierro to P. Prov. Juan Antonio de Oviedo, Yepómera, September 24, 1730, AGN, Jesuitas, II-4, exp. 38.

56. Estrada to P. Prov. Oviedo, Themeichi, November 23, 1730, AGN, AHH, Temp., leg. 278, exp. 7; this letter is translated in Sheridan and Naylor, eds., *Rarámuri,* 73–78, although the place is misidentified as Tomochi.

57. Martin, *Governance and Society,* 22–25.

58. P. Balthasar de la Peña to P. Proc. Joseph Ferrer, Satevó, February 17, 1725, AGN, AHH, Temp., leg. 970.

59. Martin, *Governance and Society,* ch. 3.

60. Martin, *Governance and Society,* 50–56; letters of P. Balthasar Ravik, Sisoguichi, October 17, 1730, and P. Ignacio Javier de Estrada, Themeichi, November 23, 1730, to P. Prov. Juan Antonio de Oviedo, both in AGN, AHH, Temp., leg. 278, exp. 7.

61. Pastor Rouaix, Gerard Decorme, and Atanasio Saravia, *Manual de historia de Durango,* 86–87, reproduces a 1731 visita report from Santiago Papasquiaro from Decorme. One of these confraternities was the cofradía of Remedios, Parroquia de Santiago Papasquiaro, Entierros, 1742, GS, no. 604830.

62. Tarahumara fiestas evolved from the colonial period, combining Christian and native elements. The matachines that are prominent, especially during Holy

Week, were apparently introduced by the missionaries, although it is not clear when this practice began; Carlo Bonfiglioli, *Fariseos y matachines en la Sierra Tarahumara*, 219–225.

63. For a discussion of the need to understand the local context of these evolving roles and the meanings of ritual celebrations, see William L. Merrill, "Rarámuri Easter," in Spicer and Crumrine, eds., *Performing the Renewal of Community*, 365–421.

64. Tanck, *Pueblos de indios*, 35, 42, 68; in Santa María de Parras, where Tlaxcalans had established a community in the late sixteenth century, by the early eighteenth century they reported having 4,000 pesos in their caja (or arca) de comunidad; land and water dispute, Parras, 1722–23, BPE, AJANG, Civil, caja 50, exp. 5.

65. Informe de la situación y estado de Huejotitlán, P. Juan Antonio Núñez, October 25, 1745, MPC.

66. P. Juan Joseph Díaz de Valdés, to Gov. Agustín de Vildósola, Badiraguato, March 24, 1742, BN-AF, caja 38, 843; Francisco Javier Veitia to Hilario Joseph Martínez de Lapisco, June 23, 1731, Archivo de Mocorito, Informes Matrimoniales, 1720–40, June 1740, GS, no. 676717.

67. Contra Juan Antonio Gamboa, de oficio herrero, por haber pretendido tener pacto con el demonio, San Francisco de Cuéllar, April 15, 1717, AGN, Inquisición, vol. 777, part 1, exp. 24; case of P. Felipe de Calderón, 1721, AGN, Inquisición, vol. 791, exp. 31.

68. P. Cristóbal Bravo to P. Proc. Laris, Tamazula, May 19, 1713, AGN, Jesuitas, I-14, fol. 107. Hundreds of memorias can be found in AGN, AHH, Temp.: for eighteenth-century examples, see legajos 282, 321, 2016, and 2017. The transport of goods between Mexico City and the missions took three to four months, and freight charges were very high.

69. ". . . que es el único regalo que se puede tener por estas partes . . ."; P. Matheo Sánchez to P. Proc. José Ferrer, San Gregorio, May 20, 1738, AGN, AHH, Temp., leg. 2016, exp. 2.

70. See the compilation by Juan Esteyneffer, S.J., *Florilegio medicinal de todas las enfermedades* (1712).

71. Memoria, Santo Tomás, May 30, 1736, AGN, AHH, Temp., leg. 282, exp. 24; P. Pedro de Estrada to P. Proc. José Ferrer, August 15, 1735, AGN, AHH, Temp., leg. 970; history of the Hospital de San Juan de Dios, ca. 1720, AGI, Audiencia de Guadalajara, leg. 206. Before this, treatment of mine injuries and illnesses had been even more rudimentary.

72. P. Pedro de Retes to bishop, Santa Catalina, August 15, 1749, Archivo de la Catedral de Durango (ACD), Varios, Año 1749.

73. P. Rector Miguel de Castillo to P. Prov. Cristóbal Escobar y Llamas, Parral, December 15, 1744, AGN, Jesuitas, II-9, fols. 47–50.

74. Report of P. Francisco de Bañuelos, Santa Catalina, June 16, 1689, AGN, AHH, Temp., leg. 285, exp. 32; P. Juan de Guendulaín to P. Prov. Arjo, Chihuahua, May 12, 1725, AGN, AHH, Temp., leg. 2009, exp. 99; P. Mateo Sánchez to P. Prov. Andrés Nieto, San Gregorio, August 16, 1728, AHPM, 1404; P. Juan Joseph de Nava

to P. Provincial, Durango, May 10, 1739, AGN, Jesuitas, I-7; P. General Francisco Retz to P. Prov. Matheo Ansaldo, Rome, October 7, 1741, AGN, AHH, Temp. leg. 314, exp. 3; estado del seminario del Parral, August 11, 1741, AGN, Jesuitas, II-9, fols. 106ff; P. Vis. Juan Antonio Balthasar to P. Prov. Cristóbal Escobar y Llamas, Chihuahua, September 29, 1743, AGN, AHH, Temp., leg. 2009, exp. 20.

75. P. Constancio Gallarati to P. Vis. Juan Manuel de Hierro, San Felipe el Real, May 12, 1735, UTNLB-WBS, 66, 213–216.

76. Alvarez, "Agricultural Colonization," 188–191.

77. See, for example, the list of debts owed by Indians from Santa Cruz (visita of Tizonazo) to Real del Oro merchant, Baltasar Silvano, October 25, 1738, Archivo Notarial de Durango, leg./año 1760, exp. Partido de Oro, 1738–1741.

78. Testimonio de un decreto y diligencias sobre el resgate de maises . . . , 1734–1735, AGN, Alhóndiga, vol. 14, exp. 4.

79. Testimony of Don Manuel Fernández de Cosío, November 8, 1734, in ibid.

80. Decree of governor, San Felipe el Real, October 19, 1739, AGN, Provincias Internas, vol. 69, exp. 1; order to Conde de Alamo, November 5, 1737, AGN, General de Parte, vol. 31, exp. 200; report of governor to king, September 12, 1740, AGI, Audiencia de Guadalajara, leg. 186. On civic responsibility and the ethos of governing, see Martin, *Governance and Society*, ch. 4.

81. Audiencia de Guadalajara to king, July 16, 1739, and September 20, 1741, AGI, Audiencia de Guadalajara, leg. 104; audiencia to king, November 6, 1741, AGI, Audiencia de Guadalajara, leg. 105.

82. On the epidemic in Nueva Galicia, see MacLeod, "The *Matlazáhuatl* of 1737-8," 7–16. A later eighteenth-century reference to epidemics uses "matlasague" and "tabardillo" (typhus) interchangeably; P. Carlos de Rojas to P. Provincial, Arizpe, January 15, 1765, AGN, AHH, Temp., leg. 17, exp. 8. The argument that it was plague has been advanced most forcefully by Elsa Malvido, who also connects it to epidemics introduced in 1545, 1576, 1641, 1692, 1761, and 1784: "¿El arca de Noé o la caja de Pandora?," 45–87. See also Miguel Angel Cuenya, *Puebla de los Angeles en los tiempos de una peste colonial: una mirada en torno al matlazahuatl de 1737*, who looks at its aftermath in terms of marriage patterns and social change; and América Molina del Villar, *La Nueva España y el matlazahuatl de 1736-1739*, who traces its transport to the north and concludes that its transmission in the north was more rapid than in the center.

83. Burial records from Santiago Papasquiaro, Santa Catalina, San Pablo Balleza, and Valle de Allende, 1720s and 1730s, GS, nos. 654993, 604871, 1222928, 162655; and petition of vecinos of Santiago Papasquiaro, Durango, October 17, 1740, AGN, Jesuitas, I-17. Small children account for a third of the death total from the epidemic in Santiago Papasquiaro.

84. Report of Francisco Alvarez Barreyro, August 10, 1730, AGN, Provincias Internas, vol. 69, exp. 4; Gerhard, *The North Frontier*, 169.

85. Dispatch of Viceroy-Archbishop Juan Antonio de Vizarrón, México, September 15, 1738, copies in BPE, AJANG, caja 48, exp. 14, and AGN, General de Parte, vol. 31, exp. 253.

86. Decree of governor, San Felipe el Real, May 11, 1740, AHP, r. 1740, fr. 3–7.

87. P. Pedro de Hualde to P. Prov. Matheo Ansaldo, Durango, December 30, 1739, AGN, Jesuitas, I-17.

88. Informe sobre los perjuicios . . . mandamientos, probably written by a Jesuit in the upper Tarahumara, ca. 1740, BN-AF, caja 12, 210; report of P. Juan Isidro Fernández de Abee, Carichi, July 8, 1744, Naylor and Sheridan, eds., *Rarámuri*, 82–83.

89. Declaration of María Magdalena García Valdés, Santiago Papasquiaro, October 19, 1739, AGN, Jesuitas, I-17.

90. P. Juan Ramírez to P. Prov. Mateo Ansaldo, Pueblo Nuevo, June 31 [*sic*], 1739, AHPM, 1402; razón de misiones de la Sierra de Topia, San Andrés y Piastla, 1740, AGN, AHH, Temp., leg. 1126, exp. 4.

91. Oidor Martín de Blancas to Marqués de la Regalía, August 12, 1744, AGI, Audiencia de Guadalajara, leg. 113. His official title was "juez privativo subdelegado superintendente general de ventas, medidas y composiciones de tierras de Nueva Vizcaya."

92. Real cédula, April 10, 1742, AGI, Audiencia de Guadalajara, leg. 106; P. Pedro de Estrada to P. Rector Francisco Xavier de la Paz, Satevó, February 19, 1743, AGN, AHH, Temp., leg. 316, exp. 5; P. J. A. Balthasar to P. Prov. Cristóbal Escobar y Llamas, Chicorato, December 28, 1744, AGN, AHH, Temp., leg. 1126, exp. 3; P. Benito Rinaldini to P. Prov. Andrés García, Huejotitlán, October 13, 1749, AHPM, no. 1389; composiciones in AGI, Guadalajara, 113, and AIP-TA, lib. 28, exp. 141; lib. 22, exp. 2.

93. Juicio de residencia del gobernador Belaunzarán, AGI, Escribanía de Cámara, leg. 394; land title of Cristóbal Marques, February 8, 1742, AIP-TA, lib. 14, exp. 1. For an analysis of how this office functioned in New Mexico, see Charles R. Cutter, *The "Protector de Indios" in Colonial New Mexico, 1659–1821*.

94. P. Lorenzo Reino to P. Prov. Escobar y Llamas, Chihuahua, January 19, 1745, AGN, Jesuitas, I-16, exp. 32.

95. P. Benito Rinaldini to P. Prov. García, Huejotitlán, October 13, 1749, AHPM, no. 1389; P. Francisco Xavier de Lora to Dr. Don Salvador de Bezerra, Tamasula, July 2, 1744, ACD, Varios, Año 1744; P. Manuel Ignacio de Cartagena to P. Vis. Marcelo de León, Tamasula, March 1748, AGN, Jesuitas, I-16, exp. 1.

96. P. Diego Manuel de Cardaveraz to Vildósola, San Juan, October 20, 1741, and P. Marcelo de León to Vildósola, San Juan, November 6, 1741, BN-AF, caja 38, 840, fols. 9–11.

97. Real cédula, July 12, 1739, BPE, AJANG, Civil, caja 166, exp. 3; Gov. Belaunzarán to king, October 24, 1741, AGI, Audiencia de Guadalajara, leg. 186.

6. JESUITS TAKE STOCK

1. For examples: Apologético Defensorio, November 1657, AGN, Historia, vol. 316, fols. 359–426; información sobre malos tratamientos . . . , 1672, BPE, AJANG, caja 8, exp. 15. Such charges were common throughout the Americas: Dauril Alden,

"Indian versus Black Slavery in the State of Maranhão during the Seventeenth and Eighteenth Centuries," in Garner and Taylor, eds., *Iberian Colonies, New World Societies*, 71-102. On Bourbon regalism, see my ch. 8, n. 4.

2. Charges of Huidobro, 1735, BPE, AJANG, Civil, caja 93, exp. 3; decree of governor, San Felipe el Real, March 1, 1735, AGN, Jesuitas, I-11.

3. P. Bernardo de Gaspar to governor, n.d. (mid-1730s), Papigochi, AGN, Jesuitas, I-11.

4. P. General Francisco Retz to P. Provincial, Rome, August 1, 1740, AHPM, no. 1306.

5. Instructions to P. Vis. Juan Antonio Balthasar, 1742, AGN, AHH, Temp., leg. 2009, exp. 47.

6. Consejo de Indias to Viceroy Fuenclara, January 21, 1742, AGI, Audiencia de México, leg. 515.

7. P. Retz to P. Provincial, January 8 and April 2, 1740, AHPM, nos. 1307, 1308; Audiencia de México to king, February 14, 1744, AGI, Audiencia de Guadalajara, 135.

8. See, for example, the Jesuit philosophical defense against episcopal visitation of missions, n.d. (eighteenth century), AGN, AHH, Temp., leg. 2009, exp. 23.

9. P. Retz to P. Escobar y Llamas, Rome, January 25, 1744, AHPM, no. 1311; Balthasar visita documents in AGN, AHH, Temp., leg. 2009, exp. 20.

10. Puntos del parecer que el señor Auditor de Guerra . . . expresó al Virrey Conde de Fonclara, July 4, 1744, AGN, Historia, vol. 20, exp. 4, fols. 95-113. As a result of these criticisms, the Jesuits became concerned that they had been lax in their book-keeping on missions: Respuesta a la consulta de las misiones . . . , August 15, 1745, AGN, AHH, Temp., leg. 2009, exp. 20. See also María del Carmen Velázquez, *El marqués de Altamira y las provincias internas de Nueva España*.

11. Real cédula, July 19, 1741, AGN, Reales Cédulas Duplicadas, vol. 98, exp. 96; real cédula, November 13, 1744, AGN, Reales Cédulas, vol. 67, exp. 32, fols. 133-144; consulta del Consejo de Indias to king, Madrid, May 12, 1744, CP, vol. 32, pp. 219-246.

12. Escobar Memorial to king, November 30, 1745, copied in AGN, Reales Cédulas, vol. 67, exp. 32, fols. 106-132.

13. Ibid., fol. 120.

14. P. Balthasar to P. Escobar, Parras, May 15, 1743, AGN, AHH, Temp., leg. 2009, exp. 20. Distances traveled by Father Balthasar will be given in leguas (leagues): 1 league is approximately 3 miles or 4.8 kilometers.

15. José Antonio de Villaseñor y Sánchez, *Theatro americano: descripción general de los reynos y provincias de la Nueva España*, 345.

16. P. Balthasar to P. Escobar, Cinco Señores, May 23, 1743, AGN, AHH, Temp., leg. 2009, exp. 20.

17. P. Lucas Merino to Bishop of Durango, Cinco Señores, June 29, 1749, ACD, Varios 1749; P. Vis. Agustín Carta to P. Proc. Juan María Casati, Durango, February 21, 1751, AGN, AHH, Temp., leg. 327.

18. P. Balthasar to P. Escobar, Parral, September 18, 1743, AGN, AHH, Temp., leg. 2009, exp. 20; P. Pedro de Retes to P. Prov. Escobar, Santa Catalina, November 4, 1745, AHPM, no. 1404.

19. Report of P. Francisco Medina Ibarra, Santiago Papasquiaro, February 20, 1691, AGN, AHH, Temp., leg. 279, exp. 114.

20. The estimates come from mission reports of 1690 in AGN, AHH, Temp., leg. 279; 1731 in Gerard Decorme, S.J., *La obra de los jesuitas mexicanos durante la época colonial, 1572–1767*, vol. 2, 78–82; and 1743, P. Balthasar to P. Escobar, Santiago Papasquiaro, May 31, 1743, AGN, AHH, Temp., leg. 2009, exp. 20. Santiago Papasquiaro is one of the few missions for which I have found reasonably reliable serial data on deaths in the eighteenth century; they clearly show the high death toll from the 1739 epidemic; Parroquia de Santiago Papasquiaro, Entierros and Informaciones Matrimoniales, GS, nos. 604830, 654993, 658011, 658012. Before the late eighteenth century, demographic data (collected primarily by the missionaries and occasionally by government officials) are random and inconsistent. Ethnic information is not included systematically; even as non-Indians increasingly took up residence in the mission pueblos, they were not always enumerated as to ethnicity. Missionaries routinely divided their counts into two categories: Indians and surrounding vecinos. Some counts provide total numbers of inhabitants; others give numbers of families. To determine an average family size, I collected all the cases in which both numbers of families and total population were given and averaged them. I arrived at an average Indian family size of 3.7; the figure for non-Indians was much higher at 7.5 (perhaps representing extended families or including servants). Ortiz Zapata visita report, 1678, *DHM*, 4-3, 301–419; Guendulaín visita report, May 18, 1725, AGN, AHH, Temp., leg. 2009, exp. 99; 1749 reports in ACD. On the problems and use of demographic data for colonial northern Mexico, see Jackson, *Indian Population Decline*, and Radding, *Wandering Peoples*, ch. 4.

21. On relations with the secular clergy, see order of jueces hacedores de las rentas dezimales, Durango, March 14, 1744, ACD, Varios, Año 1744. Much of the documentation on the case of Hualde is in AGN, Jesuitas, I-17; other references are in P. Gen. Retz to P. Provincial, Rome, October 7, 1741, AGN, AHH, Temp., leg. 314, exp. 3; and report of P. Pedro Retes, August 2, 1737, AGN, Historia, vol. 392.

22. P. Antonio de los Ríos to Bishop of Durango, July 11, 1749, ACD, Varios, Año 1749.

23. P. Retes to P. Escobar, Santa Catalina, November 4, 1745, AHPM, no. 1405; P. Antonio de los Rios to bishop, Santiago Papasquiaro, July 11, 1749, ACD, Varios, Año 1749.

24. P. Manuel Ignacio Cartagena to P. Escobar, August 7, 1745, AGN, Jesuitas, I-17.

25. Fundación, progresos y estado presente de esta misión de Santa Catalina . . . June 19, 1745, in MPC; P. Retes to bishop, Santa Catalina, August 15, 1749, ACD, Varios, Año 1749; Parroquia de Santa Catalina de Tepehuanes, Bautismos and Entierros, GS, nos. 604834, 604849, 604871.

26. Ibid.

27. Informe de la misión de N.S. del Zape, P. Manuel Vivanco, June 23, 1745, MPC.

28. P. Pedro Hualde to P. Proc. Joseph Ferrer, Zape, August 30, 1736, AGN,

AHH, Temp., leg. 2016, exp. 2; P. Balthasar to P. Escobar, June 9, 1743, AGN, AHH, Temp., leg. 2009, exp. 20; P. Lázaro Franco to bishop, Zape, August 8, 1749, ACD, Varios, Año 1749; Pedro Tamarón y Romeral, *Demostración de vastísimo obispado de la Nueva Vizcaya, 1765,* 85–86.

29. P. Balthasar to P. Escobar, Tizonazo, June 9, 1743, AGN, AHH, Temp., leg. 2009, exp. 20; Don Lucas Miguel de la Peña, governor of Santa Cruz, to P. Provincial, Santa Cruz, February 26, 1746, AGN, AHH, Temp., leg. 297, exp. 6; P. Juan Antonio de Landa to P. Pedro de Retes, Santa Cruz, March 7, 1746, UTNLB-WBS, 1744, 217–218; P. Manuel Vivanco to bishop, Tizonazo, September 2, 1749, ACD, Varios, Año 1749; autos de entrega, Tizonazo, September 7, 1753, AGN, Californias, vol. 64, exp. 14. For an understanding of the variable nature of debt peonage and the inadequacy of Chevalier's formulation as a universal model to explain it, see Eric Van Young, "Mexican Rural History," and David McCreery and Murdo J. MacLeod, "Debt Peonage," *Encyclopedia of Latin American History and Culture* (1996), vol. 2, 360–362.

30. Visita of Gov. López de Carvajal, Bocas, February–March, 1724, AHP, r. 1724b, fr. 731–756; Guendulaín visita report, Chihuahua, May 18, 1725, AGN, AHH, Temp., leg. 2009, exp. 99; case of Manuel de la Pro, 1734, AGN, Inquisición, vol. 853, fol. 287; confirmaciones de tierras, Don Juan Joseph de Arespacochaga, San Felipe, July–August 1753, AGI, Audiencia de Guadalajara, 120.

31. Decorme, *La obra de los jesuitas mexicanos,* vol. 2, 76; P. Balthasar to P. Prov. Escobar, Bocas, July 17, 1743, AGN, AHH, Temp., leg. 2009, exp. 20; P. Bernardo Treviño to P. Joseph Calderón, Parral, December 15, 1744; AGN, Jesuitas, II-9, exp. 32; P. Pedro Retes to P. Joseph Calderón, Santa Catalina, November 27, 1745, AHPM, no. 1673; P. Balthasar to P. Proc. Juan María Casati, Colegio de San Gregorio, February 7, 1747, AHPM, no. 1387; P. Miguel de Castillo to P. Prov. Escobar, Parral, December 22, 1746, AGN, Jesuitas II-9, fol. 40; Presbítero Nicolás de Guzmán to P. Prov. Escobar, Santa Bárbara, December 28, 1746, AHPM, no. 1399.

32. P. Calderón to P. Escobar, Bocas, February 28, 1746, UTNLB-WBS, 1744, 215; P. Retes to P. Prov. Escobar, Santa Catalina, July 17, 1746, AHPM, no. 1406; Parroquia de San Pablo Balleza, Entierros, 1730s, GS, no. 1222928.

33. P. Benito Rinaldini to P. Prov. Andrés García, Huejotitlán, October 13, 1749, AHPM, no. 1399; mandamientos de repartimiento, 1723–1726, AHP, r. 1723d, fr. 2554–2561.

34. P. Balthasar to P. Escobar, San Pablo, July 8, AGN, AHH, Temp., leg. 2009, exp. 20.

35. Informe de la situación y estado de Huejotitlán, P. Juan Antonio Núñez, October 25, 1745, MPC.

36. Ibid.; P. Benito Rinaldini to P. Procurador, Huejotitlán, October 29, 1748, AGN, AHH, Temp., leg. 974, exp. 1; Rinaldini to P. Prov. Andrés García, Huejotitlán, October 13, 1749, AHPM, no. 1399.

37. P. Benito Rinaldini to P. Proc. Josef Ferrer, Nabogame, April 28, 1735, AGN, AHH, Temp., leg. 2017, exp. 3. For comments on the art and architecture of this mission and others among the Tarahumara, see Bargellini: "At the Center"; *Misiones y presidios,* 61–102; and *Sur de Chihuahua: Itinerarios del pasado,* 41–71.

38. P. Balthasar to P. Escobar, Santa Cruz, August 6, 1743, AGN, AHH, Temp., leg. 2009, exp. 20; P. Cristóbal de Moreno to bishop, Santa Cruz, July 27, 1749, ACD, Varios, Año 1749.

39. P. Felipe Calderón to bishop, Las Cuevas, July 21, 1749, ACD, Varios, Año 1749. See the discussion of land tenure and usufruct in Radding, *Wandering Peoples*, 171–182. The notices of land sales by Indians in Nueva Vizcaya mission areas are infrequent before the 1750s, but there are mentions in the formal transfers of missions to diocesan control regarding Huejotitlán and Santa María de las Cuevas. In one case, we know that the "owner" was the Tarahumara governor of the pueblo, perhaps indicating that officials were more privileged in terms of landownership. See AGN, Californias, vol. 64, exp. 14, fols. 50, 64–66.

40. P. Balthasar to P. Escobar, Nuestra Señora de la Asunción de las Cuevas, September 5, 1743, AGN, AHH, Temp., leg. 2009, exp. 20; nóminas de los indios . . . , AHP, r. 1728a, fr. 157–170; P. Felipe Calderón to bishop, Las Cuevas, July 21, 1749, ACD, Varios, Año 1749; autos de entrega, Santa María de las Cuevas, October 11, 1753, AGI, Audiencia de Guadalajara, leg. 137, fols. 519–525.

41. P. Pedro de Estrada to P. Francisco Javier de la Paz, Satevó, February 19, 1743, AGN, AHH, Temp., leg. 316, exp. 5; P. Balthasar to P. Escobar, San Javier de Satevó, September 7, 1743, AGN, AHH, Temp., leg. 2009, exp. 20; P. Balthasar to P. Escobar, December 28, 1744, AGN, AHH, Temp., leg. 1126, exp. 3.

42. Report of Balthasar on the state of the Tepehuana and Tarahumara Baja missions, Chihuahua, September 18, 1743, AGN, AHH, Temp., leg. 2009, exp. 20.

43. Francisco Antonio Carrillo report on Jesuit temporalidades, October 5, 1770, AGN, AHH, Temp., leg. 21, exp. 2.

44. An interesting indicator of the poverty of Topia is the ruling of the Jesuit provincial in 1744 that mission provinces would have to donate to the costs of the order's lawsuit against Gov. Huidobro. The amounts were based on the financial capacity of each district. Topia was the only one of six missionary provinces that was not required to contribute because it was so impoverished; P. Balthasar to P. Escobar, Santa Cruz del Río Mayo, October 1744, AGN, AHH, Temp., leg. 1126, exp. 3.

45. Razón de las misiones de Topia, ca. 1740, AGN, AHH, Temp., leg. 1126, exp. 4; P. Balthasar to P. Escobar, Badiraguato, January 4, 1745; AGN, AHH, Temp., leg. 2009, exp. 42; P. Joaquín Basurto to bishop, Badiraguato, June. 13, 1749, ACD, Varios, Año 1749.

46. Letters of P. Joaquín Basurto to P. Proc. Diego Verdugo, Badiraguato, July 13, 1748, March 2 and 5, 1749, AGN, AHH, Temp., leg. 974, exp. 1; Juan Francisco Vitorica to bishop, Culiacán, May 18, 1749, ACD, Varios, Año 1749; various land titles, Badiraguato, AIP-TA, lib. 28, exp. 104; lib. 38, exps. 5, 6, 8, 12, lib. 39, exp. 5; Parroquia de San Benito, Bautismos, 1747–48, GS, no. 675802.

47. P. Baquio Silay to P. Proc. Joseph Ferrer, Cariatapa, June 24, 1737, and June 15, 1738, AGN, AHH, Temp., leg. 279, exp. 45; razón de las misiones de Topia, ca. 1740, AGN, AHH, Temp., leg. 1126, exp. 4; P. Balthasar to P. Escobar, Cariatapa, January 4, 1745, AGN, AHH, Temp., leg. 2009, exp. 42; P. Laureano Bravo to P. Proc. Diego Verdugo, Tubares, May 1, 1748, AGN, AHH, Temp., leg. 974, exp. 1; report of

P. Joseph Chávez, Cariatapa, July 18, 1749, ACD, Varios, Año 1749; report of Visitador General Rodríguez Gallardo, August 18, 1750, AGN, Provincias Internas, vol. 176, exp. 6.

48. P. Gregorio de Valdés to P. Proc. Joseph Ferrer, Tamazula, June 12, 1726, AGN, AHH, Temp., leg. 282, exp. 48; razón de las misiones de Topia, ca. 1740, AGN, AHH, Temp., leg. 1126, exp. 4; P. Francisco Javier de Lora to Dr. Salvador Bezerra, Tamazula, July 2, 1744, ACD, Varios, Año 1744; Balthasar visita report, Tamazula, January 11, 1745, AGN, AHH, Temp., leg. 2009, exp. 42; land titles, San Ignacio de Tamazula, April 1746, AIP-TA, lib. 8, exp. 9; P. Fernando Caamaño to P. Balthasar de Porras, Durango, January 22, 1748, AGN, AHH, Temp., leg. 974, exp. 1; P. Manuel Ignacio de Cartagena to P. Vis. Marcelo de León, Tamazula, March 11, 1748, AGN, Jesuitas, I-16, exp. 1.

49. P. Fernando Caamaño to P. Proc. Diego Verdugo, Tamazula, October 8, 1749, AGN, AHH, Temp., leg. 974, exp. 1; reports of P. Caamaño and Juan Francisco Victorica to bishop, June 21, May 18, 1749, ACD, Varios, Año 1749.

50. P. Manuel Gutiérrez to P. Provincial, Piaba, April 10, 1685, AGN, AHH, Temp., leg. 278, exp. 39; P. Matheo Sánchez to P. Prov. Andrés Nieto, San Gregorio, August 16, 1728, AHPM, no. 1404; report of P. Diego de Poza, Alaya, June 30, 1744, AGN, Jesuitas I-14, fol. 157; Balthasar visita report, Alaya, January 15, 1745, AGN, AHH, Temp., leg. 2009, exp. 42; P. Manuel Ignacio de Cartagena to P. Proc. Diego Verdugo, Otatitlán, July 4, 1748, AGN, AHH, Temp., leg. 974, exp. 1; fragment of a report on Topia mission, n.a., n.d., UTNLB-WBS, 1744, 471–474.

51. Correspondence between P. Manuel Ignacio Cartagena, P. Vis. Marcelo de León; and the priest of Cosalá Pedro Joseph Salcido, March–July 1749, AHPM, nos. 1409, 1614, 1615; title histories, 1743–1801, AIP-TA, lib. 47-1, exp. 5.

52. Report of P. Francisco Serrano, Remedios, n.d., AGN, Historia, vol. 308, fols. 562–566; autos hechos para que los indios vayan a trabajar, AHP, r. 1707, fr. 4-19, 81–98; razón de las misiones de Topia, ca. 1740, AGN, AHH, Temp., leg. 1126, exp. 4; Balthasar visita report, Remedios, January 30, 1745, AGN, AHH, Temp., leg. 2009, exp. 42.

53. Report of P. Miguel Joseph González, Los Remedios, June 22, 1749, ACD, Varios, Año 1749. An almud is equal to about 4.6 liters; the total yield from an average milpa would have been less than three-quarters of a bushel.

54. Vecinos de los Remedios to bishop, May 23, 1749, ACD, Varios, Año 1749.

55. Balthasar visita report, San Gregorio, February 11, 1745, AGN, AHH, Temp., leg. 2009, exp. 42; P. Matheo Sánchez to bishop, San Gregorio, May 12, 1749, ACD, Varios, Año 1749.

56. Report of P. Antonio Marín, n.d., AGN, AHH, Temp., leg. 179, exp. 43; Balthasar visita report, Otaez, February 16, 1745, AGN, AHH, Temp., leg. 2009, exp. 42; P. Cartagena to bishop, Santa María de Otaes, June 16, 1749, AHPM, no. 1616. Lobos were usually a mixture of negro and india, while coyotes were a lighter combination of mestizo and india, but these terms were very imprecise.

57. Report of P. Juan Boltor, San Ignacio, May 25, 1691, AGN, AHH, Temp., leg. 279, exp. 46; Balthasar visita report, San Ignacio, January 21, 1745, AGN, AHH,

Temp., leg. 2009, exp. 42; P. Marcelo de León to bishop, June 30, July 25, August 4, 1749, ACD, Varios, Año 1749.

58. Cabildo eclesiástico, Durango, to P. Antonio de los Ríos, Durango, December 1, 1747, AGN, Jesuitas, I-17; cabildo eclesiástico to Gov. Vildósola, Durango, December 1, 1747, ACD, Varios, Año 1748; gobernadores de la misión de Piastla to P. Prov., San Ignacio, ca. 1744, AHPM, no. 808.

59. P. Juan Antonio de Oviedo to P. Prov. Escobar, Mexico City, December 4, 1746, AGN, AHH, Temp., leg. 1126, exp. 3.

60. Medidas de dos sitios de tierra . . . San Gerónimo de Ajolla, 1744, AIP-TA, lib. 37-1, exp. 5.

61. Title issued by Gov. Diego Ortiz Parrilla, San Miguel de Horcasitas, January 26, 1751, ibid.

62. Balthasar visita report, Santa Apolonia, January 22, 1745, AGN, AHH, Temp., leg. 2009, exp. 42; P. Diego Manuel de Cardaveraz to P. Proc. Diego Verdugo, San Juan, August 5, 1748, AGN, AHH, Temp., leg. 974, exp. 1; P. Cardaveraz to bishop, Santa Apolonia, June 26, 1749, ACD, Varios, Año 1749.

63. P. Matheo Sánchez to P. Procurador, Yamoriba, February 4, 1703, AGN, AHH, Temp., leg. 301, exp. 1; P. Gregorio de Valdés to P. Procurador, Humacen, May 16, 1711, AGN, Jesuitas, I-14, fol. 195; petition of Antonio Joseph Vidaurre, por el común . . ., May 16, 1720, AGN, Indios, vol. 44, exp. 43; testimony of P. Procurador Diego Verdugo, April 17, 1744, AGN, Indios, vol. 68, exp. 33; P. Sebastián Morillos to bishop, Pueblo Nuevo, June 29, 1749, ACD, Varios, Año 1749.

64. P. Cartagena to P. Prov. Escobar y Llamas, Durango, October 22, 1744, AHPM, no. 882; P. Cartagena and P. Fernando Caamaño to bishop, San Pedro de Guarisamey, June 9, 1745, ACD, Varios, Año 1745; Balthasar visita report, San Pedro, May 20, 1745, AGN, AHH, Temp., leg. 2009, exp. 42; P. Cartagena to P. Escobar, Durango, August 7, 1745, AGN, Jesuitas, I-17; P. Luis Pastrana to bishop, Guarisamey, July 29, 1749, ACD, Varios, Año 1749.

65. Balthasar visita report, Pueblo Nuevo, June 2, 1745, AGN, AHH, Temp., leg. 2009, exp. 42; P. Fernando Caamaño to P. Prov. Escobar, Pueblo Nuevo, June 25, 1744, UTNLB-WBS, 1744, 203-204; P. Sebastián Morillos to bishop, Pueblo Nuevo, June 29, 1749, ACD, Varios, Año 1749; certification of the transfer of Pueblo Nuevo, December 3, 1753, AGN, Misiones, vol. 13, fols. 24-30.

66. West and Parsons, "The Topia Road," 408.

67. P. Balthasar to P. Escobar, Parral, July 23, 1743, AGN, AHH, Temp., leg. 2009, exp. 20.

68. P. Fernando Caamaño to P. Balthasar de Porras, Durango, January 22, 1748, AGN, AHH, Temp., leg. 974, exp. 1.

69. Ibid.; P. Pedro Retes to P. Prov. Escobar, Santa Catalina, November 4, 1745 and August 16, 1746, AHPM, nos. 1405 and 1407, respectively; P. Gen. Retz to P. Prov. Escobar, April 2, 1740, AHPM, no. 1308; Jesuit personnel records, 1748-1766, AGN, AHH, Temp., leg. 326, exp. 5.

70. P. Agustín Carta to P. Prov. Balthasar, San Juan de Topia, February 23, 1753, AGN, AHH, Temp., leg. 2009, exp. 41.

71. P. Joseph Guerrero Villaseca to P. Prov. Diego de Almonacir, Satevó, September 25, 1695, AGN, Jesuitas, I-12, exp. 251; charges against P. Ignacio Javier de Estrada, Temeichi, November 23, 1721, AGN, Inquisición, vol. 780, exp. 28; P. Juan Lorenzo Salgado to P. Prov. Ignacio Calderón, Ciribie, June 28, 1759, UTNLB-WBS, 66, 27–28. See Calderón's charges against Cristina de Villanueva, Parral, 1721, AGN, Inquisición, vol. 791, exp. 31.

72. Agustín de Vildósola to P. Prov. Matheo Ansaldo, Buenavista, October 4, 1742, AGN, Historia, vol. 17, exp. 1.

73. P. Matheo Sánchez to P. Prov. Andrés Nieto, San Gregorio, September 20, 1745, AGN, AHH, Temp., leg. 1126, exp. 3; carta annua del Colegio de Durango, 1751–1757, ARSI, Provincia Mexicana, vol. 18, fols. 493–494; visita de la Provincia de la Sierra de San Andrés de Topia, Durango, June 3, 1745, AGN, AHH, Temp., leg. 2009, exp. 42.

74. P. Agustín Carta to P. Balthasar, San Juan, February 23, 1753, San Pedro de Iscatain, March 10, 1753, both in AGN, AHH, Temp., leg. 2009, exp. 41.

75. Report of P. Andrés Javier García, ca. 1740, AGN, AHH, Temp., leg. 1126, exp. 4.

7. "STUCK TOGETHER WITH PINS"

1. Martin, *Governance and Society*, 24–25.

2. Exchanges on these issues between the Audiencia de Guadalajara and the king, 1739–1742, in BPE, AJANG, Civil, caja 166, exp. 3; real cédula, October 4, 1742, AGI, Audiencia de Guadalajara, leg. 106; audiencia to king, September 3, 1743, AGI, Audiencia de Guadalajara, leg. 105.

3. Soto y Troncoso to viceroy, San Felipe el Real, September 1, 1744, *DHM*, 4-4, 39–47. His recommendations are similar to the arguments submitted to him by the Jesuits in the early 1740s; undated draft in Biblioteca Nacional, Archivo Franciscano, caja 12.

4. Case against Juan Ignacio, mulato esclavo, por el feo pecado de bestialidad, Chihuahua, January 14, 1721, AGN, Inquisición, vol. 791, fols. 529–535.

5. P. Balthasar to P. Escobar, Chicorato, December 28, 1744, AGN, AHH, Temp., leg. 1126, exp. 3.

6. P. Balthasar to P. Escobar, Durango, March 12, 1745, AGN, AHH, Temp., leg. 2009, exp. 20.

7. P. Pedro Retes to P. Joseph Calderón, Santa Catalina, November 27, 1745, AHPM, no. 1673; P. Lucas Merino to P. Prov. Escobar, San Felipe el Real, January 20, 1746, AGN, Jesuitas II-9, fol. 86.

8. Copies of this document, which will be referred to as the Escobar Memorial, are in AGN, Misiones, vol. 22, fols. 212–239; and AGN, Reales Cédulas, vol. 67, exp. 32, fols. 106–132.

9. Real cédula, December 4, 1747, AGN, Reales Cédulas, vol. 67, exp. 32; dic-

támenes de los señores fiscal y auditor . . . México, December 7, 1748, AGN, AHH, Temp., leg. 278, exp. 42.

10. Ordenanza del virrey, October 31, 1746, ACD, Varios, Año 1753 (copy in UTNLB-WBS, 842). On Jesuit attempts to get their concerns to the viceroy through informal channels, see P. Pedro de Retes to P. Joseph Calderón, Santa Catalina, November 27, 1745, AHPM, no. 1673. In this case the conduit was the Jesuit confessor of the viceroy's secretary. The call for schools to teach Spanish anticipated by eight years a royal order to this effect, but was surely influenced by "enlightened" advocates for this practice in New Spain; Tanck, *Pueblos de indios,* 165–166.

11. Causa criminal contra Pedro Villalobos por haber maltratado a Vicente López, indio tepehuan del pueblo de San Pablo, Parral and Santa Bárbara, 1745, AHP, r. 1745, fr. 264–290; P. Manuel Ignacio de Cartagena to P. Vis. Marcelo de León, San Luis, June 23, 1747, AHPM, no. 1613.

12. Viceregal order, October 31, 1746, UTNLB-WBS, 843. Again we see a parallel with shifts in the center-south that were designed to bring more secular control of Indian pueblos. Tanck, *Pueblos de indios,* passim.

13. Auditor de guerra to viceroy, October 2, 1747, AGN, AHH, Temp., leg. 278, exp. 40.

14. For the commercial and genealogical ties of the powerful Sánchez de Tagle family, see Velázquez, *El Marqués de Altamira,* 11–20.

15. Bishop to viceroy, February 9, 1749, carta circular of the bishop, March 27, 1749, and Juan Francisco Victoria to bishop, Culiacán, May 18, 1749, all in ACD, Varios, Año 1749.

16. Expediente de tierras . . . San Ignacio de Piastla, September 1751, AGN, Tierras, vol. 1424, exp. 14; land titles Badiraguato, 1750s, AIP-TA, lib. 39, exp. 6; lib. 41, exp. 1.

17. P. Miguel Joseph González to bishop, Los Remedios, June 22, 1749, ACD, Varios, Año 1749.

18. P. Joaquín Basurto to bishop, June 13, 1749, ACD, Varios, Año 1749.

19. P. Manuel Ignacio de Cartagena to bishop, Otaez, June 16, 1749, and P. Fernando Caamaño, Tamazula, June 21, 1749, both in ACD, Varios, Año 1749.

20. P. Mateo Sánchez to bishop, San Gregorio, May 12, 1749, ACD, Varios, Año 1749.

21. On February 23, 1753, P. Vis. Agustín Carta wrote to P. Balthasar that there were only three missions in Topia that were not substantially inhabited by gente de razón; AGN, AHH, Temp., leg. 2009, exp. 41.

22. Padrón in P. Marcelo de León to bishop, San Ignacio, June 30, 1749, ACD, Varios, Año 1749.

23. P. Marcelo de León to bishop, San Ignacio, June 30, 1749, ACD, Varios, Año 1749. P. Juan Lorenzo Salgado to P. Ignacio Calderón, June 28, 1759, UTNLB-WBS, 66, 27–28. See the discussion of native cures in the region of San Ignacio de Piastla, relaciones topográficas, Bachiller Joseph Miguel León de Abena, December 4, 1777, BN (Madrid), ms. 2450, fols. 46–48.

24. P. Marcelo de León to bishop, San Ignacio, June 30, 1749, ACD, Varios, Año 1749.

25. Quejas de los gobernadores de la misión de Piastla, San Ignacio, ca. 1750, AHPM, no. 808.

26. For variations in the system, see Brooke Larson and Robert Wasserstrom, "Consumo forzoso en Cochabamba y Chiapas durante la época colonial," *Historia Mexicana* 31 (1982): 361–408; and Chance, *Conquest of the Sierra*, 103–111, 177–184.

27. P. Prov. Andrés García to bishop, Zacatecas, February 11, 1749, ACD, Varios, Año 1749; P. Joaquín Basurto to P. Proc. Diego Verdugo, Badiraguato, March 2, 1749, AGN, AHH, Temp., leg. 974, exp. 1.

28. P. Manuel Ignacio de Cartagena to P. Vis. Marcelo de León, Otatitlán, March 30, 1749, AHPM, no. 1614; Cartagena to León, Otatitlán, April 21, 1749, AGN, Jesuitas, I-16, exp. 1; Pedro Joseph Salcido to P. Marcelo de León, Cosalá, July 8, 1749, AHPM, no. 1409; P. León to P. Prov. Andrés García, San Ignacio, July 28, 1749, AHPM, no. 1410b; P. Agustín Carta to P. Balthasar, San Juan de Topia, February 23, 1753, AGN, AHH, Temp., leg. 2009, exp. 41.

29. Vecinos de los Remedios to bishop, May 23, 1749, ACD, Varios, Año 1749.

30. P. Lorenzo Reino to P. Prov. Escobar, Villa de San Felipe, January 19, 1745, AGN, Jesuitas, I-16, exp. 32; juicio de residencia del gobernador Belaunzarán, AGI, Escribanía de Cámara, leg. 394; confirmaciones de tierras, 1753, AGI, Audiencia de Guadalajara, leg. 120.

31. Padrón de Nombre de Dios, 1778, BN-AF, caja 16, 328, fols. 17–18; on carboneros, see West, *The Mining Community*, 41–46.

32. Jesuit response to viceroy's queries, November 8, 1745, AGN, Misiones, vol. 27, fols. 301–302; inspección y nómina . . . del Valle de San Bartolomé, July 19, 1750, AGI, Audiencia de Guadalajara, leg. 110.

33. P. Manuel Vivanco to P. Antonio Ruiz, Tizonazo, October 29, 1745, UTNLB-WBS, 1745, 359; P. Pedro de Retes to P. Prov. García, Santa Catalina, November 4, 1745, AHPM, no. 1405.

34. P. Pedro de Retes to P. Prov. García, Santa Catalina, September 15, 1749, AGN, Archivo Provisional, Temp., caja 5.

35. P. Carta to P. Prov. Balthasar, Durango, February 18, 1751, AGN, AHH, Temp., leg. 2009, exp. 39.

36. P. Antonio de los Ríos to bishop, Santiago Papasquiaro, July 11, 1749; and P. Pedro de Retes to bishop, Santa Catalina, August 15, 1749, both in ACD, Varios, Año 1749; P. Pedro de Retes, August 7, 1750, AGN, Jesuitas, II-29, fol. 291; land titles, Santiago Papasquiaro, 1743-64, AIP-TA, lib. 28, exps. 223, 224, 225, 232.

37. P. Antonio de los Ríos to bishop, Santiago Papasquiaro, July 11, 1749, ACD, Varios, Año 1749.

38. P. Pedro de Retes to bishop, Santa Catalina, August 15, 1749, ACD, Varios, Año 1749.

39. Parroquia de Santa Catalina de Tepehuanes, Entierros, 1728 ff., GS, no. 604871; many of the entries are recorded by the sacristan.

40. P. Lázaro Franco Coronel to bishop, Zape, August 8, 1749, and P. Manuel Vivanco to bishop, September 2, 1749, both in ACD, Varios, Año 1749; Pedro Gómez Castellano to Teniente Salvador de Acosta, Santa Cruz, August 24, 1749, ACD, Varios, Año 1749.

41. Information on land titles and holdings in AGN, Jesuitas, II-29, and AIP-TA, lib. 33-1.

42. P. Pedro Retes to P. Prov. Andrés García, Santa Catalina, September 12, 1749, AGN, Archivo Provisional, Temp., caja 5.

43. Petition of Indians of San Miguel and San Gabriel de las Bocas, May 4, 1722, AGN, Indios, vol. 46, exp. 54; P. Juan Francisco Hauga to bishop, San Miguel de las Bocas, June 30, 1749, ACD, Varios, Año 1749; Carta visita report, April 9, 1751, AGN, AHH, Temp., leg. 2009, exp. 41.

44. P. Benito Rinaldini to bishop, Huejotitlán, July 29, 1749, ACD, Varios, Año 1749.

45. Case of Joseph Manuel Antonio García, Parral, 1753, AGN, Inquisición, vol. 1231, exp. 6.

46. P. Moreno to bishop, Santa Cruz, July 27, 1749; Nicolás Paez de Guzmán to bishop, Santa Bárbara, October 18, 1749, Juan Joseph de Ochoa y Herive to Canónigo Antonio Joseph Melo, Parral, October 23, 1749, all in ACD, Varios, Año 1749. Accounts from the Hacienda de Santa Ana de Torreón of Pedro González de Almoyna relating to confirmation of land titles, Chihuahua, 1752, AGI, Audiencia de Guadalajara, leg. 120; report of Bachiller Juan José Ochoa de Herive, Santa Cruz, September 24, 1753; ACD, Varios, Año 1753.

47. P. Felipe Calderón to bishop, Las Cuevas, July 21, 1749, ACD, Varios, Año 1749.

48. P. Gaspar del Trujillo to P. Prov. García, Parral, October 24, 1749, AGN, Jesuitas, II-9, fols. 29-30.

49. P. Juan Antonio Núñez to bishop, Satebó, July 19, 1749, ACD, Varios, Año 1749; Juan Joseph de Ochoa y Herive to Canónigo Antonio Joseph Melo, Parral, October 23, 1749, ACD, Varios, Año 1749. Although the numbers of Indians in Satevó were on the rebound in 1749, by 1799 there were three times more non-Indians than Indians in the village; noticia del curato . . . San Francisco Xavier de Satebó, January 21, 1799, Bancroft Library, Mexican Manuscripts, 1793:3.

50. The bishop of Durango referred to these as "semicofradías" in a letter to the Jesuit provincial, Durango, Jan 28, 1750, AGN, Historia, vol. 393, fols. 150-152. The dedication of some livestock to the support of the patron saint fiesta was a common practice in all the missions, whether formally constituted as cofradías or not. On food offerings for the dead, see P. Núñez to bishop, Satebó, July 19, 1749, ACD, Varios, Año 1749; Kennedy, *Tarahumara of the Sierra Madre*, 149-153; and Merrill, *Rarámuri Souls*, 162-172.

51. In midcentury Inquisition cases, non-Indians and natives intermingle in pacts with the devil and flying witches; AGN, Inquisición, vol. 1169, fol. 17, and vol. 980, exp. 21.

52. Jesuit draft, n.d., ca. 1750, BN-AF caja 12; Gov. Puerta y Barrera to king, Chihuahua, July 15, 1750, AGI, Audiencia de Guadalajara, leg. 110.

53. Carta visita report, Chihuahua, June 7, 1751, AGN, AHH, Temp., leg. 2009, exp. 41; and June 25, 1751, AGN, AHH, Temp., leg. 2009, exp. 39.

54. P. Rinaldini to P. Prov. García, Huejotitlán, October 13, 1749; AHPM, no. 1389; Hadley, *Minería y sociedad,* 211–212; viceroy to corregidor, February 25, 1751, ACD, Varios, Año 1753.

55. P. Retes to P. Prov. García, Santa Catalina, September 15, 1749, and P. Joseph Pérez de Aragón to P. García, Durango, October 31, 1749, both in AGN, Archivo Provisional, Temp., caja 5; P. Cristóbal Moreno to P. Proc. Verdugo, Santa Cruz, November 23, 1749, AGN, AHH, Temp., leg. 1076; P. Juan Antonio de la Fuente to P. Balthasar, Utais, October 10, 1750, AGN, Historia, vol. 393, fol. 154; carta annua, Colegio de Durango, 1742–1751, AGN, Jesuitas, leg. III-15, exp. 3; memorial of the cabildo eclesiástico, Durango, February 24, 1757, AGI, Audiencia de Guadalajara, leg. 71.

56. Vecinos de San Buenaventura to viceroy, April 15, 1749, AGI, Audiencia de Guadalajara, leg. 120; Porras Muñoz, *Iglesia y estado,* 370.

57. Robert H. Jackson looks at these conditions for the Chumash of Central California in the late mission period in "Agriculture, Drought, and Chumash Congregation in the California Missions, 1782–1834," *Estudios de Historia Novohispana* 19 (1999): 69–90.

58. Porras Muñoz, *Iglesia y estado,* 370–371; P. Prov. Andrés Xavier García to bishop, Mexico City, July 20, 1749, ACD, Varios, Año 1749.

59. James C. Scott, *Seeing Like a State: How Certain Schemes to Improve the Human Condition Have Failed,* 1–3.

60. Berroterán report on Nueva Vizcaya, Mexico City, July 17, 1751, AGI, Audiencia de Guadalajara, leg. 137.

8. RENDERING UNTO CAESAR AT THE CROSSROADS OF ETHNICITY AND IDENTITY

1. Report of José Rafael Rodríguez Gallardo, August 18, 1750, AGN, Provincias Internas, vol. 176, exp. 6, fols. 268–279.

2. Dictamen del auditor de guerra, Mexico City, December 23, 1749, AGI, Audiencia de Guadalajara, leg. 191.

3. The entire report was edited by Germán Viveros and published as *Informe sobre Sinaloa y Sonora, 1750.*

4. Nancy Farriss, *Crown and Clergy in Colonial Mexico, 1759–1821;* D. A. Brading, *Church and State in Bourbon Mexico: The Diocese of Michoacán, 1749–1810;* William B. Taylor, *Magistrates of the Sacred: Priests and Parishioners in Eighteenth-Century Mexico.*

5. *Instrucciones que los virreyes de Nueva España dejaron a sus sucesores,* 2 vols., 30–43; consulta del Consejo de Indias, Madrid, July 7, 1752, AGI, Audiencia de Guadalajara, leg. 61; real cédula, February 1, 1753, AGN, Reales Cédulas, vol. 73, fols. 35–38;

viceroy (Marqués de Amarillas) to Julián de Arriaga, México, March 1, 1756, AGN, Correspondencia de virreyes, 2d series, vol. 1, exp. 37; real cédula, June 23, 1757, AGN, AHH, Temp., leg. 2161, exp. 1; Taylor, *Magistrates of the Sacred,* 84. Tanck, *Pueblos de indios,* 161–168, connects the secularization process with royal mandates to establish schools in Indian pueblos designed to teach Spanish.

6. P. Balthasar to P. Retz, México, April 17, 1754, AGN, Misiones, vol. 22, fols. 382–391; P. Ignacio Calderón to P. Proc. Pedro Ignacio Altamirano, México, November 6, 1753, AGN, AHH, Temp., leg. 540, exp. 2.

7. Naturales del pueblo de Santiago Papasquiaro . . . , August 13, 1749; respuesta del fiscal, October 10, 1749; parecer del auditor, October 20, 1749; and viceroy to bishop, October 26, 1749, all in ACD, Varios, Año 1749.

8. P. Vis. Agustín Carta to P. Prov. Balthasar, April 9, 1751, AGN, AHH, Temp., leg. 2009, exp. 39; P. Antonio de los Ríos to P. Prov. Balthasar, April 18, 1751, AGN, Archivo Provisional, Temp., caja 5.

9. Naturales de los pueblos . . . , n.d. ca. 1750, ACD, Varios, Año 1749.

10. Incitativo de justicia, December 11, 1752, AGN, General de Parte, vol. 38, exp. 89.

11. P. Vis. Carta to P. Balthasar, Huejotitlán, April 9, 1751, AGN, AHH, Temp., leg. 2009, exp. 39.

12. Correspondence of P. Marcelo de León with superiors in Mexico City and Topia missionaries, San Ignacio, July 1749, in AHPM, nos. 1409, 1410, 1410A; P. Prov. Balthasar to P. Proc. Juan María Casati, October 1752, AGN, AHH, Temp., leg. 327.

13. P. Vis. Carta to P. Prov. Balthasar, Santa Cruz, October 4, 1753, AHPM, no. 1390.

14. This term was not used until the late eighteenth century, but a certain amount of land, depending upon the location, was considered to be "tierra por razón del pueblo" and part of the bienes comunales (community assets) of Indian pueblos. Tanck, *Pueblos de indios,* 77.

15. P. Vis. Carta to P. Prov. Balthasar, Durango, May 27 and July 2, 1753, both in AGN, AHH, Temp., leg. 2009, exp. 41; instructions of the bishop, July 27, 1753, ACD, Varios, Año 1753; P. Vis. Carta to P. Prov. Balthasar, August 14, 1753, and October 4, 1753, in AGN, Jesuitas, I-17, and AHPM, no. 1390, respectively.

16. P. Gen. Ignacio Visconti to P. Prov. Balthasar, Rome, January 1, 1753, AHPM, no. 1340; report of auditor de guerra and order of viceroy, January 22, 1753, and respuesta fiscal, January 9, 1754, AGI, Audiencia de Guadalajara, leg. 137; P. Gaspar Trujillo to P. Vis. Carta, Parral, May 20, 1753, AGN, AHH, Temp., leg. 2009, exp. 41.

17. Bishop's instructions, July 23, 1753, AGI, Audiencia de Guadalajara, leg. 137; copies in AGN, Misiones, vol. 13, fols. 7–9, and Misiones, vol. 22, fols. 6–7.

18. August 14, 1753, AHPM, no. 1391A.

19. The ways in which indigenous peoples came to use the Spanish legal system and its institutions to their occasional benefit were multiple. Andeanists have been particularly creative in showing how some peoples reinforced collective identities without negating Spanish principles of authority; see, for example, Sergio Serulnikov,

"Disputed Images of Colonialism: Spanish Rule and Indian Subversion in Northern Potosí, 1776–1780," *Hispanic American Historical Review* 76, no. 2 (May 1996): 189–226.

20. Autos de entrega, Tizonazo, September 7, 1743, and Huejotitlán, September 28, 1753, both in AGI, Audiencia de Guadalajara, leg. 137.

21. Título de merced, December 7, 1759, AIP-TA, vol. 30, exp. 17; extracto de la entrega, 1754, Manuel Ignacio de Cartagena, AGN, Jesuitas I-7.

22. Gov. Mendoza to king, Durango, May 16, 1754, AGI, Audiencia de Guadalajara, leg. 401; consulta del consejo to king, June 12, 1754, AGI, Audiencia de Guadalajara, leg. 545; Conde de Revillagigedo to Marqués de Amarillas, November 28, 1754, in *Instrucciones que los virreyes*, 31.

23. Dictamen del auditor de guerra, December 23, 1749, AGI, Audiencia de Guadalajara, leg. 191; real cédula, January 20, 1753, AGN, Reales Cédulas, vol. 73, fols. 7-15; autos sobre presidios, Mexico City, February 1, 1753, AGN, Provincias Internas, vol. 14, exp. 5; instructions for the governor of Nueva Vizcaya from the Junta de Hacienda y Guerra, Mexico City, October 16, 1753, AGN, Provincias Internas, vol. 94, exp. 3.

24. Bishop to viceroy, February 26, 1750, ACD, Varios, Año 1749; petition of Indian officials, Lorenzo Madueno, Christóbal de Estrada, and Tomás de la Cruz, to viceroy, November 1754, ACD, Varios, Año 1755. It is worthy of note that at this late date primarily indigenous officials had last names. Mission counts listed all but the officials by first name only.

25. Viceroy to bishop, November 14, 1754, ACD, Varios, Año 1755.

26. Alcalde mayor to provisor y vicario general, Santiago Papasquiaro, February 12, 1755, ACD, Varios, Año 1755.

27. Bishop to viceroy, March 7, 1755, ACD, Varios, Año 1755.

28. Bachiller (Br.) Juan Joseph Ochoa de Herive to bishop, Parral, February 20, 1754, ACD, Varios, Año 1753.

29. Viceroy to governor of Nueva Vizcaya, Mexico City, November 18, 1754; AGN, General de Parte, vol. 38, exp. 161.

30. Viceroy to Gov. Mendoza, May 15, 1756, AGN, Provincias Internas, vol. 94, exp. 2, fols. 351-352. The protectores often usurped Indian lands and water rights for their own use; see, for example, petitions from San Francisco de Conchos, 1717, AGN, Indios, vol. 42, exp. 51.

31. Fernández de Sierra to Br. Juan Joseph de Ochoa Herive, Satevó, October 23, 1753, ACD, Varios, Año 1753.

32. San Felipe el Real, July 2, 1752, BN-AF, caja 12.

33. Report of Franciscan comisario general, Fr. Juan Antonio de Abasolo, San Luis Potosí, March 9, 1753, BN-AF, caja 15, 274.

34. Fernández de Sierra to corregidor, Satevó, November 3, 1753, ACD, Varios, Año 1753.

35. Corregidor to Fernández de Sierra, San Felipe el Real, November 7, 1753, ACD, Varios, Año 1753.

36. Bishop to corregidor, Durango, November 22, 1753; corregidor to bishop, San Felipe el Real, January 12, 1754; Ochoa de Herive to bishop, Parral, February 20, 1754; bishop to corregidor, Durango, May 12, 1754; all in ACD, Varios, Año 1753.

37. Bishop to viceroy, Durango, May 2, 1754, AGI, Audiencia de Guadalajara, leg. 206; informe de los curas y demás eclesiásticos del Obispado de Durango, July 3, 1755, AGI, Audiencia de Guadalajara, leg. 547.

38. Mendía to Miguel Liborio Martín, Ciénaga, June 17, 1755, ACD, Varios, Año 1753.

39. Joseph Joaquín de Loya and Miguel Liborio Martín to bishop, Huejotitlán, June 19, 1755; Martín to bishop, San Pablo, June 20, 1755; Juan Delgado to bishop, Santa Cruz, June 28, 1755; Ochoa de Herive to bishop, Parral, June 30, 1755; all in ACD, Varios, Año 1753.

40. Bishop to governor, Durango, June 30, 1755; bishop to Ochoa de Herive, July 10, 1755; both in ACD, Varios, Año 1753.

41. P. Balthasar to viceroy, n.d., 1754, UTNLB-WBS, 1719; annuas de la misión del Señor Juan Baptista de Tonachiqui, 1757, AGN, Jesuitas, II-7, exp. 20.

42. Land titles, 1760, AIP-TA, lib. 33, exp. 6; entrega de San Gregorio, December 24, 1753, AGN, Misiones, vol. 13, fols. 43–50; petition of Juan Francisco de Vitorica and Domingo Joseph Pando de la Granda, San Miguel de Culiacán, January 21, 1754, AGN, Misiones, fols. 85–87; provisor Joseph Antonio de Melo to king, Durango, February 26, 1754, AGI, Audiencia de Guadalajara, leg. 121; informe de los curas . . . , July 3, 1755, AGI, Audiencia de Guadalajara, leg. 547.

43. See Taylor, *Magistrates of the Sacred*, 79–83, 99–100, for discussions of the periodic competitions for appointment to vacant offices and classifications of parish priests. He describes the assistants (*vicarios*/unbeneficed assistants and *coadjutores*/coadjutors) as very transient.

44. Informe de los curas . . . , July 3, 1755, AGI, Audiencia de Guadalajara, leg. 547; indios del pueblo de Santa Cruz to bishop, Santa Cruz, October 1756, ACD, Varios, Año 1757; Ochoa y Herive to Miguel Joseph de Arenibar, Parral, November 2, 1755, Parroquia de Belisario Domínguez/San Lorenzo, Bautismos, 1755–1763, GS, no. 162584; Marcos Núñez de Quevedo to provisor, Pueblo Nuevo, November 1760, ACD, Varios, Año 1760; autos de concurso de los curatos de este obispado, Durango, May 20, 1762, ACD, Varios, Año 1762.

45. Governor to bishop, San Felipe el Real, August 8, 1760, ACD, Varios, Año 1760. These practices continued unabated, according to the Indians of San Francisco de Conchos, July 29, 1768, AGN, Indios, vol. 62, exps. 38, 39.

46. Joseph Ramón de Zúñiga to Gov. Joseph Carlos de Agüero, Huejotitlán, November 26, 1767, AGN, Provincias Internas, vol. 94, exp. 2, fol. 72.

47. Gerhard, *The North Frontier*, 169–171. The 1790 padrón for the intendancy of Durango estimated Indians to be less than a quarter of the total population; AGN, Historia, vol. 522, fols. 268–271.

48. Parroquia de San Pablo Balleza, Entierros, 1754–1760, GS, no. 1222928; P. Juan Manuel de Hierro to P. Prov. Ignacio de Calderón, Temosachi, January 11,

1755, UTNLB-WBS, 66, 21–22; P. Hierro to Capt. Gabriel Gutiérrez de Rivas, Temosachi, February 6, 1755, AGN, Jesuitas, I-16, exp. 54. Some missions were heavily indebted to merchants, muleteers, and landowners; list of creditors, July 1, 1766, AGN, Inquisición, vol. 1079, exp. 6.

49. Carta annua, Coyachi, n.d., 1757, carta annua, Blas de la Palma, Santo Tomás, November 25, 1757, in AGN, Jesuitas, II-7, exps. 14 and 21, respectively.

50. Capt. Berroterán to Gov. Agüero, September 25, 1762, AGN, Provincias Internas, vol. 94; vol. 95, exp. 1, fols. 1–240 also details Apache raiding activities. The reorganization of presidios contemplated in the 1750s had not been effective; real cédula sobre extinción del presidio de Pasaje, October 30, 1759, AGN, Reales Cédulas Duplicadas, vol. 107, fols. 36–38.

51. William L. Merrill, "Cultural Creativity and Raiding Bands in Eighteenth-Century Northern New Spain," in Taylor and Pease, G.Y., eds., *Violence, Resistance, and Survival in the Americas,* 124–152; P. Joseph María Miqueo to P. Proc. Pedro Reales, Temeichi, July 7, 1763, AGN, Jesuitas, I-16, exp. 53.

52. Parroquia de San Pablo Balleza, Entierros, 1750s–1760s, GS, no. 1222928.

53. Parroquia de Huejotitan, bautismos, 1760s, GS, no. 1222908: the frequent notation of the priest was "dicen ser español." Case of Margarita Rodríguez, 1763, AGN, Inquisición, vol. 1387, exp. 8.

54. P. Joaquín Trujillo to P. Vis. Barolomé Braun, Tutuaca, April 6, 1764, UTNLB-WBS, 66, 17–19.

55. Venta de tierras, Indé, 1760, BPE, AJANG, caja 60, exp. 1; land titles, 1730–1764, Santiago Papasquiaro, AIP-TA, lib. 28, exps. 223, 224, 225, 232; título de adjudicación, January 24, 1760, AIP-TA, lib. 33, exp. 1; Br. Benito Batres to juez de tierras, Santiago Papasquiaro, April 15, 1763, Archivo del Gobierno de Durango (AGD), cajón 3, exp. 25; copy of real cédula to bishop, ca. 1768, ACD, Varios, Año 1749.

56. Visita of Bishop Tamarón y Romeral, March 11, 1765, AGI, Audiencia de Guadalajara, leg. 556; land title, San Ignacio de Piastla, January 8, 1765, AIP-TA, lib. 35, exp. 1; land titles, Badiraguato and Cariatapa, 1770, AIP-TA, lib. 32, exp. 8; litigio acerca de las tierras . . . ubicadas en la municipalidad de los Remedios, 1777–1782, AGD, cajón 7, exp. 58.

57. Br. Joseph Ramón de Zúñiga to Gov. Agüero, Huejotitlán, October 26, 1767, AGN, Provincias Internas, vol. 94, exp. 2; Francisco Antonio Carrillo report on Jesuit temporalidades, October 5, 1770, AGN, AHH, Temp., leg. 21, exp. 2; land titles, Papigochi, 1770s, AIP-TA, lib. 40, exp. 9; lib. 41, exp. 43. Criticisms of the Jesuits escalated after 1765, and they had perhaps tried to preempt unfavorable action against them by offering to secularize the rest of their missions in 1766. See P. Prov. Salvador de la Gandara to viceroy, Mexico City, n.d. 1766, AGN, AHH, Temp., leg. 325, exp. 12; consulta of April 8, 1766, AHPM, Consultas, tomo 4; viceroy to bishop of Durango, October 11, 1766, ACD, Varios, Año 1766.

58. Case against Romano, Santa Catharina de Tepehuanes, January 1771, AGN, Inquisición, vol. 1109, exp. 1; Parroquia de Santa Catalina de Tepehuanes, Entierros, GS, no. 604871.

59. Gov. Joseph Carlos de Agüero to Viceroy Marqués de Croix, Durango, March 20, 1757, AGN, Provincias Internas, vol. 94, exp. 1; list of vecinos, Santiago Papasquiaro, December 8, 1768, AGN, Provincias Internas, vol. 98, exp. 1.

60. Report by parish priests of San Ignacio de Piastla, May 6, 1778, BN-AF, caja 35; padrón de la alcaldía del real de Copala, June 1778, BN-AF, caja 34, 743.

61. Relación topográfica de Tamazula, July 31, 1777, BN (Madrid), ms. 2450; vecinos del real de Copala to alcalde mayor, June 28, 1779, BPE, AJANG, Civil, caja 80, exp. 7. In 1793, only five villages were listed as having a total of 113 tributaries; matrícula de tributarios, Culiacán, 1793, BN-AF, caja 35, 791.

62. Expediente sobre la sublevación . . . , Real de Copala, April 1771, AGN, Provincias Internas, vol. 167, exp. 1; testimony of María Magdalena, January 11, 1771, AGN, Inquisición, vol. 1109, exp. 1. See the analysis by José Luis Mirafuentes Galván, "Identidad india, legitimidad y emancipación política en el noroeste de México (Copala 1771)," in Jaime E. Rodríguez O., ed., *Patterns of Contention in Mexican History*. For comparative context, see Eric Van Young, "Millennium on the Northern Marches: The Mad Messiah of Durango and Popular Rebellion in Mexico, 1800-1805," *Comparative Studies in Society and History* 28 (1986): 385-413.

63. Acuerdo del comandante general, May 12, 1781, BN-AF, caja 34, 751.

64. Gov. José Fayni to Viceroy Bucareli, Durango, April 24, 1773, and Br. Pedro Fermín de Estavillo to Gov. Fayni, San Miguel de las Bocas, June 11, 1773, both in AGN, Provincias Internas, vol. 43, exp. 1; resumen de las hostilidades . . . , June 30, 1797, AGN, Provincias Internas, vol. 44, exp. 1; relación topográfica, Chihuahua, February 6, 1778, BN (Madrid), ms. 2449; report of Fr. José García Rico, Bachíniva, March 23, 1778, BN-AF, caja 16, 328; prevenciones hechas al comandante inspector para defensa . . , Chihuahua, April 18, 1778, AGI, Audiencia de Guadalajara, leg. 267; muster lists, 1779, AHP, r. 1779a, fr. 3-48. For a comprehensive explanation of the political economy of this raiding, see Merrill, "La economía política de las correrías: Nueva Vizcaya al final de la época colonial," in Hers et al., eds., *Nómadas y sedentarios*, 623-668.

65. Description of upper Tarahumara region, n.d., n.p., post-1780, *DHM*, 4-4, 117.

66. Documentos sobre estado del asunto de infidencia, February 1, 1787, AGN, Provincias Internas, vol. 254, exp. 4; sobre providencias para contener la infidelidad de los tarahumaras . . . , 1787-1789, AGN, Provincias Internas, fol. 162, exp. 7.

67. Padrones, Sianori, San Andrés, Santiago Papasquiaro, San Diego del Río, November 1787-February 1788, AGD, cajón 9, exps. 15, 124; padrones, Nueva Vizcaya, 1787, AHP, r. 1787b, fr. 1378-1385.

68. Testimonio de superior despacho . . . , n.d. 1777, AHP, r. 1777a, fr. 446-451.

69. Fr. Juan Treviño to Custodian Fr. Juan de Dios Fernández de la Cueva, Babonoyaba, March 21, 1778, BN-AF, caja 16, 328.

70. Reports from the Borica visita, 1790-1791, AGN, Provincias Internas, vol. 162, exps. 3, 5, 6.

71. Swann, *Migrants in the Mexican North*, 112-160.

72. Gerhard, *The North Frontier*, 169–172; César Navarro Gallegos, *Durango: las primeras décadas de vida independiente*, 59; census of Durango, 1803, AGN, AHH, leg. 917, exp. 2. The latter actually calculates the indigenous population at only one-fifth of the total. In any case, castas made up over half the total.

73. Bishop Estevan Lorenzo to viceroy, Durango, December 10, 1792, BN-AF, caja 18, 373.9.

74. Report of Viceroy Revillagigedo on missions, December 27, 1793, AGN, Historia, vol. 42, fols. 20–26, 79–84.

CONCLUSIONS

1. Bruce Chatwin, "Nomad Invasions," *What Am I Doing Here*, 216–229.

2. Deeds, "Legacies of Resistance, Adaptation, and Tenacity: History of the Native Peoples of Northwest Mexico," in *The Cambridge History of Native Peoples of the Americas*, vol. 2: Adams and MacLeod, eds., *Mesoamerica*, part 2, 44–87.

3. See Gonzalo Aguirre Beltrán, *Regiones de refugio: el desarrollo de la comunidad y el proceso dominical en mestizo América*, and Grant D. Jones, *Maya Resistance to Spanish Rule*.

4. Solicitud del ayuntamiento de Papasquiaro sobre comprar un terreno correspondiente a los de los jesuitas, 1829, AGN, Temporalidades, vol. 38, exp. 9.

5. I have visited Santa María twice, once in the summer of 1981 and again in May of 2002.

ⒼLOSSARY

acequia: Irrigation ditch.

alaja/alhaja: (Church) furnishings.

alcalde: Indian official or judge who assisted the governor in managing the daily economic and judicial matters of a mission.

alcalde mayor: Chief Spanish governing official for one of the administrative districts that made up a province ruled by a governor; could include one or more municipalities in outlying areas.

alguacil: Chief constable in a mission responsible for law enforcement.

almud: Volume measure equal to 4.6 liters or 4.1 quarts.

audiencia: Tribunal with judicial and legislative functions; of the five for New Spain, the Audiencia de Guadalajara had jurisdiction in Nueva Vizcaya and had authority over the governor.

auditor de guerra: Chief administrative officer and adviser to viceroy in matters of warfare and defense.

auto: Case file; act.

barrio: Subdivision within a mission that may have corresponded to former ranchería organization.

bastón: Staff of office given to Indian governor of a mission.

bienes comunales: Assets held in common by an Indian pueblo.

borrachera: Spanish name for indigenous ritual drinking implying excess and indecency in celebrating.

caballería: Area measure equaling 43 hectares or 105 acres.

cabecera: Head village of mission district where missionary resided.

cacastla: Basket frames used by indigenous peoples for transporting goods and belongings.

cacique: Term introduced by Spaniards (from Caribbean Indians) to denote a native ruler or chief.

caja de comunidad/arca de comunidad: Community treasury or chest.

capitán: Military officer; chief officer of mission responsible for defense or military operations.

carbonero: Charcoal burners used in the reduction of silver ore; charcoal was manufactured on haciendas de carbón with dispersed grants of woodlands.

carga: Volume measure that varies by product.

carta annua: Jesuit annual reports on missions, composed for individual missions, and theoretically compiled and summarized for an entire mission province; written in Spanish or Latin.

casa de comunidad: Community meetinghouse.

castas/gente de casta: People of mixed race, of Indian, African, or Spanish origin.

chichimecas: Generic term (from Nahuatl) for Indians in Mexico's near and far north that connotes less "civilized."

chirimía: Reed flute.

cocolitzli: Nahuatl generic term for epidemic disease.

cofradía: Religious confraternity dedicated to the cult of a Catholic saint; often owned livestock or land.

colegio: Secondary school, largely for male children of Spanish elites in which priests—in this case Jesuits—taught a scholastic curriculum; possessed landed property to support its educational undertaking; served as a retreat and sometimes source of economic support for missionaries.

colegio incoado: Regional seminaries for teaching Indian children; certain missions received this designation and could own additional properties to support the educational endeavor.

composición: Procedure involving the payment of a fee to regularize land titles.

común: Mission community; also denotes communal land and assets.

corregidor: Chief Spanish administrative official for one of the districts that make up a province; equivalent of alcalde mayor but in a more populous urban area.

coyote: Person of mixed race, usually of mestizo and Indian origin.

cura: Priest of the secular clergy; parish priest.

derecho posesorio: Right of possession, referring here to assets including land belonging to a community by virtue of its status as a pueblo de indios.

doctrina: (1) Indian parish in areas of formerly sedentary peoples; (2) Christian doctrine, catechism.

ejido, ejidatorio/a: Communal landholding; copossessor of the lands.

encomendero: Recipient of an encomienda.

encomienda: Grant of Indians to provide tribute to a Spanish encomendero; in the far north rendered only as labor.

entrada: Expedition into unknown or unsettled areas, usually military; also associated with missionary entries into an indigenous area.

estancia: Ranch or incipient hacienda.

etnia: Ethnic group with official recognition in contemporary Mexico.

fanega: Both a volume and area measure; volume of grain equal to 55 liters or 1.5 bushels; also the land measure equivalent to that sown by one fanega of grain.

fiscal: Attorney; in missions, an Indian official delegated to enforce rules of the missionary.

fundo legal: Conventional allotment of land to a municipality; theoretically a square league in northern Indian communities.

gentiles: Unbaptized Indians.

gobernador: Governor; chief Indian officer in a mission.

hacendado: Landowner; owner of hacienda.

juez medidor de tierras: Official responsible for surveying and adjudicating land disputes.

justicia mayor: Chief magistrate of a district.

ladino: Spanish-speaking, more acculturated Indian.

legua: League; linear measure of approximately 3 miles or 4.8 kilometers.

limosna: Alms; designation given to the annual royal stipend paid for mission upkeep.

linaje: Lineage, referring to ethnic origin.

lobo: Person of mixed race, usually of African and Indian origin.

maestro: Teacher, here referring to non-Indians hired to teach reading and writing to indigenous children in Indian villages or missions.

matachín: Dance introduced by Spaniards to dramatize Christian events and symbols.

matlazahuatl: Nahuatl generic term for epidemic disease, identified variously by historians as typhus, typhoid, and bubonic plague.

mayorazgo: Entailed estate descending by primogeniture.

mayordomo: Overseer; chief officer of a cofradía.

memoria: Annual list from missionaries requesting provisions, usually supplied from Jesuit colegios in Mexico City.

memorial: Written petition.

mescal: Type of maguey cactus used by Indians for fiber, food, and drink.

mestizaje: Racial or ethnic mixing.

mestizo: Person of mixed race of Indian and Spanish origin.

mexicana (mexicana mazorral): Nahuatl or altered form of this central Mexican language spoken in the north; often a lingua franca of Indians and non-Indians in the north.

milpa: Cultivated plot of land.

montañés: Spaniard from the northern regions of Spain, particularly around eastern Asturias.

monte: Uncultivated areas, woods, or brushlands, used by Indians for hunting and gathering.

mulata: Woman of mixed race, of African and Spanish origin.

naborío/naboría: Servant or laborer on Spanish haciendas or in mines; in the seventeenth century implied a more permanent but legally servile status.

nación: Spanish term for an Indian ethnic group or polity.

natural: Native.

obraje: Spanish manufactory or sweatshop, most often devoted to manufacturing textiles.

oidor: Audiencia judge.

padre provincial: Head of a Jesuit province, in this case of their province that included all of New Spain.

panocha: Coarse brown sugar cakes.

parcialidad: Subdivision within a mission that may have corresponded to former ranchería organization.

parroquia: Catholic parish, distinguished from missions by ethnic status of parishioners.

partido: Subdivision of Jesuit mission province; another term for *pepena.*

pepena: Amount or quota of ore allowed to some Indian mineworkers to sell on their own account.

peste: Spanish generic term for epidemic disease.

pita: Fiber from the agave plant used for making course cloth.

plática: Sermon or talk about proper moral behavior delivered by a principal.

principal: Indian elder, leader, or local official.

protector (defensor) de indios: Spanish official appointed to protect or defend Indian communities against abuse by outsiders.

pueblo de indios: Indian town; implies a particular juridical status.

ranchería: Indian hamlet with dispersed dwellings; shifts in location in accordance with mixed subsistence patterns.

real: Monetary unit; eight reales equaled one peso in the colonial period.

real cédula: Royal decree.

real de minas: Mining center or town.

rectorado: Subdivision of Jesuit province including several missions.

repartimiento: System of forced, rotational labor; in the north Indians were drafted from missions to supply labor to Spanish enterprises for stipulated periods of time for 2 reales per day, usually paid in kind.

repartimiento de mercancías/efectos: Forced sale of goods in Indian pueblos.

rescatador: Itinerant merchant who was an intermediary between Indian pueblos and markets in Spanish towns; usually bought grain at low prices and sold higher.

rescate: Purchase or acquisition of grain by a rescatador.

residencia: Official review held at the end of the term of an officeholder.

serrano: Inhabitant of, or pertaining to, the Sierra Madre Occidental.

siembras de comunidad: Communal plantings on indigenous lands whose products were dedicated to meeting community obligations.

sitio de ganado mayor/sitio: Land measurement for grazing land (cattle, oxen, horses, mules) equal to approximately 4,335 acres or 1,755 hectares.

solar: Area measure, usually in towns, equal to 173 acres or 70 hectares.

temastián: Catechist.

temporalidades: Ecclesiastical properties or revenues.

tesgüinada: Ritual celebration in which maize beer was consumed.

tesgüino/tiswin: Maize beer.

tierras baldías: "Empty" or unused lands; for Spaniards, lands not being used for agricultural production.

tlatoles: Consultations among Indian elders, often associated with a call to arms or dealing with encroachments by outsiders.

topil: Indian official who served as a constable or jailer.

vara: Linear measure of approximately 33 inches or 0.84 meter.

vecinos/vecindario: Spanish or non-Indian residents, usually landholders; body of non-Indian residents surrounding a mission.

visita: (1) Subunit of a mission, under the cabecera, visited regularly (in theory) by a missionary; (2) inspection tour by a missionary or civil official.

ᴀRCHIVAL ABBREVIATIONS

ACD: Archivo de la Catedral de Durango
AGD: Archivo del Gobierno del Estado de Durango
AGI: Archivo General de Indias, Seville, Spain
AGN: Archivo General de la Nación, Mexico City
   AHH, Temp.:   Archivo Histórico de Hacienda, Temporalidades
AHN: Archivo Histórico Nacional, Madrid
AHP: Archivo de Hidalgo de Parral, Chihuahua
AHPM: Archivo Histórico de la Provincia de los Jesuitas en México, Mexico City
AIP: Archivo de Instrumentos Públicos de Jalisco, Guadalajara
   TA: Ramo de Tierras y Aguas
AJANG: Archivo Judicial de la Audiencia de Nueva Galicia, Guadalajara
ARSI: Archivum Romanum Societatis Iesu, Rome (copy in University of Saint
   Louis Vatican Film Library)
BN: Biblioteca Nacional de México, Mexico City
   AF: Archivo Franciscano
BN (Madrid):   Biblioteca Nacional de España, Madrid
BPE: Biblioteca Pública del Estado de Jalisco, Guadalajara
CP: Colección Pastells, Razón y Fe Library, Madrid (copies in Jesuit Historical
   Institute, Tucson; AHPM; and Saint Louis Vatican Film Library)
DHM: Documentos para la historia de México
GS: Genealogical Society of the Church of Jesus Christ of Latter-day Saints
   (microfilmed parish registers)
MPC: Mateu Private Collection, Barcelona (copy of documents cited in Jesuit
   Historical Institute, Tucson)
UCB: University of California Bancroft Library
   B: Bolton Collection
UTNLB: University of Texas Nettie Lee Benson Library
   JGI: Joaquín García Icazbalceta Collection
   WBS: W. B. Stephens Collection

BIBLIOGRAPHY

Abercrombie, Thomas B. *Pathways of Memory and Power: Ethnicity and History among an Andean People.* Madison: University of Wisconsin Press, 1998.

Actas del Segundo Congreso de Historia Regional Comparada. Ciudad Juárez: Universidad Autónoma de Ciudad Juárez, 1991.

Adams, David. "The Tlaxcalan Colonies of Spanish Coahuila and Nuevo León: An Aspect of the Settlement of Northern Mexico." Ph.D. dissertation, University of Texas, 1971.

Aguirre Beltrán, Gonzalo. *Regiones de refugio: el desarrollo de la comunidad y el proceso dominical en mestizo América.* Mexico City: Instituto Indigenista Interamericano, 1967.

Alberro, Solange. *Inquisición y sociedad en México, 1571-1700.* Mexico City: Fondo de Cultura Económica, 1988.

Alden, Dauril. "Indian versus Black Slavery in the State of Maranhão during the Seventeenth and Eighteenth Centuries." In Garner and Taylor, eds., *Iberian Colonies, New World Societies,* 71-102.

————. *The Making of an Enterprise: The Society of Jesus in Portugal, Its Empire, and Beyond, 1540-1750.* Stanford: Stanford University Press, 1996.

Alegre, Francisco Javier, S.J. *Historia de la Compañía de Jesús de Nueva España,* ed. Ernest J. Burrus, S.J., and Félix Zubillaga, S.J. Rome: Jesuit Historical Institute, 1956-1960.

Algier, Keith W. "Feudalism in New Spain's Northern Frontier: Valle de San Bartolomé." Ph.D. dissertation, University of New Mexico, 1966.

Almada, Francisco R. *Resumen de historia del estado de Chihuahua.* Mexico City: Libros Mexicanos, 1955.

Alvarez, Salvador. "Agricultores de paz y cazadores-recolectores de guerra: los tobosos de la cuenca del Río Conchos en la Nueva Vizcaya." In Hers et al., eds., *Nómadas y sedentarios,* 305-354.

————. "Agricultural Colonization and Mining Colonization: The Area of Chihuahua during the First Half of the Eighteenth Century." In Craig and West, eds., *In Quest of Mineral Wealth*, 171–204.

———. "Chiametla: Una provincia olvidada del siglo XVI." *Trace* 22 (1992): 5–23.

———. "Tendencias regionales de la propiedad territorial en el norte de la Nueva España: siglos XVII y XVIII." In *Actas del Segundo Congreso de Historia Regional Comparada*, 141–179.

Anderson, Gary Clayton. *The Indian Southwest, 1580–1830: Ethnogenesis and Reinvention*. Norman: University of Oklahoma Press, 1999.

Arlegui, Joseph. *Crónica de la provincia de N.S.P.S. Francisco de Zacatecas*. 1737; reprint, Mexico City: J.B. de Hogal, 1851.

Bad'ura, Bohumil. "Apuntes sobre las composiciones de tierras en Nueva España." *Historia* (Academia Praha) 24 (1984).

Bargellini, Clara. "At the Center on the Frontier: The Jesuit Tarahumara Missions of New Spain." In Thomas Dacosta Kaufmann, ed., *The Geohistory of Art*. London: Ashgate Press, forthcoming.

———, ed. *Misiones y presidios de Chihuahua*. Chihuahua: Gobierno del Estado de Chihuahua, 1997.

———, ed. *Sur de Chihuahua: Itinerarios del pasado*. Mexico City: Grupos Cementos de Chihuahua, 2000.

Beals, Ralph L. *The Acaxee: A Mountain Tribe of Durango and Sinaloa*. Ibero-Americana Series, no. 6. Berkeley: University of California Press, 1933.

Behar, Ruth. "Sex and Sin, Witchcraft, and the Devil in Late Colonial Mexico." *American Ethnologist* 14, no. 1 (1987): 34–54.

Bennett, Wendell C., and Robert M. Zingg. *The Tarahumara: An Indian Tribe of Northern Mexico*. Chicago: University of Chicago Press, 1935.

Berrojalbiz Cenigaonaindia, Fernando. "Desentrañando un norte diferente: Los tepehuanes prehispánicos del Alto Río Ramos, Durango." In Chantal Cramaussel, ed., *Asentamientos y movimientos de población en la Sierra Tepehuana*.

Block, David. *Mission Culture on the Upper Amazon: Native Tradition, Jesuit Enterprise, and Secular Policy in Moxos, 1660–1880*. Lincoln: University of Nebraska Press, 1994.

Bolton, Herbert E. "The Mission as a Frontier Institution in the Spanish American Colonies." *American Historical Review* 23, no. 1 (1917): 42–61.

Bonfiglioli, Carlo. *Fariseos y matachines en la Sierra Tarahumara*. Mexico City: Instituto Nacional Indigenista/Secretaría de Desarrollo Social, 1995.

Bonnell, Victoria, and Lynn Hunt, eds. *Beyond the Cultural Turn: New Directions in the Study of Society and Culture*. Berkeley: University of California Press, 1999.

Borah, Woodrow. "La defensa frontera durante la gran rebelión tepehuana." *Historia Mexicana* 16, no. 1 (1966): 15–29.

Boyd-Bowman, Peter. "A Spanish Soldier's Estate in Northern Mexico, 1642." *Hispanic American Historical Review* 53, no. 1 (1973): 95–105.

Brading, D. A. *Church and State in Bourbon Mexico: The Diocese of Michoacán, 1749–1810*. Cambridge: Cambridge University Press, 1994.

Brooks, James F. *Captives and Cousins: Slavery, Kinship, and Community in the Southwest Borderlands.* Chapel Hill: University of North Carolina Press, 2002.

Brown, Michael F. "On Resisting Resistance." *American Anthropologist* 98 (1996): 729–735.

Burkhart, Louise. *The Slippery Earth: Nahua-Christian Moral Dialogue in Sixteenth-Century Mexico.* Tucson: University of Arizona Press, 1989.

The Cambridge History of the Native Peoples of the Americas. Vol. 1: *North America*, ed. Bruce G. Trigger and Wilcomb E. Washburn. Vol. 2: *Mesoamerica*, ed. Richard E. W. Adams and Murdo J. MacLeod. Vol. 3: *South America*, ed. Frank Solomon and Stuart Schwartz. New York: Cambridge University Press, 1996–2000.

Campbell, Ysla, ed. *El contacto entre los españoles e indígenas en el norte de la Nueva España.* Vol. 4 of *Colección conmemorativa quinto centenario del encuentro de dos mundos.* Ciudad Juárez: Universidad Autónoma de Ciudad Juárez, 1992.

Caraman, Philip. *Lost Paradise: The Jesuit Republic in South America.* New York: Seabury Press, 1975.

Case, Bradley W. "Gods and Demons: Folk Religion in Seventeenth-Century New Spain, 1614–1632." Ph.D. dissertation, Cornell University, 1977.

Castañeda, Carmen, ed. *Círculos de poder en la Nueva España.* Mexico City: CIESAS/ Miguel Angel Porrúa, 1998.

Cervantes, Francisco. *The Devil in the New World: The Impact of Diabolism in New Spain.* New Haven: Yale University Press, 1994.

Chance, John K. *Conquest of the Sierra: Spaniards and Indians in Colonial Oaxaca.* Norman: University of Oklahoma Press, 1989.

———. *Race and Class in Colonial Oaxaca.* Stanford: Stanford University Press, 1978.

Chatwin, Bruce. "Nomad Invasions." 1972. Reprinted in *What Am I Doing Here.* London: Vintage, 1998.

Chevalier, François. *Land and Society in Colonial Mexico: The Great Hacienda.* Berkeley: University of California Press, 1970.

Cline, S. L. *Colonial Culhuacan, 1580–1600: A Social History of an Aztec Town.* Albuquerque: University of New Mexico Press, 1986.

Craig, Alan K., and Robert C. West, eds. *In Quest of Mineral Wealth: Aboriginal and Colonial Mining and Metallurgy in Spanish America.* Baton Rouge: Louisiana State University Press, 1994.

Cramaussel, Chantal. "De cómo los españoles clasificaban a los indios: naciones y encomiendas en la Nueva Vizcaya central." In Hers et al., eds., *Nómadas y sedentarios,* 275–303.

———. "Encomiendas, repartimientos y conquista en Nueva Vizcaya." *Actas del Primer Congreso de Historia Regional Comparada,* 139–161. Ciudad Juárez: Universidad Autónoma de Ciudad Juárez, 1990.

———. "Evolución en las formas de dominio del espacio colonial: las haciendas de la región de Parral." *Encuentro* 20 (1990).

———. "Haciendas agrícolas y abasto de granos en el Parral del siglo XVII." In Guedea and Rodríguez O., eds. *Cinco siglos de historia de México,* vol. 2, 348–353.

———. "Haciendas y mano de obra en Nueva Vizcaya: el real de Parral en el siglo XVII." *Trace* 15 (June 1989): 22-30.

———. "El poder de los caudillos en el norte de la Nueva España: Parral, siglo XVII." In Castañeda, ed., *Círculos de poder en la Nueva España*, 39-58.

———. *Primera página de historia colonial chihuahuense: la provincia de Santa Bárbara en Nueva Vizcaya, 1563-1631.* Ciudad Juárez: Universidad Autónoma de Ciudad Juárez, 1990.

———. "Un projet de réductions indigènes pour la Nouvelle-Biscaye: L'avis de Nicolas de Barreda, missionaire jésuite à San Andrés en 1645." In Musset and Calvo, eds., *Des Indes Occidentales à L'Amérique Latine*, 39-54.

———. "Sociedad colonial y depredación ecológica: Parral en el siglo XVII." In Bernardo García Martínez and Alba González Jácome, eds., *Estudios sobre historia y ambiente en América*, vol. I, 92-107.

———. "Transformaciones en el medio ambiente: una laguna desaparecida en el sur del estado de Chihuahua." *Suma* 1 (1989): 5-12.

———, ed. *Asentamientos y movimientos de población en la Sierra Tepehuana desde la prehistoria hasta nuestros días.* Forthcoming.

Cuello, José. *El norte, el noreste y Saltillo en la historia colonial de México.* Saltillo, Coahuila: Archivo Municipal de Saltillo/R. Ayuntamiento de Saltillo, 1990.

Cuenya, Miguel Angel. *Puebla de los Angeles en los tiempos de una peste colonial: una mirada en torno al matlazahuatl de 1737.* Zamora: El Colegio de Michoacán, 1999.

Cutter, Charles R. *The "Protector de Indios" in Colonial New Mexico, 1659-1821.* Albuquerque: University of New Mexico Press, 1986.

Decorme, Gerard, S.J. *La obra de los jesuitas mexicanos durante la época colonial, 1572-1767.* 2 vols. Mexico City: Antigua Librería Robredo de José Porrúa e Hijos, 1941.

Deeds, Susan M. "Colonial Chihuahua: Peoples and Frontiers in Flux." In Jackson, ed., *New Views of Borderlands History*, 21-40.

———. "Cómo historiar con poca historia y menos arqueología: clasificación de los acaxees, xiximes, tepehuanes, tarahumaras y conchos." In Hers et al., eds., *Nómadas y sedentarios.*

———. "First Generation Rebellions in Seventeenth-Century Nueva Vizcaya." In Schroeder, ed., *Native Resistance*, 1-29.

———. "Indigenous Rebellions on the Northern Mexican Mission Frontier: From First-Generation to Later Colonial Responses." In Guy and Sheridan, eds., *Contested Ground*, 32-51.

———. "Land Tenure Patterns in Northern New Spain." *The Americas* 41, no. 4 (1985): 446-461.

———. "Legacies of Resistance, Adaptation, and Tenacity: History of the Native Peoples of Northwest Mexico." In *The Cambridge History of Native Peoples*, vol. 2: Adams and MacLeod, eds., *Mesoamerica*, part 2, 44-88.

———. "Mission Villages and Agrarian Patterns in a Nueva Vizcayan Heartland, 1600-1750." *Journal of the Southwest* 33, no. 3 (1991): 345-365.

————. "Las rebeliones de los tepehuanes y tarahumaras durante el siglo XVII en la Nueva Vizcaya." In Campbell, ed., *El contacto entre españoles e indígenas*, 9-40.

————. "Rural Work in Nueva Vizcaya: Forms of Labor Coercion on the Periphery." *Hispanic American Historical Review* 69, no. 3 (1989): 425-449.

Deven, Carol. *Countering Colonization: Native American Women in Great Lakes Missions: 1630-1900*. Berkeley: University of California Press, 1992.

DiPeso, Charles C. *Casas Grandes: A Fallen Trading Center of the Gran Chichimeca*. Dragoon, Ariz.: Amerind Foundation, 1974.

Documentos para la historia de México. 21 vols. in 4 series. Mexico City: Imprenta J. R. Navarro, 1853-1857.

Dunne, S. J., Peter M. *Early Jesuit Missions in Tarahumara*. Berkeley: University of California Press, 1948.

————. *Pioneer Black Robes on the West Coast*. Berkeley: University of California Press, 1940.

————. *Pioneer Jesuits in Northern Mexico*. Berkeley: University of California Press, 1944.

Esteyneffer, Juan, S.J. *Florilegio medicinal de todas las enfermedades*. 1712. Reprint, Mexico City: Academia Nacional de Medicina, 1978.

Farriss, Nancy M. *Crown and Clergy in Colonial Mexico, 1759-1821*. London: University of London Press, 1968.

————. *Maya Society and Colonial Rule: The Collective Enterprise of Survival*. Princeton: Princeton University Press, 1984.

Ferguson, R. Brian, and Neil L. Whitehead. "The Violent Edge of Empire." In *War in the Tribal Zone*, 1-30.

Ferguson, R. Brian, and Neil L. Whitehead, eds. *War in the Tribal Zone: Expanding States and Indigenous Warfare*. Santa Fe: School of American Research Press, 1992.

Florencia, Francisco de. *Historia de la provincia de la Compañía de Jesús de Nueva España*. Mexico City: Archivo Literario, 1955.

Florescano, Enrique. *Precios del maíz y crisis agrícolas en México, 1708-1810*. Mexico City: El Colegio de México, 1969.

Foster, Michael S., and Phil C. Weigand, eds. *The Archaeology of West and Northwest Mexico*. Boulder: Westview Press, 1985.

Foucault, Michel. *The Order of Things: An Archeology of the Human Sciences*. New York: Pantheon, 1970.

Frank, Ross. "Demographic, Economic, and Social Change in New Mexico." In Jackson, ed., *New Views of Borderlands History*, 41-72.

Frost, Elsa C., et al., eds. *El trabajo y los trabajadores en la historia de México*. Tucson: University of Arizona Press, 1979.

Furlong Cardiff, Guillermo. *Misiones y sus pueblos de guaraníes*. Buenos Aires: Ediciones Theoría, 1962.

Ganson, Barbara. "The Evueví of Paraguay: Adaptive Strategies and Responses to Colonialism, 1528-1811." *The Americas* 45, no. 4 (1989): 460-488.

García Ayluardo, Clara, and Manuel Ramos Medina, eds. *Manifestaciones religiosas en el mundo colonial americano.* Mexico City: Instituto Nacional de Antropología e Historia/Condumex/Universidad Iberoamericana, 1997.

García Martínez, Bernardo, and Alba González Jácome, eds. *Estudios sobre historia y ambiente en América.* Vol. 1. Mexico City: Instituto Panamericano de Geografía e Historia/El Colegio de México, 1999.

Garner, Richard L., and William B. Taylor, eds. *Iberian Colonies, New World Societies: Essays in Memory of Charles Gibson.* College Station: Pennsylvania State University Press, 1985.

Geertz, Clifford. *Available Light: Anthropological Reflections on Philosophical Topics.* Princeton: Princeton University Press, 2000.

Gerhard, Peter. *The North Frontier of New Spain.* Rev. ed. Norman: University of Oklahoma Press, 1993.

Gibson, Charles. *The Aztecs under Spanish Rule.* Stanford: Stanford University Press, 1964.

———. *Tlaxcala in the Sixteenth Century.* New Haven: Yale University Press, 1952.

Giudicelli, Christophe. "Guerre, identités et métissages aux frontières de l'Empire: la guerre des Tepehuán en Nouvelle Biscaye, 1616-1619." Ph.D. dissertation, Université de Paris III, 2000.

———. "El miedo a los monstruos: indios ladinos y mestizos en la guerra de los Tepehuanes de 1616." *Nuevo Mundo: Mundos Nuevos* (France), 1 (2001): 176-190.

Gonzalbo Aizpuru, Pilar. "Las devociones marianas en la vieja provincia de la Compañía de Jesús." In García Ayluardo and Ramos Medina, eds., *Manifestaciones religiosas,* 253-265.

González Ortega, Rutilio. "La California de los jesuitas." Doctoral thesis, El Colegio de México, 1973.

González Rodríguez, Luis, ed. *Crónicas de la Sierra Tarahumara.* Mexico City: Secretaría de Educación Pública, 1984.

———. *El noroeste novohispano en la época colonial.* Mexico City: Universidad Nacional Autónoma de México, 1993.

———. *Tarahumara: La sierra y el hombre.* Mexico City: Fondo de Cultura Económica/Secretaría de Educación Pública, 1982.

———. "Testimonios sobre la destrucción de las misiones tarahumares y pimas en 1690." *Estudios de Historia Novohispana* 10 (1991): 189-235.

Goode, Catherine Tracy. "Corrupting the Governor: Manuel de San Juan y Santa Cruz and Power in Early Eighteenth-Century Chihuahua." M.A. thesis, Northern Arizona University, 2000.

Gosner, Kevin. *Soldiers of the Virgin: The Moral Economy of a Colonial Maya Rebellion.* Tucson: University of Arizona Press, 1992.

Gradie, Charlotte M. "Discovering the Chichimecas." *The Americas* 51, no. 1 (1994): 67-88.

———. *The Tepehuan Revolt of 1616: Militarism, Evangelism, and Colonialism in the Seventeenth Century.* Salt Lake City: University of Utah Press, 2000.

Griffen, William C. *Culture Change and Shifting Populations in Central Northern Mexico*. Tucson: University of Arizona Press, 1969.

———. *Indian Assimilation in the Franciscan Area of Nueva Vizcaya*. Tucson: University of Arizona Press, 1979.

———. "Observations on the Limitations of Data on the Ethnohistory of Northern Mexico." In Hers et al., eds., *Nómadas y sedentarios*, 249–273.

———. "Southern Periphery: East." *Handbook of North American Indians*, vol. 10, 334–340.

Griffiths, Nicholas, and Fernando Cervantes, eds. *Spiritual Encounters: Interactions between Christianity and Native Religions in Colonial America*. Lincoln: University of Nebraska Press, 1999.

Gruzinski, Serge. *Images at War: Mexico from Columbus to Blade Runner, 1492–2019*. Durham: Duke University Press, 2001.

Guedea, Virginia, and Jaime E. Rodríguez, eds. *Five Centuries of Mexican History/ Cinco siglos de historia de México*. Vol. 2. Mexico City: Instituto Mora, 1992.

Guevara-Gil, Armando, and Frank Solomon. "A 'Personal Visit': Colonial Political Ritual and the Making of Indians in the Andes." *Colonial Latin American Review* 3 (1994): 3–36.

Guha, Ranajit. *Elementary Aspects of Peasant Insurgency in Colonial India*. Delhi: Oxford University Press, 1983.

———. "On Some Aspects of the Historiography of Colonial India." In Guha, ed., *Subaltern Studies*, vol. 1. New Delhi: Oxford University Press, 1982.

Gutiérrez, Ramón. *When Jesus Came, the Corn Mothers Went Away: Marriage, Sexuality, and Power in New Mexico, 1500–1846*. Stanford: Stanford University Press, 1991.

———, and Richard J. Orsi, eds. *Contested Eden: California before the Gold Rush*. Berkeley: University of California Press, 1998.

Gutiérrez Castillas, José. *Santarén: conquistador pacífico*. Guadalajara: Ediciones Canisio, 1961.

Guy, Donna J., and Thomas E. Sheridan, eds. *Contested Ground: Comparative Frontiers on the Northern and Southern Edges of the Spanish Empire*. Tucson: University of Arizona Press, 1998.

Hackel, Steven W. "Land, Labor, and Production: The Colonial Economy of Spanish and Mexican California." In Gutiérrez and Orsi, eds. *Contested Eden*.

Hackett, Charles W., ed. *Historical Documents Relating to New Mexico, Nueva Vizcaya, and Approaches Thereto, to 1773*. Vol. 2. Washington, D.C.: Carnegie Institution, 1926.

Hadley, Phillip. *Minería y sociedad en el centro minero de Santa Eulalia, Chihuahua, 1709–1750*. Mexico City: Secretaría de Educación Pública, 1979.

Hall, Stuart. "On Postmodernism and Articulation." In D. Morley and K. H. Chen, eds., *Stuart Hall: Critical Dialogues in Cultural Studies*. New York: Routledge, 1996.

Hammond, George P., and Agapito Rey, eds. *Obregón's History of 16th Century Exploration in Western America*. Los Angeles: Wetzel Publishing Co., 1928.

Hard, Robert J., and William L. Merrill. "Mobile Agriculturalists and the Emergence of Sedentism: Perspectives from Northern Mexico." *American Anthropologist* 94, no. 3 (1992): 601–620.

Haskett, Robert. *Indigenous Rulers: An Ethnohistory of Town Government in Colonial Cuernavaca.* Albuquerque: University of New Mexico Press, 1991.

Hefner, Robert W., ed. *Conversion to Christianity: Historical and Anthropological Perspectives on a Great Transformation.* Berkeley: University of California Press, 1993.

Hers, Marie-Areti. "¿Existió la cultura Loma de San Gabriel? El caso de Hervideros, Durango." *Anales del Instituto de Investigaciones Estéticas* (Universidad Nacional Autónoma de México) 60 (1989): 33–57.

———. *Los toltecas en tierras chichimecas.* Mexico City: Universidad Nacional Autónoma de México, 1989.

Hers, Marie-Areti, et al., eds. *Nómadas y sedentarios en el norte de México: homenaje a Beatriz Braniff.* Mexico City: Universidad Nacional Autónoma de México, 2000.

Hill, Christopher. *The World Turned Upside Down: Radical Ideas during the English Revolution.* New York: Viking, 1992.

Hoberman, Louisa. *Mexico's Merchant Elite, 1590–1660: Silver, State, and Society.* Durham: Duke University Press, 1991.

Horn, Rebecca. *Preconquest Coyoacan: Nahua and Spanish Relations in Central Mexico, 1519–1650.* Stanford: Stanford University Press, 1997.

Hu-Dehart, Evelyn. *Missionaries, Miners, and Indians: Spanish Contact and the Yaqui Nation, 1533–1820.* Tucson: University of Arizona Press, 1981.

Huerta Preciado, María Teresa. *Rebeliones indígenas en el noreste de México en la época colonial.* Mexico City: Instituto Nacional de Antropología e Historia, 1966.

Hulme, Peter. *Colonial Encounters: Europe and the Native Caribbean, 1492–1797.* London: Methuen, 1986.

Hunt, Lynn, ed. *The New Cultural History.* Berkeley: University of California Press, 1989.

Instrucciones que los virreyes de Nueva España dejaron a sus sucesores. 2 vols. Mexico City: Imprenta Imperial, 1867.

Jackson, Robert H. "Agriculture, Drought, and Chumash Congregation in the California Missions, 1782–1834." *Estudios de Historia Novohispana* 19 (1999): 69–90.

———. *Indian Population Decline: The Missions of Northwestern New Spain, 1687–1840.* Albuquerque: University of New Mexico Press, 1994.

———, ed. *New Views of Borderlands History.* Albuquerque: University of New Mexico Press, 1998.

Jackson, Robert H., and Edward Castillo. *Indians, Franciscans, and Spanish Colonization: The Impact of the Mission System on California Indians.* Albuquerque: University of New Mexico Press, 1995.

Jones, Grant D. *Maya Resistance to Spanish Rule: Time and History on a Colonial Frontier.* Albuquerque: University of New Mexico Press, 1989.

Jones, Kristine L. "Comparative Raiding Economies: North and South." In Guy and Sheridan, eds., *Contested Ground*, 97–114.

Jones, Oakah L., Jr. *Nueva Vizcaya: Heartland of the Spanish Frontier.* Albuquerque: University of New Mexico Press, 1988.

Karasch, Mary. "Interethnic Conflict and Resistance on the Brazilian Frontier of Goiás, 1750-1890." In Guy and Sheridan, eds., *Contested Ground*, 115-134.

Karttunen, Frances. *Between Worlds: Interpreters, Guides, and Survivors.* New Brunswick: Rutgers University Press, 1994.

Kaufmann, Thomas Dacosta, ed. *The Geohistory of Art.* London: Ashgate Press, forthcoming.

Kellogg, Susan. *Law and the Transformation of Aztec Culture, 1500-1700* . Norman: University of Oklahoma Press, 1995.

Kennedy, John G. *Tarahumara of the Sierra Madre: Beer, Ecology, and Social Organization.* Arlington Heights, Ill.: AHM Publishing Co., 1978.

Kenner, Charles L. *A History of New Mexican-Plains Indian Relations.* Norman: University of Oklahoma Press, 1969.

Langer, Erick, and Robert H. Jackson, eds. *The New Latin American Mission History.* Lincoln: University of Nebraska Press, 1995.

Larson, Brooke, and Robert Wasserstrom. "Consumo forzoso en Cochabamba y Chiapas durante la época colonial." *Historia Mexicana* 31 (1982): 361-408.

Lartigue, François. *Indios y bosques: políticas forestales y comunales en la Sierra Tarahumara.* Mexico City: Ediciones de la Casa Chata, 1983.

León García, Ricardo. *Misiones jesuitas en la Tarahumara: siglo XVIII.* Ciudad Juárez: Universidad Autónoma de Ciudad Juárez, 1992.

Levi, Jerome M. "Hidden Transcripts among the Rarámuri: Culture, Resistance, and Interethnic Relations in Northern Mexico." *American Ethnologist* 26, no. 1 (1999): 90-113.

Lockhart, James. *The Nahuas after the Conquest: A Social and Cultural History of the Indians of Central Mexico, Sixteenth through Eighteenth Centuries.* Stanford: Stanford University Press, 1992.

———. *Of Things of the Indies: Essays Old and New in Early Latin American History.* Stanford: Stanford University Press, 1999.

Lockhart, James, and Stuart B. Schwartz. *Early Latin America: A History of Colonial Spanish America and Brazil.* New York: Cambridge University Press, 1983.

Lumholtz, Carl. *Unknown Mexico: Explorations in the Sierra Madre and Other Regions, 1890-1898.* 2 vols. New York: Charles Scribner's Sons, 1904.

MacLeod, Murdo J. "Desde el Mediterráneo y España hasta la Guatemala indígena: las transformaciones de una institución colonial: la cofradía." In Pastor and Mayer, eds., *Formaciones religiosas*, 203-227.

———. "The *Matlazáhuatl* of 1737-38 in Some Villages in the Guadalajara Region." In Robert H. Claxton, ed., *Investigating Natural Hazards in Latin American History*, a special edition of *West Georgia College Studies in the Social Sciences* 25 (1986): 7-16.

———. "Self-Promotion: The *Relaciones de Méritos y Servicios* and Their Historical and Political Interpretation." *Colonial Latin American Historical Review* 7, no. 1 (1998): 25–42.

MacLeod, Murdo J., and Robert Wasserstrom, eds. *Spaniards and Indians in Southeastern Mesoamerica: Essays on the History of Ethnic Relations.* Lincoln: University of Nebraska Press, 1983.

Mallon, Florencia. "The Promise and Dilemma of Subaltern Studies: Perspectives from Latin American History." *American Historical Review* 99, no. 5 (1994): 1491–1515.

Malvido Miranda, Elsa. "¿El arca de Noé o la caja de Pandora? Suma y recopilación de pandemias, epidemias y endemias en Nueva España, 1519–1810." In *Temas médicos de la Nueva España.* Mexico City: Instituto Cultural Domecq, 1992, 49–87.

Malvido Miranda, Elsa, and Carlos Viesca. "La epidemia de cocoliztli en 1576." *Historias* 11 (1985): 27–33.

Mann, Kristin Dutcher. "Music and Popular Religion in Northern New Spain." *Catholic Southwest* 12 (2001): 7–27.

———. "The Power of Song in the Missions of Northern New Spain." Ph.D. dissertation, Northern Arizona University, 2002.

Martin, Cheryl E. *Governance and Society in Colonial Mexico: Chihuahua in the Eighteenth Century.* Stanford: Stanford University Press, 1996.

Mathien, F. Joan, and Randall H. McGuire, eds. *Ripples in the Chichimec Sea: New Considerations of Southwestern-Mesoamerican Interactions.* Carbondale: University of Southern Illinois Press, 1986.

Matthei, Mauro, ed. *Cartas e informes de misioneros jesuitas extranjeros en Hispanoamérica.* Santiago, Chile: Universidad Católica de Chile, 1970.

Mecham, J. Lloyd. *Francisco de Ibarra and Nueva Vizcaya.* New York: Greenwood Press, 1968.

Merrill, William L. "Conversion and Colonialism in Northern Mexico: The Tarahumara Response to the Jesuit Mission Program, 1601–1767." In Hefner, ed., *Conversion to Christianity,* 129–163.

———. "Cultural Creativity and Raiding Bands in Eighteenth-Century Northern New Spain." In Taylor and Pease, G.Y., eds., *Violence, Resistance, and Survival in the Americas,* 124–142.

———. "La economía política de las correrías: Nueva Vizcaya al final de la época colonial." In Hers et al., eds., *Nómadas y sedentarios,* 623–668.

———. "God's Saviours in the Sierra Madre." *Natural History* 93, no. 3 (1983).

———. "Rarámuri Easter." In Spicer and Crumrine, eds., *Performing the Renewal of Community,* 365–421.

———. *Rarámuri Souls: Knowledge and Social Process in Northern Mexico.* Washington, D.C.: Smithsonian Institution Press, 1988.

———. "Tarahumara Social Organization, Political Organization and Religion." In Sturtevant, gen. ed., *Handbook of North American Indians,* vol. 10, 290–305.

Meyer, Michael C. *Water in the Hispanic Southwest: A Social and Legal History.* Tucson: University of Arizona Press, 1984.

Mirafuentes Galván, José Luis. "Identidad india, legitimidad y emancipación política en el noroeste de México (Copala 1771)." In Rodríguez O., ed. *Patterns of Contention*, 49–68.

Molina del Villar, América. *La Nueva España y el matlazahuatl de 1736–1739.* Mexico City: El Colegio de Michoacán/CIESAS, 2001.

Moorhead, Max L. *The Presidio: Bastion of the Spanish Borderlands.* Norman: University of Oklahoma Press, 1975.

Mota y Escobar, Alonso de la. *Descripción geográfica de los reinos de Nueva Galicia, Nueva Vizcaya y Nuevo León.* Mexico City: Editorial Pedro Robredo, 1940.

Munslow, Alun. *Deconstructing History.* New York: Routledge, 1997.

Musset, Alain, and Thomas Calvo, eds. *Des Indes Occidentales à L'Amérique Latine: Mélanges en hommage à Jean-Pierre Berthe.* Paris: CEMCA/ENS/IHEAL, 1997.

Nakayama, Antonio, ed. *Relación de Antonio Ruiz: la conquista en el Noroeste.* Mexico City: Instituto Nacional de Antropología e Historia, Centro Regional del Noroeste, 1974.

Navarro Gallegos, César. *Durango: las primeras décadas de vida independiente.* Mexico City: Secretaría de Educación Pública/Instituto Mora, 2001.

Navarro García, Luis. *Sonora y Sinaloa en el siglo XVII.* Seville: Universidad de Sevilla, Escuela de Estudios Hispanoamericanos, 1967.

Naylor, Thomas H., and Charles W. Polzer, eds. *Pedro de Rivera and the Military Regulations for Northern New Spain, 1724–1729.* Tucson: University of Arizona Press, 1988.

———, eds. *The Presidio and Militia on the Northern Frontier of New Spain, 1570–1700.* Tucson: University of Arizona Press, 1986.

Nelson, Cary, and Lawrence Grossberg, eds. *Marxism and the Interpretation of Culture.* Urbana: University of Illinois Press, 1988.

Neumann, Joseph. *Historia de las rebeliones en la Sierra Tarahumara, 1626–1724,* ed. and trans. Luis González Rodríguez. Chihuahua: Editorial Camino, 1991.

Obeyesekere, Gananath. "'British Cannibals': Contemplation of an Event in the Death and Resurrection of James Cook, Explorer." *Critical Inquiry* 18 (summer 1992): 630–654.

Obregón, Baltasar de. *Historia de los descubrimientos antiguos y modernos de la Nueva España.* 1584; reprint, Mexico City: Editorial Porrúa, 1988.

Offutt, Leslie S. *Saltillo, 1770–1810: Town and Region in the Mexican North.* Tucson: University of Arizona Press, 2001.

O'Hanlon, Rosalind. "Recovering the Subject, *Subaltern Studies*, and Theories of Resistance in Colonial South Asia." *Modern Asian Studies* 22, no. 1 (1988): 189–224.

O'Malley, John W. *The First Jesuits.* Cambridge: Harvard University Press, 1993.

Orozco y Jiménez, Francisco. *Colección de documentos inéditos relativos a la Iglesia de Chiapas.* 2 vols. Chiapas: San Cristóbal de Las Casas, 1906, 1911.

Ortner, Sherry B. "Resistance and the Problem of Ethnographic Refusal." *Comparative Studies in Society and History* 37, no. 1 (1995): 173–193.

Pastor, María Alba, and Alicia Mayer, eds. *Formaciones religiosas en la América colonial.* Mexico City: Universidad Nacional Autónoma de México, 2000.

Patch, Robert W. *Maya and Spaniard in Yucatan, 1648–1812.* Stanford: Stanford University Press, 1993.

Pennington, Campbell W. "Northern Tepehuan." In Sturtevant, gen. ed., *Handbook of North American Indians*, vol. 10, 306–314.

———. *The Tarahumar of Mexico: Their Environment and Material Culture.* Salt Lake City: University of Utah Press, 1963.

———. *The Tepehuan of Chihuahua: Their Material Culture.* Salt Lake City: University of Utah Press, 1969.

Pérez de Ribas, Andrés. *Historia de los triunfos de nuestra santa fé entre gentes las más bárbaras y fieras del Nuevo Orbe*, ed. Ignacio Guzmán Betancourt. Madrid: A. de Paredes, 1645; reprint, Mexico City: Siglo Veintiuno Editores, 1992.

———. *History of the Triumphs of Our Holy Faith amongst the Most Barbarous and Fierce Peoples of the New World*, trans. Daniel T. Reff, Maureen Ahern, and Richard K. Danford. Tucson: University of Arizona Press, 1999.

Perry, Mary Elizabeth, and Anne J. Cruz, eds. *Cultural Encounters: The Impact of the Inquisition in Spain and the New World.* Berkeley: University of California Press, 1991.

Polzer, Charles W., S.J. *Rules and Precepts of the Jesuit Missions of Northwestern New Spain.* Tucson: University of Arizona Press, 1976.

Porras Muñoz, Guillermo. *La frontera con los indios de Nueva Vizcaya en el siglo XVII.* Mexico City: Fondo Cultural Banamex, 1980.

———. *Iglesia y estado en Nueva Vizcaya, 1562–1821.* Pamplona: Universidad de Navarra, 1966.

Powell, Philip Wayne. *Soldiers, Indians, and Silver: The Northward Advance of New Spain, 1550–1600.* Berkeley: University of California Press, 1952.

Powers, Karen Vieira. *Andean Journeys: Migration, Ethnogenesis, and the State in Colonial Quito.* Albuquerque: University of New Mexico Press, 1995.

Prakash, Gyan. "Subaltern Studies as Postcolonial Criticism." *American Historical Review* 99, no. 5 (1994): 1475–1490.

———. "Writing Post-Orientalist Histories of the Third World: Perspectives from Indian Historiography." *Comparative Studies in Society and History* 32, no. 2 (1990): 383–408.

Punzo Díaz, José Luis. "La mesa de Tlahuitoles en lo alto de la Sierra Madre de Durango." Doctoral thesis, Escuela Nacional de Antropología e Historia, Mexico City, 1999.

Quezada, Noemí. "Cosmovisión, sexualidad e Inquisición." In Quezada et al., *Inquisición novohispana*, vol. 2, 77–86.

———. "The Inquisition's Repression of Curanderos." In Perry and Cruz, eds. *Cultural Encounters*, 37–57.

Quezada, Noemí, Martha Eugenia Rodríguez, and Marcela Suárez, eds. *Inquisición novohispana*. Mexico City: Universidad Nacional Autónoma de México/Universidad Autónoma Metropolitana Azcapotzalco, 2000.

Radding, Cynthia. "The Colonial Pact and Changing Ethnic Frontiers: Frontiers in Highland Sonora, 1740–1840." In Guy and Sheridan, eds., *Contested Ground*, 52–66.

———. "Cultural Boundaries between Adaptation and Defiance: The Mission Communities of Northwestern New Spain." In Nicholas Griffiths and Fernando Cervantes, eds., *Spiritual Encounters*, 116–135.

———. "Ecología y cultura en dos fronteras misionales: Sonora (Nueva España) y Chiquitos (Alto Perú) en la época postjesuítica." In Bernardo García Martínez and Alba González Jácome, eds., *Estudios sobre historia y ambiente en América*, vol. 1, 265–285.

———. *Wandering Peoples: Colonialism, Ethnic Spaces, and Ecological Frontiers in Northwestern Mexico, 1700–1850*. Durham: Duke University Press, 1997.

Ramírez, Susan. *The World Upside Down: Cross-Cultural Contact and Conflict in Sixteenth-Century Peru*. Stanford: Stanford University Press, 1996.

Ramos, Roberto. *Historia de la tercera rebelión tarahumara*. Chihuahua: Sociedad Chihuahuense de Estudios Históricos, 1950.

Reff, Daniel T. *Disease, Depopulation, and Culture Change in Northwestern New Spain, 1518–1764*. Salt Lake City: University of Utah Press, 1991.

———. "The 'Predicament of Culture' and Spanish Missionary Accounts of the Tepehuan and Pueblo Revolts." *Ethnohistory* 42, no. 1 (1995): 63–90.

Restall, Matthew. *The Maya World: Yucatec Culture and Society, 1550–1850*. Stanford: Stanford University Press, 1997.

Riley, Carroll L. *The Frontier People: The Greater Southwest in the Protohistoric Period*. Albuquerque: University of New Mexico Press, 1987.

———. "The Southern Tepehuan and the Tepecano." In Robert Wauchope, gen. ed., *Handbook of Middle American Indians*, vol. 8, pt. 2, 814–829.

Riley, Carroll L., and H. D. Winters. "The Prehistoric Tepehuan of Mexico." *Southwestern Journal of Anthropology* 19, no. 2 (1963): 177–185.

Riley, James W. *Haciendas jesuitas en México: la administración de los bienes inmuebles del Colegio Máximo de San Pedro y San Pablo de la Ciudad de México*. Mexico City: SepSetentas, 1976.

Río, Ignacio del. *Conquista y aculturación en la California jesuítica*. Mexico City: Universidad Nacional Autónoma de México, 1984.

———. "Sobre la aparición y desarrollo del trabajo libre asalariado en el norte de Nueva España (siglos XVI y XVII)." In Frost et al., eds., *El trabajo y los trabajadores*, 92–111.

Rocha Ch., Rubén. *Obispos de la Nueva Vizcaya*. Parral: Imprenta Parral, 1991.

Rodríguez O., Jaime E., ed. *Patterns of Contention in Mexican History*. Wilmington, Del.: Scholarly Resources, 1992.

Romero Frizzi, María de los Angeles. *El sol y la cruz: indios de Oaxaca colonial*. Mexico City: Centro de Investigación y Estudios Superiores en Antropología Social/Instituto Nacional Indigenista, 1996.

Rouaix, Pastor, Gerard Decorme, and Atanasio Saravia. *Manual de historia de Durango.* Mexico City: Gobierno del Estado de Durango, 1952.

Saeger, James S. "Another View of the Mission as a Frontier Institution: The Guaycuruan Reductions of Santa Fe." *Hispanic American Historical Review* 65, no. 3 (1985): 493–517.

———. *The Chaco Mission Frontier: The Guaycuruan Experience.* Tucson: University of Arizona Press, 2001.

Said, Edward. *Orientalism.* London: Routledge, 1978.

Sánchez Olmedo, Guadalupe. *Etnografía de la Sierra Madre Occidental: tepehuanes y mexicaneros.* Mexico City: Instituto Nacional de Antropología e Historia, 1980.

Sauer, Carl. *The Distribution of Aboriginal Tribes and Languages in Northwestern Mexico.* Ibero-Americana Series, no. 5. Berkeley: University of California Press, 1934.

Schroeder, Susan. *Chimalpahin and the Kingdom of Chalco.* Tucson: University of Arizona Press, 1991.

———, ed. *Native Resistance and the Pax Colonial in New Spain.* Lincoln: University of Nebraska Press, 1998.

Scott, James C. *Domination and the Arts of Resistance: Hidden Transcripts.* New Haven: Yale University Press, 1990.

———. *Seeing Like a State: How Certain Schemes to Improve the Human Condition Have Failed.* New Haven: Yale University Press, 1998.

———. *Weapons of the Weak: Everyday Forms of Peasant Resistance.* New Haven: Yale University Press, 1985.

Seed, Patricia. *Ceremonies of Possession in Europe's Conquest of the New World, 1492–1640.* Cambridge: Cambridge University Press, 1995.

Serulnikov, Sergio. "Disputed Images of Colonialism: Spanish Rule and Indian Subversion in Northern Potosí, 1776–1780." *Hispanic American Historical Review* 76, no. 2 (May 1996): 189–226.

Sewell, William. "The Concept(s) of Culture." In Bonnell and Hunt, eds. *Beyond the Cultural Turn,* 35–61.

Sheridan, Thomas E., and Thomas H. Naylor, eds. *Rarámuri: A Tarahumara Colonial Chronicle, 1607–1791.* Flagstaff: Northland Press, 1979.

Sheridan, Thomas E., and Nancy J. Parezo, eds. *Paths of Life: American Indians of the Southwest and Northern Mexico.* Tucson: University of Arizona Press, 1996.

Sheridan Prieto, Cecilia. *Anónimos y desterrados: la contienda por el "sitio que llaman de Quauyla": siglos XVI–XVIII.* Mexico City: Centro de Investigaciones y Estudios Superiores en Antropología Social/Miguel Angel Porrúa, 2000.

Simpson, Lesley B. *The Repartimiento System of Native Labor in New Spain and Guadalajara.* Berkeley: University of California Press, 1958.

Spalding, Karen. *Huarochirí: An Andean Society under Inca and Spanish Rule.* Stanford: Stanford University Press, 1984.

Spicer, Edward H. *Cycles of Conquest: The Impact of Spain, Mexico, and the United States on the Indians of the Southwest, 1533–1960.* Tucson: University of Arizona Press, 1963.

————. "Northwest Mexico: Introduction." In Robert Wauchope, gen. ed., *Handbook of Middle American Indians*, vol. 8, 777–791.

————. *The Yaquis: A Cultural History*. Tucson: University of Arizona Press, 1980.

Spicer, Rosamond B., and N. Ross Crumrine, eds. *Performing the Renewal of Community: Indigenous Easter Rituals in North Mexico and Southwest United States*. Lanham, Md.: University Press of America, 1997.

Spivak, Gayatri. "Can the Subaltern Speak?" In Cary Nelson and Lawrence Grossberg, eds., *Marxism and the Interpretation of Culture*. Urbana: University of Illinois Press, 1988.

Stahle, David. "American Plague." *New Scientist*, December 23, 2000.

Stern, Steve J. *Peru's Indian Peoples and the Challenge of Spanish Conquest: Huamanga to 1640*. Madison: University of Wisconsin Press, 1982.

Stodder, Ann L. W., and Debra L. Martin. "Health and Disease in the Southwest before and after Spanish Contact." In Verano and Ubelaker, eds., *Disease and Demography*, 55–73.

Sturtevant, William, gen. ed. *Handbook of North American Indians*. Vol. 10. Washington, D.C.: Smithsonian Institution Press, 1983.

Swann, Michael M. *Migrants in the Mexican North: Mobility, Economy, and Society in a Colonial World*. Boulder: Westview Press, 1982.

————. *"Tierra Adentro": Settlement and Society in Colonial Durango*. Boulder: Westview Press, 1982.

Sweet, David. "The Ibero-American Frontier Mission." In Langer and Jackson, eds., *The New Latin American Mission History*, 1–48.

Szasz, Margaret Connell. *Between Indian and White Worlds: The Cultural Broker*. Norman: University of Oklahoma Press, 1994.

Tamarón y Romeral, Pedro. *Demostración del vastísimo obispado de la Nueva Vizcaya, 1765*. Mexico City: Antigua Librería Robredo, 1937.

Tanck de Estrada, Dorothy. *Pueblos de indios y educación en el México colonial, 1750–1821*. Mexico City: El Colegio de México, 1999.

Taylor, William B. *Landlord and Peasant in Colonial Oaxaca*. Stanford: Stanford University Press, 1972.

————. *Magistrates of the Sacred: Priests and Parishioners in Eighteenth-Century Mexico*. Stanford: Stanford University Press, 1996.

————. "Santiago's Horse: Christianity and Colonial Indian Resistance in the Heartland of New Spain." In Taylor and Pease, G.Y., eds., *Violence, Resistance, and Survival*.

Taylor, William B., and Franklin Pease, G.Y., eds. *Violence, Resistance, and Survival in the Americas: Native Americans and the Legacy of Conquest*. Washington, D.C.: Smithsonian Institution Press, 1994.

Teja, Jesús F. de la. *San Antonio de Béxar: A Community on New Spain's Northern Frontier*. Albuquerque: University of New Mexico Press, 1995.

Tello, Antonio. *Libro segundo de la crónica miscelánea, en que se trata de la conquista espiritual y temporal de la Santa Provincia de Xalisco en el Nuevo Reino de la Gali-*

cia y Nueva Vizcaya y descubrimiento de Nuevo México. Guadalajara: La República Literaria, 1891.

Textos de la Nueva Vizcaya: Documentos de San Joseph del Parral 1, no. 3 (1993). Occasional documentary publication of the Universidad Autónoma de Ciudad Juárez.

Thomas, David H., ed. *Columbian Consequences,* vol. 1: *Archaeological and Historical Perspectives on the Spanish Borderlands West.* Washington, D.C.: Smithsonian Institution Press, 1989.

Thrupp, Sylvia. *Millennial Dreams in Action.* The Hague: Mouton, 1961.

Vallebueno, Miguel. "El poblamiento del valle de Santiago Papasquiaro, Durango, hasta 1743." *Transición* (Instituto de Investigaciones Históricas de la Universidad Juárez del Estado de Durango) 8 (1991): 4.

Van Young, Eric. "Mexican Rural History since Chevalier: The History of the Colonial Hacienda." *Latin American Research Review* 18, no. 3 (1983): 5-61.

——. "Millennium on the Northern Marches: The Mad Messiah of Durango and Popular Rebellion in Mexico, 1800-1805." *Comparative Studies in Society and History* 28 (1986): 385-413.

——. "The New Cultural History Comes to Old Mexico." *Hispanic American Historical Review* 79, no. 2 (1999): 211-247.

Velázquez, María del Carmen. *Establecimiento y pérdida del septentrión de México.* Mexico City: El Colegio de México, 1974.

——. *El marqués de Altamira y las provincias internas de Nueva España.* Mexico City: El Colegio de México, 1976.

Verano, John W., and Douglas H. Ubelaker, eds. *Disease and Demography in the Americas.* Washington, D.C.: Smithsonian Institution Press, 1992.

Villaseñor y Sánchez, José Antonio de. *Theatro americano, descripción general de los reynos, y provincias de la Nueva España, y sus jurisdicciones.* 1746; reprint, Mexico City: Editora Nacional, 1952.

Viveros, Germán. *Informe sobre Sinaloa y Sonora, 1750.* Mexico City: Archivo General de la Nación, 1975.

Wauchope, Robert, gen. ed. *Handbook of Middle American Indians.* 16 vols. Austin: University of Texas Press, 1964-1976.

West, Robert C. *The Mining Community in Northern New Spain: The Parral Mining District.* Berkeley: University of California Press, 1949.

——, and J. J. Parsons. "The Topia Road: A Trans-Sierran Trail of Colonial Mexico." *Geographical Review* 31 (1941): 406-413.

White, Hayden. *Tropics of Discourse: Essays in Cultural Criticism.* Baltimore: Johns Hopkins University Press, 1987.

White, Richard. *The Middle Ground: Indians, Empires, and Republics in the Great Lakes Region, 1650-1815.* New York: Cambridge University Press, 1991.

Wightman, Ann. *Indigenous Migration and Social Change: The Forasteros of Cuzco, 1570-1720.* Durham: Duke University Press, 1990.

Wogan, Peter. "Perceptions of European Literacy in Early Contact Situations." *Ethnohistory* 41, no. 3 (1994): 407-427.

Zavala, Silvio. *Los esclavos indios en la Nueva España.* Mexico City: El Colegio de México, 1967.

Zeitlin, Judith Francis. "Ranchers and Indians in the Southern Isthmus of Tehuantepec: Economic Change and Indigenous Survival in Colonial Mexico." *Hispanic American Historical Review* 69, no. 1 (1989): 23–60.

Zubillaga, Félix, S.J., and Ernest J. Burrus, S.J., eds. *Monumenta mexicana.* 8 vols. Rome: Instituto Historicum Societatis Iesu, 1956–1981.

INDEX

CPSIA information can be obtained
at www.ICGtesting.com
Printed in the USA
FFOW02n1657151214
9488FF